GEORGE WASHINGTON CARVER

Southern Biography Series

ANDREW BURSTEIN, SERIES EDITOR

GEORGE
WASHINGTON
CARVER

A LIFE

CHRISTINA VELLA

Louisiana State University Press | Baton Rouge

Published by Louisiana State University Press
Copyright © 2015 by Christina Vella

Manufactured in the United States of America
First printing

Designer: Michelle A. Neustrom
Typeface: Whitman
Printer and binder: Maple Press

LIBRARY OF CONGRESS CATALOGING-IN-PUBLICATION DATA

Vella, Christina.
  George Washington Carver : a life / Christina Vella.
    pages cm — (Southern biography series)
  Includes bibliographical references and index.
  ISBN 978-0-8071-6074-9 (cloth : alkaline paper) — ISBN 978-0-8071-6075-6
(PDF) — ISBN 978-0-8071-6076-3 (ePub) — ISBN 978-0-8071-6077-0 (MOBI)
1. Carver, George Washington, 1864?–1943. 2. African American agriculturists—
Biography. 3. Agriculturists—United States—Biography. 4. African American sci-
entists—Biography. 5. Tuskegee Institute—History. 6. Agriculture—Research—
Southern States—History. 7. Peanuts—United States—History. I. Title.
  S417.C3V45 2015
  630.92—dc23
  [B]
                                                            2015006259

To the memory of my dear mother, Nickie Vella—
that little firecracker.

CONTENTS

Photographs appear after page 176

ACKNOWLEDGMENTS

This book would not have been possible without the help of a small army of archivists and librarians. Foremost among the individuals who led me to materials on Carver is Curtis Gregory of the George Washington Carver National Monument in Diamond, Missouri, who pulled out all sorts of records, cheerfully allowing me to take up his time for two weeks. I am especially grateful to Nanette Hardison in the Joyner Library, East Carolina University, who went to some trouble to make the Lucy Cherry Crisp manuscript available to me. Dr. Ida E. Jones of Howard University Library provided several important documents. Hayden Battle, Patricia Windham, and Arely Bel Martinez of Tulane University's interlibrary loan department were, as always, my lifeline to distant collections.

The staffs of the following university libraries were most gracious in allowing me to consult their microfilm, manuscript, and newspaper holdings. I want to thank Harvard, Princeton, Yale, Columbia, Michigan, Tulane, Loyola, Virginia Tech, and Michigan State Universities, Tuskegee Institute, and the University of New Orleans. I received valuable research help from the U.S. Department of Agriculture, the National Archives, the Library of Congress, and the Franklin Delano Roosevelt Library, all in Washington, D.C.; the Franklin Delano Roosevelt Presidential Library, Hyde Park, New York; and the Southern Regional Research Center in New Orleans. The staff of Special Collections at Iowa State University Library deserves its own line in this compendium for making available its entire George Washington Carver Collection, including its copies of materials in Tuskegee.

Among the civilians who provided assistance of various kinds, I am deeply indebted to Samuel Ferraro for his intelligent research into the Austin Curtis Papers at the University of Michigan. Dr. Wade Shields provided patient computer advice when it was needed (and it was always needed), Nathan Wexler,

M.D., offered expertise on medical issues concerning Carver, and Dr. William C. Davis tracked down information about Jim Hardwick. Harriet Swift, my longtime friend, kindly provided the index.

I feel a special attachment to LSU Press for the staff's courtesy and kindness, both past and present, and for the press's high standards. My sincere thanks to MaryKatherine Callaway, Rand Dotson, Andrew Burstein, Neal Novak, and the designers, publicists, and other contributors to the publication of Carver's biography.

Professor Ron Chapman was kind enough to read the manuscript and respond enthusiastically. Finally, I want to thank my little girls, Professors Christie Riehl and Robin Vella Riehl, for reviewing the final draft, chuckling appropriately here and there, and making many good suggestions.

GEORGE WASHINGTON CARVER

1

CARVER'S GEORGE

Though it was the most shattering event of his life, George Carver had no
memory of the kidnapping. It happened when he was only a few weeks
old, during the Civil War. He could not even remember clearly what he had
been told about it later on. He and his mother were kidnapped by raiders
who snatched them from their cabin in southwest Missouri and took them to
Arkansas, seventy miles south. He was somehow separated from his mother,
who mysteriously disappeared. Their master, Moses Carver, sent a neighbor
after them, a man named John Bentley who belonged to the local militia of
the Union Army. Carver promised Bentley a racehorse worth $300, perhaps
some money, and perhaps forty acres of farmland if he could recover the
slaves. Bentley found George being watched, if not quite looked after, by some
women he described as squaws. He wrapped his coat around the infant, tied
him to his saddle, and brought him back, traveling at night and hiding during
the day from both the Confederate and Union forces that were prowling the
vicinity. Mary, George's mother, was never seen again. Even after his name
was known all over the country, George Washington Carver could never find
out whether his mother was dead or alive or what had happened to her during
that frightful abduction. Someone said she had been sold in Arkansas. Another thought he had seen her going off with Union troops. Freed slaves were
wont to follow the army that had emancipated them in those first bewildering
months of freedom, but it is unlikely that Mary voluntarily left the area and
abandoned both her children—George, the baby, and his brother Jim, who was
still in Missouri. The exact time of the kidnapping, George's precise age, the
terms of the bargain between Moses Carver and Bentley—all these are uncertain. Even the year of George Carver's birth is undetermined.

On the other hand, enough information has been gathered about Moses
Carver to give us a fair idea of how little George lived after he was returned to

his owner—we know more about his childhood, in fact, than about many others who grew up in the aftermath of the Civil War.

Moses Carver had come to the settlement then known as Diamond Grove in 1837, some twenty-five years before the kidnapping. That corner of Missouri was "the West" in the minds of the people who migrated there—promising and foreboding. The hills were forested just as in the East, but these hills were infested with bandits. In winter, the wind that battered the Ozark peaks entered the valleys as steady, panting cold. Summer was suffocating and still, except for swarming insects. The land itself, knowing no boundaries in those days except water and mountain, was Arkansas, or Missouri, or Kansas, or Oklahoma Indian Territory, everywhere riddled with streams and thick with woods. The prairies were not the vast, undulating grasslands of the farther West but ragged, green handkerchiefs set down between moist draperies of oak and elm. Four Carver brothers, Moses, George, Solomon and Richard, arrived within a few months of each other, bringing their families. Moses Carver's patents from the government assured him of four adjoining tracts of public land and several decades of backbreaking labor.

Moses Carver was twenty-five when he began clearing his property, the hardest part of confirming his claim. Every acre of field was wrested from thicket, from tough briars that had to be burned, from trees that clung to life with ancient, stubborn roots. The tangle of brush had no paths except those made by the hooves of his animals and the feet of his family. Working alone, he pried stones out of the earth or buried them under soil that he hauled up from the banks of the stream that vacillated through his land. On the edges of the fields, undergrowth reached out to reclaim the strips as soon as he had cleared them. Yet within a few years, the woods were pushed back. The farm was laid out with crops and fruit orchards, fenced by close-set rows of black walnut trees; the barns and coops were up and filled with livestock; and Carver, the enthusiast of toil, purchased more weeds and woods to clear. By 1853, his farm spread over 240 acres, with apple and cherry orchards, hundreds of Dutch elm and cultivars, sixty-five acres of oats, potatoes, Indian corn, and more. It is no surprise that the youngster raised by Moses Carver thought unremitting overwork was a way of life.

The conventional story of Moses and Susan Carver is that they came with the thousands of German immigrants whose wagons clambered into Missouri between 1830 and 1850. George Washington Carver, with his usual imprecision when he talked about his past, once described Moses as "a German by birth." Maybe Moses was so taciturn that George never realized he had no foreign accent. It is hard to say how the notion of his German origin arose. Moses was sedulous and opposed to slavery, as were most of the German people who settled in the territory, but he was thoroughly American. The Carver brothers had farmed in Ohio and Illinois before being lured to the free wilderness farther west. In fact, Moses Carver's father and Abraham Lincoln's father had owned adjoining farms. Moses and Abe played together as children.

Moses's brother George was already widowed when he arrived in Diamond Grove with his four children and his mother-in-law. In 1839, two years after all the family was settled and long before the Civil War, this brother George and his ten-year-old daughter both died in the same month, leaving another girl and two boys. These orphans were then raised by Moses and Susan, who were themselves childless. Adoptions of this sort were commonplace, then and later. Rare was the family, whether in the city or the country, that did not shelter some dependent relative, often a motherless child. The three children lived for some fifteen years in the Carvers' log shanty, a single room of fourteen by fourteen feet. The cabin had a plank door with wooden hinges, a window without glass, a clapboard roof, a wooden floor, and no foundation. The fireplace simply sat on top of the ground. The chimney was built of rocks as far as the mantelpiece and of sticks and clay from there up. It was sufficient to let out some smoke; the rest settled in soot on the walls and furniture. In that house the size of a storage room, the five of them cooked, ate, slept, kept all their clothes and possessions, bathed in winter—at least occasionally—and tried in all seasons not to step on or smell each other. The cabin was considered adequate by frontier standards. The government required only a dwelling twelve by twelve feet square to grant a homestead claim. One claimant wrote his fiancée, "I have built a cabin of 12 by 14 so that you will have enough room to spread out."

By 1855, the brother's children had grown up and moved out. The Carvers then did a curious thing. Although they disapproved of owning people and had no other slaves, they purchased a thirteen-year-old, Mary, from an adjoining farm. Possibly the Carvers bought the girl in order to rescue her in some way. They paid a good price for a used person—$700—though she was too young to help with the heavy chores. Like all the children in the family, Mary called the Carvers "Aunt Sue" and "Uncle Mose." Susan Carver treated her with much affection. But one detail set Mary apart from the Carver nieces: her fecundity. Between her thirteenth and nineteenth year, she may have had as many as four children besides George: a daughter, twin girls, and a boy James, whose father was white. The little girls, it seems, died young, if indeed they ever lived. The 1860 census of Newton County, Missouri, lists the Carvers' slaves as Mary, age nineteen, and a "yellow" baby of seven months—Jim, as he was called—but no girls. The census also shows that a farmhand was living on the Carver property, a twenty-two-year-old white man named Jim Carroll, who may have been young Jim's father. Apparently, George was not yet born in 1860. In one of his three autobiographical sketches, George Washington Carver, answering the inevitable query about his earliest years, wrote that he had had three sisters, including a set of twins. He knew them to be dead "only as history tells me, yet I do not doubt it as they are buried in the family burying ground" (1897).

There is no documentary evidence for the birth or death of these sisters and no grave marker, though there are plenty of unmarked graves of children in the Carver cemetery. George's information no doubt came from the Carvers, and it is unlikely that they could have miscounted his sisters or been mistaken as to whether there had been a set of twins. Likewise, it's hard to imagine that George later forgot these particulars. Nevertheless, when he wrote other accounts in 1922 and 1927, he mentioned only two sisters. And in an interview he gave a journalist in the 1930s, the girls had become a single sister who died while he was being rescued from the raiders in Arkansas.

What are we to make of George Carver's garbled accounts of his early years? Generally, he was as careful of the truth as most of us and was not given to exaggeration of any kind. Moreover, the scientist who did not know when he was born was a stickler for dates—he would write the date on every scrap of paper that came under his eyes even before he read it. But Carver was peculiar. Often he did not pay the least attention to matters that other people consider significant. When writers first began asking him to supply details of his background, he did not consider his childhood sufficiently important to warrant exactitude. Verifying facts about what happened far away and long ago could be a time-consuming nuisance. As his career developed and the public became curious about him, more and more writers badgered him for details of his youth. Often he was cryptic or vague and could not recall even basic information. Sometimes in an interview he would throw out a placating anecdote to be obliging, something folksy that a journalist could enrich to fill out his story. It was only after one of the biographical articles made Carver a national figure that he realized the stickiness of his harmless little fictions. After he was well known, every inconsequential fragment was enlarged by journalistic embellishments that then clung to his life as it rolled down the years.

Regarding his birth, it's a pretty good guess that George Carver came into the dangerous world of southwest Missouri some time between 1861 and 1863. His father was a black slave owned by a Mr. Grant, the same neighbor who had sold Mary to the Carvers. The father was killed before George was born. He was hauling wood with a team of oxen and in some way fell from the load, under the wheels of the wagon. By this time, the Carvers had given their cabin to Mary and her brood and had built another cabin for themselves, a shanty larger than the first one by two meager feet.

Missouri, having few plantations, had few slaves. Small farming of corn and hogs was usual for much of the state, especially around Diamond Grove, where most people owned no slaves or only one or two. But farmers from Arkansas and Tennessee started moving into Missouri in the 1840s and 50s. These settlers were adamantly with the South on the slavery issue, though many were starvelings who themselves owned nothing and no one. In 1860, the population of the state was roughly 1 million whites added to 100,000 slaves who were located mainly on the tobacco and hemp plantations of the river counties, far away from Diamond Grove. The state had too many slaves for its people to stand together against slavery but too few to make them eager to defend the idea either. Missourians were trapped; the Missouri and Mississippi rivers ran through their state. Both the North and the South thought they had to possess these strategic waterways in order to win the war.

The boundary counties where the Carvers lived had been a battleground long before the actual start of the Civil War. Ruffians from Missouri invaded Kansas in the 1850s to drive out northerners who had settled there. In turn, guerilla bands from Kansas—"jayhawkers"—made raids along the border, carrying off slaves, robbing and murdering Missouri farmers, and destroying everything in their wake. Some of the raiders were violent abolitionists, such as the notorious John Brown, Puritan transplants from the East who had been reborn in Kansas. Brown and his party cut off the hands of some Missouri slave owners before murdering them; then they fervently thanked God for His mercy in allowing their mission to succeed. Other raiders were simply lowlife criminals indulging in casual brutality against Missourians, whom they indiscriminately regarded as "pukes"—poor white trash.

After nearly fighting its own civil war between Unionists and southern sympathizers, Missouri briefly landed in the Confederacy as an ambivalent slave state on the border of free Kansas. With the official start of hostilities in 1861, the Kansas-Missouri margin became the scene of some of the Civil War's most vicious battles. Certain farms were invaded time and again by one or the other army, Union or Confederate. When those regulars moved off to another area, bushwhackers—small gangs that belonged to no particular army and recognized no authority—would sweep in and out, plundering and destroying. Jesse James began his truculent career leading a gang of secessionist brigands on the Missouri border. The southern guerillas commonly wore Union uniforms while ravaging. Inspired by the example, the regular federal troops bent on depredation likewise stole uniforms and pretended to be Confederates. Whoever the raiders were, when they came crashing through the fields, they first seized the arms on a place. Next they gathered up slaves, if any, either to free them if the attackers were Unionists or to resell them if the pillagers were secessionists or looters from either side simply on a spree. They took the horses, drove off or killed the livestock, murdered the men, assaulted the women, burned crops, carted off food stores and everything else of value, and concluded their exertions by drinking to unconsciousness. There was no government in the region where victims could seek redress, even when the area was supposed to be under occupation. Early in the war, all the structures of justice and administration broke down completely.

Moses Carver's farm in Diamond Grove was in the dead center of the agitation, but it was attacked only twice. In one raid, bandits hung Carver up and built a fire under his feet to make him reveal where he had buried his money. Since banks had closed because of the anarchy, along with schools and stores, people were keeping their scant reserves of money in their own possession.

Carver was probably one of the few who did have an enviable hoard of specie, as he was raising racehorses (which he also kept hidden from marauders.) According to Moses Carver, his tormenters left without getting his cache, but the raiders came back, and this time they did not go away empty-handed. Moses later told George Washington Carver that he heard a group of night riders thundering out of the darkness onto his land. He ran into Mary's cabin and scooped up little Jim. "He tried to get me but he couldn't," wrote George. Mary and the baby George were spirited away to Arkansas by the bandits.

Moses immediately sent Bentley to overtake the kidnappers and try to ransom Mary and George. Tracking down the marauders may not have been as difficult as it sounds, since the attackers were frequently wild youths well known in the area who took the absence of authority as an opportunity to mistreat neighbors they disliked. Carver gave Bentley $300 for ransom money and promised to reward him with a racehorse if he brought back the slaves. In another version of the story, Bentley took the racehorse with him on the chase and gave it to the kidnappers in exchange for George.

In a memoir written in 1897, George Carver wrote that he and his mother had been "Ku Kluxed" during the Civil War, that is, snatched up by the Klan and brought across the Arkansas border to be sold. Writing about the incident again in 1927, he was more vague about the culprits, remarking only that the Ku Klux Klan was active in the area at that time. But in fact, the Klan was not founded until 1866, in Tennessee, several years after the kidnapping. There was enough lawlessness without it.

The infant that Bentley finally handed over to Susan Carver appeared to be dying from whooping cough, dehydration, and exposure. Whooping cough, like any other disease in the days before antibiotics, was a dire illness even for older children, with spasms of uncontrollable, violent coughing and choking. The spasms might well up thirty times a day and recur for months before recovery—or pneumonia—set in. Susan Carver, already caring for little Jim, was determined to save the fragile baby. Whatever she did, her care was effective: George lived, against all odds, although the relentless cough permanently damaged his vocal cords. As a child, he spoke in a raspy whisper. When he finally reached puberty, the resonance improved, although his voice remained abnormal throughout his life—high and anile, like the speaking voice of an ageing coloratura. And he remained sickly and puny for years.

Burdened once more with orphans, Moses and Susan, now in their fifties, took George and Jim to live with them in the "big" house and gave the children the only real home they would ever know. The Carvers were excellent people—one would almost say excellent parents, except that the word does not quite suit them. The two boys seemed to occupy a special position, somewhere between sons and slaves. "Like most youngsters, we were expected to be indoors at night," said George Carver, dutifully creating a readable childhood.

> My brother and I would sometimes steal out to the persimmon tree. And when we went into the house, there was Mrs. Carver waiting for us beside a jar of willow switches. But when she started toward me, I used to open my mouth and yell. And she would walk away rather than hear that awful yelling. When she turned her back, I would sob and stuff into my mouth a persimmon . . . And those persimmons did taste awful good.

George loved persimmons, but nobody had to sneak them on the Carver farm—the trees were all over the place.

Susan Blue Carver seems to have dedicated her life to doing grueling farm work and rearing other people's children. She prized the spinning wheel that had been Mary's; however, George could never get much information out of Aunt Sue regarding the spirit who haunted the little implement. If he questioned her about Mary, Aunt Sue would start to cry, so that he was never able to put together a distinct picture of his living, breeding mother. Susan did not go to church, nor did she attend the few community gatherings that took place in the "cultural center"—the one-room shelter about a quarter of a mile from the farm—that served as church, school, and recreation hall for Diamond Grove. No visitors came to the little cabin stuck away on the big farm, out of sight of the road, and there would have been no room for them to sit down if they had come. Aunt Sue was "quiet and old-fashioned," according to people who knew her, for people then as now had their notions of modernity and fashion, even in the sticks.

She was probably lonely while George was growing up, like farm wives all over the empty hills, and George was good company, that bright, lively boy. He watched, fascinated, as she boiled pokeberries and barks. She used the resulting dyes on the family's food and clothes, to touch their workaday lives with color. She taught him things that only a loving mother or grandmother would bother imparting to a little child: spinning, knitting, fine needlework—the minor arts that were the major art of country homes. George Carver's handiwork—his lace samplers which still exist—are as marvelous and intricate as spider webs. "I never saw anybody do anything with his hands that I couldn't do with mine."

Some people are adept at whatever they try. They are just good at the tasks of life. Even as a small child, George was one of those persons. The Carvers' grandnephew described him as "the smartest boy I ever saw in my life. He could sew, crochet, and cook as good as any woman, and there wasn't a musical instrument he couldn't play." Susan was not sufficiently confident with a pen to attempt her name on documents, but she seems to have taught George to read a little from an old Webster's blue-backed speller, which was her only book. Most importantly, Susan made him a gentleman. Everyone who met George Carver commented on his unfailing courtesy, his air of gentility—the good manners and consideration for others that a person either acquires as a cub or never learns at all. Perhaps it was Susan who first encouraged his drawing. One of his very early pictures survives—a precocious sketch of the family's cabin, probably done when he was six or seven. Who saved that little drawing, if not Aunt Sue?

As for Moses Carver, there is little doubt that George's well-known quirks and much of his kind nature can be traced directly to this foster father, an ambitious man of independent mind and surprising good humor. Moses Carver was self-reliant, even-tempered, and slightly cracked, but possessed of the dignity that sometimes characterizes rural eccentrics. He was born the ninth and probably not the last child in a family that did not expect to provide for children beyond adolescence, if the parents or children lived that long. He continually expanded and improved his farm—even though he could never make it turn much of a profit after the war, and even though he was already making good money from his horses—simply because he liked raising things. He could be giving toward others, but with himself and his own, he was the stingiest of men. Nothing was regularly purchased except oil, coffee, and sugar. Everything else was acquired by bartering agricultural products. On Sundays the Carvers had the usual farm dinner of chicken; whatever remained of it was brought out again for Monday breakfast and again for Monday lunch and supper. Mose hunted wild turkeys and geese to supplement their diet. Once he killed a bear that lasted the family a long time—probably too long.

Years after he could afford a frame house, a stove, separate rooms, and comfort, Moses and his wife lived in a primitive shack with a fireplace and a single candle lamp. Spaces between its logs were stuffed with mud, a stopgap that did not keep such houses from being frigid in winter and stifling in every month that was not winter. The one-room cabin was no doubt bursting with rummage—gun parts, bits of tallow, locks—for Uncle Mose did not believe in discarding anything. Odds and ends had to be saved until a use was found for them. Cornhusks were stacked as a convenience in outhouses in those years before Sears, Roebuck catalogs were employed in the humble service. The other cornhusks were also saved; they made a tough, spiny stuffing for mattresses—though there was a constant supply of husks and a limited need for mattresses. Acorns could be covered for fancy buttons, should Aunt Sue ever own a fancy dress. Around his picket fences, Moses grew pumpkin-sized gourds specifically to use as water and sugar containers. (George appropriated them as planters for his flowers.) Even ashes from the fireplace were not thrown away. They were lifted, heavy and dirty, and dumped just outside the house in a tall, open hopper, where they were added to such inexpensive supplies as rainwater and leaves. From that mixture, a liquid would eventually leak out of the bottom of the hopper—lye, which was highly poisonous and could be a dangerous attraction to toddlers. Lard was then added to the compound, which was allowed to sit in a box and solidify. After some weeks, a hardy soul would taste the brew. If it tasted like soap, it was ready to use. If not, the mixture was left for a few more weeks until it was finally ready for cutting into soap cakes. Homemade lye soap and a washboard took mud out of clothes and skin off the hands that washed them. The clothes at least were durable, having been homespun on one of the Carvers' two spinning wheels— a large one for wool and a smaller one—Mary's wheel—for cotton and flax. When they finally wore out, the clothes were reborn as rags and absorbents— anything to keep from discarding them. "Nature produces no waste," George Washington Carver would one day tell his students. Eating a piece of fruit meant storing the seed—somewhere—for replanting. A broken tool could be disassembled and its parts reused—some time. As an adult, George Carver was obsessed with putting to some good purpose what others had thrown away.

Much that he collected was utilized, famously. More was stored in some corner of his quarters and forgotten, just like the rubbish on Moses Carver's farm.

There is a 1912 photograph of Moses Carver in old age that shows him glowering but composed, like a resting prophet. Being photographed at the turn of the century meant being absolutely still for several minutes. No one dared try to hold a smile for that long—the result would have been grotesque. But despite his grim elderly image, Uncle Mose must have been playful in his energetic years, since the child who grew up in his shadow was full of fun. The Carvers' neighbor Fred Baynham once gave Jim a book of recitations, *The Dime Ludicrous Speaker*. George began culling it for farcical material as he approached the age when boys turn into comedians. He could deliver a memorable "Lecture on Women's Rights," and his rendition of "The Hard-Shell Sermon" was said to be almost as funny as the ones delivered in earnest at the Locust Grove Church. A sense of humor is not an innate talent but a susceptibility acquired early in life. If mischief and jokes are deprecated in a boy, they do not often reappear in the man. Throughout his life, George Carver was whimsical, whether talking to senators, students, rocks, reeds, spiders, or himself. Only when addressing God was he constrained to be merely witty. Someone in his crib years must have welcomed his childish laughter and his antics. Someone in his childhood showed him how to be lighthearted.

Moses Carver's neighbors believed he was a capable businessman with a fortune secreted around his farm, but they liked him anyway. He supplied the music for the few festivities that took place in Diamond Grove, since he did not scorn diversion and could play dance songs by ear. He donated some of his land for a community cemetery and with his own hands closed it in with an attractive dry rock wall to keep out wandering stock. But even after he had provided this resting place for his neighbors within sight of his own window, he refused as before to attend their funerals. Moses loved children, however. He taught George to play both the accordion and the violin, entrusting them to the child's hands even though to him the instruments must have been well-nigh irreplaceable.

Like Moses, George Carver grew up to love children, and it was undoubtedly Uncle Mose who taught him to be tender with animals. There was a story abroad that Moses once broke out of his habitual aloofness to upbraid an acquaintance for putting a decorative hat on his half-starved mare instead of feeding her. George remembered Moses saying that "a man that was mean to his horse, dog, or cow would be mean to his wife." The only switching George and Jim ever received was for riding sheep after being admonished not to. Perhaps George made up these incidents, but if he did, they were fitting stories to express what he definitely remembered: Uncle Mose was humane. He cared nothing for outward appearances and was even hostile to conventions of dress and personal beauty. In that, George grew up to be exactly like him.

In other ways, however, George was his own man. Moses Carver shunned all religious cant, although he must have been a believer of sorts, since he was a bona fide member of the Masons. George, according his own misty recollection, became "aware of God" somewhere around the age of eight; by the time he was in his twenties, he was a full-blown fanatic, swept along by the vigorous evangelism of the time. Moses Carver was a smart and shrewd man, though he could not sign his name. George Carver was literate and learned in adulthood, a lover of poetry and opera, more polished and erudite, probably, than anyone Moses ever met. But no one who knew George would have described him as shrewd.

Moses Carver's pride was his stable of sleek racehorses such as the one he traded for George's return. He owned from ten to twenty of them over the years. He had oxen to plow the farm, perhaps five or as many as ten. He also kept numerous sheep, a few milk cows, some hogs and poultry—just enough to provide for the family—and a couple of mules to drag the cart that he took into town periodically to do his trading and shopping. For the manufactured things he needed—boots, knives, tools—he could sell or trade hay, beeswax, honey, and molasses. The groceries he bought in town he had to pay for in cash: two cents for castor oil, twenty-five cents for a pound of sugar, a whopping eighty-five cents for a "tin" of coffee, and fifteen cents for a half-gallon of coal oil. His best years on the farm were before George was born, when his assets were worth around a thousand dollars.

Farm production began to fall and, except for Mose's racehorses, there would have been tight times during the hungry years of the war and Reconstruction—the years when George was growing up. As a former slave owner, Moses was prohibited after the war from voting, holding office, preaching, teaching, or practicing law. None of that would have inconvenienced him. But he was also prohibited from borrowing money from a bank on future crops, if he had been able to find a bank with any money to lend. The wretched conditions of all the former slave states, the devastation of the livestock, the raiding that continued along the Missouri-Kansas border for years after the end of the war—all made it difficult to turn a profit on a large, mixed farm such as his. Nevertheless, thanks to what he referred to as his "pretty good gang of racehorses," he was never a poor man after coming to Missouri. He only lived like one.

George remembered that Uncle Mose was an excellent bee hunter and had fifty or sixty hives. He would go out with a pan of honey and "bee bread" and burn it on live coals, giving rise to a smoke that the bees could smell from four or five miles away. When the bees had partaken and were set to return home, Moses would watch which way they went, follow them, and thus locate their tree. After nightfall, he smoked out the bees with a fire of rags and tobacco and then cut the tree down. Sometimes the tree yielded a washtub full of honey. He cut off a section of the log, put a top on it, and thus had a hive he could raid from time to time for more honey. George took no part in the operation because the bees would converge on him. He was susceptible to stings—often he was attacked by bees even without deliberately intruding on them. Uncle Mose, however, did not even wear a net. To prevent the bees from picking out another tree for their nest, he would reach in the hive, scrape around with his hand until he found the queen, and clip her wings. The other bees would not leave without the queen. Aunt Sue used some of the wax to seal her canned goods. The rest was traded for store-bought items.

In 1885, Moses Carver finally built a new frame house of one and a half stories, a mansion compared to the cabin but still quite simple—two small rooms downstairs and two small bedrooms above, four times larger than the shanty. It was lit with kerosene lamps and lovely tall windows, heated with a real parlor stove as well as a fireplace. Susan Carver, being a person of refined tastes, knitted rugs for the floors and covered the walls with delicate, floral paper. It was a cozy, modest affair, this first frame house, not built until George had been gone some ten or twelve years and Susan herself was past seventy. It would be a decent abode for Moses's next wife.

The Carver farm was an important school for George in many ways. Growing up amid cornfields and barnyards was not a bad start for a boy who would become an agricultural scientist. On the other hand, the hours he might have spent with books were squandered in the usual drudgery of farm children—

feeding the chickens, bringing water from the spring in dry weather and lugging it out to the animals or the young trees, digging potatoes, churning butter, gathering chips—that is, dried dung—for the fireplace, probably a little milking and a lot of raking. Together with his brother, he scrubbed the cabin floor and took turns in the weekly task of washing clothes and the daily tedium of washing dishes. He had no illusions about farming. He knew that the stink of the barnyard clings to boots, the smell of cows trails their caretakers, and human fatigue has its own distinctive scent.

The woods around the farm housed five or six kinds of edible wild berries that were normally preserved, along with the cherries from the cultivated trees. Gathering them was a chore—George's particular chore. Elderberries alone demanded a full summer's labor for picking the tiny beads, boiling, mashing, and straining them, all for a modest store of jelly and a rash of poison ivy to show for the effort. But the berries and the boy-hours were free and had to be availed. When the berries had been vanquished, apples made their copious appearance in Carver's orchards, and the dull autumn duty of peeling and coring began. Nature gave southwest Missouri vegetation but then threaded the bushes with invisible, ruthless chiggers. The deceitful woods sheltered more ticks and wasps than birds and butterflies.

The story is often repeated that George was too sick for mighty outdoor work and was trained instead in household chores. But the fact is that when young George Carver acquired his own stake in Kansas, he already knew a great deal about clearing, plowing, preserving seed, planting, and building. It is true that his indelible childhood memory was of being weak and tired most of the time, subject to every contagion that came along. He was "slender and frail-looking" according to the Carvers' nephew, and never completely well—always just getting over one bout of "croup" as the next one struck. Aunt Sue applied her home remedies and superstitions—she had his ears pierced to help his eyesight. Typically, the ear lobes were pierced against a piece of cork; in those germless days, broom straw was stuck in the lobes until the holes were healed. Possibly George was actually suffering from chronic bronchitis, a malady that little ones tend to outgrow, though the attacks in childhood can be fatal. Whatever ailed him, he was miles away from a doctor and eighty years away from the penicillin that would alleviate bronchitis.

Carver's little George was known as a cutup who loved to entertain people;

yet, remarkably, he had a bad stammer, so severe that it might have blighted his life. Half the time, according to people in Diamond Grove who remembered him, nobody could understand what he was trying to say. Even after he had forgotten everything else about his childhood, George remembered his struggle to overcome that stammer. "The method I pursued," he advised a young man who asked for help with his own stuttering, "was to watch myself very carefully and stop attempting to talk fast; or when I became excited or was highly nervous, to wait until I could get quiet and then take each word and each letter very slowly." The stutter did not torment him when he was singing, so he was an eager songster. As if stammering were not enough, he had a slight, ominous hump that looked to develop into a real deformity. It was still a time when the weak and sickly did not survive the era's frequent epidemics. George, wan and small for his age at every age before twenty, was not expected to grow up.

There were white kids to play with, but they were spaced far out over the deep slopes. He had his brother for companionship, but mainly he played alone, with plants. When he was hardly more than a twig himself, he acquired the habit of going into the woods early to see the dawn break and watch the wild Ozarks come to life. He observed changes carefully and learned for himself the forms that birds, insects, and flowers took in their various stages. Around Diamond he was known as the little master of useless knowledge: he could talk endlessly—to anyone who could understand him—about nests, cliffs, moths, mushrooms, and other such profitless concerns. He studied rocks riddled through with tiny crystals, trying to guess the history of such glinting miracles and finally adding them to his community of lovely stones. "Many are the basketful that I have been compelled to remove from the outside chimney corner of that old log house, with the injunction to throw them down the hill. I obeyed, but picked the choicest ones and hid them in another place, and somehow that same chimney corner would, in a few days or weeks, be running over again, to suffer the same fate" (1897).

His obsession with mushrooms was long lasting, and so was his mystical preoccupation with birds. But it was flowers that finally won the competition within. A dazzling flower would appear one morning unexpected, without a name or a past. He learned its habits, but no one around him could tell him what it was called. He started making up names for his foundlings and placing them in families of his own invention. "Day after day I spent in the woods alone in order to collect my floral beauties and put them in my little garden I had hidden in the brush not far from the house, as it was considered foolishness in the neighborhood to waste time on flowers . . . Many are the tears I have shed because I would break the roots or flowers of some of my pets while removing them from the ground." The secret garden measured about three feet by six feet. He wondered if a flower could be a crossbreed, like his brother Jim, and so planted different colors close together to see if they would mix themselves. In winter, he protected them in tin cans and squash shells, taking them out into the sun during the day and covering them at dusk. The blooms he transplanted to his plot were not the well-nourished hybrids of the horticulture garden but little runts, like him, that were hardly noticeable except in clusters, hidden in the weeds and watercress. Then as now in Missouri, white clover, yarrow, and Queen Anne's lace made a summer frost for roadside ditches and prairies. Here and there he found blue flowering chicory and sprays of blue-eyed grass sprinkled like dust on the waysides; wild iris speckled the edges of the old creek, and aster peeked out at him from the brush. In his little nursery of mostly little blossoms, only black-eyed Susans and dandelions were large.

He talked to plants and they seemed to talk to him. Before he was ten years old, people around the area—the same people who snickered at his interest in flowers—were bringing him diseased plants which he would "treat" by changing the soil or water or amount of sunlight, or by diagnosing some mold or insect attacker. He generally knew the enemies of plants and how to deal with them, even though he still did not know the names of any of them—the plants, the diseases, or the insects. "Strange to say, all sorts of vegetation seemed to thrive under my touch until I was styled the plant doctor. At this time I had never heard of botany and could scarcely read."

Wanting to preserve his flowers, he tried to draw them. Then he began drawing everything he loved. He became fascinated with color when he saw some portraits hanging over the mantel in Fred Baynham's living room. George had no paints, of course, but he concocted an assortment of pigments by boiling bark and crushing vivid leaves, berries, and flowers. He applied the colors with his fingers. Like a hungry child presented with the nuisance of a fork, he found it more satisfying to paint with his hands even after he had access to a brush. He painted on any surface he could find—cans, pieces of wood, the smooth faces of cut tree stumps, bits of glass and strips of bark. Everything a child could do to better himself, George did; but still he ached for education and for simple know-how. "Mr. and Mrs. Carver were very kind to me and I thank them so much for my home training. They encouraged me to secure knowledge, helping me all they could, but this was quite limited."

In those years, Diamond Grove was little more than a crossroads. Besides the church-schoolhouse, the "town" consisted of a general store and a blacksmith shop—the equivalent of today's gas station—with a room attached to it that served as the post office. Certainly there was no library. Far worse than any material privation in George's life was the frustration of rural isolation. To a city dweller, a little community cloistered in the hills evokes a sense of coziness and security. But to a child burning with curiosity, being immured in the backwoods without books is a life of exile. Except for the Carvers themselves, most of the adults he lived among were indifferent or ill disposed to everything he cared about. The attitudes of the Missouri farmers are still perceptible in the wills, depositions, marriage, divorce and succession contracts that marked their lives. These documents were usually dictated and signed with a nervous X. They reflect the general mentality in hamlets such as Diamond Grove: an inclination to thrift, godliness, steadiness, and contented ignorance.

One time, however, George got to see a real play. A few people in the area, attempting to form a drama club, gave one performance of *Ten Nights in a Barroom*. The play was a violent, sorrow-stricken temperance melodrama, immensely popular all over the country, a dry Bible shown in many versions. At the Locust Grove schoolhouse-turned-theater, it was performed with some comic touches. Forbes H. Brown, who grew up with George in Diamond Grove, vividly remembered one of the actors wearing a red wig and "face blackened as a slave, hiding in a barrel, disclosing his presence in his fright by raising his head, much to the merriment of the children present, including little George among us in the front row." This was the only community event Brown could recall that Moses and Susan Carver attended.

One Saturday afternoon a white playmate made a remark about going to Sunday school. The word "school" in any form was exciting to George; he was allowed to go along with his friend the next day and many Sundays thereafter. The Sunday school was held, naturally, in the serviceable building that was quite near the Carver property, the Locust Grove schoolhouse. Preachers of four denominations—Methodist, Baptist, Presbyterian, or Campbellite (Disciple of Christ) would take turns riding over from Neosho, the next town. The preacher would lead the devotions, spend Sunday night with a family of his particular denomination, and return home on Monday.

One of these farmer-preachers was an eager soul named Benny Woods. The week before it was his turn to preach, all the neighbors near his farm could hear him bellowing the homily as he rehearsed on a tree stump-turned-pulpit. "He was just in his prime of life," Forbes Brown recalled, "and really had convinced himself that he was called to preach whenever the opportunity presented itself."

> I vividly recall one of his sermons on a very warm day. He required a full hour and a half to reach his point and the climax. As he warmed up, waving his arms, he suddenly jerked one end of his narrow black string tie, released the first button of his shirt collar. Soon after he doffed his coat, then unbuttoned his rather long waistcoat, in time removing it also. Wiping his brow frequently, he was then ready for full action, which was to relieve his nervous tension by seeming to spit on the floor and stamp his foot thereon, which relieved him at once, only later to repeat the performance. The boys all referred to him as "Spit-and-Step-In-It."

After attending Sunday school, George was allowed to sit on the steps outside and listen to the grown-up service. It was the singing that he loved and waited for—the only music, in fact, that he heard regularly. However, the few other opportunities for education that the town provided for its white mediocrities were closed to its one black genius. Moses enrolled George and Jim in the Locust Grove School, and they attended one year. But, according to one of George's classmates, "People cut up so about the darkies being in the school with the whites" that the boys were told they would have to go to the colored school just established in Neosho. Jim and George were still allowed to attend church events. But on Monday through Friday, when the building turned back into a county school, they were not permitted to enter it. According to Forbes Brown, this was the reason Moses Carver disdained the town gatherings—"his method of showing resentment to all for refusing to invite little George to attend public school at Locust Grove." Jim asked Aunt Sue if there were any way he could become white. According to an oft-repeated story, Aunt Sue replied that he could eventually turn white if he worked hard and sweated a lot.

Meanwhile, a new teacher, Steven Slane, had arrived at the Locust Grove School and was boarding with the Baynhams next door. Slane began tutoring George in the late afternoons, after his own long school day, because he saw that George was "an exceptionally brilliant boy." He introduced George to Louisa May Alcott's *Little Women* and *Little Men,* the latter book just having been published in 1871. These inspired George to try to write his own novel in the Alcott mode. Slane gave some serious thought to George's future, and finally advised his extraordinary pupil to leave Diamond Grove as soon as he could and to go where he could get an education.The Neosho school was about eight miles as the crow flies from the Carver farm; but the crow did not have to trek up and down the steep hills that separated George from knowledge. Nevertheless, by the time he was about ten years old, George had made up his mind to get to that school one way or another.

In the best of all possible worlds, with the best of all possible parents, George and Jim would have been driven to and from school each day in Mose's cart, or the boys would have been permitted to drive themselves back and forth—Jim was at least twelve by this time—or Mose would have paid some acquaintance in Neosho to board the boys during the school week. None of those things happened. Instead, George wrapped a few possessions in a bandanna, including his favorite rocks, bade goodbye to his secret garden, and, with the Carvers' permission, set out for Neosho on a path he knew well, a path that started at the edge of the farm and ended right in front of the Neosho Elementary School for Colored Children.

"I do not remember much about my childhood days . . . I do not recall much about the school," wrote the thirty-five year-old Carver. In his varied narratives of his early schooling, George recalled that he and Jim went to school together at first but that Jim discovered "school was not for him" and returned to the farm. In another version, George's brother attended the school in Neosho with him and took a shine to one of the girls, but after the teacher married that student, Jim turned his back on the school. The story that finally stuck was of George starting out alone from the farm and coming out of the woods where the path dead-ended on Young Street at the school. When he arrived in the town, it was getting dark. He went into a barn by the side of the school and climbed on a woodpile. That was where Mariah Watkins found him early the next morning when she went to get kindling to cook her husband's breakfast.

In his first enthusiastic days of attending classes, he made a drawing of the school building and the Watkins house next door. It's a fine, rapid little drawing that communicates the whole personality of the site with a few deft lines. But his excitement soon gave way to disappointment. The one-room school, built in 1872, was a simple structure, "crude" and "primitive," as George invariably described it later on. It contained benches and a few slates, insufficient books, and a well-meaning black teacher. There was some instruction in reading, less in arithmetic, and a sample writing book available for those who insisted on writing. The young teacher had gone only a little further in school than his pupils, and, as George was to discover, he shared their privations and their limitations.

As for Mariah and Andrew Watkins, they were fine, solid citizens, hardworking and literate. They possessed a three-room home worth a modest $500, and a bank account, also modest. They purchased insurance, bought farm tools on installment, and participated in all the usual domestic business of middle class people. Uncle Andy was a blacksmith, a bright and kindly man who readily took George on as his helper. George's situation was not appreciably different from thousands of children across the country, black and white, who around the age of ten or twelve were put out as indentured servants and apprentices, lived with a family, learned a skill, and worked in exchange for board.

Aunt Mariah was a midwife, a direct and confident woman, well known on all the country roads around Neosho. Her clients were mainly white, reflecting the general population of the area. In between lying-ins, she was a washerwoman, like so many women of color in the 1870s. She taught George to iron like an expert, a skill more than any other that was to see him through college. On the Sundays when George did not walk back to Diamond Grove, Aunt Mariah brought him to the African Methodist Church. The preacher had to have someone read the biblical text for him. George remembered him as "a good man, such a good man." The service was rousing, as devotions go. There was always somebody converting or testifying, giving some cause for general jubilation or, occasionally, fervent repentance, which was more interesting. Aunt Mariah laughed, wept, and shouted during the service along with the rest of the congregation, but as soon as they reached home, the boisterousness was over. One of her notions was that children should not laugh on Sundays.

George was deeply fond of her. Through his whole life, he read and cherished the large Bible she gave him, keeping his place with the fancy bookmark she had watched him embroider. In her later years, she became a fixture in Neosho, queenly, snappish, and venerable. It may have been Aunt Mariah who turned George into an ardent Christian, but his mystical bent seems to have started before he even left Diamond Grove. There is a story that after whittling with one of Uncle Mose's hunting knives, he began longing to possess a small knife. According to his own account, he dreamed that he saw a cut watermelon lying in a cornfield with a tiny lady's knife beside it. The next morning at dawn he ran over fences and across furrows to the place of his dream. There he found the cornfield, the watermelon, and the knife, exactly as he had seen it in the dream. From then on, he took dreams and omens seriously, or at least as seriously as a scientist dared confess to journalists.

George stayed with the Watkins about three years. He was only thirteen, but the school next door could teach him nothing more. His craving for education was tormenting him. In Neosho, real life seemed to be eluding him, like a celebration happening elsewhere, just beyond his vision, in some place whose lights gleamed faintly from across the hills. He learned of a family that was moving to Fort Scott, Kansas. Though he was still prone to sickness and felt weak much of the time, he made up his mind to go with them. The departure of his little "son" grieved Uncle Andy, whose affection was as deep as it was silent. The elder man made a will leaving everything he had to George. This was more than Moses Carver had ever done. In turn, George solemnly wrote a will—for now he could write—leaving all his assets to Uncle Andy.

In the course of George Carver's career, various accounts were published describing his life after he left Neosho, reporting that he arrived in Kansas dressed in homespun or that he wore his Sunday best. The scientist Carver would read either version—any version—and pronounce it perfectly correct. The truth was, once he quit Neosho he could remember very little. It was decades before he was asked to recount his background in Missouri and Kansas. Writers interviewing him in later life soon realized that his clearest memories were painful; he had buried them and had no intention of exhuming the old hurts. The articles that were published about his youth were half fantasy—the fantasy of a journalist if not of Carver. Professor Carver would read a piece, write a thank-you letter commenting on the author's charming style—even when the writing was charmless—and would make no effort to correct even the most obvious inaccuracies. In fact, he was entertained by the fanciful stories. Often when he rose to speak on the lecture platform, after an introduction by someone who had consulted a magazine article for information, Carver would say, "I like to hear myself introduced because I learn so many things about myself that I never knew."

Fort Scott was seventy miles from Neosho, a trip of many days. It was a true kindness for the family to take George along, since their two wagons were so loaded that there was no room for everyone to sit; each person had to take his turn walking alongside the mules. The Carvers were furious when they found out after some months that George was in Kansas. Though his health was gradually improving, they still thought his death was imminent and he needed looking after. Education or no education, they demanded that he come home at once to live in safety and stasis. But George did not return. He worked at any job he could get, trying all the while to go to school. He was never able to attend with regularity—had he expected that? He would enroll in a school until his money ran out, then leave to take one job or another, keeping himself this side of starvation. He moved alone from town to town, a vagrant child in a disordered and harassed world. Once he had to drop out of school because a street gang of white toughs beat him up and took his schoolbooks. They thought a black boy had no business with books that could only make him "uppity." In those days textbooks were always purchased by students, just as they are in colleges today, and were necessary for school attendance. Such emergencies routinely happened to blacks and to drifters. Just as the Carvers feared, a black drifter was what their George had become.

2

DRIFTING TOWARD LIFE

The second ghastly event in George Washington Carver's life was one he recalled all too well. Half a life later, the terrible scene still flashed upon his daydreams and disquieted his elderly sleep.

For much of his young life, George had not seen many people of color. A white person was nothing special to him, for he had played with white children and went home to white people every night in Diamond Grove. In Neosho he lived with a mulatto couple, the Watkins, in a section of town that was mainly black; white people there did not treat him as an equal, but neither did they mistreat him. For the most part, he was not keenly alert to the degree of brownness in anyone's skin. That was to change in Fort Scott. A ferocious experience made him realize what it meant to be a Negro.

As soon as George arrived in Fort Scott, he lied his way into cooking for a wealthy family that needed a maid and a *cuisinier*. George assured the lady of the house that he could braise meat *au jus* and bake like a confectioner. In truth, his culinary experience was limited to cornbread, bacon, peas, and other such staples of the country table. He had never before seen an up-to-date oven or even a menu. But since most people did not follow recipes in those days and cooks varied their preparations depending on the ingredients available to them, the woman did not think it odd that George asked her to demonstrate her particular methods. Before long, he was making sauces and meringue pies.

When he had saved enough money to sustain himself for a few weeks, he left the kitchen and attended school. When his money was gone, he left school and went back to work. That became his pattern—a few months of work, a few weeks of school. There was always work available—housework, ironing, carpet cleaning. Schools in Kansas were in session for only six months, and grade placement in elementary school was somewhat casual. He could usually complete enough work during his periods of attendance to get credit for an entire term. Two indifferent years went by.

At the end of March 1879, George, who was by then about seventeen, was working in town for a blacksmith, helping out with the man's invalid wife. Sent on an errand to the drugstore, he noticed an angry crowd gathered around the county jail nearby. Darkness was falling as he went back to the house, which was attached to the blacksmith shop. No sooner had he reached home than he heard a fearful commotion outside. He opened the front door and saw a hysterical mob running past. Through the rampaging crowd he glimpsed a black man with a rope around his neck being dragged down the street, pulled by a hundred hands.

What happened was this: a twelve-year-old girl who lived near Fort Scott reported that the man, who worked for her father, had raped her while they were walking together outside town. According to the police, her panties and dress were torn, and her body showed marks of violence. For three days, a small posse had been searching for the man, Bill Howard, while the towns-people became more and more agitated about the case. The vigilantes found Howard hiding in an old coal mine and persuaded him to give himself up with the promise that they would not harm him. He was brought to the jail. While he was being questioned, the mob in front swelled to several hundred—"fully a thousand," according to the doubtful report of the *Fort Scott Daily Monitor*, including thirty masked men with drawn revolvers. In a long, confused statement, Howard admitted to tearing the girl's clothes, but with her consent, so that they could have intercourse. He claimed that she willingly agreed to have sex if he promised "not to tell." He denied using any sort of force. He confirmed, after some prevarication, that he had served five years in a penitentiary in Missouri for the attempted rape of a white married woman and had been out of prison about six months. The questioning took two hours. Meanwhile, the crowd waiting outside had swelled into an enraged battalion, throwing rocks at the building and screaming for blood. Finally, they overpowered the jailers, tore the iron railings from the window of Howard's cell, and dragged him out.

They tied a rope around his neck and pulled him down the street past the house where George was standing frozen at the door. According to an account he gave long afterward, he watched aghast as they threw the man to the ground and dashed his brains out onto the sidewalk. They then picked him up and continued dragging him toward the town square, five blocks from the jail, where they hanged what was left of him from a lamppost. Even after the body had been dangling for fifteen minutes, the crowd remained in a frenzy. A few people tried to restore calm, but the attackers were still not appeased.

Shouting "Burn him, burn him!" they took the body down and dragged it to the center of the square, where they made a fire of cardboard boxes and coal oil. Whooping and screaming, they roasted Howard's corpse in an enormous blaze. When his feet and legs had been completely consumed by the flames, a trembling and traumatized policeman picked up the smoldering remains, put them in a dry-goods box, and brought the box to the engine house of the fire station on the plaza.

The reporter describing the incident in the newspaper considered Howard a "demon" and a "black beast" but was nevertheless appalled at the savagery of the crowd. He opined that a quiet lynching would have sufficed to punish the miscreant. About sixty-four white men and forty-nine blacks had been lynched all over the United States during the general period of the Fort Scott incident, but none of the incidents had involved such a rabid display of crowd hysteria. The writer lamented that the reports of bloodthirsty crowds running amok downtown would damage the reputation of the town. The only explanation he could offer for the vicious outburst was that most of the participants were rabble—"country people" he called them—from the coal banks outside the town, an altogether rougher sort than the city folk. Fort Scott, like every settlement in the West with at least three houses, a store, and a clothesline, longed to think of itself as sophisticated.

George, who had never seen a whipping and rarely witnessed a fight, was paralyzed with shock and terror. Inside the house where he passed the night quaking and shuddering, the stench of burning human flesh hung in the air. He threw his few possessions together without quite realizing what he was doing. Before it was light enough outside to see the blood that stained the street, he had fled Fort Scott. He could never flee its hideous memory. Sixty years later he wrote, "As young as I was, the horror haunted me and does even now."

The next three or four years were probably the loneliest in George Carver's long life. He drifted from place to place, cleaning stables, sawing wood, binding up harvests of wheat and oats on the prairies, washing clothes for a dollar here and there, and tending greenhouses for free wherever he could find them, for the joy of nurturing plants. He stayed a night, a week, two weeks in places whose names he forgot as soon as he moved to another little town, living always among strangers. Somewhere he bought a large accordion for seven dollars, his only traveling companion. He amused himself at night by playing it—badly, he thought.

Despite the frightful incident at Fort Scott, hatred of black people was not pervasive in central Kansas, though prejudice was strong against Native Americans. The booster spirit of the West thrived on openness. There was no bias at all against transients who were on their way to settle somewhere. The population was always on the move, and little towns competed with each other to attract such travelers and try to keep them. Each community promoted itself as a future metropolis where men on the make would find their fortunes. An easy way to show that a "city" was destined for growth was to establish the appurtenances of urban life. Every upstart town was likely to have its own daily newspaper, at least one nice hotel with a dressy public lobby, and a school to draw in families that might otherwise continue moving. Sometimes white and black children went to separate buildings; sometimes the schools were mixed. Day laborers of any race were welcome everywhere, although the townspeople tended to look down on the rustics in outlying camps and hamlets who came into town to work.

In a few places, George stayed long enough to spend time in school—towns such as Paola and Olathe. An old grocery store in Olathe served as the one-room elementary school for forty black children—forty children and George, who was then rooming with a barber and his wife. That couple soon struck out for another town, as restless westerners tended to do, but George, for once, stayed behind so that he could continue in the school.

He encountered open-hearted people without whom he might not have survived. Lucy and Christopher Seymour, a childless couple in Olathe, took him in. Lucy was an ex-slave who had belonged to a cultured Virginia family back east. Proud as Cleopatra, she was conscious of being superior to the commoner black people in the town. But those common people were adults; toward children and mannerly young men like George, she was different— gentle and motherly. Devout Christopher attended services twice on Sundays, though the Presbyterian church was unheated. George went with him. He became a lifelong Presbyterian—or so he assumed, since he "never heard of being turned out"—but in truth, George never made much distinction between denominations and attended whatever church was near him. With the Seymour nieces and nephews, George recaptured snatches of childhood, playing all sorts of games, especially marbles, his old métier. And he went to school regularly at last, finishing all the work for the fifth and sixth grade in one term and apparently skipping seventh grade altogether. On Fridays he was the accordionist for school assemblies.

However, neither the Seymours nor anyone else were his surrogate parents after he left Diamond Grove. No one appears to have paid for George's tuition or books during his fragmentary childhood. He was expected to earn his room and board by helping out at whatever work sustained the household. The families only gave him what he called "school privileges," that is, time off during the day to attend his classes, time that he was expected to make up after school and on weekends. Even when he had lived with the Watkins, he did chores during the school lunch recess. He earned whatever pocket money he needed by taking on odd jobs outside.

The Seymours moved to Minneapolis, Kansas, around 1880, and George followed them. Here he was able to attend high school in a primarily white school. Students could be promoted to a higher grade as soon as they had mastered all the subjects at each level, so George did not need to attend a full year to get a year's credit. "High School" consisted of grades eight, nine, and ten; youngsters completing ten years of school were considered high school graduates. In the eighth year, that is, the first year of high school, the fledgling scholars were fatefully placed on either a science or classics track. The scientific curriculum included bookkeeping, physiology, botany, zoology, chemistry, and geology, besides various types of literature, history, and math. The classical curriculum offered physiology and "natural philosophy"—the old-fashioned name for physics—and included three full years of Latin, all the way through Cicero. Presumably George took the scientific course; however, he later mentioned that in high school he had learned "some Latin and Greek," maybe by teaching himself with the schoolbooks available. Tuition for the public school was $1.50 per month.

George had been a loner in elementary school, but when he at last entered high school, he had a wonderful time. He played in quartets and quintets, acted in plays, and participated in everything cultural the school or community offered. At home he helped Aunt Lucy with her laundry business, especially with the fancy ironing that was his forte, and did all kinds of household work after school for other families. Summers he worked as a field hand on the farms outside town.

According to George's recollection, when he was about nineteen he went back to Diamond Grove to spend the summer with his brother and the Carvers. It was not an expensive trip; he was still so small the conductor, commenting that he was rather young to be traveling alone, charged him half-fare. Some sixth sense must have led him back to the farm at that particular time—it was probably 1882. He had had little contact with Jim in the nine years they had been separated. Jim had done some drifting himself, going off here and there to learn various skills. He had returned Diamond Grove by the time of George's visit and was listed in the 1880 U.S. census as a paid farmhand of the Carvers. A photograph of George and Jim together for the last time shows Jim as an alert, strapping fellow, apparently proud of the book or document he is holding and not averse to showing off his rings. George is wearing his first store-bought shirt and some larger man's suit. He stares out blankly from his nest of clothes.

Though vaccination for smallpox had been used on the American continent since the late eighteenth century, Newton County experienced an epidemic the year after George's visit. Jim succumbed to smallpox in 1883 in the railroad town of Seneca, twelve miles from Diamond Grove, where he was working as a plasterer. He died in a pest house, apparently a quarantine facility for indigents. For some lost reason, he was not buried in the Carver family cemetery, though contemporaries averred that Moses Carver paid for Jim's Seneca tombstone. It appears that Jim, like George, did not receive support from the Carvers, whether he needed it or not, once he left the farm. George's last blood relative, his beloved half-brother, was gone. When describing that period, he sometimes referred to himself as a "defenseless orphan." He felt, and he was, alone.

George went back to Minneapolis and finished his last two years of high school. No longer staying with the Seymours, he was living by himself in the neighborhood called "Poverty Gulch." If there is a story behind his separation from the Seymours, it is not one that we will ever know. With "George Carver's Laundry" he was able to support himself, remit his school tuition, and pay five dollars a month rent for his shack with its lean-to and clotheslines in the back. Some curious documents survive from this period. Between July 29, 1880, and January 31, 1882, George made five real estate transactions with Citizens National Bank of Minneapolis, purchasing two lots for $100 and selling them eight months later for $500. It was probably this money that had allowed him to take the trip back home. He was making his way in the world, but slowly.

Two events nudged him into his future. He learned that there was a white George Carver in Minneapolis who was receiving some of his mail, so he began distinguishing himself as George W. Carver. When someone got around to asking him what the W stood for, he answered carelessly, "Washington." He had no idea he would still be lugging that heavy middle name through years of renown when both his name and a consistent way of writing it were deemed important. The other development was a happy one that raised his confidence and his prospects for adult satisfaction. He started growing like a poplar. In the space of one sudden year, he reached his full height, a bit over six feet. Despite his unchanged girl's voice, he finally looked like a man.

George made a close friend who was a year or two ahead of him in school, a venturesome fellow named Chester Rarick. Chester went to Kansas City after graduation from Minneapolis High School and, aflame with the entrepreneurial spirit of the times, opened a business school. The summer after his own graduation in 1884, George joined him, supporting himself with a job in the Union telegraph office as a stenographer. During his churchgoing years, George had learned the organ, in the same way that he had "picked up" a dozen other arts. He thus taught Chester the organ in exchange for typing and shorthand classes in Rarick's new school. The arrangement came to an end one Saturday morning when Chester invited George to breakfast. Eating in a restaurant, even a very simple diner, was an event for George, who never allowed himself such extravagance. However, when the two friends took stools at a counter downtown, the waiter would not serve George. "Never mind me," George kept repeating as they both left the diner, "Go back in. I'll find my breakfast all right." George walked off, "and I never saw him again," Chester recalled.

In any case, George knew that he did not belong in a stenography school. Since he had finally finished high school, he had to find a way to go to college. Encouraged by the advertised "spirit of openness" in the college brochures he consulted, he gathered letters of recommendation and, in 1886, made an eager application to a Presbyterian college in northern Kansas, on the Missouri border. The college sent him a gracious letter of acceptance. It was a coeducational school of fewer than 100 students in a town that was hardly more than a village. Small, sectarian institutions had appeared like primroses on the prairie during the robust years when migrants were still spilling out from the East onto the plains—when every community was hoping for more settlers. All of England during these years had just four degree-granting colleges for its population of 23 million, whereas the state of Kansas, with a population of a million and a half in 1880, had forty-four. Just as every hamlet with a store and a hitching post styled itself a city, every institution with a handful of acolytes called itself a college, in the optimistic expectation of a future student body. Afterward, there were ghost colleges just as there were ghost towns on the prairie, buildings abandoned when the prospective students had passed the town by or had never arrived.

Entering college was a momentous step for George, the exciting culmination of his years of labor and want. Like a man about to embark on a long voyage, he made one more nostalgic trip home. He was visiting Mariah Watkins in Neosho when her nephew Cal Jefferson stopped by, outfitted in his Sunday best and driving a smart buggy. "Seeing George with all his brains and me with none and all dressed up, it made me feel ashamed," Cal recalled. In Diamond Grove, George attended the Sunday service with the whites and saw his childhood friend Forbes Brown.

> George appeared with a broad smile and we were all delighted to see how tall he had grown, though still very slender . . . Learning of his plans to seek a school in Kansas where both whites and Negroes could attend . . . Father expressed the belief that we should have a good visit together where we could sing many of the old songs and Negro spirituals of which we were all so fond . . . George seemed quite tall for his years . . . so gracious in bearing, so appreciative of the invitation to be with us, the only one of its kind, before taking leave of home ties and seeking a life career.

When the little gathering at the Forbes home had run through all the old favorites, the young people sang some of the newer songs.

It was really remarkable the proficiency he revealed in following us with his accordion. He possessed a clear soprano voice, mellow, blending with ours perfectly . . . Mother had asked that we keep "Swing Low Sweet Chariot" for our closing number, "the nearest thing to Heaven." Father remarked that we had always had family worship at the close of the day and invited George to remain for it. He was much pleased to do so and I recall how gentlemanly he was in showing his appreciation by standing and bowing to Father . . . Father's closing sentence in prayer was always the same: "And may our last days be our happiest is our earnest prayer." There was a quiet moment as we all stood, George searching our faces, then each shook his hand, wishing him well. Father was the last near the door, and as he grasped his hand, he said, "George, you can go out into the world and you may make a lot of money; someone could steal it from you. You get a good education and no one can ever take it from you." I never saw him again.

Almost fifty years later, when Carver was a renowned scientist, Brown wrote to him and received George's warm reply: "I feel you and your family are part of my life . . . May He who notices even the sparrow's fall continue to guide and protect you and yours."

The father's advice was not as bromidic in the 1880s as it may seem to us now. The whole country in those days, and especially the West, harkened to the gospel of wealth, the idea that material well-being was a sign of goodness, that poverty was a mark of depravity, and that success in life meant financial success through business, not unproductive book learning. By choosing to spend money and time on an education rather than starting an enterprise, George was swimming against a vogue for moneymaking that surged like high tide over the youth of his generation.

George took leave of his friends, made his way north back to Kansas, and went directly to the college. Zebulon Pike seeing the Blue Peak rising from the mists could not have felt more rapture than George as he looked up at the college building. It was a nice building, not the jerry-built hall of many such lyceums. He walked around and around it as in a dream, noticing the campus shrubbery, taking pleasure in the tidy halls as he searched out the admissions office. Finally, proud and blithe in his dress-up clothes, he presented himself to the college registrar. The college was no fly-by-night school, but one of the earliest ones founded on the prairie. The principal (for in those days, the heads of small colleges were satisfied to call themselves principals) was a Reverend Brown. He looked at the letter of acceptance and stared with bewilderment at the smiling face before him. "But we only accept Indians here," he stammered, "not Negroes. You didn't tell me you were a Negro." The interview that was to be one of the happiest events of his life took less than five minutes.

George walked back down the corridor and out of the building that had seemed so grand a few minutes earlier. College. To be a college student, to be going to college, majoring in this, minoring in that. It was for others, those boys and girls strolling nearby along the walkways, chattering happily, but not for him. In later years, he usually refrained from mentioning the name of the institution when describing the bitter event. The school that rejected him, to its everlasting embarrassment, was Highland College. In 1979, long after the Wizard of Tuskegee was buried with his honors, Carver's assistant Austin Curtis remarked that Highland still would not acknowledge that it had rejected George Washington Carver.

George had spent almost all his money to get to Highland; much as he reviled the place, he could not afford to leave. He turned to his old stand-by, laundry work, which required practically nothing except cheap soap, a cheap fifteen-cent washboard, a tub or even a barrel, and other people's rather more expensive dirty clothes. Despite his bitterness against the Presbyterian college, he attended a local Presbyterian church (one of four in the little town) where a few people who had heard of his rejection befriended him. The John Beeler family, owners of a big apple farm, took George into their house as a general helper. Soon he was filling in as sous-chef for Mrs. Beeler, satisfying the finicky taste of her husband, who would have been a gourmand except for the inconvenience of having no teeth.

A wave of immigration was washing over Highland as people rushed out to claim public lands in western Kansas that were being reopened by the government. Across the great West, settlement was largely propelled by railroad building—indeed, the railroads sometimes offered free transportation to newcomers going to their just-purchased land. Backwoods villages that heard their first train whistle were suddenly transformed into flourishing cities. Other upstart communities were not as lucky. Railroads were built, as anticipated, but many of the trains went "from nowhere in particular to nowhere at all," as the *New York Times* once observed. Many lines were "booster railroads," laid across the blank plain in the hope that farmers and businesses would settle along their routes. A railroad company might run out of money before it could extend a line to its intended destination, leaving only the tracks to mark its brief, metallic tenancy in the red grass. Then there were the disappointed towns that had been bypassed by the railroad altogether—clean, well-planted little prairie towns with fresh wooden sidewalks but no train. Without any newcomers to fill the streets, they faded into a clutch of rundown fences and phantom buildings dotting the desolation of the plains.

When free lands were opened, any head of a household could claim a parcel by paying a ten-dollar fee and pledging to abide by the terms of the federal grant. With the vigor of youth and the pluck of inexperience, the Beeler's enterprising son founded his own town, consisting of his store and a garden plot. He set it in Ness County, expecting that a new railroad would come through it, but the railroad landed about a quarter mile southwest. So the "town" pulled up stakes and moved closer to the tracks. The entire county had only 4,000 people, not all of them literate, but no less than four newspapers to keep up with exciting events. True to young Beeler's expectations, other residents arrived after him, including his friend George Carver, who came the next year and staked a claim on 160 acres. Though the little town of Beeler never turned into a thriving hub of commercial activity, it survived and kept its name, unlike many western communities whose names were breezily changed whenever the municipal council sought to refresh the town's public image. Today Beeler has a population of around 100 and maintains a handsome historical marker to Carver.

Ness County, Kansas, was the farthest west George had ever been. Gone were the green hills of the Missouri-Kansas borderlands, the sheltering woods, and the trees full of birdsong. Here were empty vistas, rare poplars, clean plains with tides of copper grass moving across them and changing color, and a bright line here and there of emphatic sunflowers pushing up from the great beige tableland. As he stood in the middle of his level plot, surrounded by the prairie with its restless grass, the county might have been a continent.

The patents concerning George's 1886–1888 homesteading venture are interesting records that document his indefatigable energy. He was required to show that the grazing land he staked out had no native timber and that he owned no other property of substantial worth. After building a dwelling at least twelve feet square, living there for one year, and making significant improvements to the property, he would be granted a homestead certificate. He could apply for full title after five years of continuous residence. The Homestead Act of 1862 that made his claim possible offered the free land on equal terms to married or single whites, Indians, Negroes, and women. Not far from his plot, houses were set haphazardly on the roadless prairie sod, as if they were about to stray off in different directions. Nothing seemed permanent.

George threw himself into homesteading. If his farm had been a success, he might have disappeared then and there from history. He dug for water several times with a shovel and found more dirt, but he managed anyway to build a house made of sod, boards, and tarpaper, fourteen by fourteen feet, large enough to accommodate a quiet body and an active mind. It was well appointed, for a soddy, since it had plastered walls, a framed window, and bushes that he planted all around. Whitewashed with lime and valued at fifty dollars, it was built to last longer than the six or seven years that was the usual term of a soddy. His furniture was a cook stove, a bedstead and bedding, a cupboard, two chairs, a table, a washtub and board, and a flat iron—he still picked up laundry from customers in town. His neighbor Beeler attested in an affidavit that he had seen George build the house himself and turn over seventeen acres. On ten of these acres, George planted no less than 200 forest and 200 fruit trees, mainly apricot, along with corn, Indian corn, landscape shrubbery, and "a good garden." His only tools were a shovel, a hoe, and a corn seed planter—a simple device with a tube and a long handle, operated with a foot pedal. Where he got the water for orchards is a mystery—possibly he hauled it in buckets from the clayey pond on the Beeler property, three-quarters of a mile from his stake, across the gentle swell of prairie. But let us hope there was an easier supply.

While he waited for his plants to grow, George worked as a laborer on a large ranch next to his property. That ranch was owned by George Steeley, who was owned by his mother. She was visiting Steeley, "getting him settled," as she put it. To make sure her son did not overwork, she hired George Carver, pointed out his place in the hierarchy of the ranch, and kept him in it for the duration of her visit. Kansas, for all its abolitionist fever during the Civil War, was by now spread with transients from the East and South, a few of whom despised black people. The local postmaster, for example, cursed George on sight, volubly and at length. George, quite equal to the situation, responded by laughing. The more eloquent the diatribe became, the more George laughed, until the postmaster could not stop himself from laughing, too. But George could hardly laugh at Mrs. Steeley, whose insults were more subtle.

As county commissioner, Steeley had a house slightly more comfortable than the newer preemptors—it had glass windows brought in by train from the nearest city. His dishes were made of tin, and his table was a simple contrivance of boards, like a picnic table. Rough as it was, George was not allowed to sit at the table with Steeley and his mother. He took his meals separately, an indignity that was commonplace with both white and black domestics in the South but which George had not previously experienced in homes of the West. He took comfort from his friendship with the only other servants on the ranch—the horses, especially Jesup, the gray whose name one day would be known on hundreds of farms in connection with George Carver. George spent his days off playing with the horses, caressing them by the hour, crooning lullabies to them in his melodious woman's voice, teaching them tricks. When Mrs. Steeley sold them, he grieved and worried like a slave mother whose child had been auctioned away.

Mrs. Steeley finally ended her visit and left. From then on, George and his boss worked amiably side by side, companions in toil. Together they raised a dozen sod buildings on the ranch—from barns and sheds to chicken coops. Sod was essentially mud in which dense, thick-rooted grass was embedded— often buffalo grass, so called because it had nourished the now-vanished herds of buffalo. The tough sod was cut in blocks about two feet long, a foot wide, and two to four inches thick. The blocks were laid one on top of the other, like bricks, with the grass side down and the long side out. The wall of a sod building was thus as thick as the length of the block—two or more feet. The wooden frames for the door and window were set before the sod was laid. Later on, shingle roofs would be seen on soddies, but on George's house, and presumably on the other structures he built, the roof was sod laid over some parallel poles, some tarpaper, and some straw, with a hole cut for the stovepipe. In the deep recesses of the window, flowers could bloom year round. The floor was typically dirt, or dirt covered by a carpet. Few homesteaders could afford split logs for the floor, much less the wide, rough-cut planks that could only be bought from some distant sawmill.

With their thick, insulating walls, sod houses were reputed to be cool in the broiling Kansas summers and warm in the biting winters. But when the ground around the house was frozen, the ground within the house was freezing cold as well. Straw spread on the floor made it warmer, but fleas tended to share in the comfort the straw provided. The roof usually leaked, unless the house was double-sodded. George's own house was whitewashed with lime to keep out some of the grating sand and soil, but no sod dwelling was sanitary. The dirt inside was not ostentatious, however, since all soddies were cave-dark.

The wood stove that was a godsend in forested Missouri was an everlasting tribulation on the treeless plain. Without wood, the stove had to be fed with sunflower stalks, big weeds, and above all, dung—dried "chips"—from cows, horses, or long-gone buffalo. The 15 million buffalo that had roamed the western plains were exterminated within twenty years after the coming of railroads, but buffalo droppings, blessedly dry, still stippled the prairie. Beside every wood stove was a bucket of what were euphemistically known as chips. A pile of chips perhaps ten feet high was kept next to the hut, stinking gently on the rare rainy days; grains of the dung would blow unwanted through the window. Chips burned hot but fast, so they had to be constantly replenished. The mealy dung would spill during the many trips to and from the pile, adding to the normal mess around a chip-fired stove. All during the cooking time, the voracious fire had to be stoked—stirred and fed more fuel—and the hands that did the stoking were supposed to be washed each time before they touched the food again. The quick-burning chips produced immense quantities of ash, so that the heavy stove pan was emptied—and spilled—continually. No sooner did a bucket of chips come in than a pan of ashes had to be taken out, and the traffic began again. The satisfaction of owning a bit of earth consoled some homesteaders for their strenuous labors. But it is not surprising that out of the two and a half million western settlers who bought or were given patents under the Homestead Act, some two-thirds eventually abandoned their parched farms and either went back east or emigrated to milder conditions. Many of those who went back had to bid goodbye forever to a husband, wife, or children who were left behind to spend eternity under the wind-swept carpet of the prairie.

It was not all misery. George built a lean-to on the south side of the Steeley house, a sort of crude greenhouse where he kept plants blooming. The path between his house and the greenhouse was trampled hard and bare. Life on his own farm, on the little scrap of Kansas where he was the solitary potentate, seems not to have been unpleasant. His outside garden was a rock garden, an island of gray in the shaggy grass. He grew fond of the plains and even liked the desert farther west where he first saw cacti. The main road was a deeply rutted trail, frozen hard in winter. He would follow it, riding all day to see a vista he had heard about, and come back with a painting of the scene. He drew yucca or cactus when he could get to them, the wine-stained prairie when he could not. Just as there are occasional rainbows to gladden the eastern heart, there were amazing mirages in the western desert to surprise the traveler. Large, fine stones were everywhere. And surrounding George every night, enveloping him, were the cascading fountains of stars in the clear, brilliant sky.

Without many women on the prairie, the bachelors living around the Gregg-Steeley ranch did whatever they could to keep themselves content and civilized. Though they had no sheet music, they formed a quartet and spent long, nostalgic evenings in Steeley's hut or in his store, lost in song. Steeley played the violin, his partner Gregg the guitar, Beeler the B-flat coronet, and Carver the organ—or the guitar, or the violin, or the accordion. These were the years, the late 1880s, when towns first heard the ping of cash registers in stores and the clatter of typewriters in offices. Cities were lively with tramways. Some houses had refrigerators and electric lights, phonographs and telephones. But the lonely farmers gathered in Beeler's store had only stars, the moon, the keening of coyotes, a wasteland of snow surrounding them in winter, and the music they made themselves.

George had been wandering around Kansas for almost a dozen years. He was not always isolated—according to the *Ness City Times,* he was elected assistant editor of a literary society in 1887. But the period during which he was farming his claim were successive years of disheartening drought when many homesteaders were forced to seek other pastures. His first winter, 1886–1887, was the worst in memory. Temperatures plummeted to 68 degrees below zero, people froze to death a few steps from their houses, and cattle perished by the thousands in the cold. In September, grasshoppers might suddenly appear like mile-long strips of smoke eating up the fields, leaving nothing intact on a farm but the mortgage that had paid for planting the crops. Besides all that, it may be that George realized he could never be satisfied in any place without access to knowledge. In 1888, he borrowed $300 from the Bank of Ness County, not for farm implements but, as he explained to the vice president, to further his education. In lieu of repayment, George deeded the claim over to the banker's son three years later for one dollar "and other valuable considerations." Meanwhile, he had taken off for Iowa, bringing with him as many of western Kansas's cactus specimens as he could carry. Sometimes, when recounting his life, he forgot completely about the homesteading years in Beeler.

He "drifted," in his word, north to Winterset, near Des Moines, and got a job as head cook in a large hotel, the Schultz. Three years had gone by since he was rejected from Highland College. He was twenty-five or twenty-six, neither happy nor unhappy, but haunted by a niggling whimper of disappointment. As was his custom, he attended whatever religious services were nearby and thus found himself one Sunday evening sitting in the last row of a white Methodist church. He sang along with the congregation and the choir, his tenor ringing out in the little building. The choir director, Mrs. Milholland, noticed George's fine voice and the next day sent her husband to bring the talented stranger to their house. It was a "splendid residence," according to George.

"I had to sing quite a number of pieces for her, and agree to come to her house at least once a week; and from that time till now, Mrs. And Mrs. Milholland have been my warmest and most helpful friends." (1897)

In time, George Carver forgot practically everything about his youth, but he always recalled the details of his first introduction to Mrs. Milholland. She asked him to give her art lessons; she in turn would teach him singing. Soon he was invited every day. And every day the Milhollands reminded George that it was time for him to fulfill his life's ambition: it was time to go to college.

Never were friends more ideally suited to each other than the Milhollands and George. Aside from her musical activities, Mrs. Milholland was an avid gardener, with her own little greenhouse. She was an amateur painter. And most of all, she and Dr. Milholland were warm, pious, cultivated people. At Christmas, George played Santa Claus, with a white beard under his "rosy" cheeks, not deceiving even the youngest Milholland. In 1928, forty years after leaving Winterset, George wrote to Mrs. Milholland, who had expressed interest in writing a sketch of his life: "You know of my early struggles as but few people do, and in other ways you know me probably as no one else does."

George's job at the Schultz Hotel ended when the owner's son, who had left to seek his fortune as a violinist, came back to secure his future as his father's cook. George had never stopped reading and studying alone. He had opened a laundry in Winterset and was able to save a little toward tuition—to some college, somewhere. The Milhollands were insisting, day and night, as George recalled, that he enter an art school, although it seems not to have occurred to them to question how he would sustain himself after he got in, a problem that caused George himself great anguish. They had even picked out Simpson College, founded by the Methodist Episcopal Church, as the right place for him. It took him a year to save up what he owed on his laundry equipment and the full tuition for his first term—about seventy-five dollars. He left it to Providence and desperate hope that he would somehow manage to continue financing the successive three terms. He walked the twenty-five foodless miles to Indianola, Iowa, thinking all the while of his last attempt to enter college. He arrived wary and footsore at the registrar's office. But this time he was not rejected.

3

A REAL HUMAN BEING

I n fact, from the day he arrived, Simpson College cherished him as if he were already its most famous alumnus. If there was a turning point in George's youth, it was the autumn day in 1890 when he walked into Simpson's airy art studio and took his place among a dozen students who were all eager to sit next to him. Suddenly, he was no longer an outsider with his dark face pressed against the glass doors of a college. A chair was waiting for him in every classroom.

"I shudder to think what might have happened if Simpson College had closed its doors . . . when I came, hungering and thirsting for an opportunity to develop as God gave me light and strength. They made me believe I was a real human being."

Simpson College at that time consisted of three schools—business, art, and music—with 426 students in all and a faculty of seventeen. Of the twenty art students, all except George were young women; some were married. The art room, housed in the science hall, was described in the college catalog as "elegant," as indeed it must have been, for it boasted steam heat and skylights. The Milhollands had chosen well; Simpson College offered serious courses: perspective, geometric drawing, figures, landscape, flower painting, China painting (much in fashion), and handwriting, which was included, a little apologetically, in order to meet the needs of those students who might not prosper as painters and would subside into public school teaching—the majority. Students attended classes four hours a day, in addition to having two private lessons each week. Because of the lacunae in his haphazard education, George was placed in the preparatory division, taking arithmetic, grammar, essays, one art course, and etymology—a study which was then in academic vogue because of the pervasive respect for Latin. After he paid his fees (tuition was fifteen dollars), he had ten cents left.

"For quite one month I lived on prayer, beef suet, and corn meal, quite often doing without the suet and meal." (1927)

Penury is one life experience that is never forgotten. Instead of fading, the memory of it becomes more vivid with time. In Carver's 1897 sketch of his life, the suet-and-meal episode had lasted only "one whole week." Thirty years later, his memory had stretched it to a famished month. Suet is the hard fat that gave flavor and cholesterol to bean soup and other vegetable concoctions before modern cardiac research all but outlawed it. "Had his Winterset friends known of the very slender purse he carried, his first days there might have been very different," Mrs. Milholland later wrote—disingenuously, since she knew better than anyone that George was destitute.

The president of the college gave him permission to live in an abandoned shed on the edge of the campus. In those days there were no little amenities in offices and trains such as plastic cups and sugar packets that one might take along for later use. George moved into the shed's one unheated room, which meant simply walking in with his rucksack and settling in on the floor with the mice and insects who held a prior lease. He did not have so much as a broom or a dish. George asked his art teacher, Miss Budd, if he might saw her stove wood in lieu of payment for the obligatory private lessons. Recognizing her pupil's exceptional talent and his exceptional poverty, she mobilized the townspeople to give him work.

"The news soon spread that I did laundry work and really needed it, so from that time on, favors not only rained but poured upon me. I cannot speak too highly of the faculty, students, and in fact, the town generally. They all seemed to take pride in seeing if he or she might not do more for me than someone else."

In 1956, an old classmate described George's first weeks at Simpson:

> As he was the only Negro who had ever enrolled at our college, he was the center of interest to the student body. Like many of the other students, I was anxious to meet him . . . There were a few colored people living in Indianola, and they were all accepted and respected members of the community. And in young Carver, as we came to know him, we saw so much

beyond the color that we soon ceased to sense it at all . . . I felt a special interest in him, realizing how lonesome he must be as the only one of his race among so many . . .

I sought him out in the little shack which he had been permitted to occupy rent free. He had no furniture so we sat on boxes the merchants of the town had permitted him to take. I saw the old battered and broken cook stove which he had retrieved from a dump, and the boiler and wash board and tubs which he had secured on credit.

I well remember that in taking my laundry and in going for it, I always took occasion to sit a while and visit with him. I could tell him of college customs and sports . . . and something about the advanced studies, and he could tell me of his experience and of his insight into nature and into his fellow beings.

The town, too, opened its white arms to him. The Listons, owners of the local bookstore, made him one of the family after George's art teacher told them that he needed a family. "He was a constant surprise to all who knew him," Mrs. Liston wrote. When she first approached his shack, he "timidly opened the door for me; so modest was his demeanor that I scarcely knew how to approach him. Something in his quiet manner made it difficult for me to state my real errand"—which was to rescue him from semistarvation. She noticed in one corner of the room "an old black bread pan half filled with corn meal and water, and an old stove on which was a boiler filled with shirts and collars he was laundering for the students." Like George, Mrs. Liston was an artist and religious mystic. She signed herself "Your mother" in the letters she regularly wrote to him for the rest of her life. Sometimes students or the town folk put money under his door while he was at school or slipped in a ticket to a concert or lecture. Increasingly and unwittingly, he captured them all in a sort of irregular fascination.

"The people are very kind to me here and the students are wonderfully good," he wrote to the Milhollands. "They took it into their heads I was working too hard and had not enough home comforts so they clubbed together and bought me three real nice chairs, a bed, and a very nice table. They left them for me while I was at school. I never found out who did it. Of course I had my suspicions and accused a number of boys, but they stoutly denied it."

One of the citizens described passing George's little dwelling after he had furniture.

> I frequently would see him seated at the table with the door open. I could not help noticing how nicely everything was arranged, just as precise as though he were entertaining company. Then, too, I frequently passed him on the streets carrying very carefully an armful of fine, white shirts which he had laundered. (This was when shirts had to be polished very shiny and stiff.) How did he look? Tall, angular, and somewhat stooped. He dressed plainly, and was neat and clean. His voice was very peculiar.

There is no doubt that George was a great favorite among the young women who were his classmates and that he had an easy, jovial rapport with all of them. He had a nickname, "Pleney," for his easel partner. "He was lean, tall, and hungry-looking," Pleney recalled; "Miss Budd insisted we call him 'Mr. Carver,' but we called him 'George' when she wasn't around." But if the girls met George on the street while they were with friends, he casually crossed over to the other side to save them the awkwardness of having to introduce him. Despite George's soulful, penetrating gaze and his handsome mien, there were no romances or even flirtations. He did not need to be warned to keep his distance from young white females.

He loved being in the middle of the college bustle—singing in the chapel services that were required of all students, but also joining the voluntary clubs and attending every cultural event he could afford. He was on the baseball team; active in the literary societies and the student Y.M.C.A.; he took both voice and piano instruction, paying for his lessons with paintings that the teachers, straitened enough themselves, tactfully and generously accepted.

"They are very kind and take especial pains with me; I can sing up to high D and three octaves below."

He played music when the college gave concerts in nearby towns. All of his grades except in geometry were in the 90s. And still he grew all kinds of flowers around his little hole of a house, his borrowed shed. In his spare time, which was spare indeed, he wrote bantering letters to the Milhollands—the letters of a merry collegian—though always closing them solemnly, "Your humble servant in God."

Intellectually, at least, he was promiscuous. He tried to make all the sciences his own—geology, entomology, mycology, ornithology, and botany, especially. He was at ease with any musical instrument he cared to play and was talented in a number of arts, everything from lace making to sculpture. He loved poetry. With his capacious appetite for learning and creating, he could have succeeded in any of a dozen fields. But it was only in science that he could hope to provide himself with that vexatious necessity, a livelihood. George knew this. Nevertheless, during the three terms that he was at Simpson, truly happy for the first time in his life, he had no thought but to be an artist. Like any son writing about incidents that he knows will give his parents pleasure, he wrote to the Milhollands, "I have the name, unjustly, of having one of the broadest minds in school. My teacher told me the other day that she is sorry she did not find me out sooner, so she could have planned differently for me." He was then embarrassed at his boasting and added, "Well, this subject is getting a little monotonous to me and was before I begun it, but I thought you would like and be interested in knowing what they thought of me. Please don't let anyone see this letter but the home folks."

The teacher who would have "planned differently" for him was his art professor, Etta May Budd. As the end of his two-year curriculum drew near, she began to think about the career prospects of her protégé. Young as she was—hardly older than George, who was about twenty-seven—she correctly foresaw that in the America of the dawning century, a black man was almost certain to have a beggarly life as a painter, irrespective of his talent. Botany—specifically agriculture—would offer him significantly more opportunities.

It was difficult to convince George to give up his dream of being an artist, to push him out of the snug nest of Simpson College, where for once he was part of a community, and nudge him forward to unknown ground. But Etta Budd had persuasive arguments for drawing him away from art and into botany. Iowa State College of Agriculture and Mechanic Arts in Ames—fifty miles from Indianola—was the Harvard of agricultural institutions. From its faculty would come three U.S. Secretaries of Agriculture, one of whom, Henry A. Wallace, would be Franklin Roosevelt's vice president. Even in the 1890s, no other college enjoyed its outstanding reputation in agriculture. But would

Iowa Agricultural College accept George Carver, with his sporadic schooling and his black-coffee complexion? Of course it would. Miss Budd's father, Joseph Budd, one of the nation's eminent botanists, was Iowa State's professor of horticulture and the handsome head of its department of agronomy. At one point he even served as the college's acting president.

George was not elated at his admittance. Depressed at the idea of leaving the precincts of art, he struggled with the decision to abandon his easel. What finally seems to have swayed him was the realization that as an agricultural researcher he could be of much greater service to his race than as a painter. The brutality he had witnessed at Fort Scott and the nicks he had suffered in his own journey to college had convinced him to dedicate his life to uplifting his people. The undernourished blacks all over the country needed agronomy; they would only need painting when they had enough to eat. But even as he prepared to leave Indianola, he had not quite made up his mind that the transfer to Iowa State would be permanent. The Simpson college newspaper, referring to "our friend, Mr. Carver," wrote that he planned to return and graduate from the art school the next year. The newspaper lamented his leaving; George lamented it more. Once he had made the decision to choose agriculture and not art, he locked up his paints and canvases and could not look at them for a long time, so sharp was his yearning for them and for his classmates. Those friends did not forget him. They sent him a bouquet as a token of remembrance even after he had been at Iowa State for a full year. When he came back briefly the next year, Simpson treated the visit as a special occasion that warranted an article in the campus weekly.

As for sensitive, sensible Miss Budd, she fades back into obscurity after launching her star pupil. She taught art for many more years and then died poor in a retirement home. She lived long enough to take pride in George's fame as a scientist. Her family home in Ames, where George had repaired the porch and cleaned the shed to pay for his lessons, is now a recovery house dedicated to rehabilitating wayward youth.

In 1894 Iowa State College, set amid the sparse population of the open country, was a world away from the superstition and squalor that had almost buried George in his adolescent years. Iowa State had been the first of the nation's land-grant colleges dedicated both to scholarship and practical instruction in farming and engineering. The Morrill Act of 1862 awarded public lands to the states for the support of higher education. Land-grant colleges agreed to provide certain services, such as military training. The Hatch Act of 1887 supplemented the Morrill Act, offering federal funds for the establishment of agricultural experiment stations connected to the colleges. Iowa State was an exciting place, expanding and forward-looking, from the new Agricultural Experiment Station with its sparkling laboratory to the Sanitary Building that housed the just-formed dairy department. Though they were recent, the campus buildings were stately and graceful, not at all like office architecture or like the stone immensities of northeastern colleges. The academic halls might have been the fine, gabled houses of suburban dowagers. Lest the students feel isolated on their cantle, a little tram—the Dinky—ran to and from town every two hours. George had always dreamed of possessing books; now he had 8,000 just at hand in the library. Classes were small because the student body was small—about the same size as Simpson's—but growing, like everything in the area. The four-year course in agriculture was a focused curriculum of algebra, horticulture, chemistry, livestock, elocution, principles of heredity, dairying, and entomology. Sophomore horticulture as yet had no textbook because, up until then, no one on the sweeping prairies had thought about growing anything but corn and hogs.

Iowa State, full of the song of progress, should have welcomed its first black student. People of color had long been scattered all over the West. Substantial numbers had worked as cowboys on the plains and served in the U.S. cavalry on the open range. However, Ames, Iowa, was not a frontier outpost but a city that saw neither cowboys nor cavalry in any numbers. George was a singular oddity. Some of the townspeople had seen a few black people, but they were still taken aback by George. His anthracite complexion went against their notion that the only smart colored people were those with some white blood. On the campus he could not have been more conspicuous if he had appeared among them with his curly head upside down. Many of the students at Iowa State had never looked into a black face until they encountered George's gentle gaze, and they had certainly never shaken a black person's hand. Though the admissions office accepted him, the students did not—at first.

Tuition and room were free, but students were expected to bring their own linens, carpet, and furniture. George had neither bed nor bedding; of all the poor students who attended the school, he was undoubtedly the neediest. The college officials decided it was better not to try to install him in the white dormitory. What to do with him? Professor James Wilson solved the problem by turning over his office in North Hall to serve as George's room. Years later, when George was one of Iowa's most celebrated graduates, several professors jealously claimed credit for having sacrificed their offices so that the homeless boy could have a place to sleep.

Unlike the public secondary schools in the West, where many of the teachers were barely literate, Iowa State's faculty members were versatile and learned people of high academic standing, all trying to make their mark. Etta's father, Joseph Budd, won distinction by proving that farms in Iowa could profitably grow a variety of fruits—and by writing that much needed horticulture book on orchard growing. He could not have imagined, when he lectured to George and the other students, that his ideas would soon be transplanted to the South's clay hills.

The head of the new experiment station was Louis H. Pammel, eventually to become a national authority on weeds and poisonous plants and the author of a standard reference work for botanists and veterinarians. George, who was quickly adopted by the liberal-thinking botany faculty, naturally became close to its chairman Pammel and, in time, to Pammel's wife and six children. Pammel, born in 1862, was about George's age and, like him, a young prodigy. He had not yet received his Ph.D. when George studied under him, but he was already an expert on parasitic fungi; it was Pammel who sponsored George's serious research in mycology. George and Pammel were to write to each other regularly for more than thirty years until 1931, when Pammel died. George then continued corresponding with Mrs. Pammel and the children until his own death.

Henry C. Wallace, a graduate of Iowa State, was a farmer and the publisher of a farm journal. He earned a bountiful salary teaching in the dairy department at Iowa—$1,700 a year (the school's first woman engineering professor was paid $300.) Almost thirty years after George met him, Henry C. Wallace would become U.S. Secretary of Agriculture (1921 to 1924). Like all of the faculty, he was fond of George and watched out for him. George sometimes took Wallace's six-year-old son on field trips in the woods. "George Carver introduced me to the mysteries of botany and plant fertilization . . . [he] deepened my appreciation of plants in a way I could never forget," said the younger Wallace who, like his father, eventually served as U.S. Secretary of Agriculture. Wallace the son was to reenter George's life in later years, as he followed his father's wide trail into politics.

James C. "Tama" Wilson was perhaps the most interesting and interested of all the luminaries who befriended George at Iowa State. His six-year tenure as a professor exactly coincided with George's attendance. Born in Scotland, Wilson was the eldest of fourteen children. His family immigrated to the United States when he was fifteen, as pioneer farmers in Iowa. He managed to graduate from a public high school and a small Iowa college, but he possessed no advanced degree, except the honorary doctorates that were later conferred on him—and his own advanced degree of practical imagination. He did not grow up black like George, but he well understood the pungent details of hardship. Wilson had already won prominence as a two-term U.S. congressman and had just come back to Iowa State to teach when he first met George. He was no stranger to college life, having served as a regent of the school for some years. At fifty-four, he was a generation older and a century wiser than the young professors who were George's contemporaries.

Wilson was no ordinary politician. He was a straightforward, earnest man, a visionary who wanted above all to make the United States self-sufficient in food. It is hard now to remember that there was a time when this country was not feeding the world with its farm surpluses, a time when America was importing staple grains. Wilson's unassuming manner masked prodigious energy and ambition. He was determined to make agricultural studies both scientific and practical and to elevate the status of agronomy within academe. About the time George received his master's degree and left the college, Wilson was picked by President William McKinley to be U.S. Secretary of Agriculture, a post he retained under Presidents Theodore Roosevelt and William Howard Taft. Though it strains the imagination to think of the homey Wilson adapting himself to the pretensions of Washington, he in fact became the longest serving cabinet secretary—sixteen years—in the history of the United States, *after* spending twelve years in Congress. He was the consummate Washington insider. He transformed the Department of Agriculture from a small data-collecting bureau into a major branch of government that initiated bushels of legislation dealing with all phases of farming and forestry. He set up experiment stations throughout the country where serious scientific research was applied to agriculture. He started farm demonstration programs in the South. At the turn of the century, he initiated cooperative extension services in agriculture and home economics, in consultation with George Carver, who was by then established at Tuskegee. He improved roads across the land and instituted more careful inspection of food products. Under his direction, the lowly Department of Agriculture became this country's authoritative source for scientific knowledge about farm management, land cultivation, dams, soil investigation, and forest preservation. All of that was still in the future when Wilson turned over his office to George in 1890. Their years together would enrich them both.

Those were the teachers who became George's heroes, generous men who loved both books and cows, men who were as happy examining soil samples as listening to Bach. George wanted to be like them in every detail. If ever there was a man at the right time in the right place to launch a career in agriculture, it was George at Iowa State. Farming was in the throes of a deep depression as George entered college. Both farmers and legislators were seeking help from science as never before, trying to increase production and control crop destruction. Meanwhile, the country looked to its educated people to fill the schools that were burgeoning everywhere. Before the Civil War, only a few hundred public high schools existed in the United States (though private academies were numerous.) By 1890, there were several thousand—still only a scattering in comparison with later years, but a many-fold increase. In 1870, only 16,000 children graduated from any high school, only 9,000 from college. By 1890, those numbers had almost trebled. It was the best time ever to be a teacher and an agriculture expert.

George began his life at Iowa State by working, as usual, at menial jobs— cutting wood, cleaning barns, taking care of the chemical, botanical, and bacteriological laboratories, and working as janitor for North Hall. It was his responsibility to keep up all the flower beds on the campus—he was, in fact, the college's landscaper. Professor Budd put him in charge of the greenhouses and considered him his assistant almost from the beginning. The administrators, however, were not all as open-minded as the professors. George was told point blank that he could have a job serving in the student dining hall, but he could not eat there. He was to take his meals in the basement with the field hands. And so he did, set apart from the other students and regarded by them as a kind of school servant.

Homesick for convivial Simpson College, George wrote to his "mother" in Indianola, Mrs. Liston. He was discouraged, wondering if the transfer to Ames had been a mistake and if he should drop out. Mrs. Liston consulted Miss Budd. "Stand by him," Etta told her. "My father is going to keep him where he is." Mrs. Liston both stood and walked by him. The worthy lady took a train to Ames and spent a day conspicuously going all over the campus with George, desegregating him. At mealtime, she, too, joined the exiles in the basement. The sight of an elegant white lady with George, walking and talking in the library, the class halls, the laboratory, the auditorium, had its intended effect on the impressionable students. "The next day," George remembered, "everything was different, the ice was broken, and from that time on, things went much easier."

"I as yet do not like it as well here as I do at Simpson because the helpful means for a Christian growth is not so good, but the Lord helping me, I will do the best I can . . . I am so anxious to get out and be doing something. I can hardly wait for the time to come. The more my ideas develop, the more beautiful and grand seems the plan I have laid out to pursue, or rather, the one God has destined for me." (1891)

He was among kindred Christian spirits at Iowa. James Wilson, Louis Pammel, and George were all of them in self-appointed collaboration with the Creator. The politician Wilson was as zealous in proselytizing as any pulpit theologian. From the moment Wilson arrived at Iowa State, he made a concerted effort to get the entering freshmen "started right" and "to turn them from agnosticism, which was too prevalent at the institution." George, he wrote, was his essential messenger.

When students began to come in at the beginning of a new term, Carver and I would sit down and plan how to get boys who were Christians to go down to the depot and meet them, come up with them and help them get registered, help them get rooms, and all that; which would establish acquaintance with them and enable young men of Christian leanings to get them into prayer meetings, etc. Before Mr. Carver and I left the institution, there had been quite a reformation brought about, and now that college is famous for the firm stand taken by its students along Christian lines.

As an agricultural and mechanical college, Iowa State was aware of being considered lower class by institutions that were purely academic. It laid great stress, therefore, on providing a well-rounded curriculum with careful attention to the humanities. There were no less than seven literary clubs on campus. George, who was a strenuous joiner, turned up in all of them. He participated in the German club, the art club, and the agricultural society that he helped found. With his artistic abilities, he became the one-man decorating committee for most student events. He was active in the Welsh Eclectic Society, a jovial debating club whose stated purpose was to foster "development of the students in science, literature, and public speaking." The meetings were carried on in a mock courtroom style, putting students on trial for violating the facetious rules of the dining hall. (The days when George was banished from the dining hall were well past.) Despite his woman's voice, George was a lusty participant in the "courtroom" debates. Sometimes he sang or played an instrument to give the trials a little extra sparkle, but more often he gave standup comedy presentations, such as a satire of a concert pianist wrecking a piano. "I have been to a reception nearly every night last week and the cards are out for part of this week," he wrote the Milhollands. He was thoroughly living his dream of being a college student, despite being nearly thirty. He had begun wearing a flower in his lapel, the one and only detail of his dress that he never neglected throughout his life.

He joined the Iowa State glee club. According to one biographer, he was offered a scholarship in singing at the Boston Conservatory of Music. One wonders how Bostonians could have heard his peculiar voice singing in Iowa, but in any case, he had tamed his desultory enthusiasms by this time and was not tempted to go off into yet another field. Male freshmen and sophomores were required to undergo military drill to train them as line officers and company instructors in the army. George loved the uniforms, the marching music, military science, and the details of "gentlemanly deportment." He rose to the highest rank of student officers—cadet captain—though of course at that time no black man could have become a commander of white servicemen in the regular U.S. army. That was just as well. It was the theatrics of patriotism he liked, not the theaters of actual war, which, in fact, he despised. He joined the Y.M.C.A. of the Agricultural College—a club that was nothing if not earnest in its twice-weekly discussion groups. The topics for one Wednesday night were "Heart Purity," "How to Obtain Peace," "Cheerfulness," and "Talking and Working." He was twice chosen by the Y.M.C.A. to represent Iowa State at a national summer camp in Wisconsin. It was the only two weeks in his college life when he did not have to work.

One of the few things Carver boasted about in later life was that during these lean years, he worked his way forward.

"Probably the most unique thing in my entire growing up is that I would never allow anyone to give me money. I wanted to earn my way. I have been for months without money enough to get a postage stamp, yet would not accept money. All I asked for was a job, and did not expect and would not accept pay for trivial services rendered." (1927)

Among his many part-time jobs, he served as a "rubber" or masseur for the Iowa State football team, which helped him get to know the campus athletes. He participated in fund-raising shows for the athletic program, doing stunts and balancing acts. An eye-opening photo of George in drag was saved from some college play. There was little, it seems, he couldn't do, and nothing he wouldn't do for fun or self-improvement.

His art teacher (for he still took art classes) entered several of his paintings in an art competition in Cedar Rapids; some of his friends bought him the train ticket. Four of his paintings were picked by the judges to be exhibited at the 1893 Chicago World's Fair, including a painting done a few years earlier of the cacti of western Kansas. In those days, people dressed up when traveling, when going to a business section of town, and certainly when attending an event such as a World's Fair. George, in his oldest work clothes, was in Ames on his way to clean a professor's house when a group of his classmates waylaid him, hustled him into a department store, and forced him to try on a suit. Then they bought the suit so that he would have no excuse not to take his paintings to Chicago.

It would be difficult to think of any material gift George Carver treasured more than that set of clothes, evidence of the hard-won love of his young friends. The famous Suit gathered a long, honorable history as it and George aged. He wore it, and it exclusively, the rest of his life. It figured into a serious, failed romance. No one who described George Washington Carver in his elderly years failed to describe his threadbare, discolored, patched Suit, always worn with a fresh flower in the lapel. "I think you'd call it a Norfolk coat," averred his secretary, who first saw the surviving half of the Suit in the 1930s. "It had a belt in the back. It was brown; it was a very fine-looking suit." That is, it was fine looking when it was presented to George in 1893 so that he could make a decent appearance. At that time, it was considered "fawn-colored." In later years, the Suit changed hue about every decade. One of Carver's Iowa classmates visited him in Tuskegee just before his death and recognized the decayed remains of the Suit. Carver, he wrote, had on "an old wool cap, plaid wool shirt, run-over shoes, and an old Prince Albert coat with a wide braid around the edges. The coat was green with age." Both Norfolk and Prince Albert coats were by that time so long out of style that nobody bothered to ascertain which type of historical artifact Carver was wearing.

While some students were pressing expensive presents upon him, others still snubbed him from time to time. Once, in the dining hall, he sat down at a table where a student who had recently come from the South was ensconced. The southerner began rattling his silverware and scraping his chair to show his irritation and finally picked up his tray and moved to the next table. The students at that table who had been observing the scene began rattling their silverware and scraping their chairs and finally gathered up their own trays and moved to the table where George was sitting, the table the disgruntled boy had left.

Just as at Simpson, George was careful not to arouse rumors that he was anything more than a platonic friend to the girls at Iowa State. It should not surprise us that the only black man in the college did not attempt to court other students when, all over the country, men of his race went hanging from trees, accused of the crime of casting interested eyes on white women. Free-spirited girls at Iowa State might be amiable and solicitous toward George, but only a true rebel against convention would have taken up with him romantically, at her peril and his. George understood his unique position, his "place." Besides all that, in those days he sported a big, tangled moustache grafted, apparently, with dried roots and brambles. No woman would have wanted to be kissed by it.

"A young railroad man in Ames was killed in a train accident, leaving a widowed mother. George had one dollar which he gave her with his sympathy." (An Iowa classmate, 1945.)

In the middle of George's senior year, several of his classmates noticed that the usually ebullient George seemed worried. The young people found out that he was physically and financially exhausted and was about to withdraw from school without his degree. His friends started a subscription list to fund him through his last semester—a list headed by President Beardshear, who managed to find better-paying employment for George within the college so that he did not have to drop out.

Painting still held fast to a part of him. A few months before graduation, when he was making firm plans to earn a master's degree at Iowa, George was still fantasizing about art school. The graduate curriculum at Iowa was a two-year program, but George, always intensely ambitious, thought he could squeeze it into one. He planned to do his nonresidence work while taking a course at the Chicago Academy of Arts and the Moody Institute. "I am saving all the pennies I can for that purpose," he wrote the Milhollands.

George's notebooks attest to both his artistic ability and the seriousness with which he attended his training in agriculture. There are exquisitely detailed illustrations—of such things as the powdery mildew on cherry trees, parasites on cabbage and rutabagas, tomato rot, and microscopic analyses of botanical phenomena of every sort. A large quantity of notes is devoted to the chemistry of milk, with many graphs to show the influence of various feeds on the production of milk fat, milk sugar, and on the gain or loss of fat in the cow. One large notebook deals with the bacteriology of milk and cheese. Even in these early days, George was thinking about writing a textbook: he organized each of his studies into a unit and estimated the time it would take to teach each section adequately and to write it up as an instructional chapter.

Before he received his bachelor's degree in 1894 as Iowa State's first black graduate, he was granted a teaching assistantship and admitted to the master's degree program. In graduate school, he taught classes in microbiology and botany and served as faculty sponsor for the art club. He continued working closely with Pammel, since he was again in charge of the greenhouse and was the Assistant in Botany in the Iowa Experiment Station. Even as an undergraduate, George had published papers. In his two years of graduate work, he wrote two bulletins with Pammel and three on his own.

"I can still see him starting for the fields and woods with his long, tin specimen case swung over his shoulder and a butterfly net in his hand." (An Iowa classmate, 1945.)

Since fungi are among the primary enemies of plants, it was natural that the botanist Pammel would persuade George to make mycology his specialty at Iowa. As a graduate student, George gathered a collection of over 20,000 fungus specimens. By then, he was accompanying James Wilson on short lecture tours. Wilson would talk on agriculture and George would lecture on mycology or horticulture. Sometimes he went in place of Wilson or Pammel, so that long before receiving an advanced degree, he was becoming well known in his field. His second graduation was a celebration welcoming George into the faculty. Three girls at Simpson College sent another bouquet to their former classmate. Only three years after that graduation, his teacher Dr. Joseph Budd published an article in which he cited George Carver as his authority.

George did not need to look for a post after earning his master's degree. Iowa State expected him to remain there as a full-fledged experiment station botanist with a comfortable salary. Nevertheless, while still a student, he began getting job offers, and not only from an Ames florist, who assured George that he "could name his salary." A full year before George's scheduled graduation, the president of Alcorn Agricultural and Mechanical College for Negroes in Mississippi had written to Iowa's President Beardshear, asking about George's qualifications. "Mr. Carver has admirable tact and is universally liked by faculty and students," Beardshear replied. "He is a thorough Christian gentleman and gives good promise of marked scientific usefulness in his chosen work. We would not care to have him change unless he can better himself." The president demanded to know the salary being offered and the anticipated duties. "Please send me a copy of your latest catalogue and courses of study. In case your position proves desirable, we can give him ironclad recommendations." In other words, "We think he's probably too good for you."

Alcorn's president then wrote directly to George, offering him outright the Chair of Agriculture. George's teachers were appalled. Asked to provide letters of recommendation, they praised their protégé extravagantly. But they made it clear that they had advised George to stay at Iowa. "I have great confidence in Mr. Carver's ability," wrote Professor Pammel. "This has been backed up by having him reappointed assistant with an increase in salary. Mr. Carver has a great future before him." Professor Budd was more blunt. "Indeed, we do not like to lose him. He will get next year as good a salary as you offer." Wilson's letter was a multipage essay of disappointment over George's intention to accept the Alcorn position.

> I do not want to lose Mr. Carver from our station staff here . . . I have been more intimate with Mr. Carver than with any other student on the campus . . . In cross fertilization and the propagation of plants, he is by all means the ablest student we have here. Except for the respect I owe the professors, I would say he is fully abreast of them and exceeds in special lines in which he has a taste.

Wilson described George's knowledge of animal physiology and his particular knowledge of various feeds for stock. As for plants,

> he has a passion for them, in the conservatory, the orchard, the garden and the farm. In that direction, we have nobody who is his equal.

By the time he worked toward a close, Wilson's letter of recommendation had begun to sound like a letter of mourning for a lost colleague, full of regret for the dashed hopes he had harbored for him.

> I had designed that he should experiment along the line of developing our native plants, cross-fertilizing, and introducing such new plants from

all over the world as would be beneficial to farmers and orchardists of Iowa.

We have no one to take his place, and I would never part with a student with so much regret as George Carver . . . I think he feels at home among us, but you call for him to go down there and teach . . . the people of his own race, a people I have been taught to respect . . . I cannot object to his going. It will be difficult for me to find another student who will quietly do the religious work that Mr. Carver has been doing, who will bring the same gracious influence to bear on the boys coming here from the Iowa farms, in order that they may be started in the right direction. It will be difficult, in fact impossible, to fill his place.

These are warm words, such as I have never before spoken in favor of any young man leaving our institution, but they are all deserved. If you should conclude to take him from us, I will recognize the finger of Providence and submit.

With respect,

James G. Wilson

George did not go to Alcorn, however. In the view of many of his professors, he made an even worse choice. In April 1896, George received an invitation from Booker T. Washington to join him in work—"very, very hard work"—at Tuskegee Institute, for a yearly salary of $1,000, housing and board, but no travel expenses. Tuskegee Institute was still a primitive place with no standing in the ranks of higher education, since it functioned as an elementary school, a high school, a vocational school, and a normal school—all with a total student body of about 600. But Washington himself had a name and a reputation. He was about to receive an honorary M.A. from Harvard. His philosophy of teaching his people by starting at their present level, however basic, and training them in the fields that would reach large numbers and lift them as quickly as possible out of poverty—these were exactly the ideas of both James Wilson and George Carver.

George was not, however, immediately excited about Washington's inquiry. He really could not consider any position, he wrote, until after graduation in the fall, and he explained that he had long been in communication with Alcorn, whose offer he was preparing to accept. After another letter from Washington, George was even more cautious.

It is certainly very kind of you to take the interest you have in me. Of course it has always been the one great ideal for my life to be of the greatest good to the greatest number of "my people," possible, and to this end I have been preparing myself for these many years, feeling as I do that this line of education is the key to unlock the golden door of freedom to our people. Please send me catalogues and any other data you may have with reference to your institution, so I may get some idea of the present scope of your work and its possible and probable extension.

In his next letter, George explained that the comparatively low salary Tuskegee offered was not holding him back, so long as he might expect an advance in wages and a house. "I already have a position here as you will see by the letterhead, and one of my professors told me today they would raise my wages here if I would stay, but I expect, as I have already stated, to go to my people."

What finally decided George to choose Tuskegee was that he met Washington face-to-face when the educator was in Cedar Rapids for a speech. In person, Washington was more than charismatic: he was compelling. He drew idealists like Carver to him like Wotan beckoning followers to a misty Valhalla of heroic warriors. After their conversation, George never again thought seriously of going anywhere but Tuskegee. Professors Wilson and Wallace accompanied George to meet Washington and likewise went away under a semihypnotic spell that lasted in Wilson's case for years. They were still reluctant to let go their friend, "one of my most brilliant students." as Professor Pammel wrote. "He was the most wonderful collector I have ever known."

George harbored vague hopes of taking a leave from Tuskegee after two years in order to study art in France. That dream was never to come true. "I am looking forward to a very busy, pleasant, and profitable time at your college and shall be glad to cooperate with you in doing all I can through Christ who strengtheneth me to better the condition of our people." In truth, George had little idea of what he would be doing in Tuskegee, what the facilities were, or who (besides God) his colleagues might be. For six years, he had been in the shelter of Iowa State, the prized young genius of a group of men who themselves possessed extraordinary intellects. Washington neglected answering George's repeated requests for information about Tuskegee and even ignored his inquiry about plant samples, but that did not deter the young man. "I presume you overlooked the little slips you spoke of inserting," he wrote in May 1896. Nevertheless he continued, "Providence permitting, I will be there in November. God bless you and your work."

Few celebrations in George's life could have been more emotional than his leaving Iowa State. The *Ames Intelligencer* wrote of George, "He goes forth strong in the assurance that the best wishes of all follow him. We know of no one who failed to be won to friendship by his genial disposition . . . we wish him Godspeed." The faculty and students presented him with a superb microscope and case as a going away gift. They could not have imagined that it would be the sole piece of equipment in his "laboratory" at Tuskegee for the next decade and beyond. His well-wishers crowded the station platform. There was much hugging and waving and wiping away tears. Then George, wearing the suit they had given him two years previously, boarded his luggage, including his paintings and the botanical collections he saved from among those he donated to Iowa State. He gave a last wave and with his long legs hopped over the steps and the boarding gap onto the train. With that, he made an enormous leap of faith into a new life.

4

BOOKER

To people giving their casual attention to Booker T. Washington and George Washington Carver, the two seemed so much alike that they might have been mined from one remarkable seam buried deep in the hills. Both had been born in slavery and raised in cabins where the only book was a Webster's blue-backed speller, that venerable compendium of phonics, fables, vocabulary, Scripture, and moral instruction. Both had somehow begun reading and longed so passionately for learning that they endured years of misery in order to attend school. Both became eloquent speakers who could captivate an audience in a matter of seconds. Both had mesmerizing personalities that dissolved the partition of race. And both wanted to dedicate their lives to uplifting their people. But those who knew the two men saw that underneath their public resemblance, their characters were radically different. Carver was straightforward and transparent, really a simple man. He was never agitated by jealousy. His reaction to any flare of hostility he encountered was to pour love on it. He was self-effacing. Booker* was complex, competitive, and always strategizing. He had an elaborate secret life. He displayed multiple personalities to fit his various public roles and managed conflicting ideals within himself. He loved what Carver hated: political intrigue and pitting himself against adversaries. His reaction to hostility was to outsmart and outmaneuver his enemy without openly confronting him. He was egotistical. It is not surprising that for the entire nine years Carver and Booker worked together at Tuskegee, they made each other wretched.

In *Up from Slavery*, Booker gave one version of his childhood. The name Booker Taliaferro (pronounced Tolliver) Washington was one he adopted as an

---

*Booker Washington trained students at Tuskegee to chant, "Booker! Booker!" when gathered for certain assemblies. The moniker, which is easy to remember and instantly identifies him, offers us a simple way to distinguish him from all the other Washingtons in the text.

adult, with a nod to an unloved and unlovable stepfather called "Wash" Fergu-son. Booker was his only name when was born in either 1858 or 1859, a slave on what he described as a plantation in Franklin County, Virginia. His father was a white man whom he never knew but who bequeathed him a light com-plexion and burning gray-green eyes. The cabin where Booker grew up was larger than the one in which George was born but more primitive; it had a dirt floor where the children—Booker, a half-brother, and a half-sister—slept on what he described as "a pile of filthy rags." Although his mother Jane was the cook for both the whites and the slaves of the plantation, food was not abun-dant, according to Booker. He remembered his mother waking her children in the middle of the night to eat a purloined chicken she had cooked for them. Their weekly treat was a few tablespoons of molasses that the masters allowed her to take back to her cabin on Saturday nights. Molasses stirred with lard and spread on bread was considered a tasty snack. None of the slaves sat down to eat a meal together. Each ate a little here and there—a cup of milk at one time, a piece of bread at another, vegetables consumed directly out of the cooking pot at random times and usually without a fork or spoon. Booker wore wooden shoes and a homespun flax shirt that was a pricking torture to sensitive skin. His older brother John used to perform the memorable kindness of wearing Booker's new shirts until they were broken in. The farm itself was unkempt. Though he was only about seven when he left it, he remembered gates hanging off their hinges, weeds in the yard, and slovenliness even in the "big" house.

The conditions Booker described were, in fact, typical of black plantation life. But his earlier autobiography, *The Story of My Life,* and the research of his best biographer, Louis R. Harlan, show that his situation was somewhat easier. He was born on a poorish small farm, not a plantation with many field hands, and had the softer life and better food of house servants. In one magazine arti-cle, he recalled that on Christmas Eve, grown slaves hung their stockings on the mantel in the master's bedroom and the next morning entered the room bear-ing the Yule log and singing. Nevertheless, his growing up was hard enough.

When freedom came, Booker's family stayed on the farm for three months. They finally parted from their former owners with sadness and kept in com-munication with them the rest of their lives, for the masters had been mild and decent, according to their lights. Booker's mother took her children and followed the black man he called his stepfather across the state border to West

Virginia. If there was a villain in Booker's story, it was this stepfather. He insisted that Booker work, first in a salt furnace and then in the coal mines, instead of attending one of the schools that was being set up for former slaves. In both the schools and the Sunday schools of the county, the only book used was the blue-backed speller, a basic home remedy for the common ailment of the times: ignorance. His mother procured a speller for him. He taught himself with it until he was able to convince a kindly schoolteacher to give him private lessons at night, after work. For a while, his stepfather permitted him to attend regular school on condition that he put in a total of five or six hours of paying work in the early morning and late afternoons. This proved impracticable, and he was forced to resort again to a night school. The night school that had been established in his area was several miles from where Booker worked, and often the instructor was only a semiliterate himself who had little to teach him. Meanwhile, his mother adopted an orphan boy named James, who became a member of the family.

The salt refinery and coal mine where Booker worked in Malden, West Virginia, were owned by General Lewis Ruffner. Booker worked as a houseboy for Ruffner and his wife from 1868 to 1872. Viola Ruffner had herself grown up in a poor family with seven children and had worked as a governess and a schoolteacher before her marriage. She would later become a friend and one of Tuskegee's sturdiest benefactors. With her Puritan insistence on punctuality, order, and cleanliness, she had gained a reputation for miles around as a Yankee harridan, but it was from her that Booker learned what it meant to live in a thrifty, well-managed household with all the agreeable details of civility: table settings, made-up beds, shirts with intact buttons. Mrs. Ruffner's ideas of domestic order were to stay with him all his life. While he was with the Ruffners, he heard of Hampton Normal and Agricultural Institute, a school in Virginia where students could work to defray the cost of board and tuition and at the same time learn a trade. The six dollars monthly he earned working for Mrs. Ruffner was being pocketed by his stepfather; nevertheless, he made up his mind to get to Hampton Institute one way or the other.

He started out for Virginia with $1.50 in his pocket and made the five hundred-mile journey on foot and by borrowing rides on wagons. When he had no place to sleep at night, he kept himself warm by walking. In Richmond, Virginia, still eighty-two miles from Hampton, he slept several nights on the ground under a slightly elevated sidewalk. He worked during the day unloading pig iron from a ship until he had accumulated enough money to buy his food for the rest of the trip. He arrived half-starved and filthy, but he must have already possessed some of the charm that was to serve him in later years. He managed to talk the lady principal into giving him a job as janitor and admitting him to what to him was the Promised Land.

Hampton Institute, one of the first "colleges" for black students established after the Civil War, was founded in 1870 by General Samuel Chapman Armstrong, a former Union officer. Many of the teachers were white educators from aristocratic northern families, but so dedicated were they to helping blacks that they happily joined in performing the dirtiest tasks if their services were needed, and they usually were. Most of the students were mature men and women in their thirties, eagerly grasping the opportunity for learning. All of them planned to use their education not to rise into a higher economic class themselves but for the betterment of their fellow people. General Armstrong found a Massachusetts benefactor who paid Booker's tuition of seventy dollars a year for the four years he attended Hampton. His board of ten dollars a month was paid by his work as a janitor. Now and then his brother John would send him whatever little money he could spare.

As an army man, General Armstrong naturally knew and prized military organization and routine. He valued the kind of training that would turn disparate individuals into a corps with a collective spirit and collective aims. In the military, instruction is focused on a specific task or skill, not on general education. Just as in an army that trains soldiers to go out and do battle, the education at Hampton was not aimed at teaching a man to think independently, nor was it directed at enriching the individual intellectually. It was, in fact, training, not education—training to make the students competent in a trade or industry. They would then go out and train others until the whole "army"—the black race—was an effective force, capable of sustaining itself in the economic battle it had been thrown into. At Hampton, Booker learned how to eat with a napkin and sleep in a bed with sheets (lying between, not over or under them). He submitted along with the other students to daily inspection of his clothes, which had to be clean and in good repair. Like everyone at Hampton, he was required to bathe daily, brush his teeth regularly, and sleep in a nightshirt. Except for his research activities in a debating society, he seems not to have had great exposure to books. But he was exposed to the person who would exert the predominant influence in his development: General Armstrong—"the most perfect specimen of man, physically, mentally, and spiritually, that I had ever seen," as Booker described him. Here at last was the father he had always needed and the model he could look up to for the rest of his life.

The instruction at Hampton was practical and moral—religious study, to be sure, but also learning the Christian ideals of humility and helping one's fellow man. According to Booker's analysis, the prevalent attitude of former slaves was that education was supposed to be a gate for escaping the brutal labor of the field and the stresses of work in the household. By and large, according to Booker, black people wanted to acquire enough book learning to allow them to preach or teach. More than anything, they wanted finally to have a last name, preceded by two initials (their "entitles," as they called them). They dreamed of being addressed as "Mister" by their colleagues in church or school and being able to sprinkle a few polysyllabic words into their speech. Booker remarked that in the early days of freedom, every black man who learned to read would receive a "call to preach" within a few days after he began decoding words. Relatively few realized the dignity and necessity of learning a useful trade. And none expected that after attending school he would ever again plow a field or pick a harvest.

At Hampton, Booker was imbued with the lifelong idea that manual labor gave an individual independence and self-reliance, a sense of satisfaction quite apart from its financial value. With the example of the great General Armstrong before him, he valued labor and unselfishness—service to one's fellow man—above any sort of intellectual attainment. Hampton was in those days an agricultural and trade school, not a college except in name. Students came out of the backwoods, still living as they had lived in their rude slave cabins, and were taught to read, write, raise a garden, sew attractive clothes, prepare not merely food but meals, build furniture, whitewash a house, and live in it like the respectable white people lived.

As deprived as George Carver was, from the beginning he had enjoyed more advantages than Booker. Though his family was illiterate, they were civilized to certain habits. Forks, clean wooden floors, mealtimes, and beds, for examples, were part of his upbringing. In contrast, the details of hygiene and deportment that Booker learned at Hampton constituted a revolution in his life, and like a revolutionary, he could hardly wait to press its benefits on others.

One of Booker's first jobs after he graduated from Hampton was as a teacher in Malden, West Virginia, where his brothers lived. There he established a day school, a night school, a Sunday school, and a little library. He saved enough money to send his brother John to Hampton Institute, and after John's graduation, the two of them saved enough to send their foster brother James. (His younger sister Amanda is largely absent from his narrative of his youth.) Booker then spent eight months in 1878 and 1879 in Washington, D.C., attending Wayland Seminary. This was probably the most advanced academic instruction he ever received. He disparaged the school in his memoirs, however, because it did not have an industrial component which would train the students in a skill such as their parents were following in order to pay for their children's academic education. But the seminary, too, was not primarily concerned with learning. Its goal was to produce proselytizers who would make converts. The school intensified Booker's missionary tendencies, his idea that his whole life and all his energies must be put into starting another Hampton, as it were, which would then send forth more imitations. By 1879 he was back at Hampton Institute, first as a commencement speaker, for he was gaining some reputation for his rousing rhetoric, and then, along with teaching in the night school, as dormitory supervisor to the people then referred to as Indian students. The fatherless Booker now spent two more years under the aegis of the strict, strong, loving, selfless man who did more than anyone else to shape his destiny. Through General Armstrong, the opportunity came to him to begin his life's work as the principal of a new school in the Deep South. Two men wrote to General Armstrong asking if he knew someone with the will and ability to establish and direct a normal school for blacks in Alabama. General Armstrong sent them Booker.

Tuskegee was a town of a few thousand in 1881, set in the 200-square mile area of Macon County, Alabama. During the days of slavery, the town had been a center of education for white people; hence, the population was more cultured and ambitious than average and had a more tolerant attitude than Booker expected. The largest hardware store in the town was operated jointly by a white man and a black man—a highly unusual partnership that lasted until the white man died. With the arrival of Booker, the new normal school had a principal, but it had no building or even land on which to put a building. Indeed, the school consisted only of eager students who looked to the twenty-five-year-old director to provide a place for learning.

Booker started the school in a falling-down black church that was donated. When he was not teaching, he traveled around the countryside by mule, visiting the people in their homes and advertising the school. This was the population from which his first students would come, and he wanted to know their background. What he saw in his visits did not surprise him, for black sharecroppers and tenant farmers in Alabama lived much the same as blacks and poor whites in the backwoods of Virginia and West Virginia. As a rule, whole families slept in one room, which they shared with the visitor. They ate fat pork, corn bread, and black-eyed peas boiled in plain water, as they had no gardens and used every inch of land allotted to them to plant cotton. In the cabin homes, he found showy clocks costing twelve or fourteen dollars, though no one in the family could tell time, or a costly organ which no one could play, or some other symbol of culture. The elementary schools were in session three to five months during the year, had practically no books, and employed teachers who could barely read.

No one could say that the black people in Alabama did not long for education. Booker opened his school and within a month had fifty students, most of them public school teachers. He recalled that they claimed to have mastered high-sounding subjects, such as "Banking and Discount," although they had never known anyone who even had a bank account. Booker was irked that some of the girls could locate the Sahara Desert on a globe but could not locate the proper place for knives and forks on a dinner table. Most of the students could do neither. According to Booker, they all wanted an education so that they would not have to work any longer with their hands, and certainly not work in farming, the way 85 percent of Alabama's blacks made their poor living. Booker was soon to disabuse them.

After a few months, Booker acquired, for $500, a hundred bare acres and an abandoned plantation, the new site of the school. He might never have raised the purchase money, nor the money for many, many subsequent expenditures, except for three individuals. One was Olivia Davidson, a Hampton graduate who came to work with him and was soon going all over the country to raise funds for Tuskegee Institute. She was so light-skinned she might have passed for white, and she could make the northern audiences she solicited feel that she was one of them, trying to do the noble work of uplifting the "others." Moreover, she was indefatigable, fully as devoted as Booker to building the Institute. She not only arranged large fund-raisers in the North; she canvassed the countryside around Tuskegee for small-change donations from whites and blacks. She gave countless fairs and festivals at Tuskegee where residents of Macon County donated cakes, chickens, and services for auction.

Olivia Davidson had an interesting background. Born a slave in 1854 in Virginia, she moved with her family to Albany, Ohio, where she eventually became a schoolteacher. She and her brother went to Mississippi in 1870 to teach in a Freedman's Bureau school, but the brother was murdered, possibly by the Ku Klux Klan. Olivia fled to Memphis to teach, but her school was closed by a yellow fever epidemic. She then spent two years at Hampton Institute but found the educational standards inferior. She decided to return to school and for two years attended the Framingham State Normal School in Massachusetts before deciding to dedicate her life to Tuskegee.

Booker's wife, Fannie N. Smith, was from his old home in Malden, West Virginia. She bore one daughter, Portia, before her death in 1885. Marriage to Booker and to Booker's enterprise was an exhausting proposition, as Olivia Davidson found out that same year when she became Booker's second wife. In four years, Davidson gave Booker two sons and thousands of donors all over the country. She died, worn out, in 1889. Booker had a building at Tuskegee named after her and ordered his own resting place beside her. He married a third time, in 1893, to Margaret James Murray, who hungered for his love for the next twenty-three years. She was a conscientious wife, stepmother, and administrative partner; two decades of their correspondence does not reveal a scintilla of tenderness or intimacy between them. Margaret adopted her orphaned nephew and niece when the little girl was very young; Booker became attached to the child, reared her as his own, and squandered on her his frugal store of affection.

The other lifelong supporters of the school were exceptional men, one a black ex-slave, Lewis Adams, and one a white ex-slaveholder, George W. Campbell. They were the two who had written to General Armstrong asking if he knew anyone who could be principal of the school they wanted to establish. Adams was a mechanic, and also a shoemaker, harness maker, and tinsmith. He had never been to school, although he could read and write. He gave Booker the practical guidance he needed in setting up the trade division of the school. Campbell was a merchant and banker. He eventually served on the board of Tuskegee and, time and again, gave money to the school. Booker was a young fledgling himself, hardly prepared to be a father to his teachers as General Armstrong had been. The only school he had known well enough to use as a model was Hampton; yet he had none of the resources of Hampton and none of the long army experience of General Armstrong in organizing multiple projects. But he set out to frame his life and work after his idol and to make Tuskegee a replica of Hampton Institute in every particular. He made it a point, for example, to ride around the campus on horseback when making his inspections; General Armstrong had surveyed his domain at Hampton from a saddle.

The students—at the beginning and always—provided the labor for building and cultivating the school and its farms. "We began with farming," Booker wrote, "because we wanted something to eat." Indeed, in order to board the pupils, all of whom were required to work the better part of the day, it was necessary to raise food. The first building was named Porter Hall after the northern white man who lent the money for its construction; another white man in Tuskegee who owned a lumber mill lent the wood. Privation was the normal condition of life during the first years of the school. The cooking was done out of doors. There was insufficient crockery and the food was scanty, but even worse, the cooks—that is, the students—seemed to have no idea that meals should be served at a designated time.

The school had only a few blankets for the boarding students, so that during one severe cold spell, three youngsters suffered actual frostbite. Students slept on the floor at first until other students could make mattresses—cloth bags stuffed with pine needles. The students were charged eight dollars a month for this Spartan board, which was paid for by their labor. Eight dollars was not cheap—many families survived on much less. The tuition of fifty dollars a year was requisitioned from anybody who would donate it. By the second year, enrollment was up to 150. Just as at Hampton, the students were required to use a toothbrush, to bring a napkin to meals, to bathe daily (outdoors, which was the only facility provided, with cold water winter and summer), and to wear nightshirts. In true military style, they were made to wear uniforms and attend chapel each night where their clothes were inspected as they marched in and out. Students performed guard duty at night. Everyone lived by seventeen bells that began sounding at five in the morning and continued until evening lights-out at 9:30.

For countless students, Tuskegee fulfilled a civilizing mission. For example, Mathew Woods walked out of the hills to Tuskegee, with little but the clothes on his back, and asked for work and schooling. After giving up his two guns, he was put to work in the horse barn and sent to learn how to drive an automobile so that he could become Booker's driver—Booker expected to obtain a car at some point. Woods received a degree in agriculture in 1908; his three daughters then attended Tuskegee. Once he arrived at Tuskegee, destitute though he was, his future was set: his children and his children's children would not grow up in ignorance. William Holtzclaw was the son of a slave who, before attending Tuskegee, had never worn an undershirt or drawers, slept on sheets, or used a toothbrush. After he left Booker's school, Holtzclaw went on to found Utica Institute in Mississippi, a Tuskegee spin-off, and to maintain a quite literate, thoughtful correspondence with his friend and former teacher, George Carver.

From the outset, Booker was beset by a wrongheaded obsession: he wanted to add buildings to the campus constantly. For these never-ending construction projects, the quality of the school was compromised. On one hand, Booker had to bring order out of chaos just to establish Tuskegee Institute; yet at the same time, he was caught up in a frenzy of construction, intent on enlarging a school that still did not have sufficient textbooks. To raise money for the unceasing expansion, Booker traveled and made speeches to white audiences or called upon wealthy individuals in northern cities, especially Boston. A hall would be rented, a "meeting" of citizens with an interest in black education would be held, and Booker would make an address, followed by an appeal. He became a sought-after speaker for commencement addresses at Negro colleges. Little by little, his name and the name of his school spread. The Slater and Peabody Funds, the railroad magnate Collis Huntington, and Andrew Carnegie were significant early donors. Within twenty years, Booker had erected forty buildings on the grounds. Buildings and fund-raising went together. It was easier to get a philanthropist to finance a building that would bear his name than to donate money for textbooks or laboratory equipment. It is small wonder that brick making became one of the school's most important industries. Booker often recounted that after two failed attempt to build a kiln in the very early years of the school, he pawned his watch for fifteen dollars to get the money for a third kiln, which worked. The school used the bricks; the students, at least in theory, used the training to become bricklayers.

Early on, Booker established a night school. Students were to work at Tuskegee ten hours a day and attend school for two hours each night. After two or three years, the money from their day labor accumulated sufficiently so that they could pay regular tuition and attend the day school for four days a week, continuing to work at trades for two days a week. No student was ever excused from manual labor. Although at first Tuskegee accepted only students above the age of fifteen who had had some previous schooling, within a few years children could start in the fifth grade, with no entrance requirement except willingness to conform to the curriculum. Thus, many students who began in the night school stayed at Tuskegee twelve or fifteen years before graduating. For these students—and there were many—Tuskegee served as a kind of plantation where they mainly worked in fields and shops, acquired some skills, and received a middling grade school education. Booker was convinced—and in this he was right, up to a point—that higher education was not as important as some education. "While a great deal of stress is laid upon the industrial side of the work at Tuskegee, we do not neglect or overlook in any degree the religious and spiritual side." That is to say, no stress at all was laid on academic achievement. Because the students were treated as a kind of standing work force, they were shifted from one job to another depending on where hands were needed. Many letters to Booker from the faculty complained that the students were not allowed to stay in one area—say, brick making—long enough to gain an understanding of how to carry a project to its completion. They spent one day raising the wall of a building, for example, but then were moved for three days to the fields and then were shifted to repairing fences.

Although black people gave money to Tuskegee Institute within their modest means, there was never any question that the school survived and grew because of northern white largesse. When Booker T. Washington appeared before white audiences, their first reaction was shock. His talk was poised, polished, splendidly grammatical, and affecting. He came to public notice during the era of grand rhetoric, when common people as well as uncommon would travel long distances to hear a lecture on some aspect of morality. Fine, stentorian speakers were important entertainers and were feted, like the entertainers of any generation.

Booker was not the first great black orator; that distinction belonged to Frederick Douglass, who died in 1895 the acknowledged leader of his race. But whereas Douglass was frizzy, angry, and ugly, Washington was handsome; he looked like a white man as much as he looked like a Negro, and he told white people things they were happy to hear. Douglass could move an audience to tears describing how white slave breakers whipped and starved him. Booker left them dry-eyed and cheerful by telling them that the blacks had received quite as much benefit from the institution of slavery as the whites. Douglass remarked that he had prayed for deliverance for twenty years but received no answer until he prayed with his feet. But Booker and God chattered back and forth easily, every day, in fact. The two would even have brainstorming sessions where God would make suggestions as to what project Booker should next undertake. Douglass said it was not light that was needed to solve the inequality of the races, but fire, thunder, and earthquake. Booker said that the wisest people of his race understood that agitating questions of social equality was the most extreme folly. Find out what a people will submit to, Douglass said, and exactly that much wrong will be imposed upon them. Booker said that if the black man succeeded in the trades, especially agriculture, he could lay a foundation on which his children and grandchildren could grow to higher and more prestigious things in life. In short, Booker was the white man's ideal Negro, the black man who averred that in all his contact with the white people of the South, he had never received a single personal insult. If he could turn out hundreds more just like himself—striving, admiring, industrious, and uninsulted—surely he deserved some financial help in order to try.

Booker was not wrong in much that he said. He was not wrong in advising black people not to let their grievances overshadow their opportunities, nor in holding that there was as much dignity in tilling a field as in writing a poem, nor in noting that the black man of his day needed tools more than he needed opera tickets. He was not wrong in advising black people not to shun the trades and farm work but to seize those occupations that were readily available to them and excel in them so that their labor would be satisfying to themselves and valuable to others. His great flaw was that in his self-righteousness, he went too far. There was as much claptrap in Booker's sermons as wisdom.

He was not merely willing to get along with whites and try to show them the black person's potential for success; he was fulsome in his sympathy for rich people who suffered "countless demands" upon their generosity. In preaching the dignity of labor, he became sincerely anti-intellectual. He was proud, he said, that his son and daughter, who might have studied under the country's finest professors, had instead chosen to attend Tuskegee and learn trades. One of his repetitive themes was aggrandizing lowliness for its own sake, not merely because labor was necessary to both the worker and the society at large. It was reasonable to advise blacks to tend the farms where they lived and abandon their illusions that learning a pretentious bit of Latin or Greek would lead to a life of ease. But it was absurd to imply that chopping row after row of cotton was as satisfying as reading a book, as if a farm laborer who could have a machine do the chopping would eschew it. In using himself as an example to show what a disadvantaged black person could accomplish in life, he exposed relentless egotism (in his books, he quotes laudatory newspaper articles about himself in their entirety), self-promotion, and a messianic complex that was far from attractive.

Booker became a national celebrity in 1895. He had been raising money in Boston when an invitation came to give a talk in Atlanta to a convention of Christian workers. The talk was only to last some five minutes, but it was an opportunity, as Booker correctly viewed it, to expose his ideas to a white southern audience. He had already discovered that flattery—whether it was sincere, as it usually appeared to be, or cynical—paid off. He was able to keep expanding Tuskegee Institute with the contributions that were forthcoming as long as he kept traveling and making speeches. With the 1895 talk in Atlanta, he would find that sycophancy could also bring him personal fame. In order to make the five-minute talk, he had to travel thirty hours each way by train. He arrived from Boston a half hour before he was scheduled to speak, gave the brief talk, and then within the hour boarded a return train. But what a riveting few minutes he gave them! In terms of his own career, the trip was worth all the effort. His talk was so well received that it led to an invitation to address the Atlanta Cotton States and International Exposition as the representative of his race, the speech that marked the turning point of his early work. Frederick Douglass had just died. The race was ready for a new leader. The Atlanta Exposition speech contained Booker's famous advice, "Cast down your bucket where you are," meaning that the black man would find his salvation not in some foreign colony or through some illusory political power that would be granted to him, but in the white world where he found himself, in the workaday occupations of farming and industry where he was. The oppressor and the oppressed were bound together, he asserted, and must share the same fate. "In all things that are purely social," he said, "we can be as separate as the fingers, yet one as the hand in all things essential to mutual progress." Referring to the proportion of blacks in the South, he said "We [Negroes] shall constitute one third and more of the ignorance and crime of the South, or one-third its intelligence and progress; we shall contribute one-third to the business and industrial prosperity of the South, or we shall prove a veritable body of death, stagnating, depressing, retarding every effort to advance the body politic."

It was a stirring and prophetic talk, and it catapulted Booker into national prominence. The speech was published in full in newspapers across the United States and was greeted ecstatically by southern whites. Booker, not one to hide his light under a bushel of sweet potatoes, sent a copy of the address to President Grover Cleveland and was rewarded by a letter of thanks and, some time later, a personal meeting. The objections of a few black leaders to the speech were buried under the cascades of praise. Encouraged by the success of his ideas, Booker went on to state that political rights would not be won by outside or artificial forcing, "but will be accorded to the Negro by the Southern white people themselves, and . . . they will protect him in the exercise of those rights." He believed in both a property and an educational requirement for both black and white voting, and wrote that "The Negro, instead of voting against whatever the white man advocated, should more and more be influenced by those of intelligence and character who are his next-door neighbors." It is an ironic detail that the day after the Atlanta speech, one of the teachers at Tuskegee Institute was bringing Portia Washington to college in Massachusetts when a train conductor on the Southern Railroad, a line managed by a Tuskegee trustee, beat up the teacher in a racial altercation.

* * *

With the speech in Atlanta, Washington built himself a trap from which he never escaped, as a recent biographer noted. He bargained away the fight for political equality and desegregation, accepting an inferior status for blacks in return for racial peace—a proposition that became known as the Atlanta Compromise. But that peace never arrived. In fact, the following decades saw ever-increasing racial violence. Years of appeasing white people did not improve the black man's position in the slightest. But by the time Booker realized the failure of his policy, he had spent too much time defending it and too much effort suppressing his critics to change.

The year after the Atlanta speech, 1896, he was invited to give the commencement address at Harvard University and was awarded an honorary Master of Arts degree. In reporting the address, *The Washington Post* urged Booker's appointment as a member of President William McKinley's cabinet; it was a rhetorical suggestion that McKinley dared not implement. From that time on, Booker gave continuous speaking tours. The lecture fees and contributions that came to Tuskegee in the wake of his talks financed the growth of the institution, a growth that he took care to ensure was phenomenal.

Booker was on his way back from his Harvard triumph, making a lecture stop in Cedar Rapids, Iowa, when he met George, who traveled the hundred miles from Ames to talk with him. Neither Carver nor Wilson, who accompanied George, was braced for the spell that Booker could cast on anyone that he cared to mesmerize. James Wilson could not have been more impressed during his brief meeting than if he had had a personal interview with a black archangel. George, who had been hesitant and ambivalent about accepting the Tuskegee job offer, came away wholeheartedly convinced that his destiny lay in an obscure trade school in the red clay of Alabama.

Six months later, George and his ideals arrived in Tuskegee, ready to dedicate his life to Booker Washington.

5

DOMINION OF POVERTY

His life and more Booker T. Washington expected. By the time Carver arrived at Tuskegee Institute, the school had been in existence for fifteen years. Booker had turned a barely habitable shelter into a functioning campus of new buildings that had earned acceptance, or at least resignation, from the white community around it. But Tuskegee Institute in 1896 was far from the church of sterling goals and well-regulated bustle that Booker described to prospective donors.

The school that visitors saw made a fine impression: an industrial nucleus surrounded by 2,000 acres of farm, with new buildings under construction. Booker demanded that the grounds be neat and attractive. When visitors were expected, the lawns were specially "landscaped"—teachers were sent out to the woods to cut flowers and foliage and stick the cuttings in the ground along the walkways. When the occasion had passed, the branches were left to die and fall over onto the paths. The road leading into the campus was a mess of dust in summer and a mess of mud in winter. Booker was careful to see that the wicks were trimmed on the oil lamps lining the road so that it was well lighted for visitors, but in between times, the lamps blew out and the nighttime campus was blind dark. Though a new chapel was about to be built, in 1896 the school's interdenominational services were still being held in a dirt-floor pavilion with plank benches.

The Institute ran on the energy of a relentlessly overworked faculty who, like Carver, had been drawn there by idealism. Young, fervid, and coming, most of them, from the background of Hampton Institute, where Washington recruited his teachers, they readily submitted to the principal's brusque dictatorship. Once they saw that Tuskegee was not in fact a chrysalis of Hampton, many left after one or two years. Tuskegee consistently lost about ten faculty members a year, a quite large turnover for a small school of some fifty teachers.

Other teachers remained, though unhappy, because of the paucity of jobs. A large archive of Tuskegee correspondence indicates that its teachers lived like sedulous courtiers, trying to carry out the myriad projects of the monarch, having neither time nor permission to launch initiatives of their own. Those who made up the core staff were typically tired, contentious, and addicted to gossip.

The highest ten salaries at Tuskegee were above Carver's wage of $1,000 a year plus board. However, many were paid less. Junior faculty might scrape by on as little as $250 a year. This was lower than other black private schools and colleges, but Booker rejected all recommendations that he increase salaries in order to hold on to his best teachers. He wanted only teachers so dedicated to Tuskegee's mission, he said, that they would work there at a lower salary than they could earn elsewhere. The school took no responsibility for teachers who fell ill. If they could not work they were not paid, although they might be granted an unpaid sick leave, provided they were expected to recover. Tenure did not exist. An incident of insubordination could result in summary dismissal. But if teachers found other positions during the summer after signing a contract to return to Tuskegee, Booker hounded them in their new posts, charging them with unethical conduct. There were many such cases. Nevertheless, teachers were better off at Tuskegee, a private facility, than they would have been in a public secondary institution. In the South, both white and black teachers in the public schools earned roughly the pay of first-class convicts—between $100 and $300 a year.

Besides the toil of the faculty, the manual work of students and some paid staff workers kept the school going. Student labor might be as inefficient and absent-minded as slave labor, but it raised buildings, planted and harvested crops, more or less cleaned classrooms, more or less cooked meals, sewed pillowcases and tablecloths, and provided nearly all the necessities of a self-sufficient—albeit randomly insufficient—colony. Despite the public talk about keeping the surroundings neat and in repair, everything on the campus deteriorated during Booker's long absences, particularly departmental supplies and food. Usually he traveled half the time. While on the road, he sent a barrage of instructions to the faculty and tried assiduously to remain tyrant-in-chief with his thumb on every department. But even the students could assess the conditions and discern whether or not Booker was in town. In one of their many epistles concerning the food, students noted that the greens were not washed, the dishes and forks were dirty, the potatoes sour, the meat rotten, and the syrup sour. In a word, "When Principal goes away, the meals are very much worse than when he is here."

Carver soon realized that the school had two kinds of equipment: rudimentary and nonexistent. This is not surprising considering what Tuskegee Institute started with. But it was in stark contrast to the way Booker presented the school to people who did not see it from the inside. Carver had been promised a laboratory and an apartment (on his side of the correspondence, he referred to the promise of lodging as a "house"; Booker did not refer to it at all after his initial letter). Carver had brought books and journals with him but had no room to unpack them. When he tried to dig out a journal so that he could prescribe for a sick cow, he found that his boxes were piled up in a storage facility where the books were being enjoyed by mice and roaches and his prized collections of specimens were growing mold. "At present I have no room to unpack my goods," he wrote to the finance committee. "I beg of you to give me these, and suitable ones, too, not for my sake alone but for the sake of education." He was assigned a single room in Porter Hall, the dormitory for male students, and no room for his books. Like the other faculty, he took his meals in Alabama Hall with the students. As for the laboratory, it consisted of the microscope George brought with him from Iowa and a lamp that warmed his hands, reflected light on his microscope, and served as a Bunsen burner. His purchase requests, once dropped on the desk of any Tuskegee official, disappeared like worms on topsoil, never to be seen again.

The man who had got himself through school with no more resources than a washboard and a borrowed tub was not to be thwarted by the emptiness of his one equipment cabinet. He searched the trash piles behind the kitchen for broken cups and cracked bowls to use as mortars. He pulverized material with a flatiron. Reeds served as pipettes, and old bottles as test tubes. "Equipment is not all in the laboratory, but partly in the head of the man running it," said George gamely. To get zinc sulfate, he used the zinc tops of fruit jars he found in the trash. He even had to make his own sandpaper, after consulting his subconscious in a dream to remember the exact procedure.

What surprised and bitterly disappointed him was the cold reception he received from his fellow teachers and the staff, with the exception of Warren Logan, the treasurer, and Emmett Scott, Booker's secretary. Carver found himself an unwelcome interloper in a small, trapped community whose members competed for everything—funding for their departments, students in their classes, student workers to help with the manual labor, salaries, offices, and living accommodations. Most of all, they competed for the favor of Booker T. Washington.

In general, the industrial and agricultural teachers were self-taught or half-taught people who were looked down upon by the better-educated academic faculty. Carver, being an agricultural teacher but also being smarter than his academic colleagues, came in for resentment from every side. The faculty and staff who were not alumni of Hampton were from Tuskegee itself, having graduated and immediately begun teaching their former classmates. In the case of the paid staff—the secretaries, repairman, and the like—these were often students who had dropped out of formal course work but remained at the school. At the time he came to Tuskegee, Carver was the only teacher with an advanced degree and the only one who had attended a white university. Moreover, he had been on the faculty of a prestigious university, a credential none of the other Tuskegee people could dream of possessing at that time.

The hostility of the teachers was complicated. On one side, they were eaten up with jealousy over his intellectual superiority. But there was a side that sincerely regarded Carver as their permanent inferior, for he was the only faculty member who had no white blood. In group pictures of the Tuskegee "family," his face stands out like a token Negro in a group of semi-Caucasians. They were not only light skinned at Tuskegee; they were thin-skinned. They expected Carver to defer to them, to display a self-conscious demeanor that would show he was aware of being a black set down among almost-whites. In later years, Carver told a story of how, soon after his arrival, a cabal of three teachers tried to embarrass him in front the school officials and Booker. They gathered some plant specimens, which they insisted he identify on the spot during an executive council meeting. They were armed with reference books to check his answers. Carver was reading a report when the first teacher interrupted him.

"Can you tell me what this is, Professor?" the man asked suddenly, holding up one of a bunch of plants.

Carver looked up from his paper. "That? It's *Datura stramonium*. It's what is called Jimson weed." And he went back to his report. A low rustle ensued while the interrogators checked the answer in their textbook.

"And what's this, Professor?"

Again, Carver stopped reading and looked up from his paper. "That's *Asarum canadense*—wild ginger." Another pause, while the textbook was consulted.

"Here," Carver said impatiently, "give me those. This is *Ambrosia artemisi-ifolia*—ragweed." He tossed it down. "This is *Oenothera biennis*—evening prim-rose; *Marrubium vulgare*—horehound; *Dioscorea villosa*—wild yam; Sarracenia purpurea—pitcher plant. There, that's the end of it!" What Carver assumed was a graceless joke he discovered later was actually a plot by teachers who thought they would expose him as a fake. The unmasking scene was planned with the knowledge and acquiescence of Booker, who never minded intrigue. He had told the cabal they would have to furnish proof if they asserted that Carver was not the plant expert he pretended to be.

Rejection was the last thing Carver expected. He had descended from the white world where he had enjoyed a comfortable niche in order to bring light to his people. Far from appreciating his sacrifice, the staff couldn't see that they really needed him. "What we need is a dairyman, not a scientist," said John (J. H.) Washington from behind the shrubbery of his beard. Booker's brother J. H. had been the foreman of railroad construction at Hampton and was against Carver's appointment from the beginning. He had no common ground with a university scholar, even if that scholar also happened to be an expert on dairy management and much else. Besides installing J. H. as an of-ficer of the school, Booker had made his foster brother James the postmaster of Tuskegee Institute. Each of Booker's wives served in succession on his ex-ecutive council. Like any uneasy potentate, Booker surrounded himself with retainers who would not cross him. Loyalty from his people was far more im-portant to him than knowledge in any field.

George began to wonder whether he had made a mistake in choosing sci-ence over art as the area where he could do the most good for his race. He was no doubt a little full of himself in the beginning, which did not enhance his popularity. Seeing that his specimens were relegated to a leaky room despite his respectful requests for storage space, he lectured the finance committee: "Some of you saw the other day something of the valuable nature of one of my collections. I have others of equal value and along agricultural lines. You doubtless know that I came here for the benefit of my people, no other motive in view. Moreover, I do not expect to teach many years, but will quit as soon as I can trust my work to others, and engage in my brush work, which will be of great honor to our people showing to what we may attain, along science, literature, history, and art." Arrogance had no more effect than courtesy. The collections remained in their unprotected boxes, nourishing the vermin for many more months.

Snubbed by the faculty and subjected to the random stings of their petty malice, Carver stayed away from their gatherings, taking his breakfast at six in the morning before either students or teachers were in the dining hall, and cooking dinner for himself in his room, much of the time, on a hot plate. For companionship, he turned to the only other people at Tuskegee, the students, and though he was only thirty-four, he became a surrogate father to boys and girls who were as lonely and homesick as he was. Every pupil who knew Professor Carver, without a single recorded exception, loved him. Since he lived among them in a dormitory, they made it a point to make as much noise as possible when coming up the stairs just by his room. He would come out and scold them with mock school-marmish vexation. His tirade would end by his smacking them with a rolled up newspaper and chasing them down the hall. Part of the Carver lore describes one of the many jokes the kids tried to play on him. They mounted an insect assembled from the body parts of a variety of bugs, practiced holding a straight face, and presented it to Carver. "Can you tell us what kind of insect this is?" they asked. "We've been looking in all the books, but we can't find it." Carver studied the specimen, also maintaining a grave countenance. "This, I think," he answered slowly, "is probably what we would call a 'Humbug.'"

The students who came out of the fields to Tuskegee were more varied than he could have predicted. A thousand were enrolled by 1896. Fifty percent would drop out within two years. Some had to be coerced to observe minimum standards of hygiene. Booker periodically went on inspection rampages in their rooms to see that they owned nightshirts and toothbrushes. Brushing teeth was still a novel idea at the turn of the century to country people in both America and in Europe, where enlightened landowners encouraged it among their peasants and servants. The principal liked to tell the story of three new girls, roommates who, when questioned as to whether they owned a toothbrush as required by the school, proudly produced the one toothbrush they had purchased for the three of them. On the other hand, hundreds of letters from pupils to the faculty and administrators show that the students were often as literate and genteel as their teachers who, though bitchy, were themselves people of some refinement; they had been through Hampton Institute's finishing school. In the numerous microfilm reels of Tuskegee correspondence from students or ex-students, there exist scrawled missives splattered with misspelled words, but these stand out; they are not the norm.

Carver's title was Director and Instructor in Agriculture and Dairy Science, with five designated assistants—in farm management, stock raising, truck gardening, horticulture, and dairying—an impressive-sounding faculty for a division that had no systematized course of study and only thirteen students. Though agriculture was supposed to be the cornerstone of Tuskegee Institute, and though an agriculture building was being constructed, the department did not in truth exist until Carver's appearance. He was supposed to create it and then be the head of it. His five assistants were also largely chimerical, since each of the individuals had multiple titles and duties and was not necessarily available to help out in the farm and dairy work when Carver needed him.

In addition to his obligations to teach his classes and carry out research, Carver was dismayed to receive a two-page list of duties. He was responsible in every detail for supervising two school farms (1,600 acres); the dairy (191 cows); the barns, livestock, and poultry yard (about 1,500 animals); the orchard; the beehives; and pastures. He was called to account if so much as a rake was left out overnight for, according to Booker, such negligence made the school look like the abode of "common country people." But although he was answerable for every problem, he had no authority whatever to run the operations according to his judgment.

Carver was the school veterinarian. Some cows dropped dead in a pasture—a peach orchard, in fact, where cows were allowed to graze. Students pruning the peach trees had left the branches on the ground. Carver identified hydrocyanic poisoning and saved the rest of the herd, making him the man of the hour—but only for that hour. It was up to Carver to see to it that all the school's animals were productive. Booker demanded a daily report by 8:30

a.m. on the number of eggs, fowl, and pigs in the poultry yard and farm, and the amount of milk and butter coming from the dairy. If the report arrived late, or if production fell, Carver would receive a curt note. But he did not have permission or means to feed the animals in a way that would increase their yield. He was obliged to advise the skeptical J. H., his chief antagonist, that you could not get butter from the milk of cows that were fed on cottonseed meal, the cheapest food, and that the bees would not produce much honey until they had access to buckwheat. Whether Carver's suggestions were followed was up to J. H. At any time Carver might be ordered to look after anything that did not clearly fall under someone else's authority, such as "the matter of reckless driving about the grounds" or buzzards eating the school's pigs.

During his first years at Tuskegee, it seemed to Carver that nobody on the place—not the students, the teachers, or the staff—had two cells of common sense. Three times Booker wrote to Carver asking him to recommend the best type of separator. Three times Carver suggested brands and prices but advised Booker in each letter that the dairy really did not need a separator. When the machine arrived anyway, no one knew how to assemble it, so Carver put it together. He was surprised that the separator did not seem to be working, until he discovered that the students were innocently dumping the separated cream back into the milk. There was a notorious incident when he was called upon to cure scab that was showing up in the sheep. Carver prescribed a dip and gave the formula to the man in charge of the treatment, a Mr. Green. Carver took it for granted that Mr. Green would send for him to approve the solution before the sheep were put in it. The solution mixed up by Green (or his student workers) had four times the prescribed quantity of quicklime, which caused the liquid to boil. Not only did Green fail to let Carver inspect the dip, he left the entire operation to the students. The first sheep died immediately on being plunged into the solution, but the students nevertheless immersed another fourteen hapless creatures, one at a time. No less than fifteen had been scalded to death before the boys decided to find Mr. Green to ask if they were doing something wrong. Green then sought out Carver to inquire whether he should continue with the dipping J. H. went to Carver, too—in high dudgeon. As he saw it, Booker's esteemed scientist had killed a slew of animals.

From the time Carver started working in November, he was presumed by everyone to be the school's landscaper. "The people of our race have never had a carpet of grass to walk on," said Booker. "Every city park has signs saying 'Keep Off.' I want my people here at Tuskegee to have green grass to walk on." That was enough to set Carver eagerly grading and terracing so that planting could begin in the spring. Through James Wilson's sponsorship, Carver established a weather station at Tuskegee, measuring rainfall, displaying white and red weather flags, and sending daily observations to the regional weather station in Montgomery. The "closets" and waste facilities were partly his responsibility. Being the one-man Sanitary Committee obliged him to gather and analyze samples from wells all over the county. Month after month, he reported finding *Escherichia (Bacillus) coli*; he recommended that a pump and windlass be installed to make the wells safe at Tuskegee. Month after month he was ignored. Once he found typhoid in a stream, wrote to the Surgeon General in Washington, D.C., and conferred with the public health official sent by that office. The school was not in the habit of taking such things seriously, of examining a stream for bacteria merely because a calf had been found dead in it.

Nothing shows Booker's distorted priorities so clearly as the deplorable condition of Tuskegee's sanitary facilities, nor does any other issue illustrate as sharply Carver's frustration when he tried to address serious matters at the school. From the time Carver arrived in 1896, he expostulated with Booker over the raw sewage that flowed out on the grounds near buildings and contaminated the school's water supply. Dr. J. A. Kenney joined the staff as school physician and surgeon in 1903; he became the personal physician to both Booker and Carver. From his first walk through the campus, Kenney was appalled at what he found in out-of-the-way spots, although he noted that on the roadways, "where everyone walks and sees, conditions are more favorable." Kenney addressed his findings to three officials, including J. H. Washington, to no avail. Finally, he wrote an exhaustive fourteen-page report detailing the heaps of rubbish and repositories of sewage he found in "the places shielded from public view." The grounds in the woods behind Rockefeller Hall "are filthy and polluted. The whole place is one general toilet and the odors . . . are fierce." The students regularly threw "slop water" out of the dormitory windows, including contents of chamber pots. Together Dr. Kenney and Carver—

the enlarged sanitary committee—fought relentlessly to get Booker to install proper drainage, clean up the wells, put in screens throughout the campus, and build a decent sewer system.

At the turn of the century, a country family typically had an outhouse—a closed wooden shack containing a wooden toilet set over the bare ground a little distance from the dwelling. Waste fell through the hole in the seat and eventually broke down in the soil where it landed, aided by plentiful maggots. Without exception, outhouses stank horrifically, which served to insure that they were not placed right next to living quarters. Institutions such as Tuskegee usually had earth closets. An earth closet, too, had a wooden commode where the person using it could sit down. Under the seating hole stood a large bucket containing a few pounds of loose dirt to receive the waste. In addition, a container with fine earth was sometimes placed next to the commode, so that after using the toilet, more dirt could be shoveled over the excrement. Fancy models were equipped with foot pedals that allowed the user to release a small quantity of earth into the toilet from a holding container. The fine earth was something of a deodorant, especially when mixed with a little lime, and rapidly broke down the fecal matter. When the bucket under the commode had been used several times, it was supposed to be emptied in the fields or where the contents could fertilize plants. In cities and institutions such as Tuskegee, a night soil cart was designated to receive the waste from the buckets and cart it off to some spot where it could be safely deposited.

The essential problem at Tuskegee was that there were too few earth closets, gathered in small areas, to serve 1,500 people. No one was emptying the buckets, and there was no drainage outlet for the overflowing sewage, which seeped out into the grounds and ground water. "The toilet is . . . filled," Kenney wrote regarding one of the boys' earth closets, "a large heap of excrement is behind it, and the urine seeps down into the sand from the urinos with no provision for its removal. The sight and stench are revolting." Instead of using the earth closets, the boys had turned two nearby fields into a general toilet "and the odors are fierce." Kenney wrote, "I can't blame them, for what human being can voluntarily consent to use that place?" The "toilet field" was adjacent to the bathhouse that unmarried teachers had to use, though it reeked "frightfully." As for the night soil cart, "a more repulsive object you need not wish to see," wrote Dr. Kenney. "I'll not disgust you by description." Because it leaked, it stank so mightily that it frightened Kenney's horse. Moreover, the cart was being dumped, when it was dumped at all, not on fields, but a little way from the toilets at the bottom of a hill, adding yet more odor to the mephitic air.

The toilets were not the only chronic sanitary problem. The stench from the slaughterhouse invaded the main road and the area around the hospital. The butchers were throwing all the offal and refuse from the campus slaughterhouse into a pen. The pen was studiously avoided by every mobile creature except buzzards, but people trapped in the hospital could not escape the smell, which nauseated those patients who were not already vomiting from their illnesses.

For each of his complaints, Kenney offered a solution. The night soil cart needed to be replaced with a new one lined with zinc or sheet iron. In the earth closets, "Every particle of excrement should be collected in the pails and more lime or simply dry earth mixed and then hauled away. A barrel of dry earth should be in each closet and a man should be appointed whose duty it is to keep them in proper condition and see to it that this earth or lime or both are freely used quite frequently during the day." Both Kenney and Carver insisted that several of the boys' toilets must be condemned and replaced. The two men might as well have been whispering their complaints, warnings, and suggestions to God; Booker completely ignored them—for many long years.

Families had to carry water up to their houses—from a polluted well. Carver submitted various plans for drainage and the cleaning of what he insisted were unsafe wells all over the campus. Nevertheless, two years later, the school still had raw sewage flowing out of the ground. One well in particular was being polluted by the wastes from Dorothy Hall so that the water was deemed by Kenney "undrinkable." Four years later, shortly before a typhoid epidemic at Tuskegee, Kenney urgently warned the executive council that the sewage and waste of Dorothy Hall were flowing down a ravine right to the well from which most of the school drew its water and which was used by the dairy. After the 1907 epidemic that Kenney had predicted, Carver tested the water that was being used in the creamery and in Tatum Hall and reported that it was "almost criminal for such water to be drunk or used for cooking." The men pleaded with the executive council to screen the dining rooms and clean up the open sewers. Kenney practically screamed at the officials: "The flies feed on this excreta and then on food while their legs are laden with it . . . The hospital is seldom without a case of typhoid."

Tuskegee experienced a small pox epidemic in 1904, yellow fever in 1905, a typhoid epidemic in 1907, and continuous cases of typhoid for decades. Yet in 1909, Kenney and Carver were still calling attention to the flies and open sewage from Dorothy Hall, where, "as was stated before to you," the urine from a toilet was draining almost directly into the dormitory well. "This is criminal negligence," Kenney exclaimed. In 1910, the two were still trying to have the raw sewage cleaned up near the residences and were lodging impassioned complaints about flies in the school's creamery. These complaints were not casual recommendations. Kenney and Carver filed long, separate, detailed reports, some of them running to twenty pages, from 1903 until Booker's death—repeatedly pointing to critical problems. They were repeatedly brushed aside. The reports were either unanswered or they were acknowledged with a curt, noncommittal letter from Booker's mouthpiece, the executive committee.

Although Dr. J. A. Kenney was not appreciated at Tuskegee, he remained at the school for twenty years. In 1923, he exerted vigorous efforts to have black doctors employed at the Tuskegee Veterans Administration Hospital, a facility that was intended to serve black veterans. As the issue heated up, Kenney received a death threat from the Ku Klux Klan and fled with his wife and four children to New Jersey. In the years, however, when Kenney was trying to clean up Tuskegee Institute, the major threat to his life was from the school's drinking water, as he continually asserted.

At the same time that Carver and Kenney were sending their urgent, futile warnings, addressing them directly to J. H. and Booker, those officials were absorbed in other matters. Booker was distressed because the students were "not careful about putting flowers on the tables." He was particularly exercised over finding brooms standing on the wrong end. He sent repeated letters to six staff members to correct the broom situation. Booker had no time to tend to the earth closets when the broom closets obviously needed close supervision. Then, too, "the matter of young men students putting their hands in their pockets" was becoming "a very serious problem," along with the issue of boys walking on the girls' sidewalk. J. H., too, was preoccupied. In 1904, when Carver and Kenney were issuing their usual alarms about the dangerous condition of the sanitary facilities, the principal's brother was distracted by the seating project. He had decided that the executive council at Tuskegee, which possessed a new table, should have designated seating around it, just as President Roosevelt's cabinet had designated seats at the council table in the White House. J. H. made a careful diagram to show the proper seating of the principal, dean of women, treasurer, etc., and ordered little metal title plaques for each place.

Not all serious questions were ignored deliberately. Sometimes they vanished unexplainably in the gale of paper that swirled around Booker. Since all of the faculty served on multiple committees, the dining hall committee might consist of almost the same individuals as the disciplinary council or the finance committee. The principal convoked incessant meetings of these groups, along with regular faculty and departmental meetings. Everyone who attended these meetings came away with requests to submit reports "as soon as possible" on each issue that was deliberated. Booker liked nothing so much as paper. To any complaint or suggestion, no matter how straightforward, his invariable response was to appoint a three-person committee to look into the matter and submit a report. The teachers complained lustily about the excessive meetings. The executive council of the Institute was only one of Carver's committees. Though it sounded prestigious, it was one of the more onerous and useless diets, since all executive decisions were made solely by Booker, after the formality of circulating copious memoranda. The council was an oligarchy of fifteen to twenty officers and department heads: Booker, his wife, his brother J. H., his secretary Emmett Scott, the treasurer Warren Logan, the auditor, the dean of women, the business agent, Experiment Station Director Carver, the commandant, and a few other senior faculty. The correspondence of that committee alone could take up an hour every day, aside from the time spent in the actual meetings.

Carver was not the only overtaxed faculty member. Warren Logan, Tuskegee's treasurer, taught several classes, led the choir, managed the printing office, and sang in a touring quartet that raised money for building, along with his duties as fiscal officer. Ernest T. Attwell, as business manager, was responsible for purchasing the school's supplies and those of the boarding department—a staggering task that went on incessantly. He was charged with attracting white people to the school's commencement exercises and occasionally with giving parties for the faculty. Though wilting under his office duties, he coached the school's football team. All of the teachers were expected to teach Sunday school from time to time. The staff was under strict orders to answer all letters the same day they arrived, even if it meant staying in their offices until midnight. Everyone worked hard, but it would be difficult in the period 1896–1905 to find anyone with more duties, both regular and random, than Carver.

He was thwarted at every turn by a lack of helpers. Though he was head of his department with ten theoretical workers under him, the departments were not as separate as they appeared on paper because all the unpaid work, whether done in the dairy or the brickyard, was performed by the same group of students, and all were under the control of J. H., who could assign workers to perform a particular task—or not. Carver could not choose the individuals sent to him. His department had no firm budget, since Booker thought nothing of raiding the funds allocated to one division and shifting them somewhere else. Nor was Carver able to choose equipment when told that money was available; he could put in a requisition, but someone reviewing the order might make a substitution without consulting him or simply ignore the request. Even getting a rope to hoist the weather flag was an ordeal.

D espite all his tribulations, Carver accomplished more research and field work in his first years at Tuskegee than some scientists achieve in an entire career of muddy boots. He worked with the Alabama Polytechnic Institute on a study of the fungi of the state—a state with which he was totally unfamiliar. His collaborators were dumbfounded when he identified sixty new species, sixty-four known families, 349 genera, and over a thousand known species, and promised to double the number the next year. Carver had none of the equipment necessary to identify mycological specimens and was obliged to send his discoveries to specialists all over the country for verification. But his preliminary identifications of new species turned out to be amazingly accurate. The Department of Agriculture in Washington was trying to gather examples of all the grasses in the United States. George sent in over one hundred specimens. The Smithsonian Institution was assembling information for a catalog of America's medicinal flora. Carver discovered an immense number of official drug plants, along with plants that were thought to have medicinal properties—household remedies. "I am living closely with lizards, frogs, snakes, ticks, mosquitoes, and chiggers," he boasted to James Wilson, negligible discomforts, he thought, compared to the value of his investigations. Such zealous field work in the face of all his other duties is not entirely surprising. George, like Moses Carver before him, was an addicted collector who, except for these botanical assignments, might have gone out every dawn gathering cast-off nails or some other detritus. Working in the field and befriending the plant life also kept him from being completely frustrated. By spring he was writing to Pammel: "This is indeed a new world to Iowa. Very poor to be sure, but many things to make it pleasant. I like it so much better than I thought I would at first."

By the end of Carver's first year, the new department had seventy-six pupils—a notable increase, though the agriculture department would never attract a large enrollment. Students frankly stated that they liked Professor Carver, but they were attending college to get away from farming, the sooner the better. In 1910 Booker would complain, "Notwithstanding the thousands of dollars which we are spending on the farm, there are only two students to graduate this year from the farming department." By the standards of Tuskegee at that time, Carver was a perfectionist in the classroom, insisting, for example, on precise measurements. "If you come to a stream five feet wide and jump four and a half feet, you fall in and get drowned. You might just as well have tumbled in from the other side and saved yourself the exertion of the jump," he told them. "There are only two ways. One is right and the other is wrong. 'About' is always wrong. Don't tell me it's 'about' right."

One of Carver's projects as Superintendent of Many Things was to organize the campus trash and start a compost pile inside a pen. Neighboring farmers would see that paper, wood shavings, rags, leaves, and food waste could be used to fertilize their barren acres. He wrote a planting calendar to show farmers the ideal planting times for every crop that grew in Alabama.He planted legumes—and made a great noise about it to anyone who would listen—to enrich the nitrogen-parched soil and provide nutrition for animals. There was no crimson clover anywhere in Macon County in 1896. With Booker's consent—for Booker had to approve every seed and cutting—he planted it heavily in the pastures, along with cowpeas, hairy vetch, and velvet beans on the farm. The soja plant, later called the soybean, had been known in the United States since colonial times, but it was not widely cultivated. Carver planted it on the Tuskegee farm. Then there was the peanut. In those years, people would as soon think of raising acres of parsley as planting fields of peanuts—the peanut was simply not considered an agricultural crop. But Carver began experimenting with it in his first days at Tuskegee—or nights, for he worked day and night. It was these dead-of-night experiments with vegetables—"kitchen chemistry," Carver called what he did with his two hands and no equipment—that would lead him very, very slowly to fame.

"When my train left the golden wheat fields and the tall, green corn of Iowa for the acres of cotton, nothing but cotton, my heart sank a little. Not much evidence of scientific farming anywhere. The scraggy cotton grew close up to the cabin doors; a few lonesome collards, the only sign of vegetables; stunted cattle, boney mules; fields and hill sides cracked and scarred with gullies and deep ruts. Everything looked hungry: the land, the cotton, the cattle, and the people."

Carver was not drawn to research by scientific curiosity only. Within hours of coming to cotton country he realized that the single crop economy of the South was leading large farmers into poverty and their sharecroppers and tenant farmers into starvation. Farmers had to find substitutes for cotton. He had passed the high banks of red and yellow clay and seen from afar the sharecroppers' cabins tattooed into the hillsides. Now he began going around to inspect the country and its people up close. Tuskegee was forty miles east of Montgomery in the heart of the Black Belt, so named because at one time it was a region of rich, black soil. The town seemed tidy and relatively well supplied, its dirt roads lined with wild briar and broom sedge. But just off the main road a few miles outside the town center were the stubbly fields and gaunt animals of the rural South. The saddleback cabins set in the weeds of hard-dirt plots were hardly more than make-do shacks of uneven logs or pine slabs; rain and insects streamed through the gaps. Some 85 percent of the population was black. Carver stared at the details of privation: the homemade ladder leading up to a loft where the older boys slept with the rats, a pigpen reeking near the door, an open well too close to the pigs and to the place in the bushes that served as an outhouse, flies everywhere. These were hovels far more primitive than the slave cabin where George was born, and people worse off than any he had known. He had never before been so close to the scaly legs of pellagra, the festering skin, watery stools, wasting bodies and wretched minds of stricken tenant farmers. Pellagra, he hastened to tell them, was entirely preventable if they would only eat the collards, turnip greens, and kale that they routinely fed to their hogs. The privies and yards were alive with hookworm, "ground itch," that burrowed between the toes of barefoot children and adults, traveled through the body, and caused severe anemia, among other miseries. The overwhelming majority of farm people were infected.

C otton, which had made the South rich before the Civil War, was now the cause of its want. The large plantations of the slave days had typically been mixed farms. About a third of the tillage was dedicated to raising corn and other food for the people living on the land, and the rest was planted in cotton to be sold. When these plantations were broken up, the plots were too small, it was thought, to support both food gardens and cotton, the only crop that could be sold for cash. Trees in Alabama had been burned—millions of acres of longleaf pine—to make room for cotton. Clearing the land had seemed sensible in antebellum times, when cotton was fetching high prices. After the trees were gone, however, the topsoil washed away. By the 1890s, four out of five acres were eroded. The vast majority of black farmers and many whites as well were tenant farmers obliged to plant what their creditors dictated—cotton, though the crop destroyed untreated soil, exhausting the nutrients. A plot of ground used as a cotton patch typically wore out in three years unless fertilized. Though there was still a large market for cotton when Carver first saw Alabama, the yield was diminishing every year. No one had the money to build up the land with commercial fertilizers—the only solution the farmers knew. Instead of entering a land of cotton with its snowy white stands, Carver met endless acres of wasteland where farmers struggled against the stinginess of the soil. The tenant had a few pigs and some chickens; he had lost the art of vegetable growing. His diet consisted of meal and sorghum, corn or flour bread, and a little salt meat. He could easily have grown his own food, but instead, he typically bought it at the landlord's commissary, where invariably he was in debt. The sharecropping and tenant system locked him into destitution.

If a man possessed nothing but his labor and had to use the equipment of the landlord, he was a sharecropper who usually got to keep only a third of the crop's value. If he had his own mule and plow and could buy his seed, then he could enter into a tenancy arrangement where he kept all of his profit after paying rent. Both sharecropping, where the landlord took a percentage of the crop, and tenancy, where the farmer paid a fixed rent, depended on a hierarchy of credit that weighed most heavily on the man doing the labor. First of all, the tenant often had to mortgage his future crop in order to get the seed and equipment to plant. The tenant bought on credit whatever he needed at the store that was set up on or near the land, and ran up bills for food, clothes, and loans so that he could buy tools and perhaps a mule. The interest on these loans was cruel—50 percent or more—and the merchandise was marked up as well. A coat which cost the merchant one dollar was sold to the tenant for two dollars; a pound of meat that cost six cents was sold for twelve. The merchant, in turn, was charged much higher interest in the South than elsewhere by banks that were controlled by northern financial institutions. The tenant was never able to produce enough cotton to have a profit and get out of debt. He had escaped slavery to live in serfdom. The underlying problem, even when cotton fetched high prices, was the lack of local manufacturing. The South had an army of paupers because it sold its raw cotton abroad by the pound and bought it back by the yard in the form of cloth and thread. Moreover, where conditions were ideal for one crop, they were also ideal for that crop's predator— the boll weevil, the insect that would devastate Alabama cotton a few years after George's arrival.

The economic disadvantages of people of color in Alabama were nothing compared to their social demoralization. On his second night at Tuskegee, Carver was reminded of the rigid segregation of the world he had dropped into. When his fellow teachers noted that he had been absent at dinner, he explained, "I went to a café in town—a colored café." "You didn't need to add that," they told him. Naturally, he would only eat in a colored restaurant. Such places closed early, since blacks were not supposed to be out after dark. In the 1890s, the life of every southern black person, down to minute details, was hedged by legal boundaries and pervasive antipathy. These were the years when Jim Crow practices were fixed in law, the years of Klan activity and lynching. Just at the time when Booker was establishing himself as the Viceroy of Black People, a dominion of poverty, southern whites launched their movement to take back the rights that the Civil War and Reconstruction had given to his race. The right to vote was denied to most blacks. Segregation in the South was extended to every corner of life, with the result that blacks were forbidden to enter many public places. The right to an education, to medical care, to high culture, and to ordinary services was severely restricted. As a practical matter, segregation insured that black people would be deprived of ordinary benefits that whites could take for granted. For example, southern states had reform schools for white boys and girls, but because black juveniles could not be placed in these institutions, they were thrown in with adult criminals in the black state prison. "Separate but equal" train cars and waiting rooms meant that the facilities for black people were never cleaned. Their coach was invariably situated behind the baggage car or was a compartment of the baggage car, with one single toilet for both men and women. Black travelers could not buy coffee or food in the station lunchroom, not even to take outside; they were certainly not permitted to sit inside at the tables. Dead black people were placed in a separate section in cemeteries and in the newspaper obituaries. Presumably, black spirits went to segregated Heaven, equal but separate from white ghosts.

Where the assault upon black people was not written into state law or local ordinance, it was carried on by the heavy convention of treating Negroes like a subspecies and going beyond the law in punishing them if they did not meekly submit to degradation. No black person could approach a white stranger with the expectation of a normal human encounter, since a white could take offense at almost anything a black person did and exact any revenge he pleased without answering for it. People of color were expected to remove their hats when speaking to whites. They were to speak when spoken to but not to initiate ordinary conversation; every "yes" or "no" had to be qualified by "yes, Sir," or "no, Ma'am." They were to walk on the outside, the gutter side, of roads and sidewalks and to step off into the roadway when a white person passed. Black people were addressed by their first names—even Booker T. Washington. If their surnames were used, their titles were not—"Washington," "Carver." Blacks reacted by being acutely conscious of titles within their own precincts.

At all Negro colleges, even the younger students were punctiliously addressed as "Mr. Jones," "Miss Lincoln." Oddly, if a black person achieved some special distinction, such as a college degree, whites might address him as "Professor" or "Doctor"—but never "Mister."

Even respected black men could run afoul of their white overlords. George Carver, who got on wonderfully with whites, was caught up in a dangerous incident in 1902 while accompanying a northern white woman to Ramer, another Alabama town. The photographer Frances Johnston—"the pluckiest little woman I ever saw," according to Carver—had come from Washington on a government commission to document the lives of blacks in Alabama. On leaving Tuskegee, she unintentionally imperiled her black driver by sitting up next to him in the front of the coach. Once the coachman let her down, he was set upon by a mob. Both he and his passenger Carver fled on foot and wandered about the fields all night, hiding from the vigilantes and trying to get to the next town where they might find transportation home. Morning finally silenced the ominous night crackles, faded out the fearful shadows, and revealed an unguarded train station. They had barely escaped being lynched. At around the same period, in Ruston, Louisiana, white thugs attacked the officials of a black school because the school, which had never caused any problems for the community, was located "too close" to the town. The school had to be abandoned.

The teachers at Tuskegee were strictly prohibited from showing resentment for any insult they suffered in the town and were in fact discouraged from venturing off the campus where they could get into scrapes with the townspeople. Booker constantly reminded them that the Institute depended on the good will of whites. He set up a military-style guardhouse on the campus so that students could be disciplined internally for such offenses as fighting and drunkenness without the intervention of the town authorities. The whites in the town of Tuskegee consequently had very little idea of what went on at the Institute. They were indifferent to it, though not antagonistic. Despite Booker's frequent remark that many local whites had made donations to Tuskegee, the tabulations showed that in a typical year of nearly 3,000 donations, only twenty came from southern whites, and these totaled less than $75. As for public money, tax dollars for education were spent disproportionately on whites in the South and, indeed, throughout the United States. In both white and black schools, but especially in black schools of the turn of the century, it was common to have a school term of three months and to have no textbooks.

The explorations Carver made in the countryside both appalled and inspired him. The most ignorant farmers were also the most hardheaded and superstitious, insisting that planting after dark would spoil the crop or that eggs found tilted a certain way in the nest were "bad for you." Everybody "knew" that deep plowing would cause the land to wash away. Yet it was obvious to George that he was needed here. The world had all but forgotten these landless cotton farmers, crippled with debt and ignorance, unable to do anything but plant cotton up to their doorsteps and see their harvests garner smaller and smaller returns. The crying need was for some method of making the worn-out land productive, not just for black farmers, but for everyone involved in southern agriculture. Carver turned for help to his friend James Wilson.

6

"STAND UP FOR THE STUPID AND CRAZY"

The U.S. Department of Agriculture under James Wilson was just then setting up scientific research stations all over the country, in association with the new state colleges. The white Alabama Polytechnic University at Auburn was granted a station that was supposed to serve all the citizens but, as George pointed out, black people were unlikely to have any opportunity to use it or benefit from it. Carver therefore submitted to the Alabama legislature a detailed plan for a branch experiment station, "a colored station, to be located at Tuskegee." Thanks to Wilson's influence, the plan was approved. George Carver was named director and consulting chemist of the Tuskegee Experiment Station. Wilson's department did not have control over the way the funds were distributed for the experiment stations; that was in the hands of each state legislature, and Alabama officials saw to it that the largest share of the federal funds went to the white institutions. Lawmakers reasoned that white people paid most of the taxes collected by the government and should therefore receive a preponderance of the benefits. At the outset, the white experiment station at Auburn received ten times the $1,500 allotted to Tuskegee. In subsequent years, the Auburn funds were increased to $69,439, whereas Tuskegee station's allotment remained at $1,500. Booker pledged to supplement the meager state allowance with money from Tuskegee's Agricultural Fund. In the first flush of enthusiasm for the experiment station, he even asked a company to donate several hundred pounds of fertilizer for an experiment. The company wrote back, "We sympathize with your desire for experimentation on southern soils, but we want to be frank with you: we are convinced there is only one colored man who is capable of conducting such a scientific experiment and he, unfortunately, is in Iowa." Booker responded, "The man you refer to is Mr. George W. Carver. We have him right here and he is to conduct the experiment." The station got the fertilizer.

Being the site of an agricultural experiment station was a high honor for a white college; for a black college it was a remarkable accolade, and it came to Tuskegee in early 1897 solely because of the connections, expertise, and efforts of George Carver. But that was not all. In the summer of 1897, Carver traveled to Washington, D.C., and persuaded Wilson to come in person to Tuskegee for the opening of the new Slater-Armstrong Agricultural Building the following December.

For four months the campus went into a frenzy of preparation—a tremendous to-do of building temporary arches and structures and decorating them for the ceremonies. It was the first time any federal official had taken notice of the school, and Booker was not going to waste the opportunity. He choreographed every moment of the welcome, starting with a ten-carriage procession of local and state dignitaries accompanying Wilson from the train station to the campus. In the lead carriage was Booker in his best suit, Carver in his only suit, and Wilson, wearing the first top hat Tuskegee had ever seen. As they swept through the newly built entrance arch of the college, a thousand torch-bearing students lined the driveway, cheering and chanting, "Our Booker," while the professors sent up fireworks and rockets. The band played; the choir sang. There were invocations and commendations and congratulations. Probably at no time in the Secretary's life had people made such a fuss over him.

One of the souvenirs Wilson brought back with him to Washington was the Tuskegee Institute catalogue with its fine-sounding agriculture curriculum: Horticulture, Shop Work, Livestock, Market Gardening, Drawing, Economic Entomology, Botany, Bacteriology, Vegetable Physiology, Botany Cryptogamic (that is, fungi, algae, mosses, and ferns), Agricultural Chemistry, Principles of Heredity, Seeds and Grasses, Practical Agriculture, Applied Botany, Vegetable Pathology, and Dairying. The "curriculum" was little more than a list of courses Carver was prepared to teach immediately, should there be a demand, which, for most of the offerings, there never was. Nevertheless, Wilson was happy to show the catalogue around when he gave his enthusiastic report of his visit to Tuskegee.

Undreamed-of honors developed out of that visit, beginning with the arrival of President William McKinley on the campus in 1898, bringing his wife and almost his entire cabinet with their wives. Other dignitaries came in the succeeding months and years, including other U.S. presidents. All of Washington, D.C., learned about Tuskegee Institute, initially because of the open corridor that connected George Carver to the U.S. Department of Agriculture and the man who would be the head of it for sixteen outstanding years.

George did enough for Tuskegee in his first months there to have earned its principal's lifelong gratitude—if that principal had been anyone but Booker. Far from indicating appreciation, Booker began showing signs of resenting Carver just when the young teacher had set up the experiment station and was drawing the attention of federal officials. In 1900 on a trip through Missouri and Iowa, Carver visited the Shaw Botanical Gardens. His old dream of earning a Ph.D. in botany was reawakened. He wrote to Booker explaining that he had made arrangements to enter the graduate program at the Shaw School of Botany at Washington University in St. Louis, for a degree he believed no black man had ever taken. He had already written a draft of a dissertation. But when he later applied to Booker for his leave of absence to attend school, the principal, to Carver's dismay, insisted that he cancel his plans. Carver was needed at Tuskegee, he said, to study the "food question" and try to cut losses on the school farm. It is fair to say that these were problems that could have waited, since they had existed ever since Tuskegee's founding. Having a Ph.D. in charge of the agriculture department, a man from a prominent white graduate school, would certainly have redounded to Tuskegee's credit, and it might have opened up myriad opportunities for Carver. But George sacrificed his ambition and made perhaps the most critical mistake of his career. He allowed Booker to talk him out of pursuing his dream. It seems never to have occurred to him that Booker's real reason for standing in his way was nothing more than gnawing, insidious, commonplace, human jealousy.

By the time of President McKinley's visit in 1898, George had been at Tuskegee for two years, and he was disillusioned with the pettiness and ignorance of many of his colleagues; with the fruitless committees and their endless, empty talk; with the contrast between the way Tuskegee was presented to the world and the actual quality of the education it provided; with Booker's pathological obsession with trivial imperfections and his obliviousness to the school's serious deficiencies; with the lack of a typist to help with the experiment station's immense burden of correspondence; and with the cavalier way some budget committee or Booker himself would take funds committed to an agricultural project or to the research station and spend them— who knew where? All this he saw and complained about. And yet he remained in Booker's thrall, throwing himself into the multiple projects that were assigned to him in addition to his crushing routine. He was rarely thanked, publicly or privately; he was always criticized—because a picture in the Agriculture Building was hanging a little crookedly, "especially obvious on the day the governor visited," or because some signs on the grounds of the experiment station giving the names of the plants were not up to date: "I hope you will see such a mistake does not occur again."

Booker was a complex man. He was a deliberate and skilled hypocrite. For example, when he visited Fisk University, he pointedly complained about the condition of the boys' outhouses, although Tuskegee's, as he was well aware, were incomparably more disgusting. He was occasionally a charlatan and always a showman; the show was a one-man presentation in which he expected to stand alone on stage to receive the applause. He was a politician in the worst sense, squandering his energy in spiteful actions against other blacks he perceived as rivals or enemies. And yet, he generally had a larger purpose in mind than his own aggrandizement. It is only when we look at his covert actions—his secret funding for legal challenges to segregation, for example— that we see his stout opposition to conditions that he appeared to blandly ignore. He never lost his dedication to helping what he called "the man furthest down," the poorest, most humble, most helpless of his people. It was not only for the well-dressed and well-spoken black people of his own social class that he wanted to win the respect of the white world. His compassion was greatest, his eloquence most inspired, when he stood for those who could not speak for themselves. The men and women who worked for Booker saw through his shams. Yet they also recognized the sincerity of his larger vision and remained captivated by it.

His good side was never more evident than during the commencement exercises that took place each May. White townsfolk were invited to the graduation, to be sure, and no effort was spared to get them to attend the event. But the big yearly festivity was chiefly intended for the students and their parents.

Tuskegee was not an institution of higher education. Like Hampton, it was a secondary school. Its graduates who wanted to get a college degree had to start over as freshmen at a four-year institution, such as Fisk. Few students ever actually graduated from Tuskegee's two-year program—at best, one in ten; nevertheless, every year the whole school participated in a graduation party that celebrated education and self-improvement. Parents came from thirty or forty miles away, bringing their own parents, making a two-day trip in haggard wagons to hear reassurances that, because of their sacrifices, their children would have a better life than they themselves had known. Booker's commencement addresses rarely mentioned "success." The objective of knowledge and "know-how" was not individual success but the sharing of information with others, so that the entire community would be lifted. If you can't get a paying job, he told students, ask to work for free, for to work for free was not the same as working for nothing. You were working to improve the farm, the land, the neighborhood, the world. The commencement guests went freely in and out of the shops and classrooms, touching the equipment, listening to the choir that had been rehearsed for their pleasure, enjoying the brass music which they only got to hear at this special time, and eating a good meal they did not have to cook themselves.

If Booker had a limited appreciation of pure science and no apprehension at all of knowledge for its own sake, he had boundless enthusiasm for practical education and for any notion aimed at raising the downtrodden. Carver's mind was much broader and deeper—he was a true seeker after beauty, truth, and intellectual wisdom of every kind. But he was as ardent as Booker in wanting to reach out to the meek and deprived and, perhaps even more than Booker, he had the common touch. In his very first years at Tuskegee, Carver developed a number of projects aimed at reaching the poor. His endeavors—supported by Booker—eventually made Tuskegee Institute a place where illiterate folk could feel entirely at home—a practical university for people who might never in their lives have opened a single book. Carver undertook these time-consuming projects while teaching a minimum of five courses, managing the school's enterprises that had been thrust upon him, and running the experiment station, where he was working, unaided and unappreciated, on a dozen complicated projects. Some of his outreach projects he initiated; others were already in place at Tuskegee, and he reactivated or enlarged them.

The first community project was the Farmers' Institute, held each month. A typical Institute day began with Carver giving the attendees a simple lesson in poultry raising or erosion prevention, always illustrated with animals, plants, or soil the farmers could see before them. Was there a cheap food for hogs that was good for them? Carver walked them over to his pet sow dining happily on—acorns, which were free and plentiful and generally went to waste. He took the participants to the experiment station and showed them huge vegetables flourishing in the same kind of soil they had on their farms. The experiment station plots, using no commercial fertilizer whatever, would soon show a profit of seventy-five dollars an acre. To cash-starved tenant farmers, trying to squeeze a subsistence out of fifteen or twenty acres, seventy-five dollars was a fortune.

There was always much hymn singing at the Farmer's Institute and a session where farmers discussed their particular problems and showed off their successes—nice collards or good-looking cotton—for if they were bookless people, they were by no means speechless. The wives watched cooking and sewing demonstrations and shared ideas on how to use something that grew in abundance or how to stretch something that did not. In time, committees formed and one by one gave reports of their activities—mothers who made four dollars selling rutabagas to raise money for a summer school, a men's group that had pooled six dollars from their increased egg production toward paying their schoolteacher during the lean summer. Reading the minutes of these meetings is painfully boring; sitting through them must have been deadly. For Carver, however, they were probably no worse and surely more worthy than the committee meetings he had to endure every day at Tuskegee. For the farmers, the Institutes broke the solitary routines of rural life. Some couples started out before dawn in their mule wagons and arrived back home in cold darkness, with chores yet to face and children to bed. But still they came faithfully each month.

The Institutes gave rise to a yearly fair, which grew into the Farmers' Annual Conference, held each February, still under Carver's aegis and structured around his programs. The school encouraged its neighbors on the road to Tuskegee to clean up their yards and houses in anticipation of the visitors who would pass by. Booker even offered them free whitewash. Farmers arrived in ox carts and mule wagons all through the night preceding the conference, bringing their exhibits of livestock, quilts, canned goods, needlework, and home-cured meat. Sometimes the prize animals rode in sties specially decorated for the big day. In the old pavilion, covered with long-leaf pine for the occasion, Professor Carver displayed his cowpeas, soybeans, dried fruits, and sweet potatoes, along with hand-out pamphlets explaining how to cultivate and cook foods of particular nutritive value.

Booker would start conference day by mounting a platform and giving a little sermon on farming—rotate your crops, keep a compost heap for fertilizer, and so on. He called on individuals to recount what they had been doing in the past year to improve their land or to better their situation. The annual conference had the flavor of mild revivalism, and that was precisely its intention—to revive the South, starting with Macon County, starting with the earnest individual who slowly rose, mastered his nerves, and explained how certain advice he received at last year's gathering had indeed proved useful. Students had spent the night barbecuing and baking the meal that would be spread out at noon on the grass in the bottom land—typically sheep or ox, pink lemonade, cake and coffee. Booker could eat nothing. Years of stress and probably ulcers had ruined his stomach, but he walked among the picnickers, chatting. Their mules and oxen left piles everywhere. The people tramped over new lawns, and their children crushed just-planted shrubs at the experiment station. Neither Carver nor anyone else stopped them, though it would take a week to clean up the campus afterward. Booker Washington, who could be made furious over a ragged tree limb on a walkway or a flower bed that needed weeding, refused to put the least limitation on these visitors—sometimes numbering eight or nine thousand. Carver once repeated to a biographer Booker's words regarding the yearly visitors: "Tuskegee belongs to them," he said. "This is the only time they have the freedom to do as they please and have a good time with no one admonishing them." It was Booker's tenderness toward his people that made men like Carver cleave to him, despite everything.

Most of the conference exhibits were displayed in the chapel—electrically lighted with a dynamo installed by the students. The beautiful new chapel was like a beacon to the country folk, who were years away from having electricity in their homes. A cow would be brought in, marched up in front of the pulpit, and milked to demonstrate the most sanitary procedures, followed by a horse, which was shod before the viewers and had its teeth filed. A girl showed how to cut a dress from a pattern. She fitted it on a model and sewed it up, so that the model walked off between the pews wearing her new dress.

Theodore Roosevelt visited Tuskegee in 1905. When the assassination of President McKinley in 1901 brought Roosevelt into the White House, the new president had called Booker to Washington to consult with him about the appointment of black men to office, for by then Booker was already the arbiter of which blacks were placed in important positions around the country. A storm of protest rained down on Roosevelt for inviting Negro shoes to rest under the White House dining table. But four years later, fresh from his landslide election victory, TR was ready to cross the color line again, if only in a short, symbolic visit of a few hours. For this brief, important presidential visit, Booker put the school on wheels—minus the stinking privies—and had it roll past Roosevelt's viewing stand. Students riding on floats performed the tasks of the classroom and the field. They ginned and baled cotton, contrasted old and new methods of churning butter, made mattresses and brooms, upholstered furniture, dressed chickens, pruned and sprayed fruit trees, joined steam pipes, set type, and worked a printing press as they rolled along. Who could fail to be delighted by such a show?

All such visits involved intense preparations and added burdens for the teachers. No person of influence saw the normal operations of Tuskegee during his visit, only the displays—Potemkin villages—that were put on to impress him. Hardly had the visitor left when the school returned to its uneven rhythms. "At one time we have a classroom, at another, none. Sometimes the teacher is present, other times absent; so that the whole work is not up to the standard," Carver would write Booker, not once but many times.

Besides bringing visitors, great and humble, to Tuskegee, Carver conceived a project to bring the college to people outside. Friday afternoons he packed a wagon and traveled out to the sharecroppers farthest in the sticks, bringing demonstrations to people who for various reasons did not attend the monthly institutes or the yearly conference, people who were pleased to see "The Professor" or, indeed, any sort of company. He pulled out preserved fruits to share with them while explaining to the wives that egg white made a handy seal for canning jars. If the women were pregnant, he explained to them that the old practice of eating dirt to lessen labor pains or drinking dirt tea was dangerous. He brought along a homemade transport cage and materials for making other cages in hopes of persuading the farmers to stop the cruel practice of tying their chickens together by the feet and carrying them upside down to market. He showed the wives how to make laundry starch and syrup from boiled sweet potatoes and, for good measure, distributed sweet potato candy to the children. Again and again he urged farmers to raise their own food along with the cotton they hoped to sell instead of buying from the company store. He showed the wives how to make crafts from pine straw and corn shucks. They could slowly climb out of debt by selling their homemade crafts, quilts, and embroidery or raising extra eggs and chickens to exchange in the town shops. He showed them how to make their own whitewash from the lime in the clay hills around them: "Take a few shovelfuls of white clay from the cut bank, like this. It has some sand in it, so we'll stir it into water in the big iron wash kettle and let it stand two minutes. Now let's see—the rest of the sand and gravel have sunk to the bottom and the water can be poured off. Next we put it in a gunny sack and keep dipping it until all the clay is suspended in the water. And here is our whitewash!" In time, Carver worked out simple techniques for making color washes for the inside walls of the drab cabins, walls on which the farmers had been accustomed to nailing up newspaper. He used equipment that would be close at hand to anyone. In the more distant communities, he stayed one or two nights with the people and spoke in their churches on Sunday morning before going back to Tuskegee.

There were no farm demonstration agents at that time, only Carver with his wagon full of curiosities. In 1906, Morris K. Jesup donated the money for a wagon Carver could outfit with materials. Like the medicine and peddler wagons that traveled the countryside, the Jesup Wagon could be closed against the rain, but it opened out to reveal all sorts of products attached to the doors. How small and antique it looks now in the Carver museum in Diamond, Missouri, almost like a child's plaything! But at the time, it was a farmers' college on wheels. Carver did not get to drive the Jesup wagon that he had outfitted. It was taken out on the road by another man in the agriculture faculty, Carver's bitter rival George R. Bridgeforth. Although the reasons are not clear-cut, it seems that Booker intended to insult Carver by appointing Bridgeforth to displace him. After three months, a newly appointed county agent took over as wagoner, and then the project started by Carver became a bright success. For decades the Jesup Wagon went out on a regular schedule to communities all around Tuskegee, stopping in the spring at a farm to which all the neighbors had been summoned to demonstrate plowing and planting, coming back in time to demonstrate fertilizing and harvesting, and returning later still to show everyone how to cook and preserve the food from the harvest. Eventually, the Jesup Wagon reached seven states. In the era of the automobile, it was supplanted by the Movable School, traveling hundreds of miles and serving as the model for similar projects all over the world.

The first county agent was Thomas M. Campbell, one of Carver's best students, whose appointment by the federal government was a signal honor for a black man. After one year of going around to the tenant farmers of Macon County and trying to motivate them, Campbell wrote to Carver in frustration. Carver responded with several very long letters. Carver noted that both sharecroppers and tenants moved around within the county, sometimes every year, so that they had little incentive to improve the land or beautify a house that was owned by the landlord. "Go right to their farms," Carver advised, "take hold of their problems with them, and in every way prove that you have come to help them. Show them how to do the work by actually doing it. Talk just enough for them to thoroughly understand what you are doing." Telling people what to do would never be sufficient, Carver averred. He, too, had known frustration. "Of course, while we are talking to them they will readily agree to everything you suggest, to go and do it exactly as they have been accustomed to doing it after you leave . . . Go right with them, collect the leaves, mulch, farmyard manures, etc., and actually make some compost, spread it . . . show them how to do whatever is seasonal in the way of plowing, fertilizing, selecting seed, planting, cultivating, etc. . . . The wide-awake agent will think of this as part of his job." Carver addressed each farm activity in detail, from building toilets and pruning orchards to curing meats; he gave pages of advice. He suggested that Campbell offer seasonal prizes for the best cow, pig, garden, house, yard, outhouse. Campbell remained county agent for many years. He continually sought advice from Carver, named his son Carver Campbell, and asked his mentor to be the boy's godfather.

Not all of Carver's projects were successes, but they were wonderful experiments all the same. He still painted when he could steal the time; he got the idea of making his own paints from Alabama clay. In his laboratory he experimented with red clay and, by several stages of distillation, came up with an intense new blue with many times the color saturation of previous blues. He would decline to patent most such products. His objective, he said, was not to keep his discoveries secret nor to help paint corporations make money but to share his findings as widely as possible. The Montgomery Paint and Dry Color Works was founded in 1903 by a group of businessmen intent on marketing "Prussian Blue" and other hues developed by Carver from Alabama clay. Carver served as unpaid consultant and was not to make any financial gain from the enterprise. The company failed to find sufficient subscribers to the stock, so the project was abandoned the next year.

Meanwhile, Carver tried growing thyme and lavender with the idea— ultimately unsuccessful—that a perfume industry might be developed in the region. One of his best schemes required Tuskegee to buy a bone mill to process the bones of the farm's dead animals. Treated with cheap sulfuric acid, the ground bones would be reduced to superphosphate—an exceedingly valuable fertilizer. The Institute could offer to buy bones from farmers in the area, providing them with a little cash and supplying Tuskegee with the basis for a fertilizer that the school could use itself or sell more cheaply than commercial brands. Somehow, that project was never developed. James Wilson wanted to try the patient cultivation of silkworms as an alternative to cotton and saw to it that Tuskegee received 300 mulberry trees and shipments of eggs. "The silkworm eggs have all hatched and I have thousands of them upon my hands to feed and care for," Carver reported. "I have not counted them, of course, but there are supposed to be ten thousand." Eventually, the silkworm venture proved infeasible; it was one of many projects in Carver's endless efforts to find the answer to Alabama's agricultural crisis and Tuskegee's deficits.

The experiment station was intended from the beginning to be part of the community, not a research place with a high fence to keep out intruders. In the very first bulletin, farmers and gardeners were "not only encouraged but urged to write to Professor Carver with their problems." If they could not write, they were told to bring in their samples of soils, fertilizers, insects, feeding stuffs, grasses and water for Carver's analysis. People came to the station all day long and were welcomed, even though they were interrupting Carver's other work. One man rode an entire day and called Carver out of evening chapel to ask what to do for his ailing ox. J. H. and his confreres, including Booker, slighted and hindered the experiment station whenever they had the opportunity, raiding its funds and pretending to believe that Carver was "only" a scholar with a head full of arcane information. But the truth was that the experiment station in the early 1900s was doing the finest work of the school.

The station land consisted of twenty acres which were cultivated according to Carver's detailed directions and supervision—deep plowing with an ox-drawn plow, organic fertilizing, and all the rest—without the use of commercial fertilizer. One acre of the worst land was chosen for a soil-building experiment. In 1897, this plot's yield showed a loss of $2.40, but by 1903, the same acre was producing a profit of $94.65. Carver published the results of the experiment in an important bulletin, *How to Build Up Worn Out Soils*. The pamphlet attracted John D. Rockefeller's attention; the philanthropist requested extra copies and was inspired to finance a project on soil reclamation. But Booker was far less interested in Carver's work with the station than in increasing the yield on the school's farms. He insisted that Carver shift resources and energy from experimenting with new crops to improving cotton production. Carver was, in fact, already addressing the problem of cotton production; in his first three years at Tuskegee, he had tested thirteen varieties of cotton. By crossbreeding, he developed four new varieties on the experimental farm, all particularly adapted to the light, sandy soils of Macon County. Carver's cotton was one of the little miracles of the station: one bush could carry 275 enormous bolls. In 1897, his experiments with growing sweet potatoes resulted in the largest yield per acre ever recorded in the state—266 bushels. When the cabal around Booker intimated that Carver was exaggerating his successes, Carver was heartsick that they ("they" included Booker) "want to deny the yield because they would not go out to see it."

Despite Carver's phenomenal success with the experiment station plots, Booker thought the station consumed too much of Carver's time and too much land. "The mere fact that this large field is called an experiment field prevents it being used in producing crops that we need," he complained. By 1903, the experiment station acreage had been cut in half. Booker consistently disparaged the scientific aspect of Carver's work; he never comprehended that experiment sometimes results in failure. More and more, he was exclusively concerned with what Carver could do to make the farm more productive or the school grounds more attractive. At times, Booker approached Carver with alluring plans. He proposed, for example, enlarging the agricultural building and having it house an even larger botanical collection than the one Carver had already donated. George responded excitedly, "My most sanguine hopes have been to build up at Tuskegee one of the largest and best *working* museums in the South. One that will give inspiration to both teachers and students to pursue work along industrial, literary, and scientific lines." Not only did the museum proposal wither away; within a year, the collection Carver had contributed was in ruins.

Christmas Eve, 1902, found him pleading with Booker: "I trust you will pardon me for bringing up this matter so many times with reference to the condition of the leaks . . . and the amount of property that is being ruined." He attached a detailed table showing the days of rain in each month with the precise amounts of rainfall and the number of specimens that had been ruined on each date—all together, 578 samples destroyed. "I have been constantly reporting these conditions and as yet nothing effective has been done. What specimens remain are more or less moulded by reason of the dampness, but I am cleaning them off and placing them as rapidly as I can. I should indeed be thankful if some radical steps might be taken to stop these leaks. You can readily see that the collection will soon be a thing of the past . . . Every specimen represents a particular locality and has been collected, named, and mounted by me, and when it is being destroyed by actual neglect I cannot but feel keenly about it." Even though Carver had written to Booker repeatedly about the leaks, he courteously added, "I am writing this for your information as I am sure you do not know the exact condition and the amount of property that is going to destruction in this building." When the leaks were finally fixed, Carver wrote Booker a warm letter of thanks.

Like other station directors across the country, Carver wrote bulletins—free for the asking—to disseminate the results of his experiments: *Using Acorns to Feed Hogs, Dried Sweet Potatoes as a Coffee Substitute, Better Cotton through Cross-Breeding, Protecting Against Hog Cholera.* He wrote bulletins in the early years on tomatoes, Irish potatoes, corn, onions, beans, clover, thirteen varieties of cotton, vetch, and of course, peanuts. Publishing bulletins was considered one of the major functions of experiment stations, allowing the directors to share their findings with each other as well as with the general public. Carver took more care than others to make his writing plain so that laymen could follow his directions. His bulletins were especially designed for three types of readers: farmers, their wives, and teachers who could use the information in their classrooms. Therefore, in addition to agricultural advice, each bulletin contained recipes and a straightforward explanation of the science underlying the advice. Soon other experiment stations were copying Carver's model for writing bulletins.

To promote cowpeas, which were good for the soil and were a nutritious food, he published *How to Grow the Cow Pea and 40 Ways of Preparing it as a Table Delicacy*. Carver described the history and varieties of the little pea commonly known in the South as the black-eyed pea. He gave detailed directions for cultivation, discussed diseases and insects that might attack the pea, and suggested remedies for both diseases and insect destroyers (here Carver used scientific terms followed by common names). He explained how to prepare the peas for animal food, and then gave explicit recipes—fritters, "coffee," soups, dried pea "roast," croquettes, and cow pea custard pie. It turned out to be one of his most popular bulletins.

Carver composed several bulletins on the nutritive value of sweet potatoes and their benefit to the soil. More bushels of sweet potatoes could be grown per acre than any other known farm crop. During the first year of the experiment station, Carver himself had made a nine-fold increase in the average yield per acre, and he was discovering more and more uses for the plant. Once when he brought a bulletin to Booker for his approval, the men had one of their typical arguments. "I see you say nobody knows where the sweet potato originated," said Booker.

"That's right."

"Nobody knows?"

"Nobody knows."

"Then let's say it was Macon County," said Booker, dipping his pen and preparing to insert the words.

"Mr. Washington, you can't do that," Carver protested. "Such things must be known and classified. Don't expect me to sign that bulletin if you put something like that in it."

"Why not? What's the harm in giving the sweet potato a home?"

"The harm is that it will make us look ridiculous. Anybody with any knowledge at all knows that it couldn't have originated here. The plant series doesn't warrant it." Booker had to back down.

The more serious argument that arose over the bulletins was that, despite having no typist, Carver prepared bulletins that Booker allowed to remain unpublished for months with the excuse that the school did not have the money to issue them. After Carver waited six months to get three bulletins printed, he protested to Booker, "I do not understand where the Experiment Station appropriation goes. I am very confident I have not used it." Printing the bulletins in the school printing office was an insignificant expense in comparison to the overall budget of Tuskegee. By 1900 the Institute had become a self-contained town with forty-two buildings, including a post office, bank, shops, and power plant, financed by fund-raising speeches and philanthropists. By 1906, the size had doubled: eighty-three buildings, 1,600 regular students, and a teaching faculty of 156. The endowment was over a million dollars, but still Professor Carver could not be certain that bulletins explaining his discoveries would be printed in-house. The school was still run from the center, that is, from Booker's office, with his coterie, particularly his brother, who knew even less about science and agriculture than he did and appeared to care no more about the bulletins that issued from the experiment station than he cared about Carver's botanical collections. Comments of praise were few and cold. More characteristic were such offhand notes as: "Professor Carver, please let me have seventy-five dollars to be returned at earliest convenience. Booker Washington."

For Carver, the experiment station was at the center of Tuskegee's mission to reach out to poor people. It wounded him to realize that Booker's enthusiasm was for *having* an experiment station, not for the discoveries made there, unless these were certain of attracting national publicity for the school. Carver's little allotment was raided for such projects as erecting a new horse barn which was to be "built with an imposing front," or having all the dairy workers in white uniforms. Carver could not train research assistants because J. H. constantly switched the workers around despite Carver's vigorous complaints that he was operating "with the smallest and most inexperienced staff of any station in the U.S." and that it was "impossible to do this work without men and means."

In his first two years at Tuskegee, Carver had somehow found time to write the draft of a botany textbook, the first in a proposed series. The conventional teaching of botany, he had decided, was too abstract to be useful to 95 percent of undergraduates who took a general course. Even in prestigious universities, botany students who knew a great deal about plant chemistry could not identify the common trees and grasses in their neighborhoods. Carver's textbooks would be written mainly for agriculture students, highlighting the relationship between the various branches of biology. In learning how to raise pears, the student would at the same time be taught which pests could destroy an orchard; likewise, if he learned about insects, he would know which ones liked pear trees. Botany and entomology needed to be taught together, along with such topics as molds and fungi. Carver's textbooks would offer an integrated approach to plant cultivation.

Meanwhile, he was turning out articles intended for government officials, scientists, and farmers. In a leaflet called *The Need of Scientific Agriculture in the South,* he lucidly assessed the Black Belt farming situation. He wrote nature guides for schoolchildren and teachers—short, good books with long, bad titles. Popular magazines were beginning to request articles from him; additionally, he wrote a regular column for a Columbia University review, "Professor Carver's Advice," in which he expatiated on everything from raising mushrooms to rearing children on a farm. By the early 1900s, he was in demand as a speaker and received several invitations to teach summer programs in a variety of institutions. Despite Carver's myriad accomplishments and the praise he was garnering for Tuskegee, Booker, in his 1907 autobiography *Up From Slavery,* managed to describe every step of Tuskegee's development without once mentioning the institution's most well-known professor.

Booker was not meaner to Carver than to many others; he mistreated everybody equally. It took George years to get accustomed to a "college" that had no use for independent thinking and discouraged personal goals. Being at Tuskegee was like being in the army or in a religious order where the chief officer tried to control every aspect of one's life and thought. Booker wanted the students to be happy at school, but he had no regard for the feelings of his teachers. The teachers existed to make the institution a success. Booker resented any part of their lives that took their minds outside of Tuskegee. The families of the teachers he regarded as an inconvenience.

The wives were chronically discontented, even Mrs. Emmett Scott, the wife of his chief assistant. For one thing, the women were directed to buy their groceries at the school commissary where they were insulted, vastly overcharged, and subjected to the profanity of the storekeeper. They were made to understand, they said, that the commissary existed mainly to serve the needs of the boarding department. The Children's House where their children were schooled never could keep a kindergarten going. The mothers wanted a full term and a full day's session starting in the third grade. As was his wont, Booker appointed committee after committee to study the complaints over a period of several years but never followed up on any committee's recommendations. Despite being shunted aside by the school officials, the families were expected to host a stream of Tuskegee visitors in their homes. Their yards, houses, and housekeeping were subjected to Booker's trifling criticisms, just like all the other facilities on campus. If Booker spotted a teacher's chickens outside his yard, the owner would receive a reprimand.

The teachers were required to set an example and never to do anything that reflected badly on the school. Booker fired the school pastor, Reverend J. A. Penney, after many years of service because of a flimsy accusation by a woman student who had been quartered in his home. Penney was clearly innocent of the charge of improper conduct, as Booker knew, but the pastor was terminated anyway, to protect the school's reputation. Teachers were forbidden to smoke, drink alcohol, gamble, dance, swear, or skip chapel—which was held every evening. Staffers were not allowed to chew gum in the offices. In fact, the faculty and staff repeatedly committed all these sins and more. Some of the men were even known to visit "an improper house" in town. But Booker was determined that, insofar as he could prevent it, his teachers would not behave like normal people. No teacher had what can be called a private life. Booker did not hesitate, for example, to tell his dean of women to reprimand a teacher because she was associating too frequently with a male colleague. The teachers and even the workers did not have to be ordered to spy on each other; tattling was an accepted pastime. C. L. Diggs wrote to Booker offering the names of "Ladies who goes out with gentlemen." Several teachers wrote letters reporting—for lack of more interesting transgressions—colleagues who walked on the grass instead of the paths. J. H. Washington's son followed two teachers riding in a carriage and reported to a "morals" committee (which included his father) the information that the couple kissed—although since young Washington was following at a distance at night, the kiss could not be conclusively asserted. Another report concerned teachers playing footsie under a table. Booker was furious that two teachers got married secretly. He ordered them to start living together at once and warned the faculty that he would dismiss anyone else who married clandestinely. Considering the cloister regimen imposed on them, it is a wonder teachers ever found spouses in the first place.

C arver never finished his textbook, *Economic Botany*, although he worked on it off and on for years. Nor did he resume serious art study, another of his dreams. Every hour of his life was encumbered by his work at Tuskegee, some of it essential, some of it a waste of time, even for milder minds than his. His days were far from dull, however, after he settled into Tuskegee. In fact, in the decade after 1900, his life was exhilarating and excruciating. In that fraught period he was engulfed in a long, imperfect love affair and a bitter war. For probably the first time in his life he fell—or subsided—in love.

7

LOVE AND LYNCH MOBS

The first love affair we hear about occurred soon after George Carver arrived at Tuskegee, probably between 1896 and 1899. It was inconsequential—if matters of the heart can ever be thus described. According to the account he later gave a biographer, he was smitten with one of his colleagues and began dreaming about marriage. But then he got to know the lady and woke himself up. She said something to friends that made him believe she was ashamed of being black. Whoever this self-conscious inamorata was, she was undoubtedly light complexioned, as were all the female teachers at Tuskegee in those years. If she were embarrassed to be attached to a very dark man, then George was not the husband for her, and he realized it before he did anything foolish, such as propose. "I believe in 'What God has joined together, etc.'" he said to friends. "But what God doesn't join had better be left unjoined." The woman died a few years after the relationship ended. In their recollections, friends of Carver sometimes confused this mystery woman with Sarah Hunt, but Sarah came along a couple of years later and lived vigorously into the 1940s. George's first romance was short-lived and casual; Sarah was at the center of his life for the better part of a decade.

Sarah Hunt was the younger sister of George's closest friend at Tuskegee, Adella Hunt Logan. Adella had been with Booker almost since Tuskegee's founding. When she graduated from Atlanta University, she was offered a position there but passed up the opportunity of teaching in a smart, urban environment. Instead, she went to Alabama to help Booker educate sharecroppers and their children. In 1888, five years after coming to Tuskegee, she wed mild Warren Logan, the school's treasurer and Booker's right-hand man; Booker's left-hand man, the one he used for undercover operations, confidential payments, and spying, was his secretary Emmett Scott. Logan or Scott—one or the other—acted as principal during the six months of the year when Booker was away. In fact, it is hard to imagine how Booker could have kept Tuskegee going without those aides. Like other faculty wives, Adella filled in the spaces at Tuskegee wherever she was needed. She was the school's first librarian. At times she taught English and social studies; at other times she served as the quaintly designated "lady principal."

Adella became fast friends with George Carver soon after he started at Tuskegee in 1896. Though she did not share his background of privation, the two had much in common. They were the same age, both aching for intellectual companionship, both avid for knowledge and wisdom. They loved the arts, literature, and all the sciences and could talk together for hours. On any given day, Adella could be counted on to be interested, intense, and pregnant. She had nine children before the Logan family was complete, six of whom lived to adulthood. She was active in the rising movement for women's suffrage and in much else. As a charter member of the Tuskegee Women's Club, she organized lectures and programs in nutrition, hygiene, civics, prenatal care, and prison reform. She ran a community lending library and wrote earnest articles with titles such as "What Are the Causes of the Great Mortality Among the Negroes of the Cities of the South, and How Is That Mortality To Be Lessened?" Despite her pregnancies and responsibilities, she returned to college every summer and received a master's degree in 1905.

Adella was also something of a gadfly to Booker, insisting on better conditions for the teachers, who were always last in Booker's priorities. It was no doubt with Adella's assistance that Carver drew up a list of inexpensive additions to the breakfasts offered to teachers. He suggested serving corn muffins twice a week, fried mush, grits, milk toast or fried rice twice a week, French toast with syrup, and fruit and a vegetable at every meal. He noted that hot beverages were served cold or lukewarm. "Care should be taken," he wrote, "so that coffee and tea are really hot." His list makes one wonder exactly what was served to the teachers for breakfast, if muffins, grits, hot coffee, and fruit were lacking.

Until Carver's appearance, Adella was probably the brightest teacher at Tuskegee and maybe the loneliest. The academic program she had gone through at Atlanta was modeled on that of Yale. Atlanta University took the same kinds of raw students as Tuskegee and inculcated the same habits of cleanliness, good grooming, good manners, and personal discipline that were so important to Booker, but its primary mission was to provide rigorous intellectual training to its black student body. Indeed, the black colleges of the South—Talladega, Spelman, South Carolina State, Knoxville, Morehouse, Howard, Fisk, and others—all received students who were unprepared in both studies and civilities, gave them years of remedial training, and finally admitted them to a program that was academically more serious than Tuskegee's. Adella began to annoy Booker, as did anyone in his domain with an independent mind, by prodding him to move away from the model he had learned at Hampton and to put more stress on academic teaching. Tuskegee, said Adella, could remain an industrial school, but it should be a place where students could choose to study mathematics just as readily as bricklaying. The more Adella learned, the more she insisted that Tuskegee must have higher standards—and she was always learning.

Booker, meanwhile, wanted to reform English instruction at Tuskegee but not according to Adella's program. After reading some student essays, he complained, "There are too many big words in some of them. The sentences are too long and involved." He wanted Tuskegee students "to use the smallest words possible, and the shortest and most simple sentences. Let them use the same kind of language in writing that they do in talking." Given Booker's anti-intellectualism, the intellectual Adella was waging a losing fight. She received no support from her husband. Warren Logan was "a man of little imagination," according to his granddaughter, Adele Logan Alexander. He had been a classmate of Booker at Hampton Institute and subscribed to the philosophy of industrial education. He loved "his music, his church, his school, and his leader, Mr. Washington." George, however, was a kindred enlightened spirit who managed to encourage Adella without alienating her husband. The three had a good time together. Warren and Adella were interested in music; George could play any instrument someone handed to him. They steadily produced children; he loved children. Both the Logans were devoted to George—they felt close enough to him to borrow $800 in 1902—but with Adella especially, Carver could be free with opinions and ideas that he shared with no one else at Tuskegee.

George met Adella some ten months after a hideous event in her life. In 1895, Adella's mother had come from Georgia to visit her. In those days of open hearths, fire accidents were commonplace with both adults and children. Youngsters sometimes fell into fireplaces or ran into boiling pots hanging from hooks over the flames. While Adella's mother was rocking the newest baby before the hearth, she fell asleep, and her clothes caught fire. The baby died of his burns within hours; Adella's mother died after three ghastly weeks. A year later, Adella still needed comfort from someone with a kind, open temperament, and she found that friend in George. Because George's focus was always on something larger than day-to-day events, he was the ideal companion to bring her out of the self-absorption of deep grief.

Then and always, Carver's circle of intimate friends was small. He tended to be reserved among people he did not know well, although he was invariably good-humored and well mannered. With Adella he could be himself—lively and witty or quiet-spoken and thoughtful. She encouraged him to keep up his artwork—no one else at Tuskegee had the least interest in it. "Sometimes she would make no spoken comment at all when I showed her a painting I had just completed," Carver said. "She would just stand and look at it for a long time and say nothing. And then I would see that there were tears in her eyes. She didn't need to say anything." Even without tears, it was easy to read Adella's face: sensitive, thoughtful, and unhappy. While Carver was in Tennessee in 1904, teaching in the summer program at Knoxville College, Adella and three of her children joined him there. Adella saw to it that Carver was not alone on any holiday when she could entice him to her family table with the Logan children and her sister. It is likely that Carver was somewhat in love with Adella but accepted Sarah as a substitute.

Sarah Hunt had been teaching English at Tuskegee for some years before she and Carver got together around 1900, when she was thirty-one and he was thirty-seven or thirty-eight. She was like her sister in a dozen ways. Both were alumnae of Atlanta University. Both were frank, direct individuals, excited about women's suffrage, politics, racial issues, literature, music, and theater. Sarah lived with the Logans and took part in her sister's myriad projects. When Adella staged *Othello* in her home—for where else would black people in the hills have an opportunity to see Shakespeare?—Sarah played Desdemona. By 1903, Carver was living across the campus in Rockefeller Hall, in a couple of congested rooms that served as his library, laboratory, insectarium, art gallery, greenhouse, and rubbish center. His first-floor bachelor quarters overflowed into the corridor, where the walls were lined with his paintings. He could walk over and see Sarah every day.

The opportunities to meet people of the opposite sex were few, for Carver or anyone at Tuskegee. The town was small; Carver and all the teachers were so busy, they had no time for excursions outside the campus. Though Carver had more occasion than almost any other teacher to meet women in nearby colleges, "nearby" could mean a daylong ride in a wagon over lumpy roads or an expensive eight-hour train trip. Traveling, like much else, was especially difficult for black people. There were no black hotels or even separate accommodations in white hotels except in fair-sized cities, assuming one could afford a hotel. Lodging with white people was usually out of the question. Throughout the country, many towns did not permit black people in their precincts after dark. Carrying on a relationship over a distance of even forty miles was all but infeasible. If Carver were going to find a wife, he would have to find her at Tuskegee. And it was high time; he was already noticing threads of silver in his hair. If Sarah were to take up with a gentleman, he would probably have to come from the faculty. Sarah was an intellectual like her sister, one of the few at Tuskegee in those days. Given the paucity of unmarried people at the school, let alone erudite people, Carver and Sarah must have been delighted to find each other.

They "went together" about six years. Booker insisted on strict chastity for all unmarried teachers, students, and staff. Not only were male and female souls separated in chapel, but they had to keep to separate sidewalks, in order to prevent "promiscuous mingling of boys and girls in front of the building each night." George lived in a student dormitory, and Sarah shared her domicile with the Logans' several children. But since sex was as irrepressible at Tuskegee as it is in every place at every time, it would not be outrageous to assume that they managed during that long time to become lovers. George wrote to Mrs. Liston in 1905, telling her he was seriously considering marriage and soliciting her thoughts; this was one time he did not rely exclusively on advice from Sarah's sister. At about the same time, Sarah left Tuskegee briefly but then returned. Given the absolutism Booker imposed his teachers, there was doubtless some pressure on the couple to legitimize their relationship or break it off. Why, then, didn't they get married?

Carver never talked publicly about the affair. When asked in later years why he remained a bachelor, he gave generic responses: "I never had time for a wife" or "What woman would want a husband who was always bringing home insect specimens and tracking dirt all over her parlor?" People who knew and loved Carver implied that Sarah finally rejected him for frivolous reasons. Carver's assistant recalled—seventy years after the romance—that Carver once said Sarah was more concerned with the way he dressed than with the work he was doing.

Well, any prospective wife would have been concerned about the way Carver dressed and would have made strenuous efforts to reform him. The decay of his clothes was already legendary while he was still a young man. With his discolored, oft-patched coat, hand-crocheted and hand-dyed scarves that he frequently wore in place of a cravat, and fresh flower in his worn lapel, he might have been mistaken for a vaudeville hobo. At some point he had made a conscious decision to be conspicuous by appearing to be a bum, albeit a bum who was scrupulously clean. Possibly it was his way of irritating others without actually confronting them in an open quarrel—the "passive-aggressive" behavior psychologists describe. No doubt Carver's shabbiness infuriated Booker, whose own dress was impeccable and who insisted that the very tablecloths at Tuskegee be perfectly groomed. Carver loved having his picture taken— perhaps that, too, was a way to get under Booker's fastidious skin and thwart his mania for presenting Tuskegee as perfect. It would have been difficult for anyone as genteel as Sarah to overlook Carver's patches and introduce such a beau to her upper-class friends. But in any case, it was not his clothes or any of his other eccentricities that caused the breakup. Sarah remained with him for several years, every single day of which he appeared before her looking like a tramp; she obviously made her peace with his appearance early on.

Other faint murmurs about the romance cast Sarah as having no sympathy with Carver's mystical proclivities, his obsession with plants, his almost pantheistic and intense piety. But though these preoccupations may have irked her, they were not the sort of bedrock issues that rend people in love. The fallback explanation always suggested is that Carver was homosexual; therefore, goes the reasoning, when the time came for a critical decision about marrying, he demurred. In the first place, it seems to have been Sarah, and not Carver, who made the decision to break off. Aside from other considerations, it would not have taken Carver five or six years and the counsel of Mrs. Liston to determine that he was not sexually disposed to marriage. Even if he had been homosexual, that in itself would not have precluded marriage. In fact, it would have provided him with a shield against the sort of rumors that always circulate around bachelors. Sarah's grandniece (Adella's granddaughter, Alexander) is skeptical of claims that Carver was homosexual. If he had been, Adella Logan would likely have known it and would never have fixed him up with her sister.

The most creditable explanation as to why they did not marry, despite their enduring attraction to each other, was the difference in their coloring. Sarah was even lighter than the ivory dolls who made up most of the faculty at Tuskegee in those years. She was described as having "Caucasian" hair that reached to her knees. Like her sister Adella, she appeared to be a white person. Carver, of course, did not. If she was the whitest teacher at Tuskegee, he was the blackest. The distinction between light and dark skin was critical when it came to marrying. The Hunt family did not themselves object to Carver's darkness, according to Alexander, but they were fearful of the problems Sarah would encounter in Alabama and elsewhere. She and Carver would appear to be an interracial couple. Although white men could get by with having black mistresses and common-law wives—white men had freely used their black slaves in plantation days—a white woman with a black man was something else entirely. The two would be asking for lifelong trouble.

Social ostracism by both races was the least of it. They might face jailing, beatings, Klan burning of their house, lynching, and all the dreadful harassments that such matches provoked in both the South and the North. It was during the height of Carver's relationship with Sarah, in 1902, that the racial incident occurred with Frances Johnston in which Carver's life was in danger. In 1904, to take a random year, there were lynchings in two Alabama counties near Tuskegee; the victims were black men involved in incidents with white women. In 1908, during a race riot in Illinois, an old black man was murdered and then hanged because he had married a white woman thirty-two years earlier. No doubt George was weighing these cautionary considerations when he wrote to Mrs. Liston—not that he was unsure after five years whether he and Sarah loved each other. Does a man ever ask advice, or hear it unasked, once he sets his sights on a woman he wants, except to find out the surest way of getting her? Possibly when Sarah took a brief leave of absence from Tuskegee in 1905, she, too, sought counsel from her family and came back persuaded that marriage with George would mean a life of hardship for themselves and any children they might have. One did not have to have a small mind in the early 1900s to believe that miscegenation, or the appearance of miscegenation, was a bad idea, even if the black partner was a jewel.

There was more. Sarah and Adella and their six siblings were the children of a white Georgia tanner and farmer, Henry Alexander Hunt, who had served in the Confederate army during the Civil War. Their mother Mariah—the unfortunate victim of Adella's fireplace—was of mixed blood: white, Native American, and black. The mother had the interesting moniker "Cherokee Mariah Lilly," although she looked no more like a Cherokee than she looked like a black. She came from a prosperous, refined family that had owned slaves; thus she was able to teach her daughters to play the piano but not to cook. Their father Henry Hunt supported his large, illegitimate family in a comfortable house, gave the children his name, and saw to it that they were educated. The family even had a part-time servant. But after the Civil War, their father never lived with their mother. All of the children looked white—of course, since only one of their sixteen great-great-grandparents had been black. As their friend, W. E. B. Du Bois commented, "Any member of the Hunt family had a choice as to which race he would belong." All but one of Sarah's sisters and brothers were volunteer Negroes who attended black schools and colleges. Two of Sarah's brothers, Henry and Tom, attended Tuskegee. Henry eventually held a high position as Henry Morganthau's assistant in Franklin D. Roosevelt's Department of the Treasury. Most of the Hunt children married extremely light-skinned people like Warren Logan, who had straight hair and a face as pale as Alaska. The exception was Sarah's brother Tom who, after graduating from Tuskegee Institute, married a white woman and passed into the white world. He cut ties with his family. After his marriage, he did not receive Sarah in his home, preferring to meet her outside and by specific appointment. Clearly, Sarah and Adella both had as little color prejudice as Carver. But they knew what heartache Sarah would face by marrying "down."

The painful breakup finally came. Sarah left Tuskegee to live in a settlement in Newark, New Jersey, for about a year. George later avoided talking about the affair to any of his biographers, even those with whom he was normally quite open. It is worth remembering that the years when he became disillusioned with Tuskegee and his prospects there coincided with the years of the Sarah Hunt relationship. Was it because of her that he endured insults and never followed through on his many threats to resign? If Carver loved Sarah too much to leave her, that would explain a great deal about his behavior during the early years of the Bridgeforth conflict. But Carver continued to tolerate the intolerable long after Sarah was out of his life. Perhaps he was also loath to leave Adella. Another explanation for the breakup is that Sarah observed firsthand the way Booker mistreated his teachers and was disgusted with Carver's submissiveness. She certainly had no trouble leaving Tuskegee, as she demonstrated after she ended the relationship with Carver. In any case, the romance with Sarah ended around 1906 during the most trying period of Carver's career. The end of the affair was the most piercing event in his private life until a terrible crisis involving Adella Logan occurred a decade later.

It was also a difficult time for Booker. He was under pressure from Tuskegee's board of trustees to make the farm show a profit or at least to stanch the steady losses. Several members of the board, who may never have been near a barn, were generous with their grating suggestions as to what he ought to be doing. However, as the farm had always shown a loss, that alone was not the likely reason Booker began undermining Carver. Booker's relationship with Adella, along with other irritations, no doubt affected his attitude toward George.

The period from 1902 to 1912 was the time when Booker's position as leader of his race was being vigorously challenged by W. E. B. Du Bois and others who favored a direct assault on white supremacy. Although Booker was the favorite Negro of white presidents, senators, and entrepreneurs, the impetus among black people to gain political ground was moving past him. In a biographer's apt phrase, Booker was "the apostle of things as they were." His vision of economic success featured blacks who would become successful small businessmen at some point in the millennium, even though during his own lifetime, it was big, not small, business that was sweeping everything before it. Booker's focus was on farming at a time when American agriculture was in profound depression. He was counseling blacks to spring into the middle class by becoming harness makers and blacksmiths just as those trades were becoming a thing of the past. And his efforts were centered in the South, the country's most desperate region. Blacks could not have succeeded by following his obsolete program regardless of how diligently they pursued it, even without the deforming burden of white hostility. It did not take a radical to recognize the vacuity of Booker's plan for success.

It was whites who had made Booker the spokesman of his race—blacks had nothing to do with his rise—and it was white newspapers that made him a celebrity in the general population. In the beginning, Booker must have believed that his odd relationship with the white establishment was buying time for his race, giving black people the years they needed to catch up with whites before they began demanding political rights. But by the time Du Bois appeared, some years had passed and the position of black people was the worst it had been since Emancipation. Black education had been slowly spreading, but it was not helping to lift the race in any practical way. The proposition Booker had made to southern whites in Atlanta in 1895—that blacks would accept segregation and inferior status in return for being allowed to make progress through self-improvement—was a stark failure.

The Jim Crow era was at its height. Whites were waging a vicious campaign to disenfranchise southern blacks, subjecting them to intimidation, ballot box tampering, grandfather clauses, and outright terror. Yet during this very period, Booker was writing, "During all the years that I have lived in Macon County, Alabama, I have never had the slightest trouble in either registering or casting my vote at any election," as if he did not know he was treated as an exception. Segregation was spreading from the South into parts of the country where it had never been enforced. Black people were well aware that conditions were worsening for them every day. Lynchings increased and went unpunished, occasionally abetted by law enforcement officers who enforced no law. Yet Booker at the time was often heard describing his friendship with the sheriff of Macon County, not to mention the U.S. attorney general. In response to the constant demand for articles and books, Booker's ghostwriters diligently paraphrased his early speeches, thus setting his public thought in clichés that were continually reissued; every new development in the black struggle brought forth some variation of his familiar bromides.

As principal of Tuskegee, Booker really had little choice but to praise the benevolence and general good intentions of white people. It was white largesse channeled through him that kept his school running, raised the buildings, paid the staff, and financed "The Tuskegee Machine." But by making himself "the white man's nigger," as his adversaries labeled him, Booker had to struggle to maintain his authority over more militant activists who were coming to the forefront in the fight for equality. He remained a powerful figure in public life until his death—unquestionably the most popular black man in America, respected by both races. But by the early 1900s, he was by no means the only spokesman for the black American nor the sole black leader on the political scene. He found himself engaged in a two-front war: against his old enemies, the white supremacists, and against the black intellectuals who defected from his philosophy of submission. By 1910 it seemed that Booker represented the contemptible past; Du Bois, though he would never enjoy Booker's celebrity status, represented the future.

W. E. B. Du Bois had been Booker's friend in the early years or at least a comrade-in-arms. He was also a devoted friend to Adella, with whom he worked in the Atlanta University Conferences. He held bachelor's degrees from Fisk University and Harvard, had studied in Germany, and in 1895 became the first black American to earn a Ph.D. at Harvard. These were more impressive educational credentials than Booker could claim, with his industrial school background and his honorary Harvard master's degree. Du Bois came to be associated with those who wanted serious academic programs for black students, of the sort Adella had been recommending to Booker for years. Booker advocated industrial education—that is, grade school and trade school—as a compromise that would have practical benefits for blacks but which whites could accept and promote. Du Bois was not against industrial education, but he believed that in order to rise, the race needed college-educated leaders—as many as possible. If Booker stood for gradualism in black advancement, Du Bois spoke for the impatient intellectuals, "the talented tenth." The underlying disagreements of the two leaders erupted in 1903. With the publication of Du Bois's *The Souls of Black Folk*, containing his critical but insightful essay, "Of Mr. Booker T. Washington and Others," their friendship was over.

In 1905, Du Bois organized the Niagara Movement, which in 1909 merged into the new N.A.A.C.P. The organization's magazine, *The Crisis*, publicized Du Bois's views. Booker, in turn, was the secret part owner of the *New York Age* and other periodicals where he placed editorials and articles written anonymously by himself and his ghostwriters, promoting his leadership dominance. His manipulation of the black press was far-reaching because of secret subsidies he gave to nearly all of the newspapers; he could be sure that publicity about his work was plentiful and favorable. But his control was no longer absolute after Du Bois and his partisans gained notoriety and circulation. Lines were clearly drawn. The factional rivalry was fierce on both sides. It affected everything Booker did, in much the same way as a politician is always maneuvering against his political opponents even while he appears to be going about the straightforward business of government. Most of the antagonism was hidden from the public view, but frequently enough, the fighting erupted into print, as in Jesse Max Barber's article, "What is a Good Negro?" in *The Voice of the Negro*: "A good Negro is one who says that his race does not need the higher learning: that what they need is industrial education, pure and simple."

By 1905 Booker was on very clubby terms with rich America: the John D. Rockefellers; H. H. Rogers of Standard Oil; John Wanamaker, the department store magnate; Julius Rosenwald of Sears, Roebuck; Jacob Schiff, the financier; George Eastman, inventor of the Kodak camera; Andrew Carnegie, and others who gave him many thousands of dollars. In the North, though not in the South, he regularly crossed the color line, traveled first class, stayed in luxury hotels, and dined in the homes of millionaires. He had begun tailoring his rhetoric to fit comfortably in the pockets of these financiers and industrialists. He was for public order above all and against foreign and union labor. The New England Puritan homiletics of the early years was now modified to resemble the gospel of wealth. Booker also secretly worked for civil rights for his people—so secretly that friends and critics alike were unaware of his actions. His significant covert agitation against white rule was largely ineffective, but it serves nevertheless to reveal his underlying dedication to his race. He was an intense, devious man following a long-range vision for eventual black equality; but that vision was marred by his obsession with power and control, his feral tactics against people who disagreed with him, and his simple-minded jealousy of anyone sidling into what he considered his exclusive limelight.

Booker had long dominated black hiring in government and other fields because of his connections to bureaucracy, industry, and philanthropy. His critics now turned from attacking his philosophy to exposing "The Tuskegee Machine," the network of his influence that reached even into the White House and made Booker the arbiter of practically all black patronage and all large donations to black organizations. According to Louis Harlan, Booker's most thorough and fair-minded biographer, Washington "was ready to employ ruthless secret methods of espionage, provocation, and sabotage that seem utterly at variance with the Sunday-school morality he publicly professed," in order to keep higher-up blacks in his camp. Through his control of jobs, he was able to persecute virtually any black person who defied him, and he was not hesitant about using that power. Booker forbade anyone at Tuskegee to have truck with the N.A.A.C.P., *The Crisis,* or with Du Bois himself. He kept a number of spies who reported to him when individuals anywhere in the country defected from his party, and he also maintained a complicated skein of other operatives to bolster support for him and attack his enemies. Often, his identity was protected by his shrewd, loyal, surrogate—his secretary Emmett Scott—the only individual who knew all of his political secrets and kept his blacklists up to date.

However, once it became evident that virulent racism was out of control all over the country, Booker had more trouble stifling his challengers. Blacks and liberal whites were getting increasingly outraged; they rebelled against his ineffectual responses to the appalling events taking place. Booker had to resort to Machiavellian activities to hold on to his position. Eventually, he was expending more energy against his black rivals than against the white supremacists who were supposed to be his real enemies. In 1908, a string of race riots led to a murder spree in Illinois. While he was on tour in Mississippi, a white mob in Lula hanged two blacks where he could see them from his train window. Although he did not respond to these incidents directly, they had an effect on him, and he at last issued a plea to end lynching. "Within the past sixty days, twenty-five Negroes have been lynched in different parts of the United States . . . mob violence that threatens our civilization." But his leaflet was a classic case of too little, too late. Du Bois and his supporters were already in the vanguard of resistance fighters and by now, thinking individuals were ready to listen to someone who offered them more than "platitudes, stories, high praise for the southern white man who is helping the Negro up."

* * *

Even back on the farm, Booker was meeting resistance to his authority. He demanded unquestioning loyalty from his people, which meant bowing to his word without a murmur. But as he began hiring more qualified teachers who were not afraid of him, his policies were challenged. Even students were speaking up. "My room No 9 Central Lodge is just overflowed," complained one girl. "I had to sit in the hall all night . . . Every time it rains outdoors it rains in my room . . . I have reported it twice but nothing has been done . . . In fact, every room in this hall upstairs is wet." Overcrowding was a chronic problem. Four to seven students were assigned to one room, and boys were sleeping in the halls on cots. Still, Booker was vigorously soliciting new students.

There was a large drop-out rate at Tuskegee because Booker encouraged pupils to leave when they could not pay their expenses. The principal thought it strengthened a student's character to drop out in order to raise money for his education. (Booker himself had been supported by a donor while attending Hampton Institute and had not been compelled to drop out because of tuition.) "We have refused to follow the custom of many schools in the South, of securing personal help for our students," even though it would enable them to remain for the term. Students came and went during the year, arriving when they had saved enough money to attend school and quitting when their money ran out. The result was that of the thousands who entered Tuskegee, only a small percentage graduated. An exhaustive study by the faculty had shown the main reasons: the well-being of the students was considered secondary to the building up of the school itself. Moreover, the students were frustrated at the curriculum that did not teach them a trade.

Roscoe Conkling Bruce, a Harvard graduate who was superintendent of the academic department from 1903 to 1906, was publicly outspoken in favor of industrial education, although he brought to Tuskegee a number of colleagues who were scholars. Bruce himself had been valedictorian of his Harvard class. Privately, he was sharply critical of the school's administration. In 1906 Bruce excoriated Booker for neglecting academic education at Tuskegee Normal and Industrial Institute and for not providing worthwhile industrial training, either. The regular "undergraduate" program for a student being trained as a teacher was a seven-year course, three years of preparatory work and four years of so-called normal classes. Half of all Tuskegee students were in the preparatory division, being taught third- to fifth-grade work. This was not different from other black colleges of the time. However, work in the normal school in the academic department, which did have some intellectual pretensions, was essentially junior high school instruction; the relatively few students who graduated received the equivalent of a ninth grade education. Tuskegee had a large Bible School within the larger school, the majority of whose students were "barely able to read the Bible," according to a faculty study by W. T. B. Williams. "Of the thousand or more persons who have been members of the Bible School, only about fifty have been allowed to graduate, and these confessedly as much for the sake of getting an alumni list as for qualifications."

The emphasis at Tuskegee, Roscoe Bruce argued, was on "quick commercial value" to the school, rather than on teaching. The trades or industries had come to dominate everything, but still Tuskegee had not become a trade school; its graduates had a smattering of skills but no one trade. The pressure to complete work in building, especially, was so great that a boy might work on a project on Tuesday, but by Thursday, when he returned to it, the completion of it had been turned over to someone else and he was given a different job. Emphasis was always on production of goods that the school sold for profit, never on teaching—in fact, the "teachers" were often hired artisans whose only interest was in getting the work finished. One student complained, "I have been on this [landscape] division about ten months and have never had any instruction about the work. For example we have been putting out trees ever since Nov. and have not been told what kinds they were or how to trim them." Instruction in the shops was crippled because of lack of equipment. The cooking classes (compulsory for all girls) were held in the Carnegie Library, where there were neither stoves, dishes, refrigerators, nor running water, and where food of any sort was forbidden. "The pupils who plan to teach school," said Bruce, "have not one minute more for academic studies than the pupils who plan to make horse shoes or paint houses. The word 'normal' ought to mean something. The 'normal' pupil is at present unprepared for a real teacher training course because of glaring deficiencies in English and geography and what not . . . the truth is that the carpenter is not taught enough mathematics, the machinist enough physics, or the farmer enough chemistry for the purpose of his particular work. Much more serious is the plight of the teacher." After submitting these apt observations, Bruce resigned from Tuskegee.

Adella's criticism was not more severe than Bruce's, but she allowed her opinions to be published in Du Bois's journal and appeared to have defected to the enemy. Adella was an intimate member of the Tuskegee family. No one knew more about Booker's actions and Tuskegee's inner workings than Emmett Scott, J. H. Washington, and Adella's husband, Warren Logan. In Booker's view, Adella Logan should have been the first to cleave to him and denounce Du Bois. She did nothing of the kind, though she did make efforts to placate Booker and defuse his wrath. Adella remained close to Du Bois until her death, and Carver remained close to Adella. Even though Carver took no direct part in the Booker–Du Bois conflict, he was immovable in his attachment to Adella. Booker thus classed Carver among his enemies and began lashing out at him in every way possible, using his favorite tool of war, a proxy. That was the situation when George Bridgeforth clattered onto the turbulent Tuskegee stage.

8

WRESTLING WITH DEVILS

Hatred, though unseemly and exhausting, is one of life's great passions; Carver should have taken the opportunity provided by Bridgeforth to experience it. But, like a few great men—Napoleon, Abraham Lincoln—and certain official saints, George Carver had no knack for personal animosity and could never maintain it for long. He insisted that everything in Nature was forgivable, even a loudmouth such as Bridgeforth.

George R. Bridgeforth joined the agriculture department at Tuskegee in 1902. He was a large brash, young man, querulous and confident, with the subtlety and personal charm of a blast furnace. He had little appreciation of book science and no appreciation at all of his gentlemanly chief, Carver. In fact, though he was untaught in everything, judging from his letters, Bridgeforth considered himself vastly superior to Carver and set out from the beginning to replace him in all of his functions except director of the experiment station, where he would settle for discrediting him.

Bridgeforth was a skilled operator. He allied himself early on with those who detested Carver, especially J. H. Washington. Bridgeforth convinced J. H., who convinced Booker, that he could solve the problems of the farm and the poultry yard—the chronic sores. The farm had never been profitable in a way that would allow Booker to use it as an example to farmers trying to get out of debt—school farms hardly ever made money because their purpose was instructional. The poultry yard, too, had shown deficits for years, especially after a disastrous epidemic of sorehead swept the state. Booker, following his usual tendency to jump from one project to another and one excitement to another, gravitated to Bridgeforth as the Bright New Man and began steadily pushing Carver out of the way.

A year after he settled in, Bridgeforth was sending a barrage of condescending recommendations to Carver with copies to Booker. Carver politely declined to act on suggestions he considered impractical, but Booker would latch on to one or another idea, such as a proposal to go into large-scale cattle-raising on the school farm. Carver had to beat back the idea, pointing out that hogs could live in a small space and could be fed more cheaply than any other animal in proportion to their return. "With all these charming possibilities for the production of beef," Carver wrote to Booker, "I am very anxious that we recognize . . . that no system of farming has ever paid or ever will pay which does not give the hog a most important place in the economy of the farm." The ideas kept coming, and Booker was happy to transform them into orders that Carver was directed to carry out. By 1903, Carver was begging Booker to set "a well-defined policy and not deviate from it"—clear plans for the farm and the poultry yard "with no conflicting orders or shifting priorities."

By then, the principal was objecting to almost everything Carver did in the farm, poultry yard, agricultural department, and experiment station. Carver sensed that some conspiracy was brewing against him but claimed not to understand its source. In the executive council, always the willing instrument of Booker's majesty, one measure after another was passed over his head. Carver could not miss the insult when Booker, ignoring Carver's pleas for a secretary to help with the immense correspondence of the experiment station, gave a part-time stenographer to Bridgeforth, who had no such burden. Carver even discovered that his work in the experiment station was being crudely sabotaged. In the predawn hours he saw with his own eyes "a teacher" letting animals into the experiment station plot to eat his just-planted grain and trample his young plants. The teacher fetched out the animals before daylight and locked the gates behind him. This had been going on for several weeks before Carver's investigative vigil.

Carver contemplated changing jobs in 1904, but he was forcefully discouraged, then and later, by Secretary of Agriculture James Wilson, who remained under Booker's spell during Carver's winters of discontent. Carver had been invited to teach in Puerto Rico. "Don't do it," Wilson wrote back sharply. "They can not spare you there yet, and the work you are doing . . . is the best work . . . and you should stick right at it. I hope the people at Tuskegee will fully appreciate your value along these lines. But stay by Mr. Washington." Carver was receiving plenty of appreciation that summer, but not from Tuskegee. He had been teaching summer school in Knoxville, Tennessee, where he was received so enthusiastically that he lectured voluntarily an extra three hours on Saturdays. He came back home refreshed and assured Wilson, "I had not thought very seriously of leaving Tuskegee, although elsewhere I can do very much better financially than I can here and also not have such hard work. But I should not consider the matter very strongly until I got Tuskegee's work on a firm and solid basis . . . Mr. Washington is more and more phenomenal all the time, to me as well as to others. I come into very close touch with him and he always inspires me." Being "in close touch" with Booker was enough to make George forget all slights and hurts. Booker's charisma, his seductive talk of future accomplishments and golden ideals, invariably destroyed all of Carver's resolutions to remove himself from a situation that was increasingly fraught.

By fall 1904, Carver was under full attack. He had appointed a man named Columbus Barrows to supervise the declining poultry yard A committee looking into the operation found that everything in the poultry yard was in bad condition and Carver's reports regarding the number of fowls in the yard was inflated. Carver pointed out that it was difficult to count thousands of chickens spread over a large area. Barrows, called on by the executive council to explain the incorrect inventory, stated that Carver had instructed him to submit false reports, or at least not to report dead chickens "all at once."

It was more than he could bear, Carver wrote, "to be branded as a liar and party to such hellish deceptions." He offered his resignation. Booker warned Carver that his position was "an awkward and serious one." Everything was Carver's fault; he had either been careless, according to Booker, or involved in "the deception." Carver sent Booker his personal check to make up for the missing chickens. "If you have faith in me, I will take hold of the yard with renewed vigor and give you some chickens, a number that you will be proud of. If your committee wishes to retain me upon these terms, I assure you I shall give them honest, faithful service and never let such an error again creep in." Booker responded coldly to this emotional missive. He had already made clear "just what I wish you to do in order to . . . remain in the permanent employ of the Institute"—namely, provide an impressive quantity of eggs and chickens.

Bridgeforth was sending his own missives to Booker, insisting that, given the chance, he could make the poultry yard produce. For some time he had been defying Carver's orders. When Carver gave Bridgeforth instructions concerning a short course for farmers that he was setting up, Bridgeforth's response to the instructions was: "I do not intend to spend my time running around getting orders to work when one manly order would save all trouble and hard feeling. I want teams and means to work up the short course, and if you cannot command such, I must take the matter up with the Prin. of the school today." "Manly" was one of Bridgeforth's favorite words. Carver responded by insisting on "certain courtesies" and wanted it "clearly understood that I am not going to put up with such notes as this coming into my office from you." Bridgeforth retorted that Carver's insistence was "in every respect laughable . . . I shall not stand another bit of this bluff and you must do business like a man and take some interest in things that pertain to the school. You seem to have lost all interest in all things at the school as is noticed by all." Bridgeforth was referring to the many invitations Carver was receiving to lecture at other institutions, invitations that aroused the jealousy of the faculty. "I am here to work as a man," Bridgeforth lectured him, "and I expect to be treated as such. I am not to be intimidated by your recent threats." Moreover, wrote Bridgeforth, "I intend for my name to go directly under yours as Assistant Director." He insisted on his own stationery with his title on the letterhead. To Carver's chagrin, the committee that Booker appointed to look into Bridgeforth's insubordination declined to dismiss or even reprimand him. The committee was headed by J. H.

Bridgeforth knew when to strike. Just when Carver was frantically defending himself against the charge of lying to the council about the number of chickens in the poultry yard, Bridgeforth and J. H. put forth a scheme for the agricultural department that would remove Carver as director, take him out of the farm altogether, and put him under Bridgeforth's authority. Carver's response to the attacks, then and later, had a pathetic tone. While offering his resignation again, he pleaded with Booker not to take the poultry yard away from him but to give him another chance, since he had made up his mind that "the thing should not fail." He continued: "This is in no way intended to cover up my shortcomings . . . from now on until my work is finished, my whole heart and spirit shall be put into the work." Booker was not embarrassed to heap obviously captious criticisms on Carver during the crisis. He chose that moment to appoint an executive council committee to review Carver's exhibits in the experiment station. Among other faults, the committee noted, "No native birds appear in the exhibit." Carver protested, "In a casual way, I counted over 40 this morning that are native to our state."

At this same time, the end of 1904, Carver received an offer to be a full-time professor of both art and agriculture at Knoxville College, where he had spent the previous summers. The chance to resume his artwork was tempting, but it appears that in the end he could not bring himself to give up the experiment station. He wrote to Wilson asking if it were possible to establish another experiment station in Knoxville. When Wilson wrote back that it was not, Carver decided to stay in Tuskegee. Meanwhile, realizing that Carver might indeed resign, Booker equivocated about replacing him as director of agriculture.

Carver made an urgent request for a small barn for the experiment station, to store tools, grains, and forage, which were being kept in a wet basement. This was not much to ask of an institution with eighty-three buildings. Not only was his request refused, but accusations began to fly that he neglected the experiment station. To defend himself, Carver compiled a report summarizing his work in the station from 1897 until 1906. The three-page summary of his accomplishments should have been eye-opening. Carver's experiments had proved that organic fertilizer was superior to commercial preparations. Through multiple experiments, he had identified the best varieties of cotton, wheat, rye, barley, oats, teosinte, sorghum cane, Mexican June corn, Irish potatoes, onions, hairy vetch, crimson clover, peanuts, and pine straw for diverse purposes. In addition to many newspaper articles, he had written sixteen leaflets and seven bulletins which reached ten foreign post offices. In 1906 alone, he had made twenty trips within and without the state to give talks and distribute seed and instructional material. He was fitting up the Jesup Wagon to travel to farms with information on every aspect of rural life. He had tested 115 soil samples as well as other substances for farmers and returned detailed written instructions as to the kind and amount of fertilizers that should be used with each type of soil. He did not enumerate his many smaller experiments for fear of making his report too long. All that, in addition to teaching five *different* classes, hosting the monthly institutes and the annual farmers' fair, and managing the unmanageable poultry yard.

Both Carver and Booker were holding on to each other because of the experiment station. The station allowed Carver to do the research that was most important to him. For Booker, it was a vital part of the propaganda machine that was Tuskegee. Carver could be relegated to the sidelines in the farm and the agricultural department, but he could not be pushed to the point of resigning; if he left Tuskegee, the government would almost certainly close down the station. It was clear that Bridgeforth was already the de facto head of the farm and the agriculture department. "When I call meetings of the agriculture faculty," Carver complained to Booker, "people come if they desire and stay away if they like. I have no redress in which I am sustained." Still, he resisted giving up the poultry yard. "I promised to raise chickens. I had them there. They got away. I do not know how (much to my shame and regret.) It is my intention to give you more." When Bridgeforth became particularly obstreperous, Carver would complain to Booker; the principal would reiterate homilies about the value of teamwork and mutual consideration and tell him to settle the matter himself. Meanwhile, Booker continued to inflict stings on Carver whenever he had an opportunity.

Carver was suffering. It was not Bridgeforth who hurt him—Bridgeforth alone would have been but a blister on his sensitive skin—but rather Booker, who, by rejecting Carver, bored out his inner confidence and enthusiasm. Booker could have swatted Bridgeforth any time he cared to; he allowed him to harass Carver because Carver's discomfiture was exactly what he wanted. The best course for Carver (besides resigning altogether from Tuskegee) would have been to relinquish the headache of the poultry yard and remove himself from a vicious fight that was hardly worth winning, considering the anguish it was causing him. But Carver could not face the opprobrium of failure, or at least he could not face having failed his idol, Booker. Despite another eruption of tension in 1906, Carver continued to tolerate his "awkward" and "serious" position.

Carver finally unburdened himself to Wilson in an overwrought letter detailing his frustrations. Wilson, who was totally oblivious of the way things worked at Tuskegee and had no idea of Carver's impotence, responded with what he thought were sensible consolations. "It is evident you need help, that is all. All these things you can manage if you have subordinates enough to help you out. It is utterly out of the question that you can teach so much and take charge of all these other things . . . About half that amount of teaching would be abundant, and someone else should take the other half." Meanwhile, rats were killing hundreds of healthy hatched chickens because, despite repeated pleas for a small, rat-proof unit, Carver had no place to keep incubators, which were stored here and there all over the coops and were constantly attacked.

The next blowups came in March 1908, then in September 1908, and again in September 1909. During each one, Carver was subjected to a scalding letter of criticism from Booker. In each instance, Booker demoted Carver, making him subordinate to Bridgeforth. But when Carver tendered his resignation, Booker backed off and allowed him to keep the title of director. These titles were strictly honorific regarding the agricultural department and the farm, since Bridgeforth had long since arrogated Carver's authority to himself. Carver was still in control of the experiment station and still supervised the poultry yard. Booker probably realized that the poultry yard was bound to fail unless the physical plant were radically altered to house and protect the animals, so he left Carver in a position where he could take the blame for all deficiencies.

Under the new administrative arrangements, Carver had to beg Bridgeforth to release students to help him in the poultry yard—dispensations that Bridgeforth snippily refused. Carver had to go over his head to Booker even to get a single worker to help him clean the yard. Nevertheless, it was Carver who was harshly reprimanded when fifty bushels of potatoes rotted before they could be moved to the boarding department—as if he could lug the bushels himself—and Carver who was rebuked for throwing out eggs. "The persons testing the eggs do not know their business," Booker declared, knowing full well that the "persons" were Carver. "You may not know it," Booker informed him, "but one of the officers took two dozen eggs which you all said could not be hatched, put them under a hen and twenty of the eggs hatched out healthy chicks." One does not have to guess who this "officer" was, but it is reasonable to wonder if the eggs really hatched. Booker reproved Carver for his "mistake" in having twenty-five ganders to fifty-seven geese and for raising ducks with a large proportion of drakes. "I cannot understand why anybody who knows the least thing about raising poultry would let this go on from day to day without correcting it. See that the excess number of drakes and . . . ganders is . . . turned over to the Boarding Department at once." Carver was obliged to explain that geese naturally pair off, which the best breeders allow. If prevented from pairing, egg production falls off. As for the ducks, he was making a deliberate experiment and succeeded, in fact, in getting an increase in eggs. Booker's criticisms of the yard were "not helpful," Carver wrote. "What I need now is help, real help."

Sorehead was again striking down the chickens, and Carver was writing to veterinarians all over the country for remedies. Booker disputed Carver's diagnosis of sorehead—despite there being a severe epidemic all over the South and despite Carver's long experience with the quite visible, scabby infection. From his hotel in New York, Booker discerned that the chickens were dying because Carver was not getting the chicks out of the incubators in a timely fashion. Carver's report about the epidemic, he wrote, did "not interest me overmuch. What I want you to do is divine some means by which you can get fowls . . . it only remains now for you to determine whether or not you can raise poultry . . . Here is an excellent chance for you to show that you cannot only give instruction in the classroom . . . but can actually get results in the poultry yard . . . I think if everybody will simply stop thinking and talking about difficulties . . . and go to talking and working in the direction of getting chickens . . . and be determined to get them regardless of difficulties, that you will succeed."

"Your letter encourages me," Carver wrote back. "I am determined to raise chickens regardless of difficulties." Carver may or may not have been encouraged by Booker's insults, but he wrote again to Wilson about trying to get out of Tuskegee, even if it meant going to Liberia. Wilson responded with his typical well-meaning, innocent, and outrageously bad advice. "I think you should deliberate a long time before leaving Tuskegee. The longer you stay there, the more you will be known for your work. I do not know of any place where you could do half the good you are doing there. If your work is too heavy, you should have help; and if you cannot get help, you should confine yourself to doing what you can do." Wilson, of course, did not have to endure Booker's needling. Booker's demands regarding the experiment station became more and more unreasonable, as when he ordered Carver to have a list ready in four days of "every kind of thing that can be grown from the soil of Macon County during the months of September, October, November, December, January, and February." He was regularly dictating station policy to Carver or, rather, dictating one policy and then changing his orders. One day he wanted Carver to plant cotton; then his interest in cotton waned, and he was instructing Carver to turn the station into a sort of "demonstration farm" for growing vegetables. After vegetable seeds had been planted, he decided that grasses and soybeans should be grown instead.

Carver was still given only one ex-student to help him in the station; Bridgeforth, at the same time, had a staff of eighteen. Nevertheless, the bulletins from the experiment station continued to list the entire agricultural staff on the masthead, so that scientists at other experiment stations had no idea Carver was working alone. In 1909, after holding up Carver's publications for months, Booker had the gall to reprove him for a lack of bulletins. "Your last bulletin was gotten out in April, 1906 . . . we set aside so much land and the time of yourself and students merely to the getting out of a bulletin once in a while." He grudgingly acceded to Carver's longstanding request and granted him a part-time typist for a limited period, warning him not to "make the mistake of becoming dependent on this kind of help."

From 1909 until Booker's death at the end of 1915, Carver was enmeshed in the cynical game that wore him down and brought him many times to the edge of desperation. Booker would strip Carver of his authority in one area or another—either in his classes, the farm, or the poultry yard. Then, to keep Carver from quitting Tuskegee, he would make alluring promises, especially the promise of a splendid new research laboratory where Carver could attempt more serious investigations than he had ever tried before. But neither the demotions nor the promises were carried out. In spring and fall 1909, there were uproars when Carver was again accused of falsifying the chicken count. Booker repeated the exercise of demoting Carver in October 1910 and giving him back his posts in November. Booker's promises were worthless, whether the pledge was for a lab, the publication of bulletins, or a secretary. He would make a firm commitment, but then he would use some failure on Carver's part, usually in the poultry yard, as a pretext for changing his mind. Each time the promise of a laboratory was brought up, Carver's hopes would surge. But when he tried to order something, he was put through a rigamarole. His requisitions were delayed, lost, altered, and finally rejected. Booker wrote many times to Bridgeforth and J. H. Washington about how to manipulate Carver so that he "will be willing to teach in the same way that he has been doing in the past." When Booker reorganized the agriculture department, demoting Carver, he wrote to Bridgeforth, "This is in accord with your committee's report." The "committee" had consisted of Bridgeforth and J. H. "It must be understood," Booker wrote to Carver, "that in all matters of differences, Mr. Bridgeforth has the authority to decide."

Wilson, for once, almost understood that George was being mistreated. "I am disturbed by this news; I thought you had fitted in there and that the people appreciated your ability . . . What in the world they want to put anybody over your head for is more than I can understand, unless you are developing characteristics that are new to me . . . I do not happen to know of a place where your services would be wanted at the present time, but nobody has ever suspected that you would want to leave there." Even after learning of Booker's callousness toward Carver, Wilson was still not free of his old infatuation with the principal. Carver was writing a botany textbook and wanted to dedicate it to Wilson, but Wilson instructed him to dedicate it instead to Washington. In previous years, Wilson had told Carver of positions that were available to him offering twice his salary, but Wilson had always assumed that he could not take Carver away from Tuskegee, where he was doing his life's work.

In 1910, after a great deal of turmoil, Carver thought he had reached a settlement with Booker. Bridgeforth was to be head of the agricultural department and farm and would make all the decisions, with Carver as his subordinate. Carver would be director of research and the experiment station. Booker specifically promised Carver, in writing, that he would operate the station, publish bulletins, conduct water analyses, deliver special lectures, and retain nominal control of the poultry yard. His bulletins would be published and reprinted without delay; he would be provided with a half-time stenographer. He would teach agricultural classes only "if he desires." Most important, Carver's compensation for the humiliation that had been heaped on him was the promise of "a first-class laboratory fitted up for Professor Carver." Equipment would be purchased that would enable him to do bacteriological research as well as other, more precise, analyses. That would have been a gratifying compensation indeed if Booker had had the least intention of fulfilling the commitment.

Carver believed the promises wholeheartedly and wrote to Wilson about the happy resolution of the conflict. His friend congratulated him on his "promotion" to the "highest class of work—research . . . You certainly worked for this and earned it . . . So go on, my dear Carver. You are not going to surprise me with anything you may elaborate." Booker's amiability and Wilson's congratulations excited Carver, who thought his life was going to return to some semblance of a routine. We find his shopping list—"coal, crackers, fish, kerosene"—on an envelope that had brought congratulations from the Milhollands.

He was soon disabused. Not surprisingly, Bridgeforth, as the new director of the agricultural department, began ordering Carver around, with the result that Carver chose not to teach classes, as was his privilege under the new arrangement. That occasioned a scalding five-page rebuke from Booker in February 1911. Demonstrating severe memory loss, he averred that in the twelve or fifteen years that Carver had been in charge of the experiment station, "the school has never suggested how the experiment station should be conducted . . . or what should be planted and should not be planted." Now that a rare order was given, Carver was trying to "dilly-dally" with it. He conceded that Carver was "a great inspirer of young men and of old men" and a great lecturer. But, "When it comes to the organization of classes, . . . you are wanting in ability. When it comes to the matter of practical farm managing which will secure definite, practical, financial results, you are wanting again in ability." All this was a build-up to his real message: "I was greatly surprised . . . to find that you wish a laboratory fitted up for your exclusive use and that you do not mean to give instruction to any students in this laboratory," as if he had not promised Carver exactly such a laboratory in return for stepping down peaceably as department head. "This is a departure in the history of the school which we cannot permit. We have no right to expend so large a sum of money in the fitting up of a laboratory which is not to be used as frequently as possible in the instruction of students . . . You do not help yourself when you assume the attitude that when you make a request . . . for chemicals that there must be no modification of the requisition." Booker advised him to be like the other teachers: "Follow our orders and carry out our policy and you will be much happier, much more successful, and much more useful than you have ever been . . . we should all be sorry to part with your service, but the time has come now for perfect frankness."

Carver's spineless submission to Booker's outrages is hard to admire. Any fool could have seen through Booker's perfidy and realized that the principal's sole object was to keep the experiment station at Tuskegee. But Carver was not any fool; he was a special fool, credulous as the birds that smashed themselves against his window and guileless as the chickens in the poultry yard.

As usual, Booker had not uttered his last word and later allowed that a new lab might be fitted up "gradually." Carver went through the exercise of writing up a requisition. The executive council, Booker's mouthpiece, complained about the "superfluous" materials on Carver's list and demanded an explanation of the precise use of each item requested. Carver obediently jumped through the required hoop. The list shows how impoverished he had actually been all the previous years, doing research and analysis without even basic tools, such as precision scales. But despite Carver's patient explanations, only a few items were ever delivered. At the end of 1912, fully two years after Booker had demoted Carver with the mollifying promise of a new lab, the few pieces of apparatus Carver had received were useless because they lacked essential connecting pieces. Nor was the debacle of the chickens finished. For years, Carver had made up deficits in the poultry yard out of his own funds. When chastised because of the numbers, Carver would promise: "Your yard will start in next spring with 1,000 laying hens." The hens and eggs did not increase—ever—so that then he had no recourse but to offer his resignation yet again, always with thanks and good wishes. Wilson assured Carver, "There is plenty of work in this Department for scientists who have had such training as you have had." He urged him to write for an application to take the civil service examination.

It should come as no surprise that Carver did not resign. Broken promises notwithstanding, he worked as usual, and Booker, as usual, kept alive the hope of a lab. Booker still wanted Carver to make a soil survey of the county and to write a bulletin showing which crops could be grown in which soil. That involved the analysis of several hundred samples of soil. "I have been trying to carry this out," Carver wrote him, "but can go just so far on account of lack of apparatus . . . For some constituents, I have not a single piece of apparatus."

Bridgeforth had been in control of the farm since 1910 and had no more success with it than Carver. Booker had to ask him to try to keep the losses under $20,000 a year. That did not stop Bridgeforth from continually demanding a raise in salary, which provoked Booker to chide him for his failure. Unlike Carver, who had responded to such scoldings with abject apologies, Bridgeforth fired back an angry letter, instructing Booker to have confidence in his judgments "and, not be following the wild suggestions of the passers." Bridgeforth's usefulness to Booker was wearing out. Meanwhile, throughout 1911, Carver had used the experiment station at Auburn and the Armour meat-packing company in Montgomery (both of which were well equipped) to develop an inexpensive method of preserving meat during the summer. Booker now authorized him to do further experimentation and instructed Bridgeforth to work as Carver's subordinate—to do the actual slaughtering and preparing the pickling solution under Carver's direction.

Booker finally took the step Carver had resisted for many years: in 1913, he took the poultry yard away from Carver and gave it to Bridgeforth completely. Bridgeforth now had three of Carver's four former positions at Tuskegee— head of the agricultural department, head of the farm, and head of the poultry yard. Carver feared that he was about to be eased out of Tuskegee altogether when he was laid off for a month during the summer of 1914. He was already being paid less than his former assistant. He wondered if he should "seek a place where I can have some assurance of being cared for when I reach the point where I am not so vigorous as I am now." At a time when there were no pensions except those provided by employers to their longtime workers, old age was everybody's worry.

But finally being relieved of the poultry yard was a blessing, for it allowed Carver to devote more time and energy to research. In the four years between 1911 and 1915, Carver turned his attention to developing inexpensive paints and stains from native Alabama clays, paints that poor people could use to beautify their homes, fences, barns, schools, and churches. He had always been deeply saddened by the meagerness of the farmers' lives. For years he had taught people how to use such simple things as pine needles, burlap, and string to make mats and decorations for their wretched homes. The farmers he visited had so little comfort or beauty in their lives. He wanted above all to turn the run-down houses of the tenant farmers into the kinds of dwellings that families would be happy to return to after the day's work was done, homes they could take pride in. The lime whitewashes he developed in his early years of experimentation made the cabins more sanitary as well as more attractive. By 1911, he had created washes that common people could make themselves in no less than twenty-seven colors. The washes were used in dormitory rooms and many Tuskegee buildings over the next years.

Now he set about developing more advanced paints. After several attempts, he induced Booker to look at his paint compounds, and the principal was sufficiently impressed to charge Carver with developing an exhibit of paints and stains for the school post office. Even this modest assignment drew a snide comment from J. H., who wrote Carver that he hoped the post office exhibit would be more comprehensive and better labeled than one he had prepared for the school. Carver had no funds with which to buy appropriate wood for the stain exhibits. He had to use such wood scraps as he could find. Carver wanted Tuskegee to try out some of his stains on a campus building; J. H. refused. He was not interested in the paints unless they could be developed for widespread use. "It is easy to get up a few samples of things which can never be made practical," wrote the man who had never developed a chemical compound of any sort. If Tuskegee were going to endorse the paints even in a small way, they must "be something that can be put into commercial form and sold in competition with such material as is produced in other sections of the country." Expecting Carver to compete with commercial paint laboratories was quite a charge to lay on a man who was consistently and deliberately denied access to the most basic equipment and chemicals. It was, in fact, the kind of demand that could only have been made by an ignoramus. It soon became apparent, however, that Booker, too, was keenly interested in developing commercial paints that would bring the school money and publicity.

Some of Carver's samples were over eight years old and still holding up; he had high hopes of winning back Booker's favor. He was trying to get some "star" exhibits ready for two fairs when his requisition for supplies was rejected. "I regret this so much, as I have spent all the time here working at the clays and hoping to demonstrate facts about them that no one knows except myself," he wrote, adding, "I have to teach chemistry next week without chemicals." He asked Booker to drive by the station and look at the paints, of which he was very proud. "I have done this in the crudest manner," he wrote, "without support to work with."

What had not been good enough for J. H.'s campus buildings was prized by the town's white people who were building a new Episcopal church. Commercial stain cost four dollars a gallon, far beyond the congregation's budget. Carver provided them with a stain that cost seventy-five cents a gallon and which they used on all the interior woodwork of their new church. "Everyone who sees this stain is wonderfully impressed with its beauty," wrote a church official, "and it is hard to make some believe that it is a home product." Some other Tuskegee citizens—probably Episcopalians—also began using Carver's paint products in their homes. Julius Rosenwald, founder of Sears Roebuck and Company and a financial backer of Tuskegee, wrote a long letter to Carver after seeing his impressive paint exhibit. He even sent Carver an unsolicited gift of $125 in appreciation of his work, which Carver returned with thanks, as he did all such donations.

For all his meek compliance with the demands of Booker and J. H., Carver was sufficiently disillusioned with their promises to realize that if his work were to have any chance of widespread recognition, the opportunities would not come from Tuskegee. He made plans to explore the commercial potential of the paints outside the aegis of the school. In his innocence, Carver took as his partner and confidant Emmett Scott, of all people. Very likely, it was Scott who instigated the enterprise, in his established role as Booker's secret Grand Inquisitor and agent provocateur. For over a year, from fall 1911 through 1912, Carver and Scott conferred about a covert venture to manufacture paints and stains. "Now I am ready to go in with you . . . Just keep it mum and we will divide up," wrote Carver—a comment that suggests he had previously hesitated "going in" with Scott. They decided that they could start their new company with another of the many products Carver had already developed, one that was easier than paint to distribute—talcum and face powders. They would need some $2,000 to launch the company; Carver had this and more in a savings bank.

Carver apparently had such firm faith in the potential of the enterprise that he turned down a serious proposition from an Arkansas company that wanted to manufacture his paints. But the lack of a laboratory finally defeated the project. After the Pure Food and Drug Act of 1906, such products as face powder required testing for purity, Carver believed, which in turn required finer and more reliable measuring instruments than anything he had access to. Carver again requested the connecting parts of some equipment and was again refused. Scott, meanwhile, was keeping Booker informed of Carver's every step and syllable on the subject of the paint enterprise. He even saved Carver's "mum" note in Booker's files. Carver, disheartened with the rejection of his requisition, sent a note to Scott: "I wish so much I could get this stuff so I could complete *something*. I have part of the things but they need the connections now. We could start right now if we had them, but I am a little afraid to put it upon the market without the means of verifying its purity." Scott duly saved this confidential note along with the others. The only result of Carver's years of turning dross clay into bright paint was that Tuskegee was able to save hundreds of dollars in building maintenance.

In these twilight years of the Booker era, Carver created dozens of products that are today remembered only because they demonstrate his protean investigations. He developed a laundry blueing for, in those days, fastidious housewives added "blueing" to every white wash. People in the town of Tuskegee liked it. Then there was his powder for polishing metal and silverware which the boarding department raved over—it was a useful item when the school was dressing up for prominent visitors. He developed a poison—only partially effective—for bedbugs, which were a persistent problem in the years when Tuskegee mattresses were filled with straw. In addition to his lab work, he began cultivating pear orchards for the school and working with local teachers on a literacy program for the county. He wrote leaflets with advice on building rural schoolhouses. In 1915 he was writing to J. H. about setting up an educational arboretum. Carver never lost his love of the outdoors. Though much had changed at Tuskegee, much remained the same as when he had arrived twenty years before. The students were still devastating the shrubs and landscaped plants to get sprays, needed every day, for decorating the dining room. There was not, according to Carver, "a single spot of beautiful woodland around here that is not polluted with trash, rubbish, garbage, etc." For fifteen years, Carver had been demonstrating organic fertilizers—going against the conventional opinion of his day which held that commercial fertilizer was essential to crop yield. The idea that one could rejuvenate a field with little more than leaves and swamp muck was tantamount to telling farmers they could make the soil fertile by singing to it. He had inveighed against the common practice of burning the fields preparatory to spring planting and exhorted farmers to turn the fields over instead. Finally in 1912 Carver won out over J. H. The Tuskegee farm, though no longer under Carver's control, at last abjured commercial fertilizer.

It was during this period when Carver became more deeply involved in food research, mainly because his lack of equipment limited him to "kitchen chemistry." Booker's interest in this work, insofar as he was interested, devolved upon saving money in the boarding department. Carver, as always, was anxious to please his chief, but his abiding concern was ending the widespread malnutrition of southern sharecroppers by showing them how to raise and cook healthful food. During the five years after 1910, Carver developed recipes for the foods that he knew were both nourishing and easy to grow in Alabama: sweet potatoes, cowpeas, and peanuts. It is a commonplace now to think of peas, beans, and nuts as worthy vegetarian sources of protein; but in the early 1900s, the word "protein" was not part of the normal vocabulary, and vitamin research was still in its infancy. Carver's recognition of the dietary value of these foods was remarkable. In 1911, he proudly arranged for some cooking students to prepare a five-course luncheon in Booker's honor using only Carver's peanut recipes—fourteen of them. Nine guests were invited and partook of soup, mock chicken, creamed vegetable, salad, bread, candy, cookies, ice cream, and coffee—all made from peanuts. That such a feat was possible is noteworthy. Nobody ever said, however, either then or later (except when they were obviously straining to be polite) that Carver's concoctions were delicious. When Carver accepted invitations to people's houses, he typically brought along some "delicacy" made from cowpeas or peanuts. More than one recipient expressed delight over the gift and then quietly disposed of it after the professor had departed.

In 1912 Carver succeeded in growing alfalfa in Alabama—more than 3,000 pounds on two acres in his first harvest. One of his new hybrid varieties of cotton produced a fine patch, with stalks of more than fifty bolls and squares. Still, in his letter to Wilson announcing his successful alfalfa crop, Carver penned a plaintive postscript: "I think I shall not be here much longer. Please keep me in mind."

In 1906 and 1907 Carver had published bulletins on preserving sweet potatoes and wild plums. Now he turned to meat preservation, with the success in curing that had caused more friction with Bridgeforth. For generations, farmers had waited until cold weather to slaughter hogs, lest the meat spoil in the heat. The delay meant that they had to continue to feed the hogs after they had matured and thus ran the risk of the animals contracting hog cholera. With Carver's new process for preserving meat, slaughtering could take place as soon as the hogs were grown. Carver, moreover, was quick to supply recipes for scrapple and liver pudding. Next, he developed a pickling formula for pork that finally won Booker's attention. After seeing that Carver's pickled pork was still in excellent condition after being kept for one year, Booker ordered that no more canned meat would be purchased by the school. Instead, hogs would be slaughtered as soon as they were fully grown and then preserved according to Carver's methods. It was up to Carver, of course, to make a thorough inspection of all the pickled meat preserved by the school.

By 1915, he was experimenting with drying foods. Carver had advocated eating raw fruits and vegetables long before such advice was in vogue among doctors; however, since fresh fruit was available only in the summer, he began investigating all possible ways of preserving it. His work with dehydrated food coincided with shortages caused by the Great War—shortages of tin cans, glass containers, and especially sugar, which had become a commodity beyond the budget of poor folk. Carver gave simple instructions that anyone could follow for drying sweet potatoes, and he taught farmers how to roast and grind them for a coffee substitute. Sweet potatoes could be grown abundantly with little injury to the soil. When Carver started his experiments, the average potato yield was thirty-seven bushels an acre; by 1910, he had regularly increased that number to 266. If the farmer copied him in raising that many potatoes, what would he do with them? For starters, Carver showed the farmers' wives how to make sweet potato laundry starch and syrup.

Carver continued to plead for the laboratory that had been promised, then refused, then promised again—for eight long years. Booker went so far as to do what Booker did best—he constructed a building to house a lab. In 1909 the agriculture department moved from Slater-Armstrong to the new Milbank Hall, where there was to be an office and a lab for Carver—"God's Little Workshop." Carver's joy gave way to the usual disappointment. He remonstrated with Booker that the new lab remained unfinished for months, lacking not only equipment but even woodwork; when Booker completed the woodwork, Carver sent warm thanks, noting that the woodwork was "absolutely beautiful." But Carver could not do experiments with woodwork. The equipment for the building did not arrive. The issue of getting out bulletins had never been resolved, either. In 1912, Carver was still importuning Booker for a stenographer, since he had three bulletins ready but had neither typist nor typewriter to prepare them for the printer. Just as in the past, he had to beg Booker to have the bulletins printed. Reprints were out of the question after the initial printing of a few thousand was exhausted, although there was always demand for them and they garnered praise from everywhere. Yale University, among other schools, requested them to use as instructional materials. The man who wrote the bulletins, meanwhile, was being urged not to use too many postage stamps. When he needed fifty dollars for a dairy project, Carver had to resort to asking Wilson to procure the funds from the government. On Christmas Day in 1914, Carver wrote to Booker complaining that he had been without a stenographer for some time. He was, he wrote, making serious investigations into a practical use for feathers, which every barnyard had in abundance. He had so far developed fifty-three products from feathers and was preparing an exhibit of them. But his only office help came from Emmett Scott, who had his own reasons for staying on Carver's good side.

Bridgeforth had not stopped sniping at Carver, but as time went on, Booker peeled Bridgeforth off of Carver's back sufficiently to allow the older man to do whatever research he could accomplish without equipment. In early fall 1915, about the time Booker fell critically ill in New York, Bridgeforth wrote Carver suggesting they lay down their swords. Realizing his supporter was about to die, he expected changes in the various departments in the near future and wanted to organize a new cabal, this time including Carver, against "any further trespassing." He was sure they were going to have trouble with "a certain Dr. Brody." By then, Carver had become sufficiently detached from the agriculture department that he was able to ignore its internecine squabbles. His focus was research.

During the years when Bridgeforth was attacking him—for the ordeal lasted more than a decade—Carver preached to his students that they must repay anger with mildness, that they must never retaliate against meanness and never allow themselves to harbor ill will toward their enemies, since harsh feelings would harm themselves more than their adversaries. If he were ever tempted to give in to loathing, pure and thrilling, it was during this period—the Bridgeforth years. But there is every indication that he followed his own advice, ignoring his enemy as much as possible, even on the eve of Booker's death, when the artful Bridgeforth held out the thorny branch of reconciliation. Carver went about his lonely business, as usual.

When the talk at Tuskegee was not about someone's shortcomings, it was about religion, or so it would appear. In 1906, a group of students asked Carver to organize a boys' Bible class to be held during the thirty-five minute break between Sunday supper and evening chapel. Although they were already attending compulsory chapel every night, as well as several hours of services on Sunday, fifty boys showed up in the library for the first discussion. Attendance to the voluntary class climbed to almost three hundred within months and rarely fell below 150. Carver was a Darwinian. He explained the Creation story, he said, in the "light of natural and revealed religion and geological truths," using maps, charts, plants, and geological specimens as illustrations. He presented Genesis as a metaphorical representation of scientific fact, with the seven days of creation standing for stages of millennia. His talks were perfectly pitched to the level of the students who flocked to him. Booker was not aware that the class was going on until Carver had been teaching it three years. He was amazed to learn that students ran to it early in order to get a front row seat. But Carver's Bible class was shut down with the explanation that attendees were arriving late to the chapel services held immediately afterward.

In 1908, during the worst period of his war with Bridgeforth, Carver was invited to lecture in the Midwest. He took the opportunity to visit Missouri and Kansas and see the people who had meant much to him in his youth. He found Mariah Watkins still tough and independent and in her same house next to the school, an established character in the small town life of Neosho. For the first time since he left the West, he visited Moses Carver who was then ninety-six years old. George had hired a detective to locate Moses. He found him in Kansas, sardonic and spirited as always, living with his nephew, who was also somewhat aged. Moses was still rangy and gnarled, with a thin, pointed, white beard and sharp, knowing eyes. He wore natty striped trousers—perhaps only for certain occasions such as George's visit—and the big black hat that farmers in those days favored when going to town for church or business. Since Moses could not read or write, he had never corresponded with George. He had known ups and downs since George had left. While he was chopping wood one day on his homestead in Diamond, a chip flew up, piercing his eye. He completely lost sight in that eye and in his later years had very poor vision in the other eye.

Moses allowed that when his wife Susan died in 1891 he still owned many racehorses and some farm animals. In 1897 he married a woman named Elizabeth Love, though there appeared to be little love on her side. The marriage did not work out. Moses claimed that she stayed away from the house all day, every day; the couple divorced in 1901. "I told her it was all foolishness, this thing of parting," Moses said, "and if she was bound to go I would give her a mare, a cow, a bed, about a year's provisions—bacon and lard . . . When she went to start I begged her not to go, but she was mad and would go." Since Elizabeth could not take the cow, Moses gave her twenty dollars and told her to take eighty dollars that she had buried somewhere on his property. But after the final divorce decree, Elizabeth sued Moses, alleging that he had deeded over his property to his niece and nephews in order to keep her from getting a portion of it in the divorce. Moses deposed that he was merely providing for his future: "I made a deed and they was to maintain me, and if I got so low that I couldn't maintain myself." And in fact, he left the farm around 1906 and moved to his nephew's house in Kansas.

The deposition attached to Elizabeth's lawsuit is our only direct evidence of Moses's speech and personality. The document is almost redolent of cane-backed chairs and a country law office. "Was you expecting to marry this woman at the time you made those deeds?" Elizabeth's lawyer asked Moses. "No, I never thought of marrying," he answered. The lawyer, like everyone in Neosho, believed that Moses had a ponderable store of cash hidden away. But when asked if he had any money at the time of divorce, Moses answered, "I don't know just what I did have, not much."

"Where and how did you keep your money?" asked the lawyer.

"In different places."

"Name the places," said the lawyer.

"I don't think I ought to answer that," Moses responded.

"Tell how much there was of it."

"$200 or $300. Perhaps a little more or a little less."

This was the astute and independent man who had been George Carver's only father. When George made his visit, Moses must have been impressed with his accomplishments, as was Mariah Watkins's nephew, Cal Jefferson, and indeed the whole town of Neosho. Old Carver's clever little George had come back to them a professor, a gentleman. They could have no notion of the tenuousness of his position or the sense of shame and failure that he carried with him from Tuskegee; he had just been removed as director of the agriculture department, the department he had founded.

Moses gave George something he would treasure for the rest of his life: the little spinning wheel that had habitually been used by his mother Mary when she was Moses's slave. Before George left, he purchased a new suit for Moses—an interesting gift, considering that George apparently never bought a new suit for himself in his entire life. Moses was buried in the suit two years later, in December 1910, and laid to rest in the lovely rock-fenced cemetery he had built with his own hands on his property in Diamond. Before his death, Moses himself selected the writing on his tombstone. The epitaph must have been read to him:

> Friends and strangers as you pass by
> As you are now, so once was I.
> As I am now, so you will be.
> Prepare for death and follow me.

He could not have imagined that thousands and thousands of people would visit his gravesite solely because of the black child he and his wife had sheltered for ten years.

9

BAD DAYS AND WORSE

While George was trying to put his troubles at Tuskegee out of his mind with the trip to Kansas and Missouri, Booker was wrestling with his own devils in New York. The year 1911 may have been the worst in Booker's life. On an evening in March, after delivering two speeches, Booker left his hotel in midtown Manhattan and traveled uptown to the edge of the seedy tenderloin district. He entered the vestibule of a building occupied only by whites and studied the directory of residents. Three women who lived in the building passed him while he peered at the directory. He rang one of the bells and, receiving no answer, went outside and walked up and down for about an hour. When he returned to the vestibule, he was attacked by a white man who had been watching him as he "loitered" in the neighborhood. The man chased Booker, beating him viciously with a heavy walking stick. Booker probably would have been killed in the attack had he not stumbled into a plainclothes policeman who saved his life by arresting him, only to release him when, at the station house, his identity was confirmed as the famous Booker T. Washington. His attacker, a man named Henry Ulrich, was then charged with assault. Ulrich's "wife" meanwhile appeared at the station and claimed that Booker had accosted her in the vestibule, saying, "Hello, Sweetheart."

The incident was splashed across all the New York papers, together with Booker's carefully prepared statement that he had gone to the building to meet the white man who audited Tuskegee's books for the trustees. However, that auditor, Daniel Cranford Smith, lived in New Jersey, not New York, and at the time of the assault he was in Tuskegee, as Booker was aware, where he had been for a month. Booker may have believed that honesty was the best policy, but he liked to test other alternatives first. He elaborated his story, but he never satisfactorily explained what he was doing at that particular West Side address. There was excited press coverage of the event and of Ulrich's trial, which took place despite Booker's prodigious efforts to get him and his mistress to retract their accusations and settle out of court. Through the ordeal, Booker was deluged with supportive letters, even from W. E. B. Du Bois. It became clear at the trial that Ulrich had brutally attacked Booker without provocation; but it was also clear that Booker could not substantiate his explanation as to why he had gone to Ulrich's building. Remarkably, Ulrich was acquitted and walked out of the courtroom smiling broadly. In one of the little ironies of jurisprudence, he was rearrested in the hallway in connection with his desertion of his children and his legitimate wife, who discovered his whereabouts when she read about the case in the newspapers.

Despite their momentary truce during the Ulrich affair, the hostility between Booker and W. E. B. Du Bois intensified every year. So, too, did Booker's rage against Adella Logan. In 1912, Booker's wife Margaret became president of the National Association of Colored Women's Clubs in which Adella had long been active. One of the new president's first acts was to have Adella removed from her post as head of the suffrage division of the organization. That same September, Du Bois devoted an entire number of *The Crisis* to the topic of women's suffrage, the subject that had been Adella's foremost preoccupation all her life. Adella committed an unthinkable act of betrayal: she contributed a long article to this issue of the journal—the magazine that constantly roared its criticism of Booker across the factional divide. Moreover, she was listed in N.A.A.C.P. literature as one of that organization's ten leaders committed to women's suffrage. Adella was a leader in women's suffrage, not a leader of the N.A.A.C.P., but the distinction hardly mattered once her name was connected to that of the hated enemy camp.

Adella's open defiance of Booker trapped Warren Logan in an unenviable situation. Booker's loyal adjutant was ordered to control his wife; but Adella was a feisty woman with an altogether stronger personality than her husband's. Even in family photographs with her children she appears frangible and formidable—an energetic little being who would never be governed by the likes of meek Logan. Bewildered, resentful, and embarrassed, Logan turned his attention to a younger, pliant woman. Gossip about the Logan family spread like blight through the vines of Tuskegee. The "other woman" was allowed to remain in a position in close proximity to Logan. By mid-1915, Adella was being shunned by the people at Tuskegee who cared about pleasing Booker—that is to say, by nearly everyone. She was suffering from severe nervousness and depression. In September, she was sent off to Battle Creek, Michigan, for treatment, to a sanitarium that had one essential advantage over any southern clinic—it was far, far away.

The Battle Creek Sanitarium was a Seventh Day Adventist hospital directed by the surgeon John Harvey Kellogg, Booker's friend. Kellogg, who abjured alcohol, tobacco, caffeine, fun, and flesh in all its forms, was outstanding among several crackpot prodigies of his generation. He imposed a savorless and spare vegetarian diet on his patients in order to destroy their sex drive, the pernicious contributor to illness and, concomitantly, all populations. It was his quest for anaphrodisiac meals that led Kellogg and his brother Will Keith Kellogg to develop corn flakes, the food that eventually launched the brother's cereal enterprise. Dr. Harvey Kellogg labored assiduously to eradicate sexual activity, especially masturbation. According to the doctor, self-abuse caused cancer and epilepsy, among other plagues, so that the masturbator "dies by his own hand."

To conquer the unruly urge, he prescribed electrical shocks to the genitals and advocated circumcising pubescent boys without anesthesia to instill a connection in the child's mind between the surgery and the idea of punishment. The soreness attendant to the operation was supposed to last long enough to interrupt the vicious habit. For young women he recommended applying carbolic acid to the clitoris or cutting it out altogether. His patients young and old were subjected to rigorously controlled diets and exercise. Kellogg was part of a generation that was devoutly attentive to bowel movements; in that he was fashionable. A popular ad for "a doctor's family laxative" showed an avuncular doctor (prominently wearing his stethoscope) advising a distressed maiden, "There may be poison in your bowels! To Be a Healthy Woman, Watch Your Bowels." All patients in the hospital without exception underwent daily treatment with Kellogg's "yogurt enema machine," which forced several gallons of water and a pint of yogurt into the bowel, along with God knows how many germs.

That was the institution to which Adella was committed. Booker instructed Logan, "I advise you to drop everything and take Mrs. Logan to Battle Creek." The advice had the slightly threatening tone of an order by the time he closed his letter: "I hope certainly you will consider this matter very carefully and seriously," as if Logan were likely to treat it lightly. It is possible that Booker was not merely trying to get rid of Adella. He himself had stayed at the Battle Creek Sanitarium some weeks previously for relief from his constant indigestion, and some of his wealthy supporters such as John D. Rockefeller had found it a salutary watering place. Booker may have sincerely believed that "no hospital in the country has such fine arrangements for patients with nervous troubles." He pointed to its "machines" for special treatment. Booker insured Adella's admission by writing a tactful letter to Dr. Kellogg, informing him that "no one would know from her appearance that Mrs. Logan is colored. The same is true of her daughter, Miss Ruth Logan, who is planning to accompany her to the Sanitarium." Kellogg was a staunch believer in both segregation and eugenics, but like many white conservatives, he excepted Booker from his prejudice.

Exactly one month after writing to Kellogg, on November 14, 1915, Booker T. Washington died at Tuskegee. Adella immediately returned home to her three youngest children. The timing of her return made it obvious that Booker had compelled her to leave in the first place. What happened between Adella and Logan, either before her internment or when she was allowed to return, is not known. All we can be certain of, looking back, is that it was not a happy homecoming.

The Christmas of 1915 was perhaps the first yuletide in twenty years that did not find Carver in his lab or at his desk or in the fields, hard at work, or at the Logan dinner table with the family. He was grieving. A few days before Booker's memorial service on December 15, Adella threw herself out of the top floor window of Tuskegee's academic building. She hurtled onto the sidewalk below and, after excruciating suffering, died that evening in the Tuskegee Hospital. She was fifty-two years old.

Adella's friend Du Bois believed that Booker had driven her to despair and then sentenced her to exile. The year after her death he conceived a fable, "The Princess of the Hither Isles," in which a tragic, doomed princess lives in a remote land under the domination of an evil king. She goes through such turmoil that eventually she kills herself by leaping from a high precipice.

Some years earlier, Carver had named one of his hybrid amaryllis after this princess. Now he painted two small murals, one of Booker and one of Adella, to memorialize the people he considered his loved ones. As late as 1918, Adella was still haunting his thoughts; his bulletin "How to Grow the Tomato and 115 Ways to Prepare It" was dedicated to her: "To my esteemed friend and co-worker, Mrs. Adella Hunt Logan, who was tireless in her efforts to help the farmer and his family; and who saw in the tomato a panacea for many of his ills; and who contributed more data of real value along this line than anyone else with whom I have come in contact, I affectionately dedicate this bulletin."

Sarah Hunt moved back to Tuskegee after her sister's death to take care of the Logan family, the youngest of the six living children being only six years old. Warren Logan soon remarried. Sarah, then in her late forties, moved to Los Angeles and married her second cousin, Felix Rogers. Logan remained at Tuskegee until the 1940s.

George Bridgeforth left Tuskegee and eventually was hired by a school in Athens, Alabama. In 1927, some fifteen years after his war with Carver, Bridgeforth invited the prominent scientist to lecture at his school. Carver's two letters of reply are outstanding demonstrations of his capacity for Christian forgiveness.

June 28, 1927
My dear Mr. Bridgeforth:

I thank you for your delightful favor which reached me last night. It seems good to hear from you.

I am not sure whether I can be with you or not in your County Educational Association, as you gave no dates as to when the meeting is to take place. I have not been very well since January and at present the Doctor has me shut in. I am not teaching this year in the summer school even, as the result of it. I do not know just when he will release me. If you will let me know the dates, I will take it up with him and see if it will be safe for me to make the trip. Were it any where else except with you, I would be inclined to say no, but it would be such a great pleasure to renew our old friendship again.

With sincerely good wishes, I am, Very truly yours

Carver considerately refrained from using his title, Director of Research, and signed the letter followed only by "Department of Agricultural Research."

Up to about 1915, Carver's reputation had been mainly in the South, where he was invited to speak at black farm conferences and agricultural fairs. But in the late teens and 1920s, a screen seemed to lift from his work, allowing his labors to become visible to the biology community at large. Carver remained an ardent and audible pacifist even while Americans were being jailed for speaking out against the Great War. As yet, he was still too obscure for the government to bother harassing him for his views. Booker T. Washington's death marked the real beginning of George Carver's career as a scientist and the end of his life as a barnyard drudge, assaulted by jealous colleagues and thwarted in every area of pure research by people incapable of appreciating his knowledge or his vision.

He himself did not regard Booker's death as a release, however. He mourned deeply and slipped into a rather serious melancholy that lasted several months. It was the grief of a son who lost a demanding father without ever having succeeded in satisfying him or even winning his grudging respect. In January 1915, Emmett Scott solicited donations for a memorial fund for Washington. Carver donated half a year's salary. "I am sure Mr. Washington never knew how much I loved him, and the cause for which he gave his life," Carver wrote. Handling the donation, Scott scribbled a note to someone on the back of Carver's letter: "I don't know why, but somehow I feel sorry for the old man." Scott was forty-two at the time of Booker's death. The "old man" Carver was fifty-two. Being owned by Booker for twenty years—toiling to fulfill his incessant demands, striving to be worthy of his notice and miserly praise, anxious at all times to gain his approval and anguishing when it was withheld because of some failing, in short, being in his thrall—it was a life that would have aged anyone.

10

THE CURTAIN LIFTS

The funeral of Booker T. Washington at Tuskegee was not only reported across the country, but flags on municipal buildings both in Alabama and faraway Boston bowed to his memory. Theodore Roosevelt came and delivered a muscular eulogy. The ex-president had recently returned from a harrowing exploration of the River of Doubts (now renamed Rio Roosevelt). He had become a different extrovert since his last visit to Tuskegee—thinner (he had lost fifty pounds), ill, and haggard but still enough like his old self to pay the extravagant compliment of noticing that someone was similar to him. "There *is* no more important work than that you are doing," he told Carver. "I think you do things much as I do . . . You study first, then come to a decision, and then stick to that decision. We can neither be worked, walked, nor talked down." The two men voiced their plaintive awareness that, with Booker's death, an era had passed. Exactly four years later, Roosevelt, too, was gone.

When, after a month, the torches of memorial services across the country were finally extinguished, the task of choosing Booker's successor began. The long deliberations were reported in the *New York Times* with hardly less solemnity than if the Tuskegee board were selecting a new pope. The board passed over the obvious choice, Emmett Scott, with well-worded apologies and instead chose Robert Russa Moton to succeed Booker as president. Neither Moton nor anyone else would take Booker's place as the leader of his race and the referee of all issues pertaining to black people in the United States. That was exactly as the board intended. If the businessmen who supported the school had wanted the Tuskegee Machine to continue, they would have backed Scott, who alone knew its oiled cylinders and camouflaged wires. Instead, they allowed the machine to rust away after Booker's death. For the next fifty years, leadership would not be centered on a single individual but dispersed through

several black organizations. Marcus Garvey and W. E. B. Du Bois were influ-
ential in black affairs, but neither could step into Booker's position. Du Bois in
particular was more intelligent than Booker, but he did not have his predecessor's mesmerizing personality nor the confidence of the white public. Nevertheless, his N.A.A.C.P. grew and took its place as the leading voice of black
activism. It had a membership of 90,000 in 1919, the year when two-year-old
Lena Horne was featured on the cover of its journal. Du Bois outlived Booker
by nearly half a century and was instrumental in bringing about school desegregation. He died in 1963, one year before the passage of the Civil Rights Act.
He lived a long time—ninety-five years—but not quite long enough to see the
crowning success of the revolution he had helped begin.

Major Moton, as he was known, was an alumnus and former employee
of Hampton Institute, where he had marched through twenty years as
commandant. He believed that Tuskegee should remain a primarily industrial
school. But he was a man of different mettle than his friend Booker. For all his
military background, Moton was far less dictatorial. Reading the correspondence of the principal's office, it is easy to spot which letters were written by
Moton and which ones came from Booker: Moton's tone is courteous, respectful, and gentle.

> June 10, 1916
>
> My dear Professor Carver:
>
> Mr. Roberts gave me your note today. He of course regrets, as we all do,
> that you feel you cannot take your usual classes in botany for the coming
> year . . . I wish you would withhold your definite decision until I have a
> chance to talk with you on my return. I need not tell you that it will be
> impossible to get anybody to teach this subject as you have done, and I do
> not like to think of the students losing the inspiration and help that would
> come by your teaching. If you will kindly delay, perhaps we can come to
> some amicable adjustment that will be satisfactory.
>
> Yours very truly,
> R. R. Moton, Principal

It is hard to imagine the late Pontifex Maximus writing such a letter. Moton realized what Booker would never admit—that next to the principal himself, Carver was the foremost asset and attraction of the institution. If left alone to work in his lab and teach when he was needed, he would bring renown to Tuskegee and draw many outstanding students. For his part, Carver minded his own business, now that the incessant administrative meetings had stopped. He reported to Moton every compliment he heard about him and repeated no criticisms. Starting from the week of Booker's death, Carver never again offered his resignation nor was involved in any dispute that would have tempted him to forsake Tuskegee.

Life was still not perfect. All during the 1920s, we find Carver pleading as in the past for the reprint of bulletins. In 1926 it had been four years since any of his bulletins was reprinted. The mailing list of people waiting for them numbered 2,000, most of them whites, as Carver noted with satisfaction, including schools in sixteen foreign countries. Nevertheless, that year the business committee refused his request for a reprint because of the fifty-dollar cost. Never mind that Tuskegee, along with Hampton Institute, had just received a gift of securities worth 1 million dollars from John D. Rockefeller. Throughout the decade Carver's budget for agricultural research remained at about $2,000, with $1,800 of that assigned to salaries.

Up-to-date equipment? Carver's lab was barely supplied with common chemicals. In 1929, when he was a scientific luminary and had made the name of Tuskegee known throughout the country, Carver spent a mere ten dollars of the school's money on chemicals for the lab—the rest of the materials were donated by individuals who saw that he needed them. Still, his request for a nine-dollar grinder for pulverizing stones, the only piece of apparatus he asked for in the entire year, was turned down. At the time, Tuskegee had an endowment of some eight million. Martin Menafee, whose school in South Carolina was modeled on Tuskegee, observed, "I think Tuskegee has all kinds of money. I see no reason why they should whine and complain about no finances. I presume that it is done for style." To get the grinder, Carver had to resort to a personal request to Moton. The principal was just returning from a fundraising trip around the world where at every stop he had exhorted donors to support the institution that was the center for George Carver's research.

Carver's need for secretarial help was chronic, and chronically unmet. In July 1919, he wrote a letter of outright complaint when he was asked to take on one more chore in an overburdened schedule. "I am writing to ask you to please give me some relief. I am about to break down, my work is too heavy. Some of it is being shamefully neglected . . . I do not get to enjoy any outing because I must work night and day trying to keep up my work. I must get some rest or give up my work altogether." Moton's response was to lend Carver a part-time secretary "at great sacrifices to ourselves." However, three days after Carver's complaint, Moton increased his salary to $100 a month plus board, a sum that Moton noted warmly "does not give adequate expression of our appreciation of your service, but we wanted you to know how much your faithful efforts and loyal service have helped and encouraged me." Carver was still being paid less than the newer faculty members, and he still needed more than a part-time secretary, but he was appreciative of the gesture. "For this I am more thankful . . . than my words can express. It is the things we don't have to do but do that count for the highest and best in life after all." In his fifty years at Tuskegee, Carver never once asked for a raise in salary.

World War I had ended in 1918; the tide of reform that broke upon the prewar years had receded. For the next decade, the country would be more and more infatuated with wealth and its trappings. People had the feeling that a vigorous new epoch was beginning—that the twentieth century was ready to start in earnest. For Carver, too, there was a break with the past. Within a year of Booker's death, he began receiving many more invitations to write in national journals and give talks. At most institutions, he was obliged to give two talks—one for whites and one the next day for blacks. In 1916 he accepted an invitation from Du Bois—something inconceivable when Booker was alive—to speak in California, where he was introduced by Luther Burbank. Only six years previously he had wistfully remarked, "I am sure I shall never attain to the distinction of Mr. Burbank." Each of Carver's articles, each lecture, was a small step toward national recognition and, he thought, toward the destruction of racial barriers. When the state secretary of agriculture called a meeting of the leading teachers of the state, Carver was the only black person invited to participate—a singular event in Alabama, where it was unlikely that any of the teachers had ever before sat thigh to thigh next to a Negro in public. Carver was in fact asked to address the convention and afterward spent an hour answering questions from the assemblage. As President Moton realized, these were notable tokens for Tuskegee as well as for Carver. Even the most humble black organizations could afford to invite him, since he never charged for his appearances, as in Kentucky in 1919, where he addressed a chapter meeting of the Negro Chautauqua at "Vendevere's Groc., Lunch, Ice Cream, and Soft Drinks."

For a long, bleak period he had suffered one blow after another—the Bridgeforth conflict, the end of his long romance with Sarah Hunt, the death of Booker with their differences unresolved, and the suicide of his dearest friend. He was often sick, sad, and profoundly lonely, but he nevertheless accomplished a great deal in the five years following Adella's death. Except for his depression, those could have been wonderful years for him. He had long been creating synthetic marble from wood shavings and using it to fabricate benches—one such bench remained for years on a street corner at Tuskegee. Now he refined his procedures for producing materials from clay—plastics, pottery, washing powder, shoe polish, and especially dyes.

Until the First World War, the United States had imported most of its chemicals, fertilizers, and dyes from Germany, especially aniline dyes, those derived from benzene. When the war impeded importation, industries that required large quantities of dye, such as printing, paint, clothing, and leather, had to turn to less efficient vegetable dyes. Carver thus began searching for new plants that would yield their latent colors—not that plant dyes would ever be preferable to aniline dyes. He found twenty-eight plants whose leaves, stems, roots, or fruit yielded acceptable dyes for cloth and leather—insistent colors that would not fade in washing or in light. The woods around Carver were not especially endowed with exotic flora. Nevertheless, along with cultivars, he used plain scrub plants, weeds, and growth that might be found in any thicket. From these twenty-eight commonplace plants he drew out 536 dyes. They yielded what he described as "only basic colors"; cross-dyeing would be needed to get variegated hues. But his work with dyes eventually proved futile because the shortage of aniline dyes ended with the end of the war.

Just when he needed it—that is, the year after Adella's death—came several unexpected bursts of loud applause. On November 29, 1916, Carver was elected a fellow of the Royal Society for the Encouragement of Arts, Manufactures, and Commerce. He never knew with certainty who nominated him or how the appointment came to be made, but he suspected that the nomination originated with Sir Harry H. Johnston, the distinguished British naturalist who had visited him and paid repeated tribute to "The Wizard of Tuskegee" in his books. Considering the prestige of the British Royal Society and the very few foreigners who are elected, it was a remarkable honor to come to Carver, still in the delayed early period of his career. No more than forty-four outstanding British scientists are elected to fellowship each year, along with eight foreign members. Carver took his place beside such chanticleers of enlightenment as Sir Isaac Newton, Joseph Priestly, and Charles Darwin. With this accolade, he would never again be an unknown scientist working in a backwater.

In that same 1916, Thomas Edison, who was deaf to the ordinary bustle of life, had heard of the extraordinary work of George Carver. He wrote from Florida and sent his chief assistant, Miller Rees Hutcheson, to invite Carver to carry on research in the resplendent Edison Laboratories at a "tremendous," six-figure salary that Carver was asked not to divulge. The secrecy was understandable. Edison's stable of inventors, hearing of a huge sum paid to a black man, might have become restive with their average weekly wage of fifteen dollars. There is no documentary evidence of this offer, which was apparently made in person by Hutcheson. Carver reported the proposal (though not the specific amount of the salary) to several biographers; it was mentioned in nearly every subsequent newspaper account of Carver's accomplishments during the years when Edison was alive and could have refuted any fabrication. Besides, Carver fabricated materials, not stories. Edison sent Carver one autographed picture of himself when the offer was made, and another when it was courteously and gratefully declined. Edison renewed the temptation in 1929, after Carver had become famous, repeating the promise of a first-class laboratory. Even though Edison's letter arrived during the grinder incident, when Carver was scraping to get a nine-dollar gadget, the offer was again gracefully resisted. Carver remained on affable terms with Edison; people who wanted the inventor's attention sometimes wrote first to Carver, hoping that he would put in a good word for them—a request he always gently rebuffed. When Edison died in 1931, Carver received letters of condolence. Edison and Carver had not been close, but people thought they were.

Why did Carver dismiss his one chance to be rich, to have a playground of sophisticated equipment, to do the kind of advanced research he had always dreamed of? How could he resist making common cause with the man who vowed "to make electricity so cheap and accessible that only the rich will burn candles"?

Probably for several reasons. In the first place, working for Thomas Edison, by then America's most famous inventor and man of practical science, would have been somewhat like working for Booker T. Washington. Carver would have been the talented helot of a great man who expected to draw the largest share of approbation and publicity to himself. He would have been obliged to do research in areas chosen by Edison, to be part of the Edison machinery, just as he had been a highly constrained and controlled part of the Tuskegee Machine, but without having young people around who adored him. Edison expected mankind to benefit from his inventions after he himself had enjoyed profit and glory from them. Seeking patents was an important element of Edison's system—he accumulated a staggering 1,093. His patents were usually taken out in his name although the working models were collaborative efforts involving teams of inventors and assistants who labored long hours for tradesmen's wages. Patents mattered not at all to Carver; he was averse to competition. In fact, he was against the whole idea of selfishly trying to own his discoveries. They were intended for the betterment of his fellow man, not for gaining some capitalistic advantage. The Edison laboratories were indeed modern and supplied with every substance and apparatus a chemist could wish for. But an Edison lab would not have been Carver's exclusive workshop. One of Edison's most successful ideas was the industrial research laboratory, a complex of laboratories that allowed the development of dozens of products simultaneously. Carver was as disinclined to teamwork as he was to business and monopolies. He was no doubt aware that Edison owned fourteen behemoths such as General Electric, where an unassuming genius could vanish once he entered the maw of an immense corporate system.

Perhaps the Peanut Wizard also knew that the Wizard of Menlo Park was wily, furiously competitive, ruthless, and known for breaking promises. Edison once promised an immigrant assistant, Nikola Tesla, $50,000 if he succeeded in making certain improvements to Edison's generating plants. Tesla was being paid eighteen dollars a week; the reward would have amounted to fifty years' salary. Several months later, Tesla accomplished the assignment and asked for the bonus. Edison said, "When you become a full-fledged American you will appreciate an American joke." He even refused to raise Tesla's salary to twenty-five dollars per week, whereupon Tesla resigned. Asked to contribute some years later to Edison's obituary, Tesla, who by then had learned how to talk like a full-fledged American, summarized his former boss: "He had no hobby, cared for no sort of amusement of any kind, and lived in utter disregard of the most elementary rules of hygiene . . . He had a veritable contempt for book learning and mathematical knowledge, trusting himself entirely to his inventor's instinct and practical American sense."

It would have taken courage for Carver to leave his home of twenty years, return to the white world, and work with new, unfamiliar technology and people. However, he never indicated any underlying fear of the position. His explanation as to why he declined Edison's offer was straightforward and plausible: he said he wanted his race to be recognized through him. He had worked all his life for the southern Negro farmer. "If I were to go [to Edison Laboratories], my work would not be known as mine, and my race would get no credit. I want it to have the credit of whatever I may do." If the Edison offer had come in the harassed days of 1906, 1910, or even 1912, when walking over to the poultry yard or the farm each day was a march into battle, Carver would not have been able to resist it. But in 1916 he was happier in his work than he had ever been.

That work continued to be heavy and varied but far more in the public eye than when Booker was alive. One day he was meeting with ex-president Taft to give his eager opinion of the League of Nations and the plans for international peace. Another day he was writing curricula for barefoot schoolchildren in his county. At the experiment station, people were sending the usual earthy substances for testing—corn, sawdust, ashes. One of Carver's most significant projects was completely inconspicuous—ascertaining the minimum acreage of land needed to support a family.

As late as 1930, only 64 of the 612 farm families in Macon County owned their land. At that time, fifteen to twenty acres was considered a one-horse farm, from which the tenant was usually expected to pay the landlord about one and a half bales of cotton for rent. One problem in rural Alabama was that the land had been divided and subdivided, bringing landlords more rent but making holdings smaller than twenty acres, so small as to be mere patches. Practically speaking, wages and employment did not exist in the countryside, where there were neither industries nor farms large enough to employ labor. Cash was scarce; the tenant system operated on barter and credit. Since even the larger dirt farms could not support the families living on them, the farmers were perpetually behind on their rents and had no money to buy necessities. To be self-sustaining, either the farms had to be consolidated, which would mean evicting the impoverished families, or someone had to find a way to make a living on a small plot of land—poor land, leached by cotton. Carver, according to Carver, decided to be that someone. On part of his experiment station plot, he produced 4,000 pounds of corn and fodder and 1,000 pounds of hay, in addition to various food crops. He proved that a mere six acres was enough land to provide for a farmer and his brood.

The immediate task confronting the experiment station was to get rid of the boll weevil that was destroying the cotton crop of Alabama and Mississippi. The weevil resembles a large fly and eats only cotton plants, damaging the bolls so that they become stunted or rotten. The female lays eggs in the plant which hatch in three days; the cycle of eating and destroying the plant thus begins again. A single pair of beetles can produce twelve million weevils in one season. The boll weevil can be killed by applications of calcium arsenate, but at the time of the infestation, the compound was scarce and expensive. Since farmers could not be persuaded to give up cotton, Carver considered it his lifelong obligation to defeat the insect that was spreading despair across their fields. It was a self-imposed duty he never completely set aside but never fulfilled, either, in that he was not able to destroy the pest. The best he could do was make up some poison compounds and develop a weevil-resistant strain of cotton. From one single acre planted with that strain, he picked more than 400 pounds of seed cotton. As usual, all of his crops were grown without the use of any commercial fertilizer, and every operation was kept within the capability of the one-horse farmer.

During the Booker years, Carver's work had involved (in addition to his disastrous experiences with poultry) research on soil building, feed grains, and seeds, as well as on kudzu, alfalfa, clover and vetch. The First World War, with its need for effective transport, led him to try to produce synthetic rubber and, in fact, he did extract a rubber-like substance from the sweet potato. Certain properties in mica, he discovered, could be used in making aviation spark plugs—good news for companies eager to fill large orders for the military. The food shortages of those years inspired him to find plants that were especially nutritious. It is hard now to remember a time when vitamins, minerals, calories, and protein were not part of everyone's vocabulary. But the very word "vitamin" was not coined until 1912; the role of vitamins in controlling metabolic processes was only gradually discovered as the decade progressed—Vitamin A in 1913, Vitamin B in 1915, and so on. Until about 1925, Vitamin E was designated simply "Food Factor X." Even though he was overworked and buried in the sticks, Carver kept abreast of scientific discoveries and during the war began his own research into the dietary value of cowpeas, sweet potatoes, soybeans, tomatoes, pecans, and especially peanuts—all crops that he had long been promulgating. While the United States was at war, the Department of Agriculture wondered whether sweet potato flour might be a substitute for wheat flour in the army's food provisions and called Carver to Washington for consultation. But with the end of the war the government lost its curiosity and dashed Carver's hopes for large requisitions of sweet potatoes from Alabama. He returned to his experiments with the peanut, the work that eventually brought him the most fame. Carver had continued research on the peanut steadily throughout all the years when he was focused on other research—he had never given it up. And year by year, he had added to the peanut derivatives.

O f all Carver's peanut products, peanut milk excited the most publicity and commercial interest. A typical proposition to Carver went something like this: a group of businessmen would offer to form a company to manufacture peanut milk. They proposed selling a million dollars' worth of shares to capitalize the enterprise. In return for giving up his rights and interests, Carver would receive a quarter interest in the company, that is, $250,000 worth of stock, which would only become valuable if the product were a commercial success. No further attention would be required from Carver unless, as hoped, the company made enough money to warrant offering other Carver products.

Everybody from the government of Argentina to missionaries in Africa saw the potential of Carver's peanut milk, powdered milk, and other milk substitutes. Dried milk was known in the United States but was not widely marketed. Peanut milk, however, was not at all known and remains, even now, an oddity. Peanut milk is similar to almond milk, soy milk, and rice milk in its production: the substance is ground, soaked, sometimes heated, and then passed through a fine filter. The resulting liquid is considered the "milk." Carver admitted it would "never put the cow out of business," but it was a fine substitute for dairy milk where one was needed. Missionaries in Africa considered it a godsend. "Natives have high childbirth deaths," explained one doctor working in the Congo. "Live infants are buried with the mothers because otherwise they'll starve to death, as no mother would nurse another's baby." Goats being very few, there was no reliable source of milk. Carver sent instructions for making peanut milk and also for making soy milk, which was not then in common use. Soon he was being asked by the chemists at Johns Hopkins University to provide formulas and recipes for both soy milk and soy baby food.

In 1920 Carver investigated the possibility of patenting his peanut milk. An Englishman held a blanket patent for making all nut milk, including peanut milk. He asked for the stratospheric sum of $150,000 to permit its manufacture, plus a 3 percent royalty on each gallon. "My process is somewhat different from his," Carver wrote to one of the many people who wanted to manufacture the peanut milk, "and with a legal battle and expenditure of considerable money I might win, but I think that it is not worth such an effort."

On the root of the peanut are nodules full of bacteria that convert nitrogen into usable form. Since the plant enriches the soil, it was ideal for the parched fields of Alabama. In fact, one fourth of all the domestic peanuts sold in the United States came from Alabama, but the state had not one processing plant; the largest plant in the world was located in New York, although no peanuts were raised there. Moreover, half the peanuts bought in this country were not even domestic vegetables; they were grown in China and processed in Japan. In order to compete with these imports, peanut growers needed a tariff to protect what was still an infant domestic industry. The United Peanut Associations of America, a group of growers who joined together to persuade Congress to institute a tariff, were curious to see the products Carver had derived from peanuts and so invited him to speak at their convention.

Carver's experiences at that meeting give an inkling of the harshness that confronted him and all blacks when they ventured outside their usual precincts. To say that in 1920 he was "called to Montgomery to consult with peanut planters" hardly indicates the discomfort and indignities that all such consultations entailed. Until racial integration was finally forced on the South in the late 1960s, black people rarely made pleasure trips anywhere, since traveling was no pleasure for them. Cantles of hatred could be found, or stumbled into, all over the United States. Travel meant exposure to insults and petty humiliations in strange train stations, bus stations, and hotels in various cities where it was uncertain which places enforced separate facilities, which ones made no distinction between patrons, and which ones forbade entry of blacks altogether. In the South and elsewhere, there were no elevators for black people, even a prominent scientist, unless he were able to find a freight elevator up to a hotel meeting room or sports arena where lectures were often held. If he were thirsty after his climb up the stairs, he could not drink at the public fountain. The "For Colored Only" fountain was back down in the basement. By and large, there were no restroom facilities for blacks, just as there were almost no black hotels.

Carver arrived in Montgomery in broiling September, dressed in his year-round jacket and tie, and laden with heavy cases containing his samples. The temperature was as usual still in the nineties. The convention was being held at the Exchange Hotel, where the Peanut Association members were gathered in the conference room in front of electric fans. Before Carver could even bring his burden inside, the doorman stopped him. "What do you want here?" When Carver explained that he had come to see the president of the Peanut Association, the doorman directed him to City Hall, a long walk away, where he was sent from one functionary to another, carrying his heavy load all the while, until he was at last told that the peanut men had left for the hotel. He lugged his cases back to the hotel where again he was told that "niggers" were not allowed inside. Carver finally prevailed upon the doorman to send a note up to the peanut men explaining that he was barred from entering. Then he waited in the sun for the response. At last a bellhop appeared, brought him around to the back entrance of the hotel and sent him up to the meeting room on a freight elevator.

He was tired and sweaty when he finally addressed the meeting and showed them his box of treasures—bottle after bottle of products made from peanuts, including coffee, shoe polish, stains, ice cream, and many other wonders. *The Peanut Promoter* reported that the most impressive feature of the entire convention had been Carver's address. "After he had concluded they forgot that he was of the negro race and were loud in their approval . . . Dr. Carver verily won his way into the hearts of the peanut men." In the ears of his listeners, Carver was already "Doctor." The Ways and Means Committee of Congress was about to hold hearings for general tariff revision. The peanut association unanimously decided that Carver should be the one to plead the case for a peanut tariff; no one else could show so convincingly that enlarging the domestic peanut industry could benefit every section of the country.

The following January "Doctor" Carver received a telegram from the peanut growers: "Want you in Washington morning of the 20th. Depending on you to show Ways and Means Committee possibilities of the peanut." Carver thus arrived at the train station in Washington in his customary attire, made even more remarkable for his having spent the night in a coach seat in the dirty train car reserved for black passengers. The porter he tried to engage to carry his suitcase of samples brushed him off. He found his way alone to the committee hearing.

He sat through the day watching the men who addressed the committee being harassed, interrupted, and generally badgered by dissenting congressmen. These presenters had submitted summaries of their arguments and now those briefs were being attacked. Carver had not been told to submit a brief. At four o'clock, word came down that the docket should be cleared as soon as possible. He was the last of a long file of speakers and was told he would be allowed ten minutes to talk. The members, who had sat through recitations of statistics and all the other tedium of a committee hearing, were tired of information about walnuts and pecans. They were restless to be released. As Carver clambered forward awkwardly, there were titters at the sight of the scruffy Negro trying to get his large case to the front of the crowded room. "I suppose if you have plenty of peanuts and watermelon down South, you're perfectly happy?" a congressman jibed. Carver ignored him. The room fidgeted while Carver seemed to take a long part of his ten minutes merely setting up his bottles and exhibits. Finally, he addressed them in his old woman's voice. He was soon interrupted by a hostile question, just as others had been, so that his nervous answer took up three more precious minutes.

Finally, he was able to get into his talk. The peanut, he told the committee, had possibilities that science was just beginning to discover. He picked up specimens one after another as he talked. Here was crushed cake that could be used in all sorts of combinations, from flour to breakfast food. Here were peanut hulls ground into a powder that was useful for burnishing tin plate. There were chocolate covered peanuts, more breakfast cereal, another breakfast concoction made from a combination of peanuts and sweet potatoes. From time to time, for the amusement of the audience, he took a bite of one of the foods to assure those who could not taste it that it was indeed palatable. Another specimen was a livestock food consisting of ground peanuts, ground hay, and ground alfalfa; another was peanut flour suitable for candies, doughnuts, gingerbread, and the like. Seeing that his ten-minute period was up, Carver closed his exhibit case, thanked the chairman, and prepared to go back to his place at the rear of the room. The committee members, however, forgot about the ten-minute rule and demanded to know what else was in the large specimen case that Carver had not opened. "More, more," they called.

"We will give you more time, Mr. Carver," said the chairman.

Reopening his case, Carver showed them powdered milk and cream made from peanuts, instant coffee, pomade (a hair product then much in fashion for men), massage oils, and more. From time to time the listeners began to argue among themselves over some digressive question, such as the respective merits of oleo and butter and the risk of antagonizing dairymen by marketing peanut margarine. Carver would wait for the discussion to peter out and then continue with his demonstration. He explained that the peanut was a pea, not a nut, and showed the group a handful of peanut hearts that made the best pigeon food yet discovered. Another formula using peanut flour yielded a kind of ice cream. He showed them some peanut skins and explained that thirty different dyes could be made from them, ranging in color from black to yellow; the skins, moreover, yielded a substance that could be used as a medicine in place of quinine. "Here is another stock food," he continued. "It consists of a combination of peanut meal and peanut hay, together with molasses and chinaberries. The chinaberry has a great many medicinal properties . . . "

"War has taught us many things," said Carver in closing. "There is scarcely a vegetable product that we have not learned something about . . . When you go to the first chapter of Genesis, we can interpret clearly, I think, what God intended when He said 'Behold, I have given you every herb that bears seed upon the face of the earth, and every tree bearing seed. To you it shall be meat.' That is what he means about it, 'It shall be meat.'"

Someone asked, "Did you make all these products yourself?"

"Yes," he answered. "That's what a research laboratory is for."

"Haven't you done something with sweet potatoes?"

"107 products to date," he responded.

"I did not catch that statement. Will you repeat it please?" asked Mr. Garner of Texas.

"I said 107, but I haven't finished working on them yet. The peanut will beat the sweet potato by far. I have barely begun on it." He resumed pulling out products from his case. "Here is the latest thing . . . a vanishing cream that will take any perfume. And here is one for massaging infants to fatten them." Out came a bottle of ink, dehydrated milk flakes, a relish, mock oysters, curds that tasted like meat. "I have two dozen or so others," he offered, "such as wood dyes and stains, but if my time is up I had better close."

Garner ignored his offer to stop. "I understood you to say that if all other foods were destroyed, a person could live on sweet potatoes and peanuts?"

"That is correct," said Carver, "because they contain the necessary vitamins. Together they form a natural food for man and beast. There is everything here to strengthen and nourish, and keep the body alive and healthy."

By this time, Carver had talked not for ten minutes but for an hour and forty-five.

"What school did you attend?" asked the chairman.

"The last school I attended was the Agricultural College of Iowa. Secretary [of Agriculture] James Wilson was my instructor for six years."

Representatives John Carew and Garner then proposed, "I think he is entitled to the thanks of the Committee." And with that there erupted a spontaneous and prolonged burst of applause, a rare occurrence in the dour hearings. As the audience went home after the presentation, pleased and talkative, Carver lugged his materials back to the depot. He remained all night in the colored section of the station, waiting for the next train, and then sat up during the twenty-hour journey, staring out at the black void from his seat in the separated car. He knew that his exhibit had been a powerful argument for protecting the industry. The committee in fact wrote into the Fordney-McCumber Bill the highest tariff the peanut industry had ever enjoyed.

Carver's reception by the Ways and Means Committee was reported the next day in newspapers across the country. His peanut showcase was described in detail. The people who read about Carver's wonders had never bought sliced bread, orange soda, dried soup, cake mix, frozen vegetables, or Cheerios—these things were unknown. Many had never had potato chips or Jello, as these were still novelties. Aspirin was a wonder drug that had been developed during their lifetime. Nowadays, with our sugar-free sweets, soy burgers, frozen juices, instant coffee, and all the rest, it is hard to imagine the excitement Carver elicited when he held up a few bottles of cold cream, paint, and milk made from a single vegetable. But if we consider how many of our everyday conveniences, from canned dog food to ballpoint pens, did not appear in stores until Carver was an old man, we can understand why people marveled at his imagination. Food in 1920 had to be cooked, unless it could be eaten raw. Carver was presenting a glimpse of a future without slow simmering and endless meal preparation. The Peanut World called him "an incomparable genius" and "a miracle worker." "His contribution to the common fund of human knowledge in the field to which he has devoted his life is simply immeasurable."

Following the Ways and Means hearing, Carver was invited to Washington several times, for his name was spreading throughout the hives of Independence Avenue. He wrote a report on the Wilson dam and nitrogen plant at Muscle Shoals, Alabama, where he saw by-products going to waste that he thought could be used in the manufacture of nitrogen. He had long been interested in the possibilities of fixing free nitrogen from the air to use in fertilizers, dyes, munitions, and other applications. As a result of his report, the government began consulting him about the plant.

In the next years, the fickle collective mind of white people somehow assigned Carver a category by himself. He was not one of them, but neither was he identified with "the others," those who were likely to be chased like roaches when they showed themselves in public. In the U.S. in 1919, seventy-five Negroes were lynched. Several of the victims had been accused of murder, but others were attacked for such offenses as "making remarks about the Chicago race riot," "keeping company with a white woman," "making boastful remarks," "being found under a bed," "insulting a woman," "discussing a lynching," and "alleged misleading of mobs searching for another."[i] The number of blacks thus murdered was few in comparison to their population; but the arbitrariness of the attacks and their savagery kept the thousands who remained unharmed in a state of terror. It behooved Carver to face white audiences confidently, as if all Negroes were welcome to address them. Certainly no one thought of lynching him. Nevertheless, his success in the white establishment was not a phenomenon he could have expected in a society where nearly every Caucasian considered every Negro his unequal. In 1922 in Washington, D.C., Tuskegee's President Moton gave the keynote address at the dedication of the memorial to the Great Emancipator. He was treated courteously, but the black people who had traveled to Washington to hear him were shooed away from the dais and shunted to the edge of the crowd, lest their darker presence offend the 50,000 white people in attendance. How things would change in forty-one little years! In 1963, on the 100th anniversary of the Emancipation Proclamation, Martin Luther King gave his "I Have a Dream" speech on the steps of the same Lincoln Memorial, watched by an intense audience of 200,000 black and white people, standing together in every sense.

Moton was delighted with Carver's growing reputation and never failed to describe his work when raising money for Tuskegee. Moton's attention was not solely opportunistic. He was genuinely and deeply fond of Carver. Whereas the hand-painted cards that Carver sent Booker every Christmas had elicited polite thanks, Moton responded to such gestures with overflowing appreciation. Carver still found a little time for what he called his "brushwork." He importuned his friends to give him locks of their children's hair so that he could make his own brushes. "I really love to paint," he wrote to a friend. "My ambition is to paint a flower or a fruit so that you can see God in it."

He was invited everywhere with his peanut exhibit and was lodged, usually, with a black family. Whether in Carolina or California, Carver would follow the mother around the house as she did her chores, discussing gardening or cooking, holding murmured conversations with the houseplants, and making himself quite at home. Local journalists noted that the peanut exhibit he had brought drew more interest than any other feature of the fair or exposition where it appeared. "Carver himself attracted almost as much attention as the one hundred or more products he has discovered in the peanut," they would write, eager to expand on his derelict appearance and the dismay it invariably evoked. Bemused, Carver would remark, "If I had known they wanted new suits, I could have mailed them some. I have suitcases full of them."

First the Royal Society recognition, then his appearances before Congress, and then, in 1922 in Kansas City, Missouri, Carver received the Spingarn Medal, awarded yearly to an American Negro "who shall have made the highest achievement during the preceding year or years in any honorable field of human endeavor." With each Spingarn Medal, white people were reminded of what blacks could accomplish. If they believed in the genetic inferiority of black people, as most did, the Spingarn Medal annually obliged them to make room in their minds for one more exception. In fact, the white people in Tuskegee were the ones most eager to see the medal, according to Carver. "I must confess," he wrote to Major J. E. Spingarn, "that I do not feel worthy of such a distinction. However, I shall endeavor, with all that is within me and as fast as the great Creator gives me might, to at least make my friends have no regret that it came this way." It is a curious fact that in 1921 and 1922 Carver was increasingly being invited to speak before white organizations in the South at the same time that violence against blacks was sharply rising. Even when he appeared at black schools and colleges, whites attended in increasing numbers, and the information from his talks rippled out to the white community. White people hardly ever went into black schools to attend events—it was almost unheard of. Martin Menafee wrote to him from the Voorhees Institute in South Carolina, "I was in Bamberg this morning and I met a few white people there who were just carried away with your address here. The Mayor of the town said that you were a miracle and that he enjoyed every moment he was here. You have taken things by storm here."

There were storms of a different sort roiling Tuskegee. A veterans' hospital for black soldiers who were returning from the war had been established in 1923 on ground donated by the Institute. When it was learned that Negro physicians and nurses were to be installed there, the white people of Tuskegee angrily objected. The driving force behind the hospital had been Carver's old friend and physician, Dr. J. A. Kenney, who insisted that everyone hired by the hospital, from doctors to grounds keepers, should be black. It was rumored that the Ku Klux Klan planned to lure Kenney into the country on a sick call and then lynch him. The Klan did burn a cross on Kenney's lawn—a warning not to be taken lightly—and planned a protest demonstration on the Tuskegee campus. Kenney left town at once with his family and went to Newark, where he subsequently enjoyed an illustrious career. The one black person in a managerial position at the hospital prudently departed from Tuskegee. President Moton and Carver, the most prominent individuals at the Institute, were both advised to leave, although no specific threats were made against them. They remained on the campus. The N.A.A.C.P. asked President Warren G. Harding to send federal troops to protect the Institute and especially the hospital, with its fifteen black patients and white staff. In the end, Moton yielded to the town's pressure, agreeing that the hospital would be staffed by white doctors and nurses, assisted by black orderlies. Seven hundred masked Klansmen then paraded through the campus without incident, while the terrified students and staff huddled inside their locked dormitories and houses.

In a report to Moton, Carver described the work of the experiment station for 1923, that is to say, his work. His mail had brought the usual problems and questions, and he had done experiments of several years with grasses and insecticides. He had formulated a compound he called "Mellosoil" to correct the acidity of the soil in Macon County. Carver was especially proud of Mellosoil. Whereas he was modest about his own abilities, he endowed each new creation with a life of its own and talked about it like a father describing his versatile child. But he gave away all his children, including the formula for Mellosoil, to anyone who asked for them.

A nd so Carver, too busy by the 1920s to remain depressed, ascended to the postwar "normalcy" that President Harding urged everyone to enjoy. What was normal for George Carver?

George and his brother Jim, ages about nineteen and twenty-one, respectively, before George's growth spurt.

Dimensions of the Carver cabin where George grew up.
Courtesy George Washington Carver Monument Archives.

Fort Scott, Kansas, 1886.
Courtesy Fort Scott National Historic Site.

Carver with one of his paintings.

Courtesy Iowa State University.

Booker T. Washington.

Courtesy Library of Congress.

Dining hall at Tuskegee decorated for the holidays.

Courtesy Library of Congress.

Carver teaching a class at Tuskegee.

Courtesy the Tuskegee University Archives, Tuskegee University.

Mrs. Warren Logan

Adella Hunt Logan.

Carver.

Moses Carver in old age.

Courtesy George Washington Carver Monument Archives.

Carver with specimens and a soil sample.

Courtesy Library of Congress.

Lucy Cherry Crisp.

Courtesy East Carolina
Manuscript Collection, J. Y.
Joyner Library, East Carolina
University, Greenville, N.C.

Carver and Jim Hardwick.

Courtesy East Carolina Manuscript Collection, J. Y. Joyner Library,
East Carolina University, Greenville, N.C.

Carver working with plants in his lab.

Courtesy George Washington Carver Monument Archives.

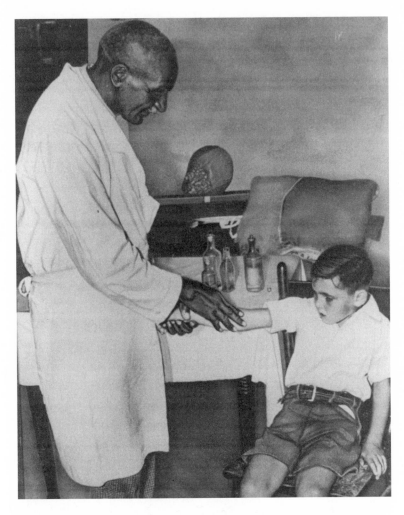

Carver with a young patient.

Courtesy the Tuskegee University Archives, Tuskegee University.

Carver with Henry Ford.

Courtesy George Washington Carver Monument Archives.

Carver with assistant Austin Curtis.

Courtesy the Tuskegee University Archives, Tuskegee University.

Carver with biographer Rackham Holt.

Courtesy the Tuskegee University Archives, Tuskegee University.

Lucy Cherry Crisp with her bust of Carver.

Courtesy East Carolina Manuscript Collection, J. Y. Joyner Library,
East Carolina University, Greenville, N.C.

Carver and Franklin Delano Roosevelt.

Courtesy Alabama Department of Archives and History, Montgomery, Alabama.

Carver's funeral.

Courtesy the Tuskegee University Archives, Tuskegee University.

11

TRYING TO BE SERIOUS

Nearly all the recollections of Carver describe an aged man, friendly when you got to know him but quiet and a little withdrawn among strangers. Of course he was remembered as old. Reminiscences of Carver were not formally gathered until the years 2001 to 2005. The people being interviewed were in some cases over a hundred years old themselves, trying to remember a man they had known as teenagers, a man who was indeed quite moldy by the time they met him. Carver himself had not been approached by biographers until he was well past middle age, so that their books, too, leave the impression that all his life he was toothless, stooped over, and shuffling. As for his aloofness, it was only after he had become a celebrity that people were called upon to describe him. They remembered a man who, whether they realized it or not, was compelled to protect himself from the hordes who stopped him on the campus, insisting on a word, or who knocked on his door simply to see if he were as unkempt as they had heard, or who telephoned him begging for a personal conference to discuss their financial problems. Fame can make anybody antisocial.

But it is true, nevertheless, that Carver always acted a bit like an old man even while he was doing the work of six strong youths. He was one of those people who can't wait to be elderly. At the time of Adella's suicide, Carver was around fifty-two but already thought of himself as getting on in years. As early as 1919 he wrote to a doctor friend that he was afraid he might die soon with so much of his work unfinished. In 1928, he remarked that he would soon be leaving the world. He was obliged to keep renewing his life's visa until 1943, when he actually did make his long-planned departure. Meanwhile, he read newspapers avidly but remained steadfastly behind the times. Thirty-five years after telephones were in common use, he was still writing "phone" in quotation marks, as if it were a novel invention and a novel abbreviation with which he was uneasy. He believed that printed typewritten letters were impersonal and impolite and insisted on writing to friends in longhand until he wore out his joints and was forced to resort to the typewriter that was finally purchased for him. As he made his way year after year into the twentieth century, his manners remained those of a nineteenth-century gentleman. Nothing on earth could make him address a friend, even a child, by his first name. And no one dared call him "George," save for two exceptions: Henry A. Wallace, the vice president, who took the unwelcome liberty,* and former students writing in jest. Even when he was young, a mere stripling of forty, he had lodged a prissy complaint in an executive council meeting: "The matter of teachers calling each other by their given names—such as 'Hetty,' 'John,' 'Bill,' etc., should be corrected . . . Also, their addressing each other thus: 'Hello! How are you?' etc." He mellowed later on, though. By the time he was sixty, students and children alike called him not Professor but "Fess," and he responded.

For the rest, he was a saint, old-fashioned by half a century, but still a saint, a man who loved everyone and lived to help them. "It's not enough that you climb the mountain," he said. "You need to throw the rope over and pull someone else over that mountain." He never took a step toward the summit without looking behind him. He gave credit to God for all of his accomplishments or benign impulses and took the blame himself for all of his failures. "My little job," he wrote, "is to interpret God as He speaks to us through the things He has created. This I am endeavoring to do as fast as He gives me light and strength."

But like many saints, he could be exasperating to live with. Carver was a collector and hoarder all his life. For some of the forty-seven years he lived at Tuskegee, his lodging consisted of two rooms in Porter Hall. Later on, he was given an apartment in Rockefeller Hall, and then a similar one in Dorothy Hall, consisting of a living room, bedroom, kitchenette, and bathroom. Every cubic centimeter of his narrow living space was crammed—with specimens he found on his daily morning explorations, with junk he picked up and thought he might find a use for, with mementoes and gifts that were sent to him. After 1909 he had an office and a laboratory, though no equipment. Those rooms, too, became the repository for mounds of what most people would consider trash. "There were stacks and stacks of things," one person recalled, "maybe a

*Not to be confused with Henry C. Wallace, father of the vice president and Carver's former teacher.

little portrait he had started in one corner and some jars in another corner of fruit he was pickling or maybe an embalmed specimen of an embryo of a pig or chicken or something." Before Booker's death, J. H. sent a memo to Carver complaining that his rooms were dirty. Carver was under heavy fire just then from all sides, since it was an intense period of the war between Carver and the J. H. faction. Carver replied with a rare show of irritation, "If my rooms are dirty it's because I don't have any help [on the farm] and no time to clean them." Early on, his messiness had led to comments that he was secretive. People who came to his door were not usually invited in. All unexpected visitors are unwelcome to those who are ashamed of their housekeeping—certainly no sinister mystery there. Insofar as it was J. H.'s business (or ours) to inquire into his domestic habits, Carver's nest was undoubtedly squalid.

However disordered his surroundings may have been, no one ever said that George Carver himself was dirty. In commenting on his notorious shabbiness, his contemporaries were careful to say that he was well shaven and very fastidious in his person—in fact, a stickler for cleanliness. "If you don't have all of the fine shirts and clothes," he told students, "you can take a shirt and wash it and hang it up to dry and then wear it the next day. You might not look like you just stepped out of the pages of *Esquire*, but whatever it is you have to wear, if you can wash it and iron it, you can come clean the next day." It should be noted that once Carver graduated from being a laundryman to being a professor, he never again ironed anything, but he did wash his shirts and protected them while working in his lab with an old, sagging, more or less white apron made from a flour sack. "He was going to be clean," said one of his former students, "but he didn't guarantee he was going to be pressed." "He could have been invisible," noted another; "it wouldn't have mattered to him." At some point during his forty-odd years at Tuskegee, the women teachers he met in the dining hall finally persuaded him to give up his discolored celluloid collar and buy a regular shirt with the collar attached. It was harder to get him to surrender his old cravat and wear a more up-to-date four-in-hand—that is, a modern tie. A fresh flower or plant could always be found in the thready buttonhole of his lapel. But we have to wonder. How hygienic can a person be underneath a coat that has not been cleaned for decades, a coat which, after the first twenty years of daily use, probably could not have withstood immersion in any sort of cleaning compound?

He was different from other people but eminently sane. His idiosyncrasies were harmless—his nearly obsessive habit of dating every scrap of paper that came under his eyes, for example, and his passion for knowing the precise name of every natural specimen that he encountered. For an old man, as he seems to have been most of his life, he was rarely cranky, except when people tried to chat about the weather. "If you don't have anything better to talk about, don't waste my time. The weather is God's business. There's nothing you and I can do about it, so let's not discuss it."

His punctuality *was* a nuisance in his later years, when people were clamoring for his time. If he had an engagement with someone who turned up a few minutes late, he would say, "Sorry you missed your appointment." Normally, Carver took breakfast at six a.m., before the cafeteria line was set up; consequently, a girl was assigned to serve him in the dining hall. Adele Mc-Queen, who was his regular server when she was a twenty-year-old student, recalled that he would go out on the porch of the cafeteria and wait for her to appear. "You're late," he'd say (regardless of what time she came) and spank her as she went up the steps. It was a routine game between them, followed by some funny little anecdote that Carver always had ready. Adele served Carver three times a day for about two years, a task she described as "a joy." Every Friday night he gave her a quarter to buy something for herself. Another student waitress remembered, "He wouldn't just let you put the tray down and say good morning and leave. He sat you down and talked to you—pearls of wisdom on how to live, how to get along. And his biggest thing was that the color of your skin wasn't a crutch or something you could fall back on . . . It wasn't anything to hold you back."

"When you are married, don't let everybody into your business," he advised. "That's between you and your mate. What works in one household might not work in your household . . . Keep your business to yourself, and that means parents and everybody else." Some cafeteria workers remembered Carver being a lot of trouble. "Coffee was the biggest problem," one recalled, because it had to be boiling in the cup when she got it to the table. If it wasn't bubbling, she had to go back. "He liked strong, black coffee, boiling hot. He'd drink it from a spoon while it was so hot."

In his advanced years and during periods of sickness, his supper was brought to him in his room at six in the evening. If the meal arrived while the campus bells were still tolling the hour, Carver thanked the porter and ate heartily. If she arrived after the clock had stopped tolling, he would greet her as usual, "How are you, little girl?" or some such pleasantry. But she would come back later to find that he had not touched the plate. Either he prepared something for himself from his own provisions or he went hungry, but he simply "lost his appetite" if the food arrived even twenty seconds late. Only one food-bringer remembered being scolded, however—a neighbor whose mother sent her with a meal for Carver. The little girl was about to set the heavy tray on top of the huge Bible in his apartment—the Bible given him by Mariah Watkins. "Oh Child, Child no! Don't do that! Don't ever set anything on the Bible," he said. That little girl eventually married the son of Dr. Kenney, the veteran campaigner for clean privies and an integrated hospital staff at Tuskegee.

Cooking was part of Carver's work as he tried to find novel uses for common crops. Thus, when he had to consume his experiments, he ate some peculiar things—perhaps all saints do. He thought nothing of making lunch with clover tops, dandelion, wild lettuce, chicory, rabbit tobacco, alfalfa, thistles, bedstraw, pepper grass, wild geranium, purslane, hawkweed, Flora's paintbrush, watercress, shepherd's purse, or chickweed. Neolithic man had survived on whatever he could find growing around him before the domestication of plants. Why shouldn't he? For a joke he would offer to make a dandelion sandwich for a child, knowing that the youngster would vanish at once on some pretext. He made pies from curled dock and used sour grass or sheep sorrel to make confections. In place of asparagus tips, he ate pokeweed and swamp milkweed, along with evening primrose and lamb's quarters, which Carver insisted had medicinal value and in fact was later discovered to be rich in Vitamin A. Students were often the unwilling testers of his concoctions. He'd put something on a little piece of cracker and say, "Son, I just made this today. How does it taste?"

"Sometimes it would taste like hell," recalled one trapped taster, "but I'd still tell him it was pretty good." Another student whose father worked at Tuskegee remembered having Carver to dinner at their house. He never failed to bring a bag of mushrooms he had gathered. Her mother would thank him graciously and set them aside, never to be eaten, since she didn't trust Carver's assurance that mushrooms were really human food. Carver could look at food and without tasting it determine that it lacked salt or was too salty, a talent that impressed Mr. Lomax, an instructor in the food division at Tuskegee who used to consult with Carver about recipes. (It wasn't so hard. Salt preserves the bright color of vegetables.)

He was a lighthearted saint, serious about things that were important and playful about everything else. "He had a twinkle in his eye that you couldn't miss," said a former student. One of his young friends asked if he thought boxing was permissible. "I think if you want to box or attend bouts it would be all right," Carver answered. "God meant that we should play and have a real good time and enjoy the things He has so wonderfully created."

Fond anecdotes abound. One describes the Bible study meeting where he told the story of Sodom and Gomorrah, at the same time fiddling with some articles on the table. The talk was drawing to a close; it was time to leave. "These wicked cities," Carver asked, "what became of them?" Suddenly, flames, fumes, and fury exploded on the table in front of him and everybody scattered, fleeing from "God's wrath." Carver had created a harmless explosion.

In Rockefeller Hall, Carver got an unlucky room assignment under the well-used piano in the boys' dormitory. He had to request a different apartment. "Dr. Moton, I am not complaining about the piano or its use. Young people are going to play and they should and will play anything and everything, night, day, Sunday and every time they get a chance, which when properly directed is perfectly permissible. The piano was put there for them to use, and they dance and everything over my head." That didn't keep him from readily complying when the girls asked him to donate a piano to their own dorm.

Carver's students paid him the highest compliment a young person can pay to a superior—they teased him. On their side, the bantering often mentioned spanking—either punishment they claimed to deserve for some venial transgression or chastisement they wanted to administer to him for not writing or being too modest, etc. "My Dear Prof, I know, yes, I know that you have laid me to the dogs and that you would like to lay the dogs (dogwood) to me, but you know I am married now and you cannot whip a married man. SEE!!!" Nobody in that innocent time saw anything unsettling about such raillery; even Carver's businessmen friends joked with him in that way. The president of the Tom Huston Company threatened to spank Carver for saying that people overestimated him. Several dozen white youths became friends with him after he lectured at their colleges. They were all full of play. "You forgot to put my street address on your letter of the 15th," wrote Wilson Newman, "but I got it all right this morning. The postman got the address off the police docket after I was arrested in my development. There you laugh! And you were the cause." After admonishing Carver for imaginary faults, he closed, "It hurts me to say these hard things to you; but they are for your own good."

Carver occasionally wrote letters concerned solely with religion, but these were usually letters of condolence, not conversation. Up until the 1930s, he mentioned God fairly often but rarely Jesus, the preferred idol of Protestant evangelicals. People speculated as to whether it was mere whimsy or more serious mysticism that inspired Carver to talk to plants. Everyone who described him, without exception, mentioned three things about Carver: his dreadful clothes; his high, squeaky voice; and his habit of chatting with flowers. At Tuskegee, new students would see an old man walking around the campus, looking intensely at the bushes, and they would think, "Who is this guy? Is he one of the gardeners here?" They were surprised when they found out he was *the* Professor Carver and astonished when they observed him whispering. If they approached him, he would tell them that he was communing with the flowers, that the spirit of God lived in them. He scared them the first time or so they heard him talk that way, but then they relaxed and wanted to hear more about this dialogue.

Actually, it was not only flowers. Carver talked to birds (loudly, in the early morning), butterflies, cattle, toadstools, stars, and rivers, in the same way that people make small talk with their pet dogs and cats. He believed that natural phenomena were reflections of the Creator. Carver was not a pantheist. God does not reside in flowers or animals, no more than an architect lives in all the houses he designs; but by observing the way the joists fit together, by knowing the foundations that underlay the floors, you could better understand the mind of the creator. If animals and plants were expressions of the divine—God "talking out loud"—then communicating with them could bring one closer to God. "Cows talk," said Carver. "Everybody talks."

He was on confidential terms with all the hundreds of tiny weeds and blossoms on roadsides and pond edges, plants that are part of our everyday lives but that we pass without noticing. He personalized every living or eroding thing, including rocks, which were ever changing, if not alive. He called things by their names. From the time that he was a frustrated child who had to resort to making up names for his flowers, he longed to know the history and background of every plant—where was its native home, who named it, how had it been interbred with some other plant, who were the other members of its family. Just as with a person, a plant, however familiar it is and however often you encounter it, is still a stranger until you know its name. Carver was a walking catalogue of biological taxonomy and information, not only about plants but about all of natural history. He was on first-name and nickname terms with everything around him and was therefore always among friends. He wanted fervently to penetrate the mysteries of disease, weather, animal behavior, planetary motion, and all the rest. It was as if, by murmuring courteously to clouds and spiders, he could induce them to yield him their secrets.

What separated Carver from normal people was not his collection of dotty habits—lots of people have cute quirks—but something more profound: his boundless and promiscuous kindness. Austin Curtis, Carver's last assistant, described him perfectly: "He was kindness itself."

Anyone who reads his enormous correspondence cannot fail to see that his thoughts were always centered on the other person, tendering comfort or encouragement. To the Milhollands, he wrote mainly about amaryllis gardening, Mr. Milholland's predilection, and the items he was turning out on his potter's wheel, which interested Mrs. Milholland. To the Rosses, his old friends in Kansas, he wrote about Dr. Ross's experiments and Mrs. Ross's cooking—and hardly a word about flowers. He wrote about astronomy to Helen Chisholm, his old companion in stargazing. To the coterie of students he met through the Y.M.C.A., he gave counsel as to how they could achieve spirituality. When he wrote of himself, it was always in terms of God's blessings or his own failings: "God has indeed dealt very generously with me. He has revealed and made it possible for me to do so many interestingly strange things. Pray for me that I may be strong and not fall by the wayside." The lowliest and meanest individuals were worthy of solicitude; the more helpless they were, the more he cared about them, for they, too, were expressions of the genius of God. To a primary class in Philadelphia who sent him a hand-decorated candy Easter egg, he responded with 500 words explaining his delight with every detail, from "the dear little sprays of lily-of-the-valley" to "the charming little clusters of forget-me-nots" which signaled "that I occupy your thoughts and am not forgotten." People who met him when they were children never forgot his gentleness. "Children didn't want to misbehave in front of him." Carver spoke to them as if they were adults. He showed them fascinating objects, such as pieces of fallen stars and petrified wood and the tooth of a mastodon. If children were making noise outside his lab, he would go and talk to them pleasantly, bringing along some peanuts. "He'd walk across the campus," recalled a friend, "and there'd be a string of kids following him on the way to the Agriculture Building."

His goodness to his students was legendary. "I can never begin to tell you what your friendship meant to me when at Tuskegee," wrote a former pupil, a mother of five. "You understood us so well. We could be ourselves in your presence. Life was better for being in your midst." The upper-middle-class boys Carver met through his interracial work were equally grateful. "I would have missed many of life's finest lessons and much of its beauty if I had never met you," wrote a young white man who, like many others, named his son after Carver. An ex-student observed, "He found a world within himself that superseded our existence here. He taught students to be honest and honorable."

C arver put almost all of his pay in savings accounts in Iowa and Tuskegee; the only time he wrote checks was to lend money. Before he had been at Tuskegee ten years, the Carver Savings and Loan operation was an established informal institution. In addition, he made plenty of donations—to found a boys' camp, for example, or for scholarships for white students at the University of Georgia. When blacks criticized him for that particular generosity, he replied, "Plenty of white people give donations so that black children can go to school. Why shouldn't I do something for a white student?" In later years he approved of the idea of admitting white students to Tuskegee. On Christmas, Carver remembered all his ever-lengthening list of godchildren and namesakes with annual checks. He loved giving presents to children and invariably responded to their thank-you notes: "Dear Prof. Carver, I do thank you so much for the knif you sent me you don't know how I appreciated it. I like it fin. I injoy being with you when you were up here. I will need my knife when I start to School To sharpened my pencle and file my fingernails. Your little Frien,

Ernest Blanks." Carver's kindliness grew in part from his own relentless striving to become what he thought God wanted him to be. "I trust you will pray for me that I may get rid of all my littleness," he would often write. "I should have been a better man."

By 1925, Carver was receiving some forty letters a day, many from former students who addressed him as "My dear Father," "Daddy," "My dearest Dad," "Old Man," "Old Boy," "Young Man," and "Fess." They signed themselves "Your son," "Your daughter," "Your boy," "Your godchild," very frequently "Your bad boy," and in later years, "Your grandchild." One girl addressed him as "My dear Georgie Porgie." Cricket, one of Carver's cheekiest former students, addressed him as "Dearie." He had called lots of students "Dearie," and many of them teased him about it. Cricket was one of the few Tuskegee alumnae who was not reverent toward the late Booker. She deplored what she judged was his passivity in the face of violence toward blacks. She was putting her faith in Du Bois, the man of action. As various cultural opportunities opened to them, the young people sought Carver's opinions on music, art, literature, and politics, since he was knowledgeable about all the arts and letters. They wrote of their love for him and described how he had taught them to take life seriously. They revealed intensely personal details—discussions of relatives who were being blackmailed, were involved in adulterous affairs, had fallen victim to alcoholism. They asked for love advice, which Carver, from his vast inexperience, tried to provide, along with prayers and sympathy. Charles Hyne gave a long explanation of why he didn't try to kiss a girl and asked Carver if he had done the right thing. Later on, when he was engaged to the young lady, he asked Carver's advice about how to handle his fiancée's excessive dependence and what to do about his sister, who was rude to her. Carver answered each letter at once, long and thoughtfully, in his large, fine hand. When Carver delayed answering for as long as a week, his friends wrote again to find out if he were well.

And they had enormous fun with him. A letter from "Your Boy," Samuel Richardson, was typical: "Hello, Prof., You see I'm pretty near to being a scientist myself and as I have always had a hankering for being familiar with great folks, I take this liberty in addressing you. Look out! I'll be calling you 'George' first thing you know." Wilson Newman, whom Carver had met while on a tour of white colleges, wrote that he missed Carver so much, he was going to show up in Tuskegee on Thanksgiving Day. He had wanted a train that arrived at midnight, so that he could see Carver arrive at the station, looking "stunning" in his nightie, but since the only train to Cheraw arrived in the late afternoon, he would nevertheless do his best, he wrote, to disturb Carver's holiday dinner. Jack Boyd sent him pages of corny farm humor. In those days, there was no end of jokes about Sears, Roebuck: the farmer tries to order "Privy Paper" and is directed to the company catalogue with its order blank for toilet paper. "Hell," the farmer writes back, "if I had a Sears Roebuck catalogue, I wouldn't need Privy Paper."

Carver's young correspondents brought the world to him at Tuskegee. During the Great War, as it was called, one wounded former student had commented that 96 percent of his fellow patients in the hospital were infected with venereal disease. A young Chinese American friend, a whole-hearted believer in Chiang Kai-shek, had joined the Kuomintang and Chiang's nationalist army. He wrote Carver long, articulate letters describing conditions in Nanking as the Nationalists tried to reunify the country and suppress the Communists. One boy who had left home was thrilled with his job as a student waiter at the University of Illinois because he was allowed to eat on the premises. "There is not a place around here where Colored can eat that really serves anything worthwhile—it means everything to a student, as you know, to get his board." Another in Chicago was fearful because he was passing as a white student in the Institute of the Radio Corporation of America, the dissimulation being necessary to gain admittance to a school of distinction. Quite a few felt that the only way to escape menial labor was to go into business of some sort—an idea that was pervasive in the white world as well—and so asked for help or guidance. One ex-student trustingly sent Carver his precious formula for growing hair on bald heads and pleaded for his endorsement. People who met Carver by chance wrote to him afterward to say that their lives were changed by the encounter. One man had determined to kill himself when he happened to chat with Carver outside a venue where the scientist was giving a talk. He left Carver with a renewed sense of the wondrousness of the world and life.

The young white people who wrote to Carver often attended schools such as Columbia and Cornell. They wrote of lectures and concerts they attended—seeing Reinhold Niebuhr preach or hearing a concert by Ignace Paderewski, the greatest living pianist. The black youngsters wrote about joblessness, by and large, and the frustration of trying to get back into school. They pleaded for Carver's help in locating scholarships. Ernest Frei, working as an elevator operator at night and attending the University of Chicago by day, fantasized about going into the woods and reading for a whole day. Even if these youths could have afforded tickets to cultural events, in most places they would not have been admitted. Tuskegee did what it could to expose its students to the arts. Carver wrote of hearing a recording of Roxy and his Gang. The great operatic contralto Ernestine Schumann-Heink volunteered to sing in Tuskegee's chapel; Carver wrote her a fervid letter of thanks.

In the 1920s, while the country as a whole was prospering, Carver's people were left behind in an agricultural depression that would lead to the industrial depression of the 1930s. For blacks, America in the 1920s was not roaring but moaning with pervasive unemployment in the larger northern cities where they had scattered to seek their fortune. On farms, it was a period of outright desperation. Many of those who addressed him as "My dear Father" turned to him when they needed money and were never refused—in 1925, for example, a typical year, he sent out some thirty checks in amounts ranging from ten to two hundred dollars. When no money was requested, but Carver knew there was need, he enclosed a book of stamps. The loans were generally made to working men with families, such as "Your boy, Greg Jones," who was a waiter in Chicago, trying to attend junior high school at night. One friend asked Carver to help his impoverished mother; Carver did and received a touching letter, the first one that the barely literate woman had ever penned. Always, there were letters from people trying to return to school but unable to pay tuition and support their families, even with night jobs. Stephen Brown was a young man with four children, two of them deaf; his mother had planned to finance his return to school, but her savings were wiped out by a fire and the death of his father.

After Carver was a national figure, his old students continued to tease him as if he were still their own cherished eccentric. "My dear friend," wrote a former student. "I miss you very much and before I left I did not get a chance to tell you goodbye and get my final beating." The "bad boy" had become chairman of a high school biology department and requested a photo of Carver to put up in his school. Over and over, Carver thanked his admirers but then said there was "only one discouraging thing in your whole letter, and that is your estimate of me, which continues to be 75% too high." It was his stock response to praise.

* * *

With every year, the pile of mail grew, and Carver complained that he never expected to see the wood on his desk again. To follow Carver in the 1920s is to see what it is like to become famous in the space of about ten years. His every step into the white world was reported in newspapers—never mind that those steps entailed inconvenience, discomfort, insults serious and petty, and courage. After each of his talks came the invariable report that the audience had been surprised and delighted by the dignified colored gentleman, as if Carver and his unwieldy trunk of magic elixirs had been brought to the gathering in a golden coach and not in an airless, smelly, steam pumpkin that was his segregated transport any time he left Alabama; as if, on arriving, he had been attended by friendly welcoming committees and alert footmen, and not required to carry his own gear through back doors reserved for kitchen deliveries and the disposal of garbage.

The newspaper reports of his appearances prompted more invitations to speak. By the middle of the decade, he had been featured in *Popular Science, Collier's, Literary Digest,* and *Time.* A journalist imprisoned in Michigan even wrote about him. Magazines were eager for contributions from Carver "on any subject you care to write about." He was in any number of educational films and in a movie documentary series called *Strange As It Seems* that was distributed to 6,000 theaters. In 1928 he was awarded that bracing academic handshake, an honorary doctorate from his alma mater, Simpson College. The degree he most coveted, however, from Iowa State College, was not forthcoming.

Everyone who wrote about him, whether in a national magazine or a four-page weekly newspaper, received a warm acknowledgement if Carver learned of the article: "I wish to thank you more than my words can express for the clipping you so kindly sent me. It certainly places a great responsibility upon me to try to live up to the many generous things you have said about the work that I am trying to do." He spent hours each week responding to publicity. Albert Einstein, in a lecture at the University of California, named Carver second among the ten greatest living scientists. One of Carver's former students was present and reported that, though there were "no more than a dozen colored people in the crowd of 2,000," the audience spontaneously applauded Carver's name. "I think it was mighty fine of the white people to raise such a fuss when your name was called," wrote the friend. Einstein repeated the accolade on the occasion of Carver's death.

Carver's life was now measured and marked by his travels, which spread his reputation although, curiously, he had to wait for years to see the one place he wanted to visit: Carlsbad Caverns in New Mexico. Northern companies began converging on him with business propositions and requests for consultations. The manufacturer of Oh Henry! candy bars had a problem with wormy peanuts finding their way into the candy. "I gather what you don't know about the peanut isn't worth knowing," remarked the company's chemist. The National Pecan Growers Exchange in Albany, Georgia, sent him some pecans and asked for a chemical analysis that would help them decide whether to market a fertilizer made from pecans. Fair enough. These were the kinds of services and information Carver's experiment station provided for countless individuals and merchants. But many businesses were clearly out to suction as much free information from him as possible. Ralston Purina executives wanted to know the precise ingredients that went into Carver's pecan breakfast food. Moreover, in hopes of manufacturing a pecan butter that might rival peanut butter, they sent Carver some pecan meats which "if you will be kind enough and disposed to do it, we will thank you to make into butter for us and will thank you further to state the ingredients you would use to put into combination with pecans." Sunmaid Raisin Company of London, England, and many others were not abashed to ask outright for his formulas. Carver did not think he was being exploited by these requests and, on the contrary, assured the companies that he would be delighted to assist them in developing their products. Black educational institutions proposed that he donate his formulas so that they might market his products and profit from them. By the mid-1920s, manufacturers were regularly asking him to solve problems with dyes and ceramics, as well as food derivatives. Carver made a list for President Moton of "a very, very few" of the larger companies he was serving: Planters Nut and Chocolate Co, Suffolk, Virginia; H. S. Whiteside Company, London, England; and twenty-one others. With individuals Carver was completely open handed, sending one his formula for a hair-growing solution based on ox bone marrow, to another an anti-itch salve. "Will you kindly tell me something that I can use on my plants to make them grow thrifty and bloom?" was a constant request. He had nothing on hand to send a young man who was determined to earn some money and asked Carver to kindly provide him with a formula for straightening kinky hair. People who couldn't find jobs often asked Carver if he had some leftover idea they could develop to make a few dollars.

Though Carver was by this time friendly with many captains of industry, he remained at heart a radical—a pacifist during war, a sympathizer with socialism during the business craze, and an independent thinker at all times. When the Llano communistic settlement in the unlikely location of Newllano, Louisiana, requested some nutritional menus for their cafeteria, Carver sent a very detailed table of seventy-five foods, giving an analysis of their water, protein, fat, carbohydrate, ash, and caloric value—along with his detailed menus. He had a soft spot for the Llano radicals because their colony was completely desegregated. "Dear Comrade," wrote their leader, George Pickett, "Quite a bit of publicity has recently been in the newspaper against aluminum ware as unfit to be used in preparing foods. Do you know whether this is just capitalistic propaganda to cause the people to purchase other kinds of cooking ware, or is it true that aluminum ware does throw off certain properties that are injurious to the human system?" Pickett closed by asking Carver please not to stop communicating with him. He had reason to fear that Carver might shun him. At the time, Communists who assembled for any reason were routinely set upon by mobs and beaten up by police, as if they were Negroes. Carver wrote back that he had not seen any authoritative studies on the aluminum question. He reassured Pickett: "To know you and keep in touch with you to me has been a very great pleasure and profit." He felt "grateful to you for all you are doing for my people."

From his magic cap Carver was steadily pulling out beauty aids with commercial potential derived from peanuts and other vegetables. He made up various types of insulating boards from peanut shells. But though he never entirely set aside research on the peanut, his mind was taken up more and more during these years with formulating paints and stains. Carver had already learned how to make house paint from waste crankcase oil. Commercial paint was selling for two dollars a gallon—serious money for farmers or any middle-class home improver. Now Carver created an array of clay-based exterior paints that could be sold for a fraction of that price and lasted fifteen years. Some years earlier he had worked out a process to make the pigment "Prussian Blue." He followed it with "Egyptian Blue," so named because it seemed to duplicate the brilliance and durability of the ancient blue that had lasted in the desert for thousands of years. Eventually he would develop an "Egyptian Purple" as well, by putting red clay through six successive oxidizing operations. The chief chemist of the Tom Huston peanut company marveled that for ten years Carver's Egyptian Blue had held up on a church without the slightest sign of drying, cracking, or losing its splendid sheen. It was "70 times richer than any other blue" and derived from a raw material—clay—that was abundant. Carver's imagination was stimulated by companies that turned to him for information. If Alabama clay could yield fine paint, a Baltimore manufacturer wanted to know, what about Florida? Would a paint factory in Tallahassee be a wise investment? That started Carver thinking, and the next week he was happily analyzing dozens of Florida clay samples.

There seems never to have been a period when Carver worked on just one product. "I am at this time being besieged from two sources," he wrote a friend, "by the Tubize Artificial Silk Company for vegetable dyes, and the citrus fruit growers." The citrus growers had the notion that Carver, if pestered, would do for orange peels what he had done for peanuts. Tubize of New York got looms of free research out of Carver. First the company asked him to make plant dyes for synthetics. Within a few months, Carver found eighty different plants that yielded permanent cloth dyes. Then they wondered if he would kindly perfect the dyeing process so that the color was uniform.

Naturally, he gave away formulas, not to mention ideas, that were patentable: a compound of mineral water; a formula for dyes made from the northern persimmon; some products he developed from the palmetto root—three grades of insulating board and a rich, black paint. Patent applications required the services of a patent attorney; they ran to thirty or more paragraphs and had to be carefully worded so as to allow many processes to be integrated and granted exclusivity under one grant. Carver believed that the attorney and patent fees could run to $2,000 each; a few patents would have wiped out his life's savings—and he didn't like to be bothered with them anyway. Yet if he did not attach his name to his discoveries, they would be patented and absorbed by white-owned companies with no recognition of the contribution made by his race. Therefore, when a group of local businessmen proposed forming a company that would apply for patents in his name and investigate any existing patents, Carver finally gave in. He hoped that at least he would be relieved of the incessant requests from companies for samples of face powder or wall paints or food recipes. He could simply refer them to the company attorney.

Under the impetus of E. W. Thompson, the Carver Products Company was formed in 1923. It was to begin manufacturing and marketing paints, stains, and cosmetics made from clay according to Carver's formulas, and was expected to extend its list of products later on. Carver was to receive 10 percent of any net profits. The company bought 150 acres of land which would supply the clay for the paints, and planned to build a paint plant. On his side, Carver developed a number of umbers and siennas; ochres, including yellows and pinks; thirty-five shades of wood stains, from baby pink to moss green; creosote stains; and cold water paints that were richer and more durable than the wall finishes then available—all derived from Alabama clay. The paints and stains, Carver hoped, might be what he had been seeking for years, an alternative to cotton agriculture. It was no wonder businessmen wanted a chance to market them. At the same time Carver was still creating a dazzling array of other products from fruits and vegetables.

At first Carver was excited about the Carver Products Company, but he found that it took up more of his time than he had anticipated. Having his name attached to a company generated more correspondence, not less—from the army's Chemical Warfare Office, or a concrete manufacturer asking him to create a white concrete that would look like marble. Allowing agents to handle his products did not seem to inhibit people from going directly to Carver for information, nor did it inhibit Carver from giving them whatever they asked for. He was more burdened than ever. A few companies tried to compensate Carver with a consultant's fee or a payment for analyzing their products. He invariably returned it. "Your company is doing so much for the development of this interesting crop," he would write back, "that I can do a little something without being paid for it."

Then at the end of 1924, Carver was swept up in a small tornado that took his mind off business entirely—in fact, for a time, took his mind off everything. Carver had often been snubbed by white organizations and scientists who refused to take a black researcher seriously. But for the first time in his career, he was attacked outright by people outside of Tuskegee itself who averred that he was a creation of publicity and not a scientist at all.

12

A REAL CHEMIST?

In November 1924 the sky fell on Carver's graying head. He had been invited to speak in New York to a religious organization that worked among Native Americans and poor southerners. He was to address an audience of five hundred whites about his work with impoverished blacks and his personal mission to give aid according to Christ's precepts—it was, after all, a church-based audience. When he took the podium, his mind was full of his latest discovery, a medicinal peanut compound. People died needlessly, he told his listeners, even while God had provided the gifts of the earth to cure them. With great earnestness Carver averred that every herb and plant could be made useful to man. "God is going to reveal things to us that He never revealed before if we put our hand in His," he said. Then he dropped the bombshell: "No books ever go into my laboratory. The thing that I am to do and the way of doing it come to me. I never have to grope for methods; the method is revealed at the moment I am inspired to create something new. Without God to draw aside the curtain, I would be helpless." The audience burst into spontaneous applause; the newspapers reporting the lecture did not.

The Baltimore Sun the next day published a favorable editorial about the talk. But a *New York Times* editorial by a writer who was not present at the speech was contemptuous:

> It is for chemists to determine to what extent Dr. George Carver of Tuskegee is worthy of recognition. Whether eminent or not, he seems to have done useful work in discovering and developing new uses for several common Southern products, and therefore it can be claimed that he has shown abilities of a sort not present in many of his race. It is therefore to be regretted . . . that Dr. Carver . . . should use language that reveals a complete lack of the scientific spirit.

Real chemists, or at any rate other real chemists, do not scorn books out of which they learn what other chemists have done, and they do not ascribe their successes, when they have any, to "inspiration." Talk of that sort will simply bring ridicule on an admirable institution and on the race for which it has done and is still doing so much. All who hear it will be inclined to doubt, perhaps unjustly, that Dr. Carver's chemistry is appreciably different from the astronomy of the once-famous John Jasper who so firmly maintained that the sun went around a flat earth.

Carver eventually composed a response that the newspaper did not publish—probably it arrived too late to be timely. It was just as well, since the letter amounted to a rambling sermon replete with biblical passages that would have confirmed the *Times*'s skepticism.

"I regret exceedingly that such a gross misunderstanding should arise as to what was meant by 'Divine inspiration,'" Carver wrote. "Inspiration is never at variance with information; in fact, the more information one has, the greater will be the inspiration." Carver quoted the disciple Paul at length, as if he, too, had been a scientist "rightly dividing the world of truth." He stated his educational credentials, which for 1924 were impressive, since the majority of people who were known as scientists did not have academic degrees higher than Carver's. He listed sixty-one scientists whose works had influenced him and whose books were in his library, alongside the leading scientific journals. To explain what he meant by inspiration, he gave an example:

> While in your beautiful city, I was struck with the large number of Taros and Yautias . . . ; they are edible roots imported to this country . . . Dozens of ideas came to me while standing there looking at them. I would follow the same or similar lines I have pursued in developing products from the white potato. I know of no one who has ever worked with these roots in this way. I know of no book from which I can get this information, yet I will have no trouble in doing it. If this is not inspiration and information from a source greater than myself . . . kindly tell me what is.

Carver closed the letter with a statement that has become one of the most often quoted "sayings" of George Washington Carver: "Science is simply the truth about anything." The remark survived somehow, even without the printed letter. Within a few days, newspapers all over the country carried the story of Carver's New York talk with either approval or sneers regarding his "divine inspiration," under such headlines as "Chemist Attributes Success to Divinity, Gives Credit to God," and "Negro Professor Aided by Heaven, Inspired by Providence." The story appeared abroad in the *Manchester Guardian* and even the *Colombo Daily News* in Ceylon.

Carver was attacked because his 1924 speech came at the end of a fractious year in which the antipathy between Darwinian evolutionists and biblical fundamentalists—between science and religion—was heating up, stoked by newspaper publicity. The mortal contest between the lions and the Christians took place a few months later in Dayton, Tennessee. A state law had just been passed forbidding the teaching of evolution. John Scopes, a twenty-four-year-old high school teacher backed by the A.C.L.U. and *The Baltimore Sun,* was willing to violate the injunction so as to test the law in the courts.

The Scopes "Monkey Trial" in July 1925 brought famous men to Tennessee: the biblical literalist William Jennings Bryan who, in effect, prosecuted the theory of evolution, and the agnostic Clarence Darrow, who defended it by attacking Bryan. More than 200 reporters, including the most popular journalist of the day, H. L. Mencken, descended on the hot courtroom. The proceedings were broadcast on radio all across the country. Hostility between religion and science had been intensifying since the publication of Darwin's work; the trial was bringing a tense national issue into sharp focus.

Scopes's defense at first proposed that evolution was compatible with biblical teaching, a viewpoint later called "theistic evolution," which Carver himself warmly supported. As the trial progressed, Scopes's lawyer Darrow ridiculed the literal interpretation of the Bible and exposed Bryan's ignorance of both science and other religions. Bryan in turn attacked Darwin's theory and derided the notion that humans were descended "not even from American monkeys, but from old-world monkeys." The trial itself was not acrimonious—Bryan even offered to pay Scopes's $100 fine when he was found guilty. But it galvanized a broad base of vociferous Christians who alarmed the scientific community to the point that the liberal press declared ideological war against fundamentalism.

The judge finally stipulated that neither the validity of the law nor the theory of evolution could be decided by the court, which could only determine whether or not Scopes had broken the law. The trial of several days thus ended unsatisfactorily for both sides, since it left open all questions concerning evolution. Afterward, the religious conservatives retreated from the public eye, partly because of a brilliant attack on them by one of Scopes's lawyers, Dudley Field Malone, but mainly because Bryan's death deprived fundamentalists of a recognized, respectable leader. Nevertheless, a movement against evolution remained alive in both the North and the South throughout the 1920s, despite the savage ridicule that such journalists as Mencken had heaped upon Bryan, the state of Tennessee, and the entire South. Present-day debates between evolutionists and creationists are deferential in comparison to the acidulous attacks exchanged in Carver's day. Long after the Scopes trial was over, northerners who knew nothing of the South beyond Mencken's vicious descriptions nursed a mental picture of a drawling and drooling population of morons under the Mason-Dixon Line, beating back enlightenment with shovels and Bibles.

Carver's vague lecture had thus added a spark to what would soon become a bonfire. His situation was ironic, since he was a devout evolutionist whose library contained well-worn copies of all of Darwin's works. In his flexible theology he believed in the metaphorical, not the literal, truth of the Bible— that God had created the universe through the process of evolution that was described allegorically in the Bible. This was a quite common view among intellectual believers who, like Carver, avoided being overly specific in their exegesis but generally believed that evolution was part of the system put in place by God. Religious fundamentalists who hated both Darwin and academia were ecstatic upon reading that Carver seemed to be on their side. Scientists were disappointed. On the whole, however, the *New York Times* brouhaha helped Carver's career by making his name a household word in intellectual households. For better or worse, scientists all over the country now had heard of him and knew something of his accomplishments.

In 1926, an inventor in Georgia, Tom Huston, also learned of Carver's work. In the years since Carver had begun his research, the peanut had become a valuable agricultural crop, especially in Georgia, thanks to his promotion of it and the protective tariffs that he abetted. Huston had just patented a narrow glassine package with a red triangle logo. Tom's Roasted Peanuts, a bag with a single serving of nuts, was introduced as a snack for people on the run. It was a great idea; however, the oil that was necessary to preserve the nuts left the snackers with sticky hands. Carver was enlisted to work on that problem and on all the others that confronted a new company manufacturing nuts. When a peanut crop failed, the cause was almost always a fungus, Carver's specialty. With his mycological research, Carver was able to identify and control the various types of fungi that from time to time threatened to devastate Huston's suppliers and destroy the entire industry. Within four years the peanut company was so prosperous that Tom Huston was featured in *Time*. He never hesitated to acknowledge that Carver was his Unpaid Chief Researcher and the scientific brains of the burgeoning company.

Carver had a special relationship with the forty-one year-old Huston and with several of his employees, such as Dana Johnson and his brother Cecil. Carver's friendship with the young Johnsons long outlasted his ties with the company. Perhaps no one in the company loved Carver more than Bob Barry, the man in charge of ensuring the quality of the nuts. Barry was married with a young child. His grandfathers had both been Confederate soldiers, one a major who after the war had sponsored a black missionary to Africa. Barry was thoughtful, unusually intelligent, hardworking, and unassuming, a little like Carver himself. He shared Carver's love of the wilderness, his sense of humor, and to some degree, his religious bent. Both his and Huston's letters to Carver ranged far beyond peanut exigencies. Barry was self-diagnosed with "Carveritis." He became Carver's oldest protégé, writing to him nearly every day, studying scientific literature his mentor recommended, and soaking up everything Carver cared to teach him about nuts and life. "Some of these days I am going to kidnap you and take you off in the woods where I can talk to you for about a week," Barry wrote. "There are so many things that I want to say to you that I do not know where to start when I have the opportunity."

The company almost went under at the beginning of the Depression because of a widespread mold that attacked all southern peanuts. Carver undertook a thoroughgoing study of peanut diseases for Huston, a project that absorbed months, but which led to his identifying the fungus that would have destroyed one of the South's great money crops. He saved the crops and the company. Neither the scientists consulted by the government nor those in other agricultural experiment stations had recognized the mold as being the same fungus that caused wilt in cotton and field peas. Carver examined all the specimens Huston's men brought to him and gathered others in the fields, so that by the time he solved the problem of the peanut mold, he had identified no less than six thousand fungal specimens. For farmers, he wrote a four-page summary of fungal diseases of peanuts (1930), followed by a staggering bibliography in which he gathered all the scholarly information available on peanut diseases up to that time, country by country and state by state. These bulletins were published and four thousand copies distributed to southern growers—not by Tuskegee Institute, but by Tom Huston. What Carver did for the Tom Huston company was, as its manager Grady Porter recognized, a godsend to all growers. In return, the company did more than Tuskegee, with its parsimonious printing of Carver's bulletins, to disseminate Carver's teaching about peanut farming. Carver was "exceedingly grateful" to the company for the opportunity to make a real contribution to southern agriculture.

Scientists in other experiment stations were not enthusiastic about Carver's eradicating the mold under the auspices of Huston's company. They claimed the project was an example of a commercial manufacturer impinging on the territory of professors; but the more likely reason for their resentment was that Huston had found expert counsel from a black man in the smallest experiment station in the country. B. B. Higgins of the Georgia Experiment Station wrote Barry a snide missive attacking Carver's credentials as a fungus expert. Carver responded directly to Higgins in an amiable letter, praising Higgins's own mycological work and inviting him to come to his laboratory for a talk. Higgins was won over after one visit, or at least was mollified into silence.

Carver's research for the Tom Huston Company was essential, and he furnished it lavishly. In truth, he was an integral part of the company, but he steadfastly resisted being connected to the business in any formal way. Huston repeatedly invited him to become a paid consultant, a position he could fill without giving up his post at Tuskegee. Carver demurred. He was working on many products, he said, not just peanuts. His principal, Mr. Moton, who had control over his time, wanted him to accept all the lecture invitations he could manage. Finally, the strongest reason: "I am clannish enough to want my people to receive credit for my work. I do not want my work to be swallowed up and lost to the race to which I belong."

Carver's lectures meanwhile continued to be Tuskegee's most effective and economical form of publicity, since wherever he went to talk, the host paid all of his expenses. When Tuskegee had to pay his travel costs, these were minimal. A one week trip to the 1928 Montgomery State Fair for seven days, including train fare, car fare, room, board, and incidental refreshments cost $28.49. Two years later, Carver's expenses for the same trip were only $19.38, prices for everything having fallen on account of the Depression. When it became impossible for Carver to carry his exhibit cases, Tuskegee allowed Harry Abbott from the central office to accompany him on his outside lectures. Carver traveled several times a month, every month of the year, so the two became close friends. Before long, Carver was referring to Abbott as his secretary and when they were home, as his assistant. Every minute that Carver was not on the road, he was in his laboratory fiddling with new products, sending someone here toothpaste, someone there acne medication or a dandruff cure made from peanuts.

Carver Products failed to attract investors, so the company never really got off the ground. Carver's lawyer Thompson did not give up, however. In 1926 we find him the manager of a new enterprise, the Penol Company, formed to manufacture a peanut emulsion developed by Carver, with hopes of marketing other peanut derivatives in the future. Again, stationery was printed and Carver traveled to Philadelphia to discuss plans for a manufacturing plant. Carver got the idea for Penol cough syrup while listening to a sermon about the death of a child in Africa. "Probably TB," Carver thought. "Can't something be done to help such sufferers?" Though it was Sunday, the one day he usually did not go to his lab, on this day he could hardly wait to get there. After some hours he had concocted the cough syrup. He took it himself, and found that a cough which had been lingering for several weeks stopped instantly. Creosote, a strong antiseptic, had long been prescribed in treating lung disorders, including tuberculosis, but when emulsified with cod liver oil it was a disgusting medicine that patients could hardly get down. Carver blended beech wood creosote with peanut juice in a stable emulsion. Not only was it pleasant tasting (relatively), but it added nutrition to the medicinal properties of the creosote. He received letters from people with ulcers who had not been able to eat normally until they began taking Penol, and in that way he discovered that the mixture was also comforting to the stomach. Before the Penol Company was even established, individuals were requesting the syrup from Carver and then sending him telegrams attesting to its curative power.

Tuberculosis was still a worldwide scourge. From time to time people had sent Carver samples of new TB medications for his endorsement, since "any statement from you will receive world-wide attention;" but he had never found any other product that was effective. Carver believed that Penol assuaged at least the coughing symptom associated with the disease, but he firmly asserted that he had not found a cure for TB. A hospital in New York with three hundred tuberculosis patients wanted to order as much Penol as Carver could send. Carver did not have to supply the syrup. He could reply that the Penol Company owned the formula. "I have nothing to do with it more than endeavoring to keep them straight in its manufacture." However, the Penol Company could never manage the distribution phase of the business. Carver was to receive 10 percent of the profits from Penol, but it never made a profit. Other commercial efforts met a similar fate. Around the same time as the Penol effort, 1928, a factory was built in Thibodaux, Louisiana, to exploit Carver's formula for sweet potato starch. Several businessmen worked on the project for four years. No less than 1,000 acres were planted in sweet potatoes to supply the factory's capacity of 1,500 bushels a day. Exactly what happened to this enterprise is uncertain, except that we know it foundered.

Some years after Carver's death, the man who had been his laboratory assistant in the 1920s discussed these business ventures. Jack Sutton emphatically denied that Carver ever actively participated in any of the business dealings. "The only thing he ever did was lend money and lose money to them," Sutton averred. "He was duped into signing papers allowing use of his name in the obtaining of patents and copyrights and in . . . enterprises which allegedly would help Tuskegee Institute obtain funds. He was naive and trusting." Carver's correspondence with his business partners and others bears out Sutton's judgment. He seemed totally indifferent to the commercial success or failure of these companies. Early on, he gave advice to one of his former students: "Under no circumstances attempt to go into business because as soon as you do, your investigations come to an end and you stop and go to money making . . . I do not permit [the Penol Company] to discuss business with me at all . . . I cannot take up my time from creative work to go into those things which I know practically nothing about."

Meanwhile, he continued to freely hand out medicinal concoctions, despite the warnings of his lawyer that it was illegal to practice medicine without a physician's license. He merely admonished the patient not to spread the word around that he had gotten his medicament from Carver. When he was convinced that any one of his formulas had important potential for healing, he sent it to his county physician to try out in the expectation that the doctor would then send the drug where it needed to go for government approval. Or at least, that is what Carver claimed he did. More frequently, he just gave the medicine to the patient, as when the son of a teacher at Tuskegee came down with typhoid. Carver gave the little boy a quinine compound of his own manufacture with instructions to put it under his tongue twice a day and "don't tell anybody, absolutely."

The fact was that Carver had no time to care about companies or government approval. He was being pulled in a dozen different directions. The Mid-Continent Petroleum Company wanted him to analyze sludge, a nuisance byproduct of oil refining, to see if something useful could be made from it. Carver produced a road-building material from the waste product, as well as paint in several colors, the formulas for which he simply handed over to the company's chief chemist. He first extracted sulfuric acid, crystallized and concentrated it, and made a rich brown stain. With the addition of copperas he made greens and blues; he added zinc for yellows and whites. Libby's looked to him for a solution to the ant infestation that was destroying their Hawaiian pineapple orchards. Carver found that the orchards were being infected by a bacterial disease spread by ants which are plentiful in pineapple paradises. Companies constantly sent him products to try out; if he liked them, they asked permission to use his name in their advertising. From time to time he received letters from women asking if he could come up with a hair dye that would color grey—something more effective and darker than the sage tea that was commonly used. News of Carver in the Nigerian *Daily Telegraph* brought many letters to him from Africa.

"You ask me what I am doing?" he wrote to one of his acolytes. "Well, it is hard to say. I have so many things going on. People from the N, S. E. and W. are coming for information." He referred to a power company, a chocolate company, and a large slate plant in Chicago which had recently brought problems to him. A representative from a company in Atlanta spent an entire day trying to persuade Carver to become a paid consultant to a "gigantic" plant where bleach, dye, and cloth were manufactured. "I do not think God wants me to sell out in that way," Carver wrote. "I am going to straighten them out on some knotty problems, but . . . Then, everybody is begging me to please come and talk . . . I cannot go now as much as I used to, as you know. I am getting along in years and cannot sit up and ride all night like I used to."

After 1925, he was no longer mistaken anywhere for a bum, to his disappointment. For years his favorite mischief had been to arrive at a meeting or a train station appearing to be a derelict black nobody, so that his hosts would bypass him while they looked for the Great Scientist. Now, that was not possible. Everybody knew what he looked like from seeing his picture in the newspapers, and all had heard about his dishabille. News stories reported his sayings and doings, his current experiments and their outcomes, his lectures. The *Times* uproar had followed on the heels of several strenuous lecture tours on white college campuses, with large audiences, sponsored by the Y.M.C.A. Despite Carver's reputation as a humanitarian, the audiences were frequently hostile at the beginning of a lecture, though at the close of his talk, his listeners typically applauded and cheered him with abandon. The tours of the 1920s were harrowing for Carver. He suffered with his throat all the time he was on the road, usually came home with severe laryngitis, and several times ended with pneumonia that kept him in bed for months.

He was loved by thousands of people who had met him and respected by hundreds of thousands who had not. They solicited his opinion about everything from child rearing to the harmful effects of smoking. His former students and the acquaintances he made on his tours kept up a constant blizzard of loving letters. Along with letters from foreign governments in the 1920s, Carver received appeals from ordinary people—high schoolers wanting information about how to grow tall or gain weight. He treated every request as if it came from President Herbert Hoover. A Georgia state school superintendent asked him to approve a science program and choose textbooks. Carver provided the educator with a five-page list of necessary apparatus for a high school chemistry laboratory, complete with pricing information—a list that must have taken him hours to compose. It was common for him to write long letters to plain folk who had somehow been moved to write admiring or supplicating letters to him as, for example, when he wrote a long letter to a distraught mother whose son had been arrested.

His public lectures were filled beyond capacity, even on Thanksgiving Day in 1925, when a presentation left 100 attendees standing outside the hall. People published songs in praise of him. But the dizzying pace of his life, his persistent throat infection, and the relentless demands made upon him by his admirers left him depleted. "I am sick and old," he complained, "worn out with traveling and lecturing, unable to go anywhere without a doctor's permission." He was sixty-three.

Though his inner life was taking a new turn, Carver's outward activities remained the same from year to year. If he was eccentric in many ways, in many other ways his habits were perfectly ordinary. He continued to teach in the summer school at Tuskegee and to run the experiment station. For decades he assisted at chapel services by passing the collection plate. He was no longer treated as an outsider by the other teachers. Tuskegee was by then attracting some of the best minds to its campus—thanks in part to him—people who were not uneasy in the presence of a man of genius. The faculty was, moreover, a much larger group than it had been in J. H.'s day, with teachers who were happy to be the friend of a renowned scientist. Some former students recall that Carver was the pet of the entire Tuskegee community; the women on campus took turns making up special trays for him and sending them to his apartment. But other alumni remarked that in the 1920s, Carver was well liked but still underappreciated at Tuskegee, an opinion that seems correct in view of the administration's stinginess towards him.

Several friends tried to write his biography, but only one succeeded, a former student, Raleigh Merritt, who took advantage of his personal knowledge of Carver to publish a book that became quite well known, *From Captivity to Fame: The Life of George Washington Carver*. Carver's old acquaintances wrote to him to say hello, now that they knew where he was and that he had made good. One of those was Cal Jefferson, Mariah Watkins's good-for-little nephew. Mariah was now quite old but still living in Neosho in the house next door to the school. Cal, acting as her curator, had mortgaged the house to get money to care for her, but the care was rare and miserly. The bank holding the mortgage suggested to Cal that he put some money back into her account, as "Aunt

Mariah" was coming into the bank and begging loans from acquaintances she met there. Mariah, who had been independent throughout a lifetime of caring for others, ended up being dependent and neglected after Andy's death. "Dear Cal," she wrote, "I will drop you a few lines to let you know I am in a poor condition. I fell down and nearly killed myself. I want you to come and see me as soon as you can. I wrote for you all to come last week and you didn't come . . . Tell your wife I hope she don't wait until I die to come. I have been looking for her quite a while. Everyone is always asking about you and said I have to have someone with me but I don't want no one but you . . . I send my love to you both." According to his curatorial account, Cal was paying his wife eight dollars a week to clean Mariah's house (the normal rate was $1.50) and was taking fifty dollars a week himself for the ostensible expense of driving his wife there. In another letter two months after the first importuning, Mariah reported, "I am yet alive but I am very poorly . . . I haven't got any kindling wood to start my fire . . . Come as soon as you can. Much love to yourself and your wife." Carver, who had not seen Mariah since his visit in 1909 and had seldom written to her, knew nothing of her troubles. When she died around 1925, the last of his childhood "family" had passed.

Carver had a few more years to get used to his notoriety before he would be hit by a deluge of publicity such as he had never imagined. It was during these quieter years that the governments of Korea, Japan, and the Soviet Union separately invited him to tour their countries and examine their soil and native products with a view toward attaining self-sufficiency in food. The United States was leading the world in an anti-Bolshevik crusade at the very time when the Soviet Union wanted Carver to come for six months in return for "a vast sum" to work on cotton production. In 1931 Carver sent an ex-student—his assistant, Jack Sutton—and recommended thirty other researchers. "No other colleges in the country would even answer their appeals," wrote Sutton. "Anti-communism was a disease, a cankerous sore . . . you can have no idea of the degree of courage it took for Carver . . . to send a group of Negro specialists to the Soviet Union." The Soviets were apparently truthful in claiming that they did not discriminate on the basis of color. Sutton soon advanced to the position of research chemist and manager of a large laboratory investigating ways to use rice straw, a waste product, in making wallboard. Sutton learned to speak Russian, married a Russian girl, and for some time seemed to be happily raising a biracial family in the Communist hinterland. After seven years, however, Sutton was caught up in one of Stalin's waves of xenophobia. He was ejected from the country, compelled to leave his family behind. After his return to the United States, Sutton received a master's degree in science from Columbia University, taught science in New York City public schools, and finally in 1946 remarried.

Carver did not try to bolster his own public image as a scientist. "Time and again he made it clear to me," Sutton wrote, "that he was primarily an artist who created good (God's creations) out of natural things. He knew that he was not a 'real chemist' engaged in even applied chemical research. He used to say to me jokingly, 'You and I are cook-stove chemists, but we dare not admit it because it would damage the publicity that Dr. Moton and his assistants send out in press releases about me and my research for money-raising campaigns.'" Of course, no one could have been a real chemist with Carver's paucity of equipment. Sutton continued, "I have known him to show momentary flashes of anger at some of the exaggerated claims [in the principal's press releases] concerning the hundreds of new products produced by his research. He would frown and then laugh, saying, 'Oh, me!' and his anger was gone."

Sutton decoded the cherished myth that Carver forgot to cash his paychecks. "Every few years the bookkeeping department and treasury would stage charades trying to 'persuade Professor Carver to deposit or cash his checks so that we can balance our books.' Had they genuinely wanted to pay him," Sutton asserted, "they could have opened a savings account in the Institute Bank in his name and deposited his monthly pay in it. What they really wanted and achieved was to have Carver 'lend' the Institute money to 'tide them over.' Most of these 'loans' were mere surrenders of his checks . . . The memory of it still hurts me." A white physician in town once commented, "Carver would do anything, even hang himself, if he thought it would help Tuskegee."

Carver was still answering thirty or forty letters a day by hand, despite several interruptions before any letter was finished, and he was daily turning aside a dozen invitations to lecture. There is hardly an example of a peremptory note in his correspondence. To Dr. Ross, who complimented him on his writing style, Carver responded, "I am glad you can read my letters. I was not aware that my spelling and grammar were even respectable." When asked for an article, he would submit it with an apology: "I have thrown together a sort of rambling, disconnected something from which you may find something fit to print. If it is not what you want, send it back with suggestions and I will take pleasure in recasting it."

In Austin, Texas, the state legislature adjourned its regular business so that Carver, who was passing through, could give an address. But on that same tour of the Southwest, he was refused when he tried to purchase a sleeping berth on a train. There was nothing very unusual in that—blacks were routinely excluded from berths in many parts of the country. But this time the president of the railway company apologized, whereupon Carver characteristically sent him a warm letter of thanks for his apology. That tour gave him a chance to stay with Dr. and Mrs. Ross. Though Ross was not young, he was inspired by Carver to begin doing medical research on animals. Carver encouraged him and seemed genuinely attached to the physician, though he had little to say to him beyond small talk. He wrote about two letters a month to him over a decade, all nearly identical, all remarking that Ross overestimates him. He reiterates how much Ross's friendship means to him, thanks him for the most recent gift, since Ross is always sending him something—often birds to cook—and closes with some compliment to Mrs. Ross.

Carver was still spry enough to run on at least one occasion. He had long cultivated a night-blooming cereus, which opened its petals only once every ten years. On the night when Carver realized the great event was taking place, he stayed up all night, watching "the miracle of God." Remembering that one of the faculty women would be coming to campus on Franklin Road, he scurried out to meet her. "Run, run, while you can still see it. Hurry!" he urged her. He brought the cereus to the yard of Rockefeller Hall and had a party with lemonade for friends who came to see it—about a dozen people, including Mrs. Long, the dormitory mother. "Watch it, watch it, watch the petals," he exhorted them.

For the rest, there was the usual passage of time marked by public milestones, when his private life intersected the traffic of historic events. Tuskegee was largely unharmed by the Great Flood of 1929, though many in the surrounding county lost their homes. Now and then students staged a protest that was reported in the papers. The Ku Klux Klan was an intermittent nuisance until the Depression gave everyone something larger than race to worry about. It had been quite a while since Carver was involved with any woman, though it was not for lack of volunteers. After noting that Carver's reputation was growing like kudzu, Bob Barry joked, "You have fought the women off for a long time but I'm afraid you're doomed now." Was that all there was then? Creative work and the admiration of friends and strangers as he faced advancing age? None of the tender, private intimacy that every man and woman longs for?

That was not all. There was another entire side of Carver distinct from his life in the laboratory and the lecture hall. During most of the 1920s, he was deeply engaged with many white students in an ongoing religious project for interracial harmony. The students were mainly well-to-do zealots from preppy colleges in the Piedmont region who embraced Carver with all the fervid devotion of youth. To all of them, Carver responded warmly. But for one, not a student but a young religious activist, he felt an immediate attraction so intense it was painful. For one person, Carver experienced again, and for an entire decade, the plangent ache of unattainable love.

13

PASSION PURE AND SIMPLE

Jim Hardwick was an intelligent, earnest young white man starting a career with the Young Men's Christian Association when Carver met him in 1923. At the time, the organization was beginning an evangelical recruitment drive intended to last several years. Carver had been invited to address the summer conference of the "Y" in Blue Ridge, North Carolina. Generally, white religious leaders addressed this gathering, and Carver's audience—boys selected from various colleges—was initially hostile to him. It was while he was delivering his first lecture at Blue Ridge, talking about Christian love to the sullen faces of southern white boys, that Carver saw Hardwick from across the hall. Carver looked into Hardwick's eyes, "those wonderful soul windows of yours." "I did not have to learn to love you," Carver declared. "I did this the first time I saw you, before you ever spoke to me. It was the Christ in you, of course."

Although some of the students had planned to disrupt the meeting and prevent Carver from speaking, once the boys heard him, they got so excited that they picked him up in a surge of youthful spirit and carried him around the hall as they cheered his name. Here as everywhere, his demeanor, personality, and polished speech cut through every stereotype, which was exactly what the organizers of the conference had hoped would happen. Suddenly, each youth sought a private meeting with Carver and wanted him to lecture at his own college. A nucleus of the young men became the Blue Ridge Boys— a self-described little family of Carver admirers. Several of them indentured themselves to him: Charles Harman, Howard Kester, Al Zisler, and a dozen others. Wilson Newman from Vanderbilt considered Carver a spiritual father and took it upon himself to arrange subsequent college tours where Carver's friendship with the individual boys was cemented. On his side, Carver was just as taken with "these fine young men, so full of possibilities, and so full of the love of Jesus Christ."

The two weeks Carver spent at Blue Ridge in 1923 marked a turning point in his life. There in the white columned hotel set high in the ashen hills, with its surrounding cottages, conference rooms, and parks, he fell in love—there is no other word for it—with one special man who became in his letters, "My Very Own, Handsome, Marvelous, Spiritual, Boy." His obsession with Hardwick took a particular form. It was merged with a pious fervor more intense and overwrought than anything Carver had previously exhibited. If, as he thought, he had inclined a group of young men toward God, it was also obvious that his contact with those youths and with Hardwick had a profound effect on him. He became immersed in an anxious fanaticism from which he never emerged completely, although it weakened considerably after about a decade. During the 1920s, his lifelong reverence for life and nature became a panting pressure to proselytize. In every discussion of nature, whether he was talking about plants, fungi, minerals, or hogs, Carver began to aggrandize the Creator in a way that previously he had only implied or imparted as a subtext. He started mentioning Satan and the need to escape the fearful clutches of Evil. For the first time, his thoughts were less about God and more about Jesus Christ, in the fashion of Protestant evangelism. Asked to write a few words of general advice to young people, Carver in those days could work himself into a rapture of several pages. "I want them to find Jesus and make Him a daily, hourly, and monthly part of themselves. O how I want them to get the fullest measure of happiness and success out of life. I want them to see the Great Creator in the smallest and apparently the most insignificant things about them. How I long for each one to walk and talk with the Great Creator through the things he has created."

His sermonizing gradually attracted a following of strangers who regularly wrote him ten or twenty ecstatic pages, true believers who were not in the least interested in science, except insofar as it affirmed the grandeur of God, but who idolized Carver as a holy messenger from Jesus. Some of the letters consisted of little more than strung-together biblical references. The writers gushed over God or nature or both, as in the single-spaced missives from one of his Blue Ridge Boys: "As I wander through the dark, encountering difficulties, I am aware of encouraging voices that murmur from the spirit realm. I sense a holy passion pouring down from the springs of infinity. I hear music that beats with the pulses of God . . . I feel the flame of eternity in my soul."

Other letters, though, show how effective Carver was in providing comfort to lost souls through his proselytizing activities. During the first Y.M.C.A. conference, Carver had struck up a conversation with a waitress serving him breakfast. She could not arrange her work schedule so as to hear all of Carver's talk at the conference, but she read about him afterwards and finally wrote him a beautiful letter, some ten years after talking with him, because she felt he would understand her.

All my life I have hunger for the Truth and until last March did I find the thing that satisfied that inner longer for knowledge. In Mr. Roosevelt address on the 4 of March when he said there is nothing in life to fear but fear. All my life I had feared every thing and every body. But when I read that I saw life different . . . And the most wonderful thing, I found out what God is. All my life I thought God was external a long ways away, and one had to suffer on this earth and when it was all over that he would go some place called heaven to rest. When last March I found God was not as I had always thought him to be. But the closest thing to me was God and at the center of my being. You can know how happy I was when I learn this truth about my God and to know he is with me always, when all my life I had felt lonely . . . I have found out where the temple of God is, within me. And right thinking is the kingdom of heaven.

Carver's attack of religiosity is not hard to understand. He persuaded himself that his helpless attraction to Hardwick was ordained by God, who had brought the two together so that Carver could lead the younger man to grace. Carver would guide Hardwick to fulfill God's plan for him, a plan that God had revealed to Carver. Carver never described his love for Hardwick without talking also of God. Hardwick would help Carver fulfill his own divine destiny. "I can feel your love," Carver wrote, ". . . I never begin a new project but what I think of you in connection with it." Almost as an act of will, Carver's feeling for Hardwick was subsumed and sanctified in a raging devotional fever.

Only a few of Hardwick's letters are available. They show that he at first responded wholeheartedly to Carver but became more guarded as time went on. Their correspondence continued with many lacunae until a few years before Carver's death, nearly twenty years after he met Hardwick. Not all of Carver's letters survive, since he did not make carbon copies for his records. He wrote Jim in longhand or typed his letters himself, even after he had a secretary, on his Carver Products stationery (with its post office box return address that was not the same as Tuskegee's). From those letters that were saved by Hardwick or someone else—eighty-one long communications—it seems obvious that for the ageing professor the relationship with Hardwick was unique.

I t is delicate and easily contorted, this question of whether Carver's love for Hardwick was an erotic attachment, overtly expressed at some point. If one had a mind to, one could find many examples of Carver verbalizing his love for close friends. He wrote without the conventional pellicle of restraint that people use to shield the intensity of their emotions. Generally in his letters to friends, Carver thanked them for their expressions of kindness and offered fatherly advice or sympathetic support in their projects. He sometimes described what he was working on and who had come to see his lab. With intimate friends such as Pammel, he occasionally added his ideas about the direction in which God was guiding his life, or shared some insight into the unknown that he had gained while making his morning collection of specimens. "I am confident that my life and career could never have been what it is had it not touched yours," he once wrote to Pammel. "You will never know in this world what your life has meant, and is still meaning, to me." He regarded the elder Henry Wallace with reverence and unabashed affection. To one other close friend, Judge Leon McCord of Montgomery, he could be very effusive but only on special occasions. He mentioned God at least briefly to everyone.

With Hardwick there is something else—a need, an anxiety, a tumescent fixation that is unmistakably different from his addresses to other dear ones. Carver poured out his innermost feelings to him in letters that were invariably long and suffused with exquisite tenderness. Carver's voice in all his letters is so clear and authentic, it is easy to discern the temperature of his feelings for various people. Regarding Hardwick, it seems clear, he was in the grip of love at first sight and remained its willing captive for years. "My precious friend Mr. Hardwick, . . . I love you for what you are and what you hope to be through Jesus Christ," he wrote in one of his early messages, four and a half months after meeting him.

I am by no means as good as you give me credit for being. There are times when I am sorely tried and am compelled to hide away with Jesus for strength to overcome. God alone knows what I have suffered in trying to do as best I could the job he has given me in trust to do, most of the time I had to work without the sympathy or support of those with whom I associated. God gave you to me for courage, strength, and to deepen and indelibly confirm my berth in humanity. And Oh, how I thank Him for you, you come to me when I needed you most.

At first Carver wrote every few days. After six months, one finds the noteworthy statement, "I have known all of the time that you could not love me as I love you"—a response to some assertion by Jim.

Somehow I love you all the more because you are having the struggle . . . I love you because you tell me things that I think you would not tell others . . . I shall reserve most of what I have to say until I see you. How I would like to see you face to face tonight, so we could sit down alone with God and talk and pray together. I love you because your spirit is longing for freedom . . . When I see you I will tell you what I saw in you when I put my hand on your head. Yes, I saw it the moment I saw you and loved you then for it and shall continue to love and pray for you . . . Don't let anything keep you from coming to see me.

Hardwick did go to Tuskegee early in 1924. Following the visit, Carver repeated some of his remarks. "I can never be to you what you are to me. I love you all the more dearly because you belong to another race." "Your visit here lingers with me . . . I love you because you are my ideal type of man. And one that I can confide in at all times." The Blue Ridge Conference was coming up again in June, and Carver was invited back, as he would be every year. "I fear that we will have very little time to be together . . . However, we must find some time. I see more progress in you all of the time. Continue to let Christ lead you."

The next missive, if it had been addressed to a woman, would be called, without hesitation, a love letter—and so it is.

Don't give me credit for loving you. I could not help it if I tried . . . More and more you are losing sight of self. I saw what God had in store for you the very first time I laid eyes upon you, and wanted to tell you so much how your very soul lifted me up. I could not do so because I felt it would be quite out of place from a stranger and also of a different nationality. God willing I will tell you some things this summer that I have never told you. I have purposely held these things back in order that you might know me better, and know that my love is absolutely genuine.

Carver often spoke of his "genuine" love, by which he meant perhaps "disinterested," "non-sexual"—or perhaps something else. "I have gotten such wonderful results in the laboratory here recently . . . All of the time I am thinking of you and God. God is using you as a medium to inspire me." He described gathering some plants for a talk. "I thought of you and longed for you while I was collecting them."

As the time for the June reunion approached, Carver became more intense. "Commune with nature," he lectured Hardwick. "Fight Satan in whatever form he appears . . . God is in you. He will fight your battles and will win every time. I doubt if I would have gone to Blue Ridge this summer if you had not decided to go. I want to be with you just as much as possible."

Carver wrote again the next day. Jim had made a recent visit. "I missed you so much when you left . . . It was so good to have you all to myself so we could talk as we wished . . . Your spirit helps me so much. It is what my very soul has thirsted for all these years. Just to think you have been here. We are to see each other in June, and that is not all. He has something else in mind for us." As a postscript, he added, "Do not worry. It is absolutely impossible for you to mean more to me than you do now, except as I grow more and more into love of Jesus, as I am trying to do. Pray for me. I have your picture before me now."

What could that mean, Jim's enigmatic worry that he would come to mean more and more to Carver? Jim had acquired a sweetheart whom Carver referred to as a "lady friend." "God will direct you in this matter as he has in others, I am sure," he commented simply. He was aware that his declarations were open to various interpretations. "I talk to you as I do no one else. Others would misunderstand me, but I think you understand me thoroughly."

Carver's second appearance at Blue Ridge had all the trappings of an old-time revival of the type that was seen eighty years earlier in the Burned-Over District of New York. Many of the boys who had met Carver the previous year wanted personal interviews—so many that Carver had to limit them to fifteen minutes each. He began at four each morning and held the last interview at midnight. "One desired to be a food chemist, another a research chemist, others desired to find Jesus in a different way than they had before. All wanted to know how to read God out of Nature's great book." They cornered him in the woods for advice on everything and in between conferences, brought their poison oak rashes and sprained ankles to him for treatment.

Carver's older "sons" and "bad boys" who had left Tuskegee were still deluging him with mail. "My dear and only Daddy," wrote one. "Now listen, I don't care what kind of a Ridge you go to next time, you have got to take me. Do you have any other Son besides me? If so, I'm going to resign . . . I am not angry, but I am real jealous." The letter was signed, "Son." Carver was still working constantly with everything from peanuts to paints to pork. And he was, as he never failed to note, getting older. The second Blue Ridge trip in 1924 came at the end of several long speaking tours. When he returned to Tuskegee, he had something of a breakdown. He was confined to bed with pneumonia for some months and then suffered repeated and severe bouts of flu. Death hovered in his thoughts. When Booker's widow sent him a get-well note, he responded with his customary unchecked warmth: "I was deeply touched when I read your beautiful note of January 30th. You are constantly on my mind; and as the links of the chain become fewer and fewer, and the chain smaller and smaller which binds us and makes us as one little group, it cannot but help make each one feel nearer to the other." Four months later, Margaret Murray Washington was dead.

When it was reported in the newspapers that Carver was ill, his correspondence multiplied. "Oh, the letters, telegrams, whole churches over 2,000 miles away praying for my recovery! My, how little it makes me feel. They came from all classes and all nationalities. I am not so good, no better than others, except they pull me up to it. What a responsibility!"

* * *

The reunion at Blue Ridge may have been tense, since Carver collapsed after it, but attending it did not diminish his ardor for Jim. "What a joy always comes to me when I recognize your handwriting in the mail," he wrote.

> You have not lost sight of self yet, but thank God, you will. As soon as you begin to read the great and loving God out of all forms of existence He has created, both animate and inanimate, then you will be able to converse with Him, anywhere, everywhere, and at all times. Oh, what a fullness of joy will come to you. My dear friend, get the significance. God is speaking. "Look unto the hills from whence cometh thy help." Yes, go to the mountains if God so wills it. Get ready to come down here for a week or so, should God ask you to do so. Somehow God seems to say to me that this may be so.
>
> As for you, my friend, you belong to me. You are mine. God gave you to me last year . . . "This is the person whom I have chosen to be of great help to you. You need him." . . . From that very time until now I have loved you so dearly. Don't get alarmed, friend, when doubts creep in. That is old Satan. Pray, pray, pray . . . Yes, my friend, you are going to grow. Your letters are always such a comfort to me. Do not get away somewhere and fail to write me regularly. You are now a part of my life and I long for your letters . . . At some of the personal interviews the boys wept. I have held my head and wept many times when I read so many of the letters they have written me. I fall, my friend, so far short of yours and their rating. Oh, my friend, I am praying that God will come in and rid you entirely of self so you can go out after soul's right, or rather have souls to seek the Christ in you.

As usual, he recorded Jim's spiritual progress. "I really think that little by little, God is burning out the dross of your nature and you will come out of it as gold tried by fire."

By early September, Carver had received over 500 letters from his "Blue Ridge Boys" in addition to all his other fan mail. But these did not satisfy him because his letters from Hardwick were now longer spaced. Under the heat of Carver's exhortations, Hardwick had begun to wilt. It must have made the young man uneasy, having Carver watch him so intently as he became dross free. Jim withdrew, first with the excuse that writing was difficult while he was traveling and then with no excuse at all. Carver explained the silence by persuading himself that Jim was unwell. "Were you in the North and I learned you were ill away from home, I certainly would get on the train and go to your bedside. This is what I think of you," wrote Carver. "I am afraid, dear friend, you are not praying for me very much. I do not feel your loving Christ-like spirit as sensibly as I used to. Just remember my love for you is just the same."

In the next two years, there was no evident communication between them. In January 1927, two years and three months after Carver assured Jim that his love was "just the same," we find him writing: "My dear friend Mr. Hardwick: What a pleasant surprise it was to me yesterday when I received your fine letter. Of course I thought of you every day, but never expected to hear from you directly again." Jim was still with his girlfriend and was now established as Y.M.C.A. secretary at Iowa State, Carver's alma mater.

Something had happened—something untoward—leaving no record of the grief it must have wrung from Carver, something that led him to think that Jim intended to cut off the relationship. Carver's comment, that he "never expected to hear from you directly again," is the sole evidence for suspecting that Carver and Jim were ever physically intimate, that Jim recoiled from some incident between them. Perhaps the incident was merely a conversation in which Jim expressed his need to back away from Carver's smothering affection. Or was there some episode that occasioned a sudden and clear decision? Except for this remark, which might mean everything or nothing, not a syllable in Carver's letters suggests that the old professor put his hands anywhere but on Hardwick's head. The rest of Carver's response is restrained: "I have missed your letters so much and your fellowship, and it is indeed refreshing to hear from you." Hardwick had invited him to come to Iowa State to lecture; Carver was in sufficient control of himself that he was able to decline politely, using the long distance as an excuse. "Trusting that God will bless you this year as never before," he signed himself "Very sincerely yours," with nary a word of love. But it's interesting to note that although Carver had been continually sick with arthritis and fainting spells, he went on an outing and walked ten miles after receiving Jim's letter.

Another year passed, it seems, before the two got "back together," a year in which Carver wrote Jim only a few letters. Though he effused about God as always, he was reserved toward Hardwick, except in closing "With a heart so full of love." In spring 1928, Carver was mistreated by a bull that, fortunately, had no horns. He was badly bruised in the attack and confined to bed for some weeks. By the time he recovered, Hardwick was haunting him again, if, indeed, he had ever been absent from Carver's thoughts. "You, my friend, seem to go with me in the laboratory, the woods and fields, and indeed when nature speaks to me in all of her loveliness, you seem to be there." Soon Carver was again writing with his old, twitching excitement because Hardwick was planning to visit him. "Thank God and praise His holy name that you are coming. I have it all mapped out what we will do or rather how we will commune with the Great Creator." At times, Carver wrote brief notes to Jim: "This is a Monday morning and I am wondering just what you are doing."

By now, whenever Carver worked in his lab, he felt Jim standing beside him. He looked forward to their regular summer reunion, although Jim warned him that their time together might be constrained. "Of course, you must see your dear mother just as much as possible, then your lady friend, and what time is left to me if possible." Admiring a new photo of Jim, Carver exclaimed, "I actually believe you are more handsome than ever. You seem to have rounded out into such an athletic figure . . . Your chest was just a little too flat when I saw you last." Jim was probably a good-looking fellow. He had been captain of the football team at Virginia Tech before graduating with a degree in agriculture. His brother Harry was head coach of the football team of the U.S. Naval Academy. Jim had written of wanting to make Harry more of a Christian. When recruiting on school campuses, the Y.M.C.A. tried to convert athletes first, believing that unabashed Christian he-men would attract others to the organization. Jim had been one of these masculine exemplars. Carver's letters grew longer and longer: "It seems impossible to stop." But he assured Jim that when he called him "Beloved Friend," he meant "God love and not Sense love." Yet each palpitating letter displayed more and more Sense love. "You were with me today . . . I want to see you so badly . . . I can hardly wait for the time to come."

Poor Jim, trying to keep Carver at a Christian distance and at the same time being haphazardly inhabited by God. "My friend, you are now losing the finite and taking on the infinite," Carver assured him. "It seems to me that I never saw you look more handsome. Why not? God's love makes your eyes bright and your face shine with a beautiful heavenly brightness." Who could be himself under such a glare?

When Carver was awarded the honorary doctorate at Simpson College, Hardwick sent a testimonial but did not come. When passing through Virginia, Carver stayed at Jim's mother's house and slept in Jim's old room, though the corporeal Hardwick remained in Iowa. The relationship settled into a pattern of Carver's continually reaching for Hardwick and the younger man backing away. Hardwick apparently made a brief—very brief—visit to Carver and then allowed several months to elapse without communicating again. "Yes, I was sorrowfully disappointed in you—your brief visit," Carver complained, when Jim finally wrote to him. "I wanted to talk with you and show you Oh so many, many things that you had never seen before . . . After your explanation, of course, I understood it all, that you really strained a point to come by at all, which I appreciate so very much."

The other Blue Ridge Boys were visiting Carver. Wilson Newman, bringing along Howard Kester, made good on his promise to disturb one of Carver's Thanksgivings. When they left, Carver felt the need to write to Jim, as he was "unusually lonesome this evening." But generally during this arid interval, he restrained himself from writing unless Jim wrote to him first; Jim did this only once in the entire next two years, at Easter in 1929. Carver wrote back of hoping to see him again "someday." He had again calmed down.

Carver contracted flu again in 1929, which once more worsened into pneumonia. Perhaps that illness prompted Hardwick to write to him, finally, in August 1930, addressing Carver as "Old Friend" and promising to keep more in touch. Jim did not write more frequently, but he did manage to visit Carver around Christmas 1930. "I do not recall ever being more happy," Carver asserted. He reminded Jim that one day he would be able to talk to God through human beings, as well as through nature, since "God lives in the hearts of men." Or perhaps most men. President Moton's sister was murdered in another state just then, but no arrest was made for a year. Possibly the murderer was a family member, since neither *The Tuskegee News* nor the *Montgomery Advertiser* reported the case, as if Moton were keeping the affair secret. The *Advertiser*, which enthusiastically informed its readers of all grisly accidents, cruelty to animals and children, dastardly swindling, and especially murders, would not otherwise have overlooked the story. Carver kept Jim informed about it.

Hardwick was now working in Montgomery, forty miles from Tuskegee, and planned another visit. "Glorious!" Carver wrote. "I want you just as long as I can have you. I have so much to talk with you about. I am positively thrilled at the prospect of seeing you some day very soon. I want to talk to you about the Artist Soul that God has so generously given you." That Christmas visit and the period following it marked the height of the relationship with Hardwick. Carver felt better than he had in years, despite having had all of his teeth removed. Gingivitis is thought to exacerbate rheumatoid arthritis and osteoarthritis. One treatment for severe gum disease, and thus for arthritis, was to extract the teeth. Carver found the procedure helped him. Jim's presence helped him even more. "I have been so happy ever since you were here. It may seem odd to you, but I seem to be in better physical condition than before. I have not been able to do but little walking for some time. If I attempted to walk much further than my office, I would become so tired that I would have to rest. January 1st I walked all afternoon and several hours in the forenoon collecting botanical specimens." The visit lifted Carver for fully three months. "I have felt so supremely happy ever since you were here," he wrote at the end of January. "I am still happy," he wrote in February. "You seem to be with me. I talk to God through you. I am now working on a piece of pink marble from Ala. I can only get a few moments at a time, but it is in these few moments that you seem so near to me. What would I do without you?" A few days later he wrote of gathering plants in the woods. "You seemed to accompany me all of the way. I could not keep the tears out of my eyes. I was supremely happy."

For more than two years they exchanged visits. In between times they wrote, with Carver unfolding himself to "My Very Own Great Spiritual Boy" about every ten days. He often mentioned some therapeutic massage oil he had concocted and the people who were being helped by it. Once in Carver's apartment, Jim had said a prayer that Carver thought induced God to come and sit with them. "Without knowing it, the spot you consecrated with your divine prayer is the spot where I do the massaging." They did not apparently talk much on the phone. Long distance calls, especially for an intrastate distance of only fifty miles, were costly and probably would have been billed to the Tuskegee account. "You are on my mind all the time," he assured Jim repeatedly, "and have been ever since God gave you to me." Virginia Tech wanted

Carver to choose a picture of himself that could be sold in their gift shop. He picked one that included Jim.

It must have been burdensome, really, even for another fanatic, which Jim surely was, to be told in every manic letter that he was gaining power from God each hour, that God was speaking through him and shaping his "artistic soul," that his spirit and Carver's had been inseparably knitted together in God's tapestry, etc. Carver repeatedly compared himself and Hardwick to the biblical Paul and "his precious little Timothy."

Rarely did real life enter Carver's letters to Jim, although Carver was, as usual, immersed in the real worlds revealed to him by his microscope. Still restless for knowledge, he crammed a dozen projects into the spaces of his mind not dominated by Jim. In 1928 and 1929 Carver was experimenting with all sorts of substances—sweet potato starch, palmetto roots, vegetable dyes, oil refinery sludge—but he was never long away from peanut research. In a comparison study made for Huston, Carver pointed out that peanuts contained more protein than twenty-five other common foods, only slightly less than California black walnuts and cheddar cheese but slightly more than some meats. In those days when nutritionists hoped for more, not fewer, calories in foods, the peanut had the highest caloric content. Carver developed new peanut recipes and included them in his reports to the Huston Company, along with several oddities such as art wallpaper made from peanut skins. Seeing that Carver needed a blanket and also that he was in desperate need of a new typewriter which Tuskegee had withheld for years, Huston provided very fine ones. Carver, who had saved the Huston Company tens of thousands of dollars and had generated untold sales of peanuts, wrote Huston that he was "semi-dazed" at such generosity and would need some time to recover before he could express his appreciation. Huston then made an even more dazzling gesture. He presented Tuskegee with a bronze bas-relief of Carver sculpted by Isabel Schultz. Before the official unveiling of the plaque on May 28, 1931, Carver tried to thank Huston, but after four paragraphs of gratitude he concluded, "All that I have said seems so flat, and the more I try to express myself, the flatter it gets." To Jim he wrote, "Your spirit seems so strong tonight that I cannot resist sending you these few lines. How I wish my precious boy could be here May 28." Jim did attend the presentation, along with several others from Carver's "little family." Huston, though dynamic and ambitious, was fundamentally shy. He assigned Bob Barry to make the formal presentation of the bust. "It is a masterpiece of art," Carver wrote to Jim. "I do not feel equal to it."

Although he was now a national figure, commercial companies continued to impose on him, and Carver involved himself wholeheartedly in their research projects, never having got the hang of competitive capitalism. From London, a seller of beer and sparkling water pleaded with Carver to give him a formula for a winter drink so that he would not have to lay off his thirty employees every fall when the season for cold drinks ended. Publishers sent pounds of books hoping for a favorable comment about them that they could quote; Carver usually tried to comply because "You can't hurt people's feelings." He often ended his lectures with a poem—he had excellent taste in literature. That little habit induced hundreds of rhymers to send him their doggerel about nature or his admirable self.

The Department of Agriculture of the State of Alabama asked him to solve the problem of peanut-fed hogs yielding a pork that was soft. So much negative publicity had been put out about the mushy pork that even in Alabama for a time it was not served to people who were rather badly fed to begin with: prisoners, inmates of the insane asylum at Tuscaloosa, and students at Tuskegee. Carver began a close and long-lasting collaboration with the Swift Company, trying to make the meat more marketable. Though he worked on the problem about four years, the best solution he could find was to feed the hogs exclusively on peanuts and then switch exclusively to corn six months before slaughtering. He created recipes for gravy that utilized the excess oil, but that hardly solved the problem. Nevertheless, those recipes, like all of Carver's cooking directions, were welcomed by people as far away as South Africa.

T he more his reputation spread, the more he was required to take long trips—several each year. He had reached the category of a garden-variety celebrity, still without any premonition of the deluge of publicity that would hit him in a few years. And he was not yet exempt from racial insults. When Carver spoke at Cornell University he was well received. But when his sponsor, Charles Hyne, one of Carver's "little family," invited him to have dinner with his social fraternity, the members refused to sit down with a Negro; the invitation had to be withdrawn. In 1931, Hardwick set up two tours for Carver throughout the South. In Columbus, the Mississippi State College for Women cancelled Carver's talk on racial grounds. When an indignant Hardwick arranged to hold the lecture in another venue, the students were forbidden to go (although fourteen of their professors attended.) One girl wrote an editorial in the college newspaper protesting Carver's treatment and, as a result, reportedly lost the scholarship she had won as an honor student. On the other hand, Carver was welcomed at the University of Mississippi and Mississippi State.

Few people realized how much the lectures drained Carver. He was anemic, had fainting spells, and was nearly always recuperating from one flu attack or another. In 1930 he reported to his friend Ross that he had coughed all night for several nights during a lecture tour and, in the Kansas City train station, feared he was going to collapse as he struggled up the stairs to the waiting room. Then there were visitors, more each year "from every direction." Because of their constant interruptions, Carver wrote, "I fear my laboratory work is about at an end." Yet he did manage, as usual, to be remarkably productive, developing such oddities as a peanut toothpaste that dentists in Montgomery gave their patients as a treatment for gum disorders. He produced seventeen different types of paving based on cotton—in Fort McClellan, Alabama, his cotton asphalt was used for a runway that long outlasted Carver. He was making rugs from spiny mallow and yucca leaves, and fabricating paper and beaverboard from straw. He was still investigating peanut fungi for Tom Huston, along with fungi that were affecting other crops. And he was still receiving pleas from remote corners of the world to identify strange tropical maladies and treat them.

People thought Carver could do anything—and would do anything. Grieving people sent photographs of their lost loved ones and asked if he could kindly—and charitably—paint "a nice, big" portrait of them with his clay paints on peanut shell paper. One doctor wrote from Belize, "Should you request, I shall send you some germs extracted from a patient with the hope that you can make the necessary analysis and prepare a drug that would eventually cure the disease." The doctor was not sure what disease Carver was supposed to cure. When pharmacies began going out of business because of the Depression, people from far away wrote to Carver to ask if *he* couldn't refill their prescriptions.

The Depression fell early on Mississippi and Alabama, in the winter of 1930, during the region's historic draught. By 1932, whole counties were closing their public schools, then allowing a few to reopen as smaller, private schools. By the following year, there were similar closings of both schools and banks across the country, even in the usually prosperous small towns of Iowa where Carver had received his desultory secondary education. Black parents naturally could not afford to maintain private schools, so black children dropped out at whatever grade level they were, most of them never to return. In Hattiesburg, Mississippi, schools were still open in 1933 but operating only eight months a year. An examination of schoolchildren in two counties in Alabama revealed that 90 percent had "terrible" teeth, trench mouth, pyorrhea, and cavities. The teachers assisting in the examinations—all unmarried—no doubt needed dental care themselves: their average pay when room and board was deducted was $1.06 a day. The price of cotton kept falling, along with everything else. A can of Campbell's tomato soup sold for eight cents; eight pounds of bulk lard ("Bring your own bucket") for ninety-six cents, a large can of "cooked brains" for twenty-three cents, and Black Draught, for "constipation, indigestion, and biliousness" sold for one cent a dose.

Some of Carver's former students, now adult farmers, wrote with anxious joviality that they hoped they wouldn't be reduced to eating their cotton. "Money is like hen's teeth in this section," wrote Alice Simmons, who signed herself "Daught." Long before the bank failures, she wrote of men leaving Mississippi in droves to find work. "There is only a road between us and the trains and we can see men beating their way into the freight car boxes—going places looking for work . . . Papa went to collect rent that should have amounted to thirty dollars last Monday, but he only got one." The pay for field work was $1.50 per day, but intensive field work was only needed in the spring and fall. Like many people who were lucky enough to have jobs, Carver had his salary reduced, from $100 monthly to $87.

It was only in the newspapers that times appeared good. Of 27,000 people in Macon County, the *Montgomery Advertiser* blithely reported that only fourteen were unemployed and that everywhere in Alabama, the jobless rate was under 1.4 percent. This was arrant nonsense, since everyone in Alabama personally knew dozens of people who were looking for work. One of Carver's friends in Columbus, Georgia, wrote that the newspapers had started putting editorials on the front page every day, trying to convince people that times were getting better, but that no one believed it. Columbus did its best to raise spirits. During the most dismal of all Christmas seasons, the downtown section was strung with colored lights as usual, though the town could no longer afford to pay for them. The merchants volunteered to finance the expenditure. Carver wrote to all the friends who usually sent him Christmas presents and asked them instead to make a gift to "some poor, hungry, sick, jobless soul."

Things were scarcely better in sections of the North. The Loom Works of Worcester, Massachusetts, announced that women whose husbands were employed would be discharged first during the massive layoffs. In Chicago, Al Capone opened a large, free soup kitchen for the unemployed. Youngsters had the hardest time of all finding work. One of Carver's young friends in Milwaukee wrote, "I have been to the various places in Kenosha and here in Milwaukee . . . So far, it is the same story—'We have so many men with dependents whom we have laid off and whom we must rehire first.'" From New York, one of Carver's student friends, Harry Ittner, commiserated that between 10 and 14 million people were unemployed in the United States (out of a population of about 120 million), yet one could still see radio, movie, and stage stars, bankers, large businessmen, and others living ostentatiously. Ittner was appalled.

It was true that the public was bifurcated psychologically between hopelessness and escapist fantasy. Newspapers were lavish in reports of society weddings and heiresses on world tours. The "Social Calendar" was a weekly feature of the press, announcing such entertainments as bridge classes for ladies of leisure. Women graduating from college were featured on the front pages of Sunday editions, while the back pages invariably reported cases of farmers killing themselves and their families and mothers of small children committing suicide. The antidote to that bleak news were comic strips, read by everybody—*Winnie Winkle, Little Orphan Annie, Bringing Up Father*. The most popular shows on radio were interviews with sports figures—Knute Rockne, Jack Dempsey, Babe Ruth. Everyone who could afford the ten-cent admission flocked to the movies to see the Marx Brothers. The good thing about it all was that much of the entertainment accessible to ordinary people was of remarkably high quality—free concerts given by idle symphony musicians trying to maintain their skills, good serialized novels, and an affluence of classical music on the radio.

In Buffalo, Harry Ittner observed, people were starving, yet the grain elevators in the harbor were full of wheat—"so much that they do not know what
to do with it." Due to the distribution system, there seemed no way to give
the wheat to people who were hungering in the very shadow of the elevators.
Ittner favored a new movement that was gaining adherents. Following the
ideas of Edward Bellamy and Thorstein Veblen, the Technocracy system would
place the entire industrial and agricultural business of the country under en-
gineers and economists who would have absolute control over production.
Ittner approved of the steps the Fascists were taking in Italy along those lines.

Certain entrepreneurs were trying various schemes to relieve the spreading desperation, but these were possibly too late and certainly too little. In
Detroit, Henry Ford was willing to provide capital of $250,000 to establish a
colony that would be worked, supervised, and managed by black people. They
would raise products on a farm, which would provide materials for a factory
connected to it. Ford hoped the enterprise could be extended to other cities where there was widespread unemployment. At the time, no black people
were farming in the rural areas outside Detroit. The organizers of the plan finally decided in March 1933 that it would take decades for the colony to make
enough profit to repay Ford. In fact, the entrepreneur and his estate could
have afforded to hold the debt for generations, but that was not the sort of aid
that Ford offered, and so the project fizzled. The following month, Ford sent
for Carver to ask his advice about what could be done.

Carver stated what every thinking person knew—that the country still possessed exactly the same manpower, natural resources, and infrastructure that
it had before the economic collapse. "Are we starving in the midst of plenty?"
he asked in an article. The South, he said, was still capable of raising peaches,
plums, figs, pears, corn, string beans, okra, tomatoes, pumpkins, and many
other foods. Yet there was hunger everywhere in the South, despite the previous summer's bounty crop of fruit and vegetables. People were not trying
to preserve supplies for winter because they couldn't afford jars, but Carver
pointed out that all those foods were delicious when properly dried. A billion
pounds of peanuts had been raised. Carver exhorted readers to use peanuts as
a meat substitute and insisted that a family could maintain itself on peanuts
and other foods that could be raised in a backyard garden. Throughout the
Depression, he continued to write articles urging the public to view the pea-

nut as a staple item of food, again and again presenting tables that compared the nutritive value of a pound of peanuts with like amounts of cheese, eggs, round steak, and various luxury fruits and vegetables. For years, people had been abandoning farming to seek industrial jobs. Now was the time, he said, to go back—not to subsistence farming but to sustenance farming, since no other sustenance was apparent—to go back even as tenants or sharecroppers, if necessary.

In his many magazine and newspaper articles, Carver urged farmers to have fruit trees. "Make up your mind now to not only live from products raised on your farm, but to always have a surplus to sell." He stressed the value of raising chickens and as many hogs a possible, since hogs could turn waste materials into meat.

Jim Hardwick still had a paycheck, but most of Carver's young friends were suffering. I. B. Talton wrote from Denver, "I have no job and have not yet been able to secure a teaching position for the winter . . . There is a certain girl in Birmingham . . . You and she seem to be the only two people in this whole world who really love me . . . Outside of my work, whatever that happens to be, you two are my only interest in life . . . I've tried several laboratories for work. It's the same story always: 'Laying off men.' . . . I'm sitting here looking at the snow-capped peaks of the Rockies, wondering just what the next six months will bring me."

People were no longer buying Tom's Roasted Peanuts to eat during their coffee breaks at work, since they had neither work, coffee, nor money for snacks. Production at the Huston plant had to be cut back. Grady Porter was let go, and there were scary days for Bob Barry. "You sure do help me want to keep on living," Barry wrote to Carver in 1931. "Please keep it up." Month after month, bankruptcy was looming. "The worst part of it," Barry wrote to Carver, "is that there isn't enough for any of us to do to be able to go home at night and feel that there was some use for living each day."

What finally precipitated Huston's business failure was a project he had begun a few years before, while the peanut company was still in its glory days. In the late 1920s, Huston had turned his practical mind to Georgia's excess peach crop. He developed a plan for quick-freezing peaches that were going to waste and marketing them in the off-season (using Carver's technical advice for quick-freezing fruits.) But just after Huston had gone into debt to launch the new product, the Depression struck and sales of the new frozen peaches plummeted. Huston's bank creditors demanded controlling interest in his peanut company and then promptly used their power to fire Huston as president. Carver continued to provide scientific advice to the new directors for many more years until his death, but there was no deep friendship with them such as he had enjoyed with Huston and Barry. The indomitable Huston went on to launch a chewing gum enterprise, "Julep Gums." In this, too, Carver appears to have been assisting him, since around the same time, the early 1930s, Carver formulated a chewy jujube candy made from peanuts. It was Carver who seems to have suggested curing the jujube and making a snack out of it. He gave Huston technical direction, as usual. According to Austin Curtis, Carver's assistant of those years, the unlucky Huston "lost his mind" some time in the late 1930s; Curtis could offer no record of Huston finding it later on.

A weird morbidity pervaded those Depression years. Suicide was so pervasive that when someone went missing, everyone feared the worst. In 1931, Wade Moss, the chemical director of the Huston company, gave a printing company an order to print 1,000 volumes of *The Trail Blazer*, a biographical booklet that had been written about Carver. Then he disappeared, leaving the printing company without distribution lists or payment but with a room full of Carver's life. It was assumed that Moss decided his own life was not worth continuing.

The strangers who turned to Carver for advice and money naturally multiplied during the Depression. A deaf man in California "who nobody cares to hear" asked how he could make a living. All he wanted was honest work—and a method for making a light brick out of clay without fire so that he could build a house for his family. A fifteen-year-old in Michigan whose father had had several operations in the previous four years needed $4,000 to keep his parents from losing their home in one of the thousands of foreclosures of the time. "Please don't let my folks know about this . . . they would give me the dickens for begging." Carver was awash in letters from youngsters who wanted to work their way through school and asked which colleges might accept them: "My father is a cripple and has no money . . . I will never be satisfied until I have a college degree." Some asked him outright to finance them, such as one white friend who needed six dollars a month to attend law school in Chicago and another who needed an entrance fee of $19.50 to start college work.

For the first time Tuskegee was forced to cancel its annual fair in 1931. The Institute claimed it was struggling to stay open and solicited contributions from its faculty—Carver gave generously. Carver estimated that the school lost about $20,000 in the bank failures. Carver lost twice that much. For all his working life, he had steadily saved whatever part of his salary of a thousand a year that he didn't give away. In 1931 he had over $7,500 in a Des Moines bank and more than $31,000 in the Macon County Bank in interest-bearing certificates. By the middle of the next year, both banks had gone under and with them, Carver's lifetime store. "I had my eggs in two baskets and they both collapsed and smashed my eggs," he wrote to Dr. Ross. The bank failure "did not leave me enough to get a pair of shoes," he remarked to another friend, "but I am not suffering nor grieving." Like thousands of other people who had scrimped for decades, he was wiped out. Moreover, in 1932 Carver had not deposited five of his paychecks. As a consequence, they were not honored, and so he lost an additional $500.

People assumed Carver was quite comfortable in Tuskegee, where his housing was assured and where he never needed to miss a meal, even a late meal, except voluntarily. And indeed, he was comfortable. He mentioned his savings loss to Jim but only in passing, in one of his letters. Though he was saddened by conditions around him, in 1932 Carver may have been one of the few truly happy people in America. He was speaking to ever-larger audiences. In Kansas City he addressed 1,300 people, surprisingly, since "It was a pay affair," meaning that the audience paid to get in. In October the popular *American Magazine* published a long biographical article about him, "A Boy Who Was Traded for a Horse," by James Saxon Childers. Carver's correspondence then doubled as letters of admiration poured in.

But more than anything else, what kept him giddy with delight through the entire year was that he and Jim were making tours together, evangelical excursions sponsored by various branches of the Y.M.C.A. For days at a time, Carver had Jim to himself, away from the interested eyes of the Tuskegee community. In between their trips, Carver wrote to Jim about God and nature, as always, and about Jim's spiritual progress and the grand work the younger man was accomplishing. Now, in addition, he chatted about the recent "fam-

ily" members—every one of his letters mentions some new boy or girl. "He
has caught the vision," he writes of one or another. These new acolytes—some
three dozen—wrote to him regularly, usually a few times a month. One was a
Rosicrucian who tried to recruit Carver; another worked with the Anti-Saloon
League; many others were aspiring poets or inventors. All were more or less
God-struck.

Carver was often sick, but even that did not deflate his enthusiasm. In April
1932, he cheerily reported going to the hospital. "My trouble is said to be fatal if
I take cold with it." In the fall he complained to Mrs. Milholland that he could
not do much walking and even riding in a car tired him. But "Thank God I
keep as well as I could expect at my advanced age"—about seventy-one. In October, he was struck down again during a flu epidemic which saw seven thousand cases in Alabama and thirty other victims in the Tuskegee Institute hospital. But he said very little about his discomfort, his chief worry being that his
health would interfere with trips he had planned with Jim. A fire raging on the
campus while Carver was writing to Jim occasioned only one sentence, even
though it completely burned a teacher's cottage and one of the largest girls'
dormitories. Such events hardly deflected Carver's preoccupation with Jim and
their special connection. He wrote about one of his walks where he collected
dead twigs—okra stalks, bean vines, dead leaves. "All were teeming with the
most simple (and in some cases) the most marvelously complex compound
microscopic life. How I longed for my great spiritual boy, the pioneer of all the
dear little family. I wanted him to see that by the thing we call death, in the
plant is only a preparation for myriads of actual microscopic plants that could
not have existed had those plants not given up their lives, as we term it." Carver
was still using the microscope his fellow students had given him in 1896.

The trips with Jim in 1932 and 1933 meant the world to Carver. He loved
traveling, and these were the most loving travels of his life. A swimming incident elicited a facetious threat: "May this soak in pretty thoroughly, dear, that
two can play mighty pretty at that water ducking business." Apparently "Jimmie" as Carver now occasionally called him, ate some raw meat during one of
their trips, for a lark; Carver chided him for it. They even had fun with the car
breaking down, an old Ford that had to be prayed over if it were to complete a
journey. While planning "the greatest trip we have ever made," they doubled
their prayers for the health of the car. In between trips there were letters, and

in between letters there were notes. Carver dreamed about Jim, complained about not hearing from him often enough, and dashed off quick messages: "My great spiritual boy: This, dear, is before breakfast Mon. morning. I just want my precious boy to know that I will pray that God will be especially near you all this week." The relationship was clearly stressful for Jim. During the Christmas visit of 1930, Carver had noted, "Your nerves are delicate, finely balanced, and are extremely sensitive to change." Jim tended to have back trouble and suffered some problems with his eyes—possibly as a result of tension, as Carver himself was aware.

At the end of 1932, Hardwick wrote Carver a letter remarkable both for its tenderness and its rarefied tone of formality. It was, as it turned out, a farewell letter, though perhaps Carver did not recognize it as such. Under Hardwick's nostalgic message, one can almost see him drawing a curtain over a stage of his life and leaving Carver behind it.

My great Friend Dr. Carver:

Apart from those in my own family circle you are and have been for years the best friend I have ever had. You are so much a part of my life, are the object of so much of my thinking and affections that it is hard to imagine life without you.

I shall treasure throughout life the many and varied experiences which we have had together. We have laughed over funny happenings until we were both almost in hysterics. We have trusted ourselves to old automobiles in some situations in which it seemed only a miracle could get us where we wanted to go. A time or two it seemed that our only hope lay in your extracting some gasoline from nearby vegetation. We have gone through dangers together, driving over flooded roads, facing antagonistic people, at times barely escaping accidents which neither of us will ever forget. Finally, as a climax, we have kneeled together many times to pray until God flooded our souls—we knew we had seen Him without whom men cannot live.

Traveling with you so much I have been made aware of many doors that neither you nor any member of your race could enter. I have seen the antagonism of some who resented your attainments merely because of your race.

Over all these experiences you have triumphed without any trace of bitterness. I came to realize you were invincible. No man could really harm you. Through you I have come to have a deeper faith in love as the way to meet all difficulties.

My sympathy, of course, is deep for the members of your race who find this life cramped and so many opportunities unavailable to them. It is deep also for those who have succumbed to such treatment—are the victims of bitterness, cynicism, and a sense of futility. My sympathy goes out as well to the apparently better situated but infinitely more pathetic members of my own race whose prejudices and selfish attitudes are responsible for such conditions.

As I close this letter I want to send you my love and express the hope and prayer that God will give you life and strength to carry on your work for many years to come.

Jim Hardwick

The occasion for the letter is uncertain—possibly an early Christmas greeting—but it marks the end of the fevered intimacy between Carver and Hardwick. They took another trip together in 1933, "the greatest trip," according to Carver, where they separated in Tucson. "It was such a trial for me to see him go after such a delightful and uplifting 16 days together," Carver remarked to Jim's mother. Carver wrote Jim fifteen letters that year, throbbing with God and ecstasy just like all the previous ones. But the tide of their relationship was ebbing, for two quite understandable reasons.

First and foremost, Jim acquired a new best friend who shared all his secrets. In 1934 Carver wrote to Jim's mother, "I confess that I have not as yet recovered from the shock of dear 'Jimmie's' marriage." It was natural and normal that Jim's new wife would replace Carver as his dearest confidante. But how the old man must have suffered, especially since the marriage came as a surprise! Hardwick's mother Helena maintained a correspondence with Carver into the late 1930s when Jim seems to have completely withdrawn from him. She welcomed Carver to the Hardwick home when he passed through the Carolinas on one of his tours. Many years after Carver's death, Helena told an interviewer:

> Dr. Carver was tall and stately . . . He always used good English. Never making a grammatical error . . . On entering the home Dr. Carver bowed very low and he was so humble, one felt very little in his presence.

Hardwick's marriage was the primary reason the bond with Carver slackened. But it was not the only reason. About a year before Jim's wedding, something occurred that interfered with Carver's obsession with Jim, interfered, in fact, with every facet of Carver's life and turned his routine thoughts and actions upside down. Even his incessant descants about God subsided.

For some years, Carver had been giving massages with his peanut oil emulsion to people who came to him in run-down condition, sickly, but with no readily diagnosable disorder. He frequently received effusive thanks for restoring their health. He gave peanut oil massages to Bob Barry and President Moton, both of whom seemed to think the medicament did them some good, and he treated the leg of a physician in Tupelo—an eye, ear, nose and throat specialist—to good effect. During one of Jim's low periods, Carver lectured him: "Your body needs building up. How I wish I was near enough to give you a good massage every evening. With prayer followed by oil I would put you to bed rather early and let you sleep late. A week of such treatment would make a new man of you physically."

Carver believed in the efficacy of his preparation, although he did not understand exactly how it worked. A former state congressman thought Carver's massages had saved his life and recommended Carver to the superintendent of a Florida cotton mill, who likewise traveled to Tuskegee for the treatments for four months. The peanut oil had started out as one of Carver's cosmetic preparations to remove wrinkles. He discovered its flesh-building properties when women who used it complained that their faces were getting fat. Carver began trying it with people who came to him with shriveled limbs. He would give them several massages and then send them home with a supply of the oil and instructions to continue the manipulations. In many cases, the massages helped; in others, not at all. But in a few cases, the results were miraculous. One of the most amazing cases was a man who had come to him on crutches but, after a period of treatment, was walking six miles (later eight and a half miles) without any sort of assistance. Another patient, a little boy, had to be carried into the room at first but after a month of treatments, astonished Carver by getting up one day from the massage table, dressing himself, and walking across the floor. Carver became increasingly aware that the massages were most effective in cases of rheumatism, St. Vitus's Dance (chorea), muscle pain, and irregular growth. The oil seemed to build muscles and rejuvenate tissue—skin tissue especially. But people hoped it could cure anything and sent for it as a remedy for such complaints as roaring in the ears. A Texas man was one of the earliest petitioners, but surely not the last, to ask Carver to send him some of the oil to remedy "a short and shrunken male organ." People who tried to order the oil from Carver were referred to the Penol Company. But the people who came to him at Tuskegee he massaged without charge at night and on weekends, after his regular work in the lab. Word spread of the oil's benefits. There was talk of giving a massage to Franklin D. Roosevelt.

In an interview in 2004, one of Carver's "miracle" patients described his massage treatment, even though her "cure" took place after Carver's death. Dr. Patricia McIntosh-Bell was in the second grade in 1947 when infantile paralysis, or polio, struck, leaving her leg withered like that of a person of ninety—"horrible looking." The doctors in a hospital in Tulsa, Oklahoma, thought that since she would always have a shriveled right leg, they should amputate it while she was still young and allow her to get accustomed to a prosthesis; it would become natural and normal for her. Her mother adamantly opposed the amputation. A doctor told her father, "Take your wife outside and talk some sense into her and then bring her back in." The father replied, "I have to live with her. You go outside with her." So it ended with Patricia coming back home with both her legs. Her mother was acquainted with Carver's treatment of crippled victims, having attended Tuskegee many years before during a mumps and fever epidemic during which Carver had treated everybody. She telephoned to Tuskegee, even though at that time, as Patricia recalled, "it was a big deal to make a long-distance call." Carver had been dead for four years. The authorities at Tuskegee went into Carver's lab, which had been kept exactly as he had left it, found the formula for his peanut oil and the instructions for the massages, copied them, and sent them to Patricia's mother.

The treatment consisted of massaging the leg with the oil for a long time, then wrapping the leg in blanket strips that had been soaked in hot water, and then further wrapping the leg with towels. The little girl's parents continued this treatment for a year before the leg "finally started to flesh up." It was smaller than the other leg, but she was eventually able to walk without a limp. She returned to school at the end of the year. "People who had the privilege to go to the hospital recovered," Dr. McIntosh-Bell recalled—noting that as a Negro she was not permitted to stay in the white hospital—"but they were in iron lungs, wheelchairs, crutches, things like that. Almost all of them had some kind of brace." But those whom Carver treated "came out of it walking, doing normal, without the aid of anything."

In 1933, Carver had given a cycle of massages to only two victims of infantile paralysis. But those two appeared to have been wondrously cured of their symptoms; that is, they came to him as severely handicapped cripples and ended the treatment as normal, functioning people able to participate in athletics. United Press got wind of the special peanut oil being used to treat victims of polio and telegraphed Carver for confirmation. Carver telegraphed back, "Do not want any publicity at this time until making further demonstrations of its efficacy." Nevertheless, Carver was about to be thrown, quite suddenly, into fame such as no one had imagined was possible for a quaint black scientist working in a primitive laboratory in the poorest southern hill country. On the last day of 1933, the last private day of his life, people all across the country opened their newspapers to read that George W. Carver of Tuskegee Institute had discovered an effective treatment—indeed, a cure—for the most dreaded childhood disease of the twentieth century.

14

---≈---

SUFFERING HUMANITY

W hen Carver began massaging limbs withered by infantile paralysis, there were seven thousand crippled children in Alabama whose parents were too poor to pay for any sort of medical treatment. In 1930, schools closed in Kansas City and other communities for fear of the infection, and in those towns, children under fifteen were ordered by the authorities to stay away from movies and other public gathering places. Infantile paralysis struck everywhere, cutting down millionaires such as Franklin D. Roosevelt and paupers living in abandoned freight cars, people with access to excellent health care and people who had no care except what they could give each other. Rich and poor lived in dread for their little ones as they saw people around them placed in iron lungs or unable to move in their beds. The story of Carver and the "cure" for polio is one of those details of medical history that flickers briefly and then fades away into the oblivion of failed research. But for Carver the "brief period" amounted to several harrowing years of overwork that destroyed what was left of his health.

Unlike United Press, the Associated Press had not sought permission from Carver to break the story about infantile paralysis, as the disease was then called. "Peanut Oil Aids Victims of Paralysis: Healing Property of Mineral Liquid Found by Negro Scientist" was the 1933 New Year's headline on front pages from Montgomery to Milwaukee.

> Discovery of a mineral [sic] oil in peanuts that has aided in the recovery
> of infantile paralysis victims and in the rejuvenation of tissues has been
> announced by Dr. George Washington Carver, noted Negro scientist and
> head of the research department of Tuskegee Institute. "It has been given
> out that I have a cure," said Dr. Carver. "I have not, but it looks hopeful."

The article went on to imply that Carver had used the oil on 250 polio patients with good results. Actually, he had used it on only two victims of infantile paralysis. The other 248 were, as Carver was the first to state, people with arthritis, stunted growth, unexplained aches and pains, and a host of other symptoms that his peanut oil massages seemed to relieve. "I am using it as a fact finder," said Carver, "and I am working out its complete pharmaceutical value."

But he was never going to have the time or proper conditions to test the specific therapeutic value of his peanut oil. Three hours after the article appeared in the morning papers, cars were lined up in front of Rockefeller Hall carrying afflicted patients who begged for a massage, then and there. By afternoon, the road leading to the Institute was full of carts, wagons and automobiles that would join the queue. On January 2, 1933, the first day of mail delivery after the appearance of the news, the Tuskegee post office was inundated with letters from "suffering humanity," as Carver called the avalanche of distress that fell on his stooped shoulders.

> "My boy . . . fifteen years old . . . one arm drawn up, the other can't bend. Holds a pencil with his mouth and draws . . . His limbs ache all the time."
>
> "Seven years old, weighs 34 pounds."
>
> "Ten years old . . . can't sit up . . . arms and legs don't grow, but is very intelligent."
>
> "I am 5 ft. 4 inches tall, 45 years old and weigh 79 pounds . . . so anxious for the sake of my husband and little girl to recover my health without incurring further hospital bills."
>
> "My five-year-old can't sit up. He seems to have right good use of his legs but his back is weak and cannot use his arms good . . . If there is any chance of getting some of the peanut oil to use on him, you cannot imagine how much I would appreciate it."
>
> "I am a dentist . . . One leg amputated because of a disease that caused the blood vessels in the legs to collapse . . . Can work a few hours a day . . . Trying to save the other leg."
>
> ". . . Sudden blindness . . ."
>
> "Dr. Carver I have a grandson and he had infantile paralysis and he lost his speech and will you sen me you peanut oil send it C O d please."

"I am writing to you to see will you please give my baby a treatment she is a little girl five years old she is underweight she doesn't talk and she slobbers all the time and keep her clothes wet all the time right on her chest so please let me know at once."

Certainly not all the patients suffered from infantile paralysis. A TB patient wondered if the oil could be massaged into the lungs to build them up. A widow, out of work and supporting her mother, wrote about her seven-year-old who had never walked. The doctors could not identify the cause. The girl could not stand, but she could kick and roll over in bed. Any number of people wrote concerning children, with and without infantile paralysis, who could not use their arms or legs, hold their heads up, or control their speech, but who seemed to be intelligent.

People wrote to him asking for a bust developer, a way to treat a tumor without surgery, to relieve epilepsy, "smothering spells," "bleeding bladder," and "Gonorier and Syphillis." To these, Carver sent back a form letter: "The oil is not manufactured commercially and will not be until I finish my investigations and get the range of its entire pharmaceutical possibilities. I have only used it on two cases of Infantile Paralysis, each of which shows decided improvement. One of the cases has left and I will not see him any more. Three others have just come to me, so that I can go on with my investigations and give you truth and directions of value."

He could not resist appending a note to most of the letters. Some people received the form letter but wrote again anyway, pleading for some word of hope. A fourteen-year-old girl had been stricken with paralysis a few months before and had not been able to sit up since. Her parents, like nearly all the supplicants for the oil, could not afford a hospital, "even though the doctors say she will never walk again unless treated in a hospital now." A few tried to make Carver feel guilty about not sending the oil, but it was easy to forgive them in the light of their misery: "I belong to Michigan and all my people helped to take your people out of slavery pleas help me out of the awful pain I have to suffer yours truly." Most people wrote with fervid, humble hope that Carver could lead them out of their despair. "I want to know what wood I have to Do to try your treatment I has had a stroke for near 3 years I can work on my leg But drage it an cant use my hand at all So please Rite Me at once."

It would have taken a tougher man than Carver to turn his back on them. Tuskegee allowed him a part-time secretary—sometimes a student, sometimes the wife of a faculty or staff member—to sort through the letters, deciding which ones should receive the form response and which letters Carver should see. The patients who received Carver's personal attention—they numbered in the hundreds—were instructed to go to a doctor and get a diagnosis, since an oil massage might be exactly what they did not need. If the doctor confirmed that no harm would be done by a massage, he asked them to send the doctor's statement describing their problems. Usually, the patient's importuning ended there, since hardly anyone in the depths of the Depression had money for yet another visit to a doctor merely to obtain his written diagnosis. Carver tried to be resolute about getting the permissions. He had been advised to proceed carefully: practicing medicine without a license was a felony that could incur a long jail sentence. When people he knew came to him for help, he dispensed with all precautions and even treated their relatives.

Sufferers who came to Tuskegee received daily massages until they had to leave. Usually they stayed at Tuskegee and paid the Institute a fee for their room and board. Carver taught them how to continue the massages at home and sent them away with instructions and a small supply of the compound. He would not accept payment for the massages or the oil. The patients were asked to write him weekly detailed reports of their progress. He soon had twenty-five infantile paralysis patients along with people with other disorders. He did not massage women, practically the only people he refused, for what he called "obvious reasons."

Peanut oil, it seemed, was good for everything—hay fever and skin problems. One man's hands "were full of sores. The skin was off some of the fingers almost all the way around. I was really afraid to touch him." Carver made up a salve from peanut oil and the yucca plant. Within days, the hands were almost completely healed. Aside from the rubdowns, he saw hundreds of patients who asked him for oral advice about various conditions—he counted fifty-two in one day alone. Whenever he massaged anyone, he tried to clear up other problems that came to his attention, mixing up a zinc ointment, for example, to cure one young man's acne.

Within a month after the first news story about his "cure" for paralysis, Carver had received over 1,500 letters. Some of the crippled patients made startling improvement after just a few weeks. These were only a few of the hundreds Carver treated, but their recovery was so radical that they could not be ignored. One boy stricken with infantile paralysis came to Carver on crutches, with a withered leg, dragging a useless foot behind him. "He now walks uphill for miles," Carver reported to his friend, Dr. Ross, who was a physician and surgeon. "He plays football and says that leg and foot are as strong as the other one and are now as large." Another case was that of a sixteen-year-old who was carried into Carver's treatment room, absolutely helpless. A few months later Carver was reporting, "Yesterday he, too, walked in without cane or crutch. He cannot go up and down steps without help."

One of Carver's first patients was W. S. Sherrill, a personal friend of Franklin Delano Roosevelt and a fellow victim of polio. He traveled by train 1,100 miles to receive three days of massages. He reported that after further self-treatment at home he was positively better and planned to return in two months. Carver explained to Sherrill that he worked first with the fatty acids of the oil, which changed their limpidity and viscosity. The isolation of acids from peanuts was not common in Carver's day. References exist from 1913 citing some German chemists who isolated lignoceric acid from peanut oil; possibly they got the idea from Carver, who by then had spent years working with peanut components. "Second. The absorptive power of the skin is given special attention. Sometimes I have to use 3, 4, and 5 of the number before I am through. Third. I single out the muscles, those that are real active, sluggish, inactive, and then proceed to wake them up by massaging. The patient is shown just what to do."

To Dr. Ross, he remarked, "With my patients I get varied results. Some respond with the first treatment, others much later . . . I have them from 50 years down to 11 years, some have been crippled thirty years and respond to the treatment . . . I do not take operable cases, of course . . . not attempting to doctor. I am simply a scientist trying to work out the efficacy of the peanut oil." To another doctor, he sent instructions on massaging: "The muscles needing it should be singled out and massaged daily. 5 or 6 drops only—gently, thoroughly. Skin and muscles should become supersaturated in about 9 days, then stop and give only friction massage for 9 days, then use oil again." His biographer Rackham Holt watched him with a patient. "He would run his long, sensitive fingers over the afflicted area and say, 'Life ends about here,' isolating the muscle so accurately he might have been dissecting it out."

The success stories were not based only on his observation; when the patients returned to their own doctors, they, too, noted improvement. "Mother took the baby [a two-year-old] to Dr. Dawson last week, and the first remark that he made was to the effect that the baby was better than he had ever seen him, and I feel that the credit goes to you. He sits in his swing for fifteen minutes at a time and works his feet to push himself up and down . . . Still unable to force his body up from the floor." Doctors, especially the doctors of patients who had benefited from Carver's treatment, wrote to him asking to receive a portion of his compound, along with instructions for the massage, so that they could try it out. Their patients were suffering from many conditions, such as multiple sclerosis and "contracture and deformity of lower extremities as a result of peripheral neuritis." Within weeks of the first news story of the "cure," fourteen physicians had eagerly written to Carver.

Carver's old friend Dr. Ross was the first to work alone with small amounts of the emulsion. Thrilled with the improvement in his patients, he bought a larger quantity of the oil from a plant. "I shall begin to use it on a baby 2 years old that is just recovering from an attack of infantile paralysis with both limbs paralyzed and if successful with this case I am going to establish a great clinic for this kind of work and see how many white, colored, and Mexicans I can help in this town with oil." A few months later Ross was writing, "My little baby patient is now able to stand on his feet and walk when led by its mother."

One of the most prominent doctors who took a wary but enthusiastic interest in Carver's work was Luther Fischer, an Atlanta physician, surgeon, and head of a large hospital that eventually became the Emory University Hospital Midtown. Fischer was no radical. In 1923 he fired a nurse at the Davis-Fischer Sanatorium for wearing bobbed hair. She appealed to Dr. Davis, Fischer's partner and former teacher, who was the father of five daughters. He reinstated the nurse. In 1935, eighteen months after news broke of the massage treatment, Fischer wrote to Carver asking for information. If Fischer could be won over to the efficacy of the treatment, he might provide the professional connection that Carver needed in order to have his work accepted by the medical community at large.

Carver described many cases to Fischer. The one that may have most impressed the doctor most was that of Emmett Cox who, like Fischer, lived in Atlanta, and had been treated by physicians with whom Fischer was acquainted. Stricken with infantile paralysis at two, he had conventional treatment in a sanatorium and underwent several operations. At Carver's request, Cox wrote to Dr. Fischer explaining his case history: "My legs were very weak and dwindled away to almost nothing [after the surgeries] so they were again put in braces, one a long brace extending from my waist down to my foot, and the other a small leg brace both of which I wore up to about three months ago. I had given up hope of ever going without braces and crutches until I was examined by Dr. Carver." Carver began massaging Cox on September 1, 1934. "Within a month," Cox averred, "legs began to grow and fill out and muscles began to strengthen considerably. In three months time my legs had grown so much that my braces were pressing against them and preventing them from growing further. I realized that I would either have to buy a larger brace or do without entirely."

After not bending his knee for twenty-two years, Emmett Cox at the time of the writing was driving a car. He gained weight, and his complexion cleared up after the treatment. "The treatment consists of a massage by Dr. Carver once a week and by myself each night. After having Infantile Paralysis for 22 years, I am now looking forward and firmly believe that I will be able to walk without crutches some time in the near future."

Carver was experimenting with forty-four oils, alone and in combinations, varying them according to the skin absorption of different individuals. He had good results with a compound of cocoa butter and olive oil but finally decided that peanut oil was overall the best. By the time Fischer became involved in his work, Carver had begun to think that it wasn't the oil at all that effected the restoration but rather the massage. He finally had to admit that he did not know what brought about marked improvement in some of the cases.

Fischer was careful. First he asked Carver for a list of his patients; to several he sent a questionnaire and an invitation to describe everything they could about their condition and Carver's treatment. They wrote him back very fully. He visited Carver a number of times, spending long hours to learn his massage technique and even bringing along one of his own patients for treatment. His excitement grew. He consulted with Carver about making additions to his hospital to equip a special section for massage treatment. Fischer, however, was not about to compromise his own position among his colleagues by formally endorsing a therapy that was still experimental. Carver once mentioned a chiropractor who was trying out the oil massages. Fischer bristled. The medical profession did not recognize chiropractics, he wrote sharply. "If it is your intention to have any relations whatever with this group I shall have to very reluctantly and with much sorrow withdraw any interest that I have in your work." In steering Carver away from chiropractors, Fischer was actually protecting him. The American Medical Association (AMA), which no medical practitioner could afford to antagonize, was at the time conducting a vicious campaign to discredit chiropractors.

There was no shortage of people who wanted to manufacture Carver's massage compound. His early biographer Raleigh Merritt, ever alert to the possibility of a Carver-endorsed enterprise, was among the first to propose a business venture with his old friend. Carver gently refused to give out any formula until he understood the process by which his patients' muscles were rejuvenated. After four months, he still had treated only fifteen cases of infantile paralysis, the rest being victims of other afflictions. Carl S. Frischkern, a doctor in Norfolk, Virginia, began distributing his own peanut oil, one that was not appreciably different from the oils already on the market, claiming that he had made the discovery of a treatment for infantile paralysis. Protective of his friend Carver, Dr. Moton was at first incensed at this effrontery, but Carver had come to the conclusion that any manufactured peanut oil would suffice for the massaging. He ended up recommending that his patients order their oil from Frischkern, since they could get it from him in large quantities at a fair price.

Dr. Fischer became alarmed at the army of people eager to exploit Carver's findings, businessmen who wanted to use both Carver's and Fischer's names in advertisements for their massage products. At one point, he warned Carver that he would abandon all his investigations into the massage therapy if Carver tried to promote his treatment without first getting the approval of the AMA. Fischer was trying to help him gain the endorsement, but it was a tricky business and he had to proceed cautiously. As the head of a hospital, he could not become associated with a "quack" therapy, as defined by the professional medical associations, regardless of his own conviction that it had merit.

Meanwhile, the occasional miracles kept turning up. After many weeks of treatment, a patient, "one of the strangest cases that has come to my attention," was brought into Carver's office.

This child, as I remember, is a poor diminutive fellow just three years old. His head rested on his chest and his feet were crossed. Could not stand, of course. Did not seem to notice anything. They told me that their doctor said that the child was defective at birth. That some of the brain cells which cause muscular coordination were not functioning, and might never, as the mother in desperation insisted that I see the child . . . A great humanitarian [Birdie Howard] took it upon herself to bring the child to see me. I didn't see anything that I could do, so I recommended the oil massage, and this seems to be the result—a reconditioning of the muscles, or rather, a conditioning of the muscles, because such have never functioned.

Most cases responded with significant, but not miraculous, improvement. But then there often followed a period where no further progress could be detected. Patients felt better. But what did that mean? How could it be measured? A typical report was: "All conditions have not been eradicated at this writing. However, the general improvement is noticeable." Commonly, patients made marked progress just after Carver massaged them and then leveled off in the succeeding weeks. We will probably never know whether this was because the subsequent massages were not done with Carver's expert technique, or because the patients had responded to Carver's personality, or whether the massages were only helpful up to a point, beyond which the patient could not improve. Fischer was as confused as Carver about the reasons for the wide variation in results among patients treated with peanut oil massage; but he conceded that since no one was harmed by the oil, and it was an inexpensive and noninvasive treatment that brought about significant improvement in many cases, the technique should be publicized by the AMA and made available to doctors.

The AMA had only recently established its hegemony over American medicine. The organization had no staff or facilities for testing the efficacy of any product before granting—or withholding—its coveted "seal of acceptance." It prided itself on being extremely conservative, the mouthpiece of orthodoxy in medicine, through its *Journal of the American Medical Association*. The monarch of the AMA was Morris Fishbein, M.D., editor of *JAMA*, whose *Modern Home Medical Adviser* was on family bookshelves throughout America. He also wrote three very popular books against medical fads and quackery. In the early

1930s he occupied such a lofty position that no doctor dared get on his wrong side. He was the archivist of a "quack file" that at one time contained hundreds of thousands of names. He had enormous control over what information reached the public and what did not, over who was branded a charlatan and who was granted professional respect. Carver had an opportunity to see the power wielded by Fishbein in a minor incident. A journalist, T. H. Alexander, had brought his own child to Carver and had been so impressed with the boy's improvement that he wrote an article about the treatment for the *Saturday Evening Post*. The magazine would not publish the piece without Morris Fishbein's approval, which was refused.

Fishbein was the foremost enemy of herbal medicine, nutritional medicine, chiropractic, and any curative generally associated with women. An Alabama black man with no medical credentials promoting a peanut oil massage did not stand a chance of a fair hearing. Nor, it turned out, did Dr. Fischer. Fishbein had been known to persecute certain practitioners who persisted in offering their findings to the public in the face of the AMA's condemnation. In the case of Dr. Fischer and Carver, however, Fishbein simply ignored the correspondence and medical histories sent to him. When it became clear that the AMA had no intention of investigating or approving the therapy, Fischer abandoned hope of adding a massage section to his clinic. It was a bitter disappointment to Carver, Fischer, Ross, and others using the therapy when they realized it would never get the large trial that it deserved. The doctors swallowed their frustration and continued to practice massage quietly.

Morris Fishbein's star waned, finally, but only after he had enjoyed years of preeminence and ruined many reputations. Eventually it came to light that he took money from drug and product manufacturers in the form of advertising fees in exchange for granting the AMA's "seal of acceptance." Moreover, he organized harassing campaigns against particular targets such as chiropractic therapy and certain cancer treatments. As early as 1937, the AMA was found guilty of antitrust violations for conspiracy and restraint of trade for attempting to destroy a doctors' group in Washington, D.C. Fishbein himself was eventually convicted on racketeering charges. During his cross-examination during a 1937 trial, he was forced to admit that he had failed anatomy in medical school, that he never completed his internship before working for the Journal of the AMA, and that he had never practiced medicine for even a day nor treated a single patient in his entire career. Not the least of his sins was that he was a staunch defender of the tobacco companies that advertised heavily in the AMA Journal. "More Doctors Smoke Camels than any other cigarette" was the slogan of the Camel exhibit at the 1947 AMA convention.

Carver seemed unaware of Fishbein's machinations; he thought his therapy was being dismissed because of honest conservatism and distrust. "I don't blame them," he wrote to Fischer. Unlike Fischer, he did not have much to lose by continuing to give massages and to instruct others in giving them, so long as he was careful not to do anything that could be interpreted as practicing medicine, such as giving injections or handing out medicines to be taken internally.

O ver the next two years, excitement over the polio "cure" subsided, although people continued to flock to Carver for treatment. The majority reported "better flexibility," "better appearance of the skin"—nothing dramatic. A young man gained feeling in his numb limbs, an inch at a time over a period of months. A little girl began "working her toes a little bit on the leg that was apparently dead, after four massages, and today she can work one of the muscles all the way up in the same leg." To Carver and his patients, such improvement after years of total paralysis was cause for jubilation, but to people looking for a clear-cut cure, the many examples of gradual progress were greeted with a shrug.

Prominent Klan members had begun coming to Carver for treatment. He was probably right in thinking that if he could give them comfort, he could modify their thinking. It was well known that Hugo Black, U.S. senator from Alabama, was a former Klan member when Franklin Roosevelt nominated him to the Supreme Court in 1937. Yet Black went on to become one of the strongest proponents of school desegregation. "The attitude of the whole section is beginning to change," Carver wrote hopefully. "Prejudice just seems to be melting away."

News of Carver's work had reached Mohandas Gandhi at the time when Gandhi was trying to establish associations of village industries. Although public opinion has sanctified Gandhi since his death, during his lifetime he was a controversial figure, hated by some of the best people. Many would have agreed with Winston Churchill, who called him "a seditious Middle Temple lawyer" and a half-naked "fakir of a type well known in the East." The Hindus, he added for good measure, were "a foul race." Churchill was himself to become a posthumous deity, but he, too, was reviled in his own time by some factions.

At the very least, everyone considered Gandhi a radical; it is not surprising that he and Carver found each other. They both believed in grassroots movements and attacking poverty at the village level, if no other level offered relief, and they both went among princes dressed like the lowest caste whose struggle they joined. However, Gandhi was a more authoritarian and prickly personality than the gentle Carver. Gandhi asked Carver to send brochures on topics that could help a people whose average yearly per capita income was $27.50. He hoped Carver's discoveries could be adapted to Indian conditions and agriculture. A correspondence ensued between the two advocates of nonviolence and indigenous products. Within a year, Carver was regularly writing to "My Beloved Friend, Mr. Gandhi," who responded with his own expressions of affection. They exchanged literature—on religious scripture, on racial segregation, and on the nutritional components of vegetables. Many people were struck by the physical resemblance between Carver and Gandhi. Gandhi outlived Carver by exactly five years; he was assassinated by a Hindu nationalist on January 30, 1948.

N otwithstanding Carver's joy when his patients improved and his willingness to sacrifice his time and energy for them, massaging was hard physical work. He was seeing twenty-five patients and giving up to seven massages every day, including weekends. He was wearing out. "I cannot venture too far, now," he wrote to Mrs. Milholland. "I am somewhere in the seventies and must take it slow . . . I have to stop here, my arm is about to give out." His friends and people who wanted to consult with him on various other matters were aware that he was doing some work with massage oils, but it never occurred to them that he was too busy to respond to their personal letters. They were living their normal lives and presumed that he was doing the same. He eventually answered all of his mail, though it's hard to see how. By the end of 1935, he had received 3,000 letters requesting information about massage therapy. He was still the head of the experiment station and was expected to keep up with its business. His old friend, J. A. Stevenson, the U.S. Department of Agriculture (USDA) mycologist, had a dozen ideas to discuss with him. A company wanted information about his cotton asphalt. Scientists in California enlisted him to find out why thousands of ducks were dying in the Salton Lake. A government patent officer wondered if Carver could make a peanut butter that wouldn't stick to the roof of the mouth. Then there were the persistent, invariably long, ravings from people such as Helen Gertrude Randle, "Dietician, Food Chemist, Psychologist, Business Builder, Personality Expert," according to her ponderous letterhead, who sent Carver reams of literature about herself and asked him to "Please get a stenographer to make a complete list of all the names and addresses of all the people who have written to you about the peanut oil," so that she could send each of them her brochure, "How to Live 100 Years Free of Disease."

In June, he wrote to his former student Helen Chisholm that he had still not opened his Christmas presents. "I keep your lovely picture on my desk," he assured his friend. "People want to know if that's a picture of my girl. If they are just 'people,' I tell them yes, and they say you are entirely too young for me." *The American,* a popular magazine, wanted to know which five books he would take along if he were forced to live on a desert island. Carver scribbled back: the Bible; *The Genera of Fungi,* by Clements and Shear; *Illustrated Flora,* by Britton and Brown; *Manual of the Study of Insects,* by Comstock; *The New Dietetics,* by Kellogg, "and also a compound microscope."

At the end of 1934, Robert R. Moton resigned as president of Tuskegee. He had been ill for some months and had been in Virginia all the previous year on sick leave. For some years, Carver had been massaging Dr. Moton. When Moton left for Virginia, Carver supplied him with oil, which Moton used everywhere; Carver even suggested he massage his troublesome prostate gland with it. Carver and Moton were true friends, bound by an affection more profound and intimate than the one-sided worship Carver had felt for Booker or the pleasant but measured kindliness he would eventually show to Moton's successor.

A number of people began asking Carver for interviews so that they could write biographies of him. Both Mrs. Liston and Mrs. Milholland, along with James Saxon Childers, had prepared drafts of his life, but by 1935, the only full-length published biography was that of Raleigh Merritt. Then along came Lucy Cherry Crisp, thirty-five years old, a very religious piano teacher from North Carolina who was introduced to Carver by Jim Hardwick during Carver's last Blue Ridge tour. Charmed by Carver's genteel manners and his merry disposition, she set about writing his life. At Carver's urging, she wrote to Mrs. Liston asking to see her draft, which Mrs. Liston apparently did not intend to finish, so that Crisp might use the information Carver had given Mrs. Liston about his early life. That straight-edged Midwesterner replied that she would turn over her manuscript only if she were given sufficient financial remuneration for the time and effort she put into it.

Crisp began her own manuscript with a description of Jim Hardwick—of the time when she first met Carver in North Carolina, on a road tour conducted by Jim. Carver was sitting in their battered old touring car at the University of North Carolina as she and Jim approached. After some conversation, Jim said that they had better stop talking so as to get Carver out of the car and inside for his lecture. "How long will that take?" Crisp asked. Jim had implied that moving Carver would require some time and effort. "About thirty seconds," Carver answered, nimbly hopping out of the car and laughing delightedly at Jim's little joke.

Crisp's biography was a workmanlike effort of several years that was never published, but her fondness for Carver lasted. In their many letters, Crisp and Carver often wrote about Jim and God, the two obsessions they shared. Carver's devotion to his protégé was as strong as ever. Jim's surprise marriage did not take place until the summer of 1934. Carver, blissfully ignorant of the changes in Jim's life, continued to write to him during the first half of that year as if their two souls were one. "I have 12 infantile paralysis cases and through the providence of God, they are getting better . . . This is our work. You have a 50% share in it." "I often wish I could see you laughing at that poor unfortunate fellow you pulled out of that upturned car. You laugh with such ghoulish delight." Carver was elated when Jim planned to visit him in Tuskegee. Regarding some arrangement Jim suggested for that visit, Carver responded, "No, no Dear, you must be here after I slip away to await your coming. The thought of your leaving me here makes me sick at heart. God did indeed put us together. I knew it all the time. And what marvelous times we have had and somehow I believe the best is yet to come. You seem to be ever present with me, sleeping or awake. It is your great spirit." That visit was a stinging disappointment. Jim brought several other people and stayed only briefly. If he had intended to tell Carver of his impending marriage, he lost his nerve. Carver was bewildered. He knew something was wrong, but what?

Jim left behind more than one broken heart on his way to matrimonial bliss. Lucy Crisp confided to Carver her own love for Jim, at a time when neither of them knew that he was engaged. "How shall I say all these things I have in my heart to say to you," she wrote to Carver. "You know how impossible it is." Carver consoled her, so that she left Tuskegee in early July with "a sense of calm and confidence," expecting to see Jim in Atlanta on her way back to North Carolina. But Jim avoided her. "It was all strangely unlike him," she wrote to Carver, "and confirmed the conviction growing in my mind that he is in the midst of some special crisis or confusion. I wanted to tell you this in order that we might together give him . . . sustaining, strengthening prayer . . . It is a great relief to be able now to talk and write freely to you about this." But within a few days, Jim had written to Crisp to tell her of his recent marriage, which he did not intend to announce publicly until September. He did not write to Carver who, when he got the news from Crisp, was deeply shocked. "My dear friend," Crisp wrote Carver afterward, "I do so hate for you to be so troubled. It came out all between the lines of your letter. Please do not let it distress you so . . . He will write you soon, I know . . . and if he is as happy as marriage is designed to make us, then both you and I should be very happy for him."

But Lucy herself was going through "the hardest weeks I have ever known. My love for him has been the central fact in my thought and emotions for more than a year—and it was all so deeply twined about the very roots of my deepest religious convictions and desires as well that it had an even greater hold upon me than I myself realized." She might have been writing for Carver. She was comforted that Carver knew about her feelings and was "definitely seeking help for me" in the form of prayer.

It was Carver who finally wrote a short letter to Hardwick, addressing him as "My Beloved friend and co-worker, Mr. Hardwick," and signing himself "Yours very truly"—quite a cool-off from his usual effusive tone. But he did not write a word of reproach or dismay, nor did he acknowledge the marriage he wasn't supposed to know about. Carver worked out a little of his longing for Hardwick by writing to Jim's mother, Helena. "I miss being with dear 'Jimmie' so much, the precious boy is a real part of my life, but I can understand why I hear from him so little now; he is on the road." Carver and Helena Hardwick kept up a correspondence and even a few visits until the end of his life. From time to time, he sent her primroses for transplanting. They bloomed intensely for some years but then very slowly withered away.

15

―≈―

FAME AND ITS DISCONTENTS

Carver was not without his own admirers, namely, one Birdie Howard. His friendship with Birdie was not in the same class as his fraught passion for Heartbreaker Hardwick, but perhaps Birdie's devotion helped to ease his sense of having been jilted. With Hardwick, Carver had been the idolater and Jim the idol. With Birdie, his position was reversed—it was she who did the adoring and he who accepted the breathless admiration and responded stiffly. Carver met Birdie in 1928 or 1929, as the result of a casual conversation with a stranger while he was on a lecture tour. After he got back home, the man he had talked with wrote to him, offering to fix him up with a genteel Georgian. "The enclosed card may assist you in recalling our talk on marriage. Now, if you were serious, write Miss Birdie H. Howard at . . . a wonderful woman and an orphan, therefore you may realize another dream." It was Birdie who apparently wrote first to Carver, beginning a long correspondence. By 1934 the two were old friends, and Carver was regularly receiving her lighthearted letters. "Get all your stars," she wrote him. "I'll wrap them around my heart and sparkle for you. Do keep well, Dearest Dear Honey . . . I hope I will know when you speak over the radio. I long to hear your caressing voice."

Birdie's appearance in Carver's life overlapped his relationship with Jim. His passion for Jim was still at its peak in 1933, when he was writing a dozen letters to Jim for every one he received in response. By that time, Birdie was completely enamored. Her whole-hearted worship of Carver—inasmuch as he would accept it—lasted until his death. Her letters were bubbly and unconstrained, full of giving and warmth; his responses were prompt, kind, careful, and short. Jim was a polished southern gentleman with family roots and a profession. Birdie was lonely, countrified, straightforward, and unselfconscious. She trusted that Carver could see through her lack of cultivation to the good heart within. She was also female and, from all indications, open to physical love—both characteristics that Carver was not looking for as his life proceeded ever more painfully toward its end.

Birdie was excited about Carver's massage therapy. She described a child of her acquaintance. "I think she has paralysis. Her people say she's marked, as her mother nursed her grandma before she was born. The poor little one is less than 4 years and can not walk. They spank her. I think she can be cured." Birdie took it upon herself to bring the girl to Carver. Over the years, Birdie brought several children to Carver for treatment, youngsters whose parents either did not have the means or the initiative to make the trip. In several letters, Birdie related dreams she had concerning Carver—multitudes of people shouting his name—that she thought were messages from God.

Birdie's love for Carver took a form he should have understood quite well— a covert and possibly unconscious sexual passion disguising itself as religious zeal. It had the same character as his fervid attraction to Hardwick. In one letter Birdie related a dream in which Carver was ill and she was taking care of him. "I saw you pack some kind of leather case full of sort of folded papers you said what is the use I've no heir then you wept and wept the people kept yelling you went out." As the dream continues, Carver comes back in and puts his head on her breast and weeps. He takes her hand and they walk out to paradise, which is a "wilderness of nature." Then they come back to the sea. "Great white waves came faster, faster just rushing on us. When they broke it seems like men fighting war. We sat down and ate oysters. Suddenly the sea was calm, the tide going out." That was the climax of the dream, but it was not the end. The vision continues with her seeing Tuskegee on fire in the distance. Carver and Birdie are on a bed and he keeps addressing her as "Dear"—"Don't be afraid, Dear." She is holding a baby and Carver writes a name on a card: "George Washington Carver, Jr."

Birdie no doubt knew nothing about Freud, but Carver, who kept up with current ideas in all the sciences, was familiar with *The Interpretation of Dreams*. Even without Freud's guidance, he must have realized the dream's symbolism, down to the oyster aphrodisiac. Then again, one can't be sure. Carver, who thought God was speaking in the humming of bees, might have taken Birdie's word for it that God was visiting her sleep with a message. In any case, he must have been moved by the good woman's sincerity and ingenuous openness, as well as her unconditional acceptance of him. She closed the dream letter remarking that she was happy his teeth couldn't give him any more trouble, since they had all been removed. "Write as soon as you can. My prayers. Much love for you always, Dearest Dear. Yours, BJH."

Birdie was right in perceiving that Carver was a little sad not to have an heir or obvious successor to carry on his work. He hoped that at his death, six or seven researchers would complete some of his projects, each specializing in one or another branch of his activities. In truth, it would take six or seven lifetimes to address even half of Carver's far-reaching projects. He particularly regretted that, because of giving massages all day long, he had not finished several manuscripts he had begun, especially his botany textbook. With the dramatic increase in Carver's correspondence and lecture invitations, he was finally allowed to have a full-time personal assistant. Like Moton, the new president, Frederic Douglas Patterson, urged Carver to travel and lecture as much as possible. After 1933, Carver was always either at his massage table with patients, on the road, or in the hospital recovering from exhaustion. Many times he got up from a sickbed to board a train for a lecture tour that had been planned months earlier. Patterson recognized that Carver was an inimitable asset to Tuskegee, attracting students, faculty, and donors, and he let Carver alone to do pretty much as he wished, so long as he continued to travel and talk. It had been years since Carver was required to teach. Patterson was as stingy as the other presidents in publishing Carver's bulletins, but he did not interfere with his research. Once upon a time, a Tuskegee principal had gone so far as to insist that Carver limit his investigations in the experiment station only to plants grown in Macon County.

The scientist's relationship to Patterson in the early years was correct, polite, and difficult to surmise, since Carver was extremely circumspect in his comments about his chief. Apparently Patterson once remarked that Carver was a "pseudo-chemist," a comment that Harry Abbott was still fuming about after years had gone by. Certainly Carver did not enjoy the intimate friendship with Patterson that continued to exist between him and Moton. There were always "certain matters" regarding Tuskegee that Carver wanted to discuss with Harry in person and could not reveal in letters, as these went through the campus mail service.

In 1930, before Moton's departure and to the accompaniment of much fanfare, Carver had finally received some new equipment. The bounty came not through Moton's efforts but as a gift from Henry Ford, who visited Carver's lab and noted its appalling poverty. All of Carver's close assistants, Jack Sutton, Harry Abbott, and Austin Curtis, felt that Patterson and Tuskegee had not shown Carver adequate respect and appreciation; consequently, after Carver's death, none of the assistants donated his papers to Tuskegee, papers containing Carver's personal correspondence. Abbott gave his collection to the George Washington Carver National Monument in Diamond, Missouri, as did James Hardwick. Austin Curtis—who had other reasons for disliking the administration—left his archive to the Benton Historical Library of the University of Michigan. Relations between Carver and Patterson markedly improved, however, with time. After Patterson settled in, a few amenities that had been promised for years finally came to Carver. Regarding his salary, Carver had always said, "When they feel I'm worth more, they'll pay me more." Without being asked, Patterson raised his salary to $115 a month and gave Carver at least some of the secretarial help and lab assistance he had been pleading for since the experiment station was first set up. Harry Abbott nevertheless maintained that the school never came to "a full appreciation of what you mean to her."

Carver developed warm relationships with all of his part-time secretaries—usually middle-aged ladies—and all of the young men who served as his assistants. The first youth in whom Carver took a fatherly interest was Emile Hooker, the Nicaraguan student who had been engaged to help sort out the avalanche of infantile paralysis letters. Carver kept in touch with Emile's mother after the young man went off to Cornell to do graduate work. Emile later came back to Tuskegee to teach agriculture and help out from time to time with Carver's mail. When Carver's secretary Mrs. Walcott had to go into the hospital in 1937, Hooker and a student helper, "Buster," were brought in and proceeded to play one practical joke after another on Carver. On receiving some sort of make-believe "document" from Hooker, Carver forwarded it to Mrs. Walcott: "Now this is what I have to put up with daily, hourly, and momently," Carver wrote in mock exasperation. "You just tell the doctor that it is most important that you get out and help me because I can't stand it any longer . . . they come and spread their feet in my office, knowing they will get beat up about it. I found this document on my desk, and I am sending it to you so that you will see how very urgent it is for you to come and help me." When Carver himself had a prolonged stay in the hospital the following year, Mrs. Walcott moved into his apartment. Carver and Mrs. Walcott and Hooker remained friends to the end of Carver's life.

John Sutton, Carver's first assistant, had been a volunteer, since Tuskegee would not pay anyone to help him until late in his career. "Jack" was an atheist who deified his mentor long before the world discovered him. Sutton came to Carver as a twenty-year-old student in 1917 and from that year on, spent the rest of his life writing and thinking about his teacher. As an old man, thirty years after Carver's death, Sutton was still working on a biography of the scientist.

> How does one write about a harmless little old man who rejected wine, Eros, money, and power; a man who taught Sunday School each Sunday morning and a Sunday evening Bible class, and was thoroughly disliked by the Tuskegee Institute chaplain because he, Carver, believed that *agape*, love given without expectation of return, as Jesus loved, applied to all people, even to Communists in godless Russia . . . who averred that he never entered 'God's Little Workshop' . . . without first engaging in meditation and prayer.

Jack Sutton's father was a Hard-Shell Baptist who beat him in an effort to save his soul from hell fire, all the while quoting Scripture: "Be sure your sins will find you out'; "The wages of sin are death," etc. As a result, Jack hated religion, but he willingly attended Carver's Bible study groups. Sutton's parents had arranged for him to enter Tuskegee with the understanding that Carver was to be his surrogate father and Jack was to be his unofficial postgraduate assistant; he had already completed a teacher's normal course and was therefore not required to attend chapel services, wear a cadet uniform, drill, or observe 10 p.m. lights out. "I was given a laboratory next to his and saw him every day at his office and went to his 'dormitory lab' each evening for work in systematic botany and mycology and the microscopic examination of plant diseases in Macon County."

According to Sutton, Carver repeated Matthew 10:16 each morning on awakening, before setting out on his walks: "Behold, I send you forth as sheep in the midst of wolves; be ye therefore wise as serpents, and harmless as doves." The younger man could never resign himself to remaining "harmless." As an unbeliever, he could not accept a submissive program, nor could he bear to see Carver suffering Tuskegee's vicious infighting without striking back. Sutton left for a time to attend graduate school at Iowa State and Cornell but was drawn back to Tuskegee to work again with Carver. To the end of his life, he could recall Carver's favorite biblical quotations and his religious meditations. "Look unto the hills from whence cometh my strength," was Carver's constant advice to him. "But I had such a built-in resistance to religion," Sutton wrote, "that none of it ever seemed real." Even the gentleness of his surrogate father could not erase Jack's association of religion with paternal cruelty.

Jack was with Carver on and off for fourteen years before he took the opportunity Carver provided for him to go to the Soviet Union in 1931, and he was with him again intermittently after his return in 1938. According to him, Carver believed in dreams, in some psychic phenomena, and in mental telepathy, which the two often played with. "I engaged in sending telepathic messages and receiving them from him for many years," Sutton wrote. "Even when I was employed in Soviet Russia some 5,000 miles away from him, he sent me messages about my research problems, particularly when I was working on the problem of utilization of rice straw as a fiber replacement for jute. With his help I solved the problem. But," he added, "without the Bible."

Sutton began seriously trying to write a biography of Carver a few years before his mentor's death, along with dozens of other people, and he was still chewing on it until his own demise. Somehow, he could never get past Carver's unwavering connection with religion. "It has been the one single obstacle that has done more than anything else to prevent me from finishing the reams of material I have written about him in the past twenty years," Sutton wrote in 1974. He had just discovered documentary evidence that Carver had been interested in the ideas of the Christian Scientists, although never a member of their church—just as the Christian Scientists had long maintained but could not prove.

* * *

Harry Abbott, the man who had been transferred to Carver's office from Tuskegee's administrative precincts (specifically the printing plant), became Carver's second surrogate son, after Sutton, the first assistant to work and travel with him outside the lab. He was protective of Carver, insisting, for example, on comfortable accommodations for his frail charge. In 1930 Carver was not allowed to purchase a ticket to a Pullman car Abbott had reserved for a train trip from Oklahoma City to Dallas, one part of a longer journey. He and Abbott were compelled instead to ride in the segregated coach which did not have sleeping facilities. Abbott's complaint to the railroad company stirred up a storm of publicity. The law in Oklahoma called for "separate but equal" facilities for the races, a law that the railroad companies found burdensome. It was expensive to provide Pullman cars for the segregated sections of the train, since they frequently went empty. The president of the Atchison, Topeka, and Santa Fe railroad tried to deflect criticism by writing Carver a hearty letter of apology, which the traveler graciously accepted. Carver was then criticized by the black press for letting the railroad off so easily and not filing a lawsuit. Abbott remonstrated that, "like Banquo's ghost," the incident would not go away—largely because he was himself forwarding to newspapers the exchanges between him and the railroad. After some months, and probably to Abbott's disappointment, the brouhaha subsided.

Carver and Abbott remained devoted to each other from 1927, when Abbott first began traveling with Carver, until the old man's death in 1943. When Abbott worked for Tuskegee, he and his wife Marguerite lived in a house on the Institute grounds. When he left in 1935 to work at the University of Chicago, Carver was bereft; for a while, he continued to take his daily walk over to the little cottage with its abandoned garden plot. Abbott's wife constantly sent Carver delicacies from the Midwest, but Carver lamented that he lost his appetite when he no longer had Harry to share his meals. Remarking about a recent illness, Carver wrote, "To tell the truth about it, I think that was part of my trouble, that I cannot adjust myself to your being away." A year later, he was still writing plaintively, "There is so much that I had planned for us to do."

In some of their long and tender exchanges, Abbott recalled trips they took together. "I thought those were great years!" he wrote; "physical separation cannot destroy real friendship." A 1937 trip through Iowa, Oklahoma, and Colorado was made two years after Austin Curtis had replaced Abbott as Carver's assistant; yet Carver refused to make the tour unless Abbott could accompany him. On New Year's Eve, Abbott tried to express how profoundly he had been affected by the years at Carver's side. Thanksgivings and random holidays found Abbott visiting Carver, though the younger man could hardly spare money for travel. "I don't see how I can get along without these visits," Carver wrote. "The chats we had seemed to refresh me so much, and if I could get them now I know that I would feel better. I am confident that some of my disabilities come from the fact that I can't see my friend, Harry. That may seem rather odd to you; nevertheless, it is true. I did indeed miss you at the banquet [the celebration of Carver's fortieth anniversary at Tuskegee], which was so unique and positively beautiful. And such a fine group was there. But through it all, I wanted to see you there." Since Carver by that time could not manipulate a pen, the letter was signed for him by Emile Hooker.

Although Carver addressed his letters to "My beloved friend, Mr. Abbott," in private he sometimes called Abbott "Harry-O." Abbott took the nickname for one of his businesses—"Harrio Stationers." He shared Carver's interest in chemistry and farming and, after settling in Chicago, wrote a book about making specialty soaps. Both he and Carver loved to cook and eat fatty food in those wonderful days when no one thought about cholesterol. Carver wrote to him about having had some "fat back," which was not cooked as well as "the H. O. Abbott style." President Patterson had taken Carver for an automobile ride. "They tried to fry some fat for me, but it was nothing like as good as the bacon you prepared for me." Even when he was at death's door, he wrote to Abbott that a friend had sent him a generous piece of "the most delicious" barbecued pork, "just the kind that you and Mrs. Abbott would not eat. In fact, nobody wants this kind except myself as it is all fat and barbecued to a turn." The next year, after visiting Abbott, he wrote, "There is one thing that I was disappointed in as I expected that you would leave me a real fat-backed sandwich to take on the train with me." (Excluded from the dining cars, black travelers had to bring their own food.) "Mrs. Abbott would not have approved of it at all. But then, you and I can do things that no one else approves of except us." Carver went on to describe exactly how he would have wanted the imaginary sandwich prepared.

Food became more and more important to Carver as he aged, as it does to many people whose excitements are limited. And like many thin people, he talked about food more than he ate it; that is, he took tiny portions of everything. He often described to Abbott what he had for supper and lamented that he had none of Marguerite Abbott's delicious coffee to put into his cup. "His cup" had been given to him by Henry Ford from his family collection. It was a special thing designed for a caffeine addict. It "must have held one quart," Helena Hardwick remarked after she saw it; she noted that when Carver had breakfast in her home in Virginia, he contented himself with only three regular coffees. His predilection for odd food had not waned with the years. Abbott sent him some pig tails, which lasted him for several suppers. Carver was delighted when someone gave him a quart of samp—a porridge made from coarse hominy; so Abbott found a place in Chicago where he could purchase it. Carver thought it was worth the extra time one had to spend cooking it, as he liked samp better than grits and, besides, a quart lasted him a good long time.

Carver warned Abbott to be prudent and to "feel the pulse of the public" in investing in a business venture—modish words from a pecuniary simpleton. Despite the advice, Abbott was in debt the next year, and Carver sent him money. "Now all that explanation that you are giving me," Carver wrote, when Abbott tried to thank him, "you could have saved it, as you know, quite well as I know, how our relationship stands, and that little dab that I enclosed is just an indication to pick up any little thing that you think I would like. With so much love and best wishes." The Abbotts finally got out of debt by the end of 1940.

Carver tried to arrange his tours so that Abbott could come from Chicago to meet him—in Oklahoma, Minnesota, or wherever. The schedule then became a closely guarded secret. "Coming back from St. Paul I will have a two-hour layover. Don't tell anyone so we can have the time to ourselves and I can talk over some matters that are most important in line with your letter. Also have some other things that I want you to know.

Abbott's replacement as Carver's right arm was Austin Curtis, who was hired in September 1935. There are signs that Curtis may at first have resented his predecessor. "Well, jealous or no jealous," Carver wrote to Abbott,

"I think people understand pretty well now how inseparable we are." Despite Curtis's frequent, smug assertion that "Others had been tried and Carver felt they didn't measure up to what he wanted in an assistant," the indications are that Carver resented having to change sons, perhaps because Abbott's departure had not been entirely voluntary. Abbott once referred to "misunderstandings" with Tuskegee that had made it advisable for him to leave. Curtis was hired without Carver ever having met him. His father, Austin Curtis Sr. (nicknamed "Soybean" because of his extensive work with that plant) was Director of Agriculture at West Virginia State College. When Carver reviewed the paperwork for young Curtis's employment, he wrote to Patterson: "You will note that my designated assistant receives . . . quite twice as much as the person he is supposed to assist." He wondered if some of that money couldn't be diverted to printing a bulletin he had ready. Even with an adjustment, Curtis was paid a good deal more than Carver, as President Patterson noted in later years. ("So why didn't he simply give Carver a raise?" Austin Curtis responded, when told of Patterson's remark. "That was within his power.")

When Curtis arrived at Tuskegee, a friend brought him to Carver's apartment. They rang the bell for a long time before Carver opened the door a tiny crack. "Carver, this is Curtis, who is to be your assistant," the friend said.

"How do you do and goodnight," Carver replied and closed the door.

The next morning in his office, Carver instructed Curtis to go around the campus and learn how things were done—how to place orders for equipment "and that sort of thing." Curtis continued reporting to Carver every day, but it was six full weeks before Carver gave him anything to do. For his living quarters, Curtis was assigned to a room in Phelps Hall, the dormitory for single male teachers. He was soon to wed and would be moved to the modest facilities for married staff. Carver meanwhile was living in a three-room ground floor apartment in the student dorm, Rockefeller Hall.

Carver continued writing as always to Abbott. "I really believe that you have a greater opportunity where you are now than when you were here. Personally, I can hardly put up with the fact that you are not here, as I miss you so many, many times per day, you and Mrs. Abbott. And I do miss running into your house and having a genuinely good dinner or supper or whatever you choose to call it, and then the lovely little chats that were so helpful to me." That was two years after Curtis had begun working with him. Nevertheless, Carver got used to Curtis and relied on him increasingly in the eight years of Curtis's tenure. Whereas Carver had come to consider Harry Abbott a friend and an equal with whom he could exchange counsel, his relationship to Curtis was much more that of a father who had to physically—but not psychologically—lean on his adult child. People took to calling Curtis "Baby Carver," and the name stuck, so that Carver routinely referred to him as "Baby," and Curtis was delighted to sign all his correspondence to Carver with that nickname.

Their mutual attachment was a little odd. Carver was modest and truly indifferent to money. He was profoundly dedicated to the poor of Alabama and the Deep South, where he could help "the man farthest down." Curtis, in contrast, had an unmistakable mercenary streak. He was not backward about taking the credit for having facilitated awards that came to Carver. And after Carver's death, he left the South almost at once to seek his fortune where he expected to find less prejudice. Carver certainly was not more fond of Curtis than he was of Harry Abbott, although he was forced to be more dependent on him. Nevertheless, they clearly got on, or Carver would have got rid of Curtis. There were hundreds of young men eager to take his place.

Carver remained preoccupied with his massage therapy for two years or more after Curtis's arrival. He was on the road constantly, except for his frequent bouts of illness, and, when he was home, chained to his "massage room" (a little space cleared out in his living room). A very popular national radio show, *Strange As It Seems*, devoted half of its program to Carver at the end of 1935. That precipitated another deluge of mail, including congratulations from friends such as Abbott, who heard the program in Chicago. Carver was then invited to give regular radio talks. Raleigh Merritt, still trying to capitalize on his familiarity with Carver's discoveries, was inspired by the new burst of publicity to try to patent Carver's peanut coffee. For some years, J. A. Stevenson, the Chief Mycologist of the U.S. Department of Agriculture, had regularly been consulting Carver. In July 1935, Carver was formally appointed a collaborator in the Bureau of Plant Industry, division of mycology and disease survey. He sent the department a new series of over 800 collections; the list ran to twenty-one pages—a striking contribution from a man who was spending much of his time confined to bed.

In the 1930s Carver went through a new phase of religiosity. He maintained a correspondence with Glenn Clark, an English professor in Minnesota who began writing to Carver in 1928 at the urging of Jim Hardwick because both men were especially interested in fostering interdenominational cooperation. Clark and Carver corresponded exclusively about religious matters and made appointments to pray "together," that is, at the same time, although they did not meet in person for seven years. After a visit in 1935 and subsequent meetings, Clark wrote a brochure about Carver, "The Man Who Talks With the Flowers." He distributed 200,000 copies, a prodigious quantity considering that the population of the country was under 132 million. The brochure was by itself a potent amount of publicity and engendered yet more articles and inquiries from people wanting to write book-length biographies. The articles and booklets that were coming out were actually better publicity for Carver and Tuskegee than books would have been; more people read newspapers and magazines than ever picked up a biography.

Despite his burden of patients, Carver was still thinking of new products, such as a milk made from a magnesium compound. Dr. Fischer waved Carver away from that idea. "The only satisfactory Milk of Magnesia I have ever seen was made by Dr. Phillips, who was a colored man in Chicago years ago. His one formula made him rich. No one has ever been able to make a satisfactory magnesia except this one. He did a great deal of rubbing, mixing, and dissolving to get his formula."

In 1936 a chef's school was established at Tuskegee to train cooks for hotels. Black people had of course been cooking in white homes for some 150 years. But when they worked in restaurants and hotels, they were kept in the kitchens, out of view of the dining rooms, so that the public had not been much aware of them. Only a few years before, restaurants in the South had received threats after hiring black kitchen help. The chef's school was an announcement of sorts that blacks trained in cooking would be seeking employment in white businesses, despite it being a time when thousands of whites were themselves desperate for jobs. Racial attitudes were softening but not regarding black waiters. It had been more than forty years since a white student at Iowa State had indignantly left her place at the dining table because a brown hand, George Carver's hand, had placed a sugar bowl in front of her and she did not want any Negro to handle her food. A classmate who witnessed the incident wrote, "I do not remember that girl's name or anything else about her, where she was from or where she has gone . . . but every intelligent person of this world today knows who that waiter was, and where he is, and what he is doing."

As for Carver, he was ambling around the campus as always, apparently lost in thought, stopping now and then to examine some plant that caught his eye, and murmuring to himself and to the flowers in his squeaky voice. A student recalled that in 1936 a dean at Tuskegee was a woman with a heavy voice like a man's. To listen to them in the dining hall deep in conversation was "interesting."

The year 1936 marked Carver's fortieth anniversary at Tuskegee. The celebration climaxed with a ceremony, speeches, and readings of congratulatory letters and expressions of appreciation solicited from eminent personages. A bronze bust of Carver was unveiled, a sculpture that was financed by contributions of "not more than one dollar" collected by Austin Curtis. Carver's talk in the chapel concerned a strip of plastic he carried to the podium; he had made it from soybeans. The event was reported in *Time, Life,* and in the newspapers. At such special times, Carver still thought of Jim Hardwick. He wrote to Jim's mother, "Wish so much that you and dear Jimmie could have been present at the unveiling. I do not see him very often now, or even hear from him. I know that he is very busy and it may be that he is a little like myself, that he begins to feel the weight of years and the strenuous work that he has . . . The moving picture people, radio people, etc. are making very definite demands upon my time . . . The exercises were unusually good. You can imagine, however, what a strain they were upon me. It was such an unusual ceremony. One which rarely comes to an individual who is yet living."

Baby Carver could not enjoy the occasion—his wife Belle was in Mt. Sinai hospital in New York. Though Carver badly needed him to deal with the swarm of journalists and the correspondence that poured in, he insisted that Baby remain in the North with his wife for several weeks. Carver's hand had "refused to write" for several years, although he could still massage with it, a work that he enjoyed "so much." The day after Belle Curtis died in New York, Austin sent a telegram to President Patterson, explaining that he hesitated to cable Carver directly for fear that the news would be a great shock. "The dear boy spared me," Carver noted, appreciatively. Two years later, Curtis remarried.

Birdie Howard's tenderness toward Carver endured. "Dear Marvelous Man," she wrote him early in February 1936. "I imagine your quiet (almost silent) dignified manner as you receive visitors and go among your patients. You are utterly selfless and there is no other and we will never have another man like you." Although Carver had come to believe that the restorative effect of the treatment lay in the massage and not in the particular oil he used, Birdie claimed to know better. "Honey, you'll fine to the world sufficient proof that Infantile Paralysis can be cured by your formula." She exhorted him to rest. "Should you ever take time for a little rest you must come over here Dear and let me take care of you. Love to my Valentine. God will not fail us in this. Bye. Yours Lovingly."

Having seen all the publicity about the anniversary, Jim Hardwick, addressing Carver as "My great Friend," scrawled a short letter—very short—inviting him to attend a retreat he was holding in Montgomery for two days. Hardwick was not hoping merely for the pleasure of Carver's company, as in the old days. He wanted him to bring his peanut exhibit, his clay exhibit, and all the signs to go along with them. This was quite a favor to ask of a man whose health was very precarious and who was at that moment overwhelmed with prestigious requests for his appearance. Although Montgomery was a mere forty miles distant, Carver responded with a conventional letter of regret that his doctor would not allow him to travel. He understood that Jim's interest was not in seeing him but in capitalizing on his notoriety. Jim was trying to take advantage of him; the realization must have hurt.

The publicity surrounding the fortieth anniversary generated a spate of honors. More were to come in the next years. The permanent parade of visitors and sightseers that had long been a nuisance to Carver ("I'm not here just to be looked at") was by now a horde that descended on him every time he ventured out of doors or even opened the door to his apartment. He was a tourist attraction. No one who came to Tuskegee for any reason wanted to leave without taking a look at Carver. He grumbled to President Patterson: "Everyone wants to see 'the public curiosity.' Some want to see whether he wears a dress or pants, some want to see how feeble he is, others want to see what complexion he is." Always "being on display," as he put it, was one more thing wearing him out. After each illness, he seemed to take longer to get his strength back. "People are beginning to feel just a little bit alarmed and are giving me the protection now that I should have had a long time ago," he commented to Harry. "They are keeping people from crowding me and worrying me nearly to death." The "protection" meant that while Carver was in the hospital in 1938, visitors were allowed in for only five minutes at a time—but still, there was a perpetual line outside his room. The hospital might as well have allowed one person to stay all day. Having made so many wearisome trips at the behest of Tuskegee Institute to attract good will and donations, he was disgusted that his health now prevented his going to those events he really wanted to attend. Carver was sickly throughout his entire life but, naturally, much more so in his last decade. He complained that he had to be "carried" everywhere he went, using the southern expression for "brought." "You know how inconvenient it is," he wrote to the man who had for years done the carrying, "and how I hate it."

Metro-Goldwyn-Mayer wanted to produce a film short on Carver, but Austin Curtis considered the company's offer of $500 a paltry honorarium. Carver had always refused to accept any remuneration for articles, lectures, interviews—everything. In the face of Curtis's rejection, MGM withdrew the movie proposal. In June 1937, *Reader's Digest* reprinted James Saxon Childers's article about Carver just as several illustrated magazines were featuring a picture of Carver surrounded by stacks of letters. Carver's mail, which had subsided, now resurged. A photograph was widely disseminated showing Carver exchanging warm greetings with Franklin Roosevelt, who stopped at Tuskegee during a southern tour. Unless he wanted to wear a disguise, Carver would never again be able to go anywhere in the United States unrecognized.

Fred Allhoff's article, "Black Man's Miracles" in the January issue of *Liberty Magazine,* provoked more mail than Tuskegee had ever before received about anything. As with the announcement of Carver's polio "cure" on the last day of 1933, the second deluge of letters washed over Carver at the beginning of a new year, but this tidal wave was even larger. The article described Carver's experiments in treating various health problems with peanut oil. The resulting inquiries that poured in came mainly from people afflicted with poliomyelitis, acne, arthritis, and stunted growth. Many also came from physicians, chiropractors, physical therapists, beauty consultants, masseurs, and people who wanted to market Carver's oil. Each of the thousands of people who wrote received an answer, if only a form letter explaining that Carver could not supply samples of the oil.

In 1937, a new movement and a new term had gained popularity. "Chemurgy" was an effort to focus the discoveries of chemistry and related sciences toward practical ends, especially in the area of farming. Scholars from Massachusetts Institute of Technology and Johns Hopkins contributed to the publications of the chemurgic national council. The movement was largely the project of Henry Ford, who made Carver its most honored member. Nevertheless, at the Dearborn banquet given by Ford, Carver, a special guest, sat outside the hall until everyone had eaten rather than subject his host to criticism from segregationists for violating the fierce convention against interracial dining. Famous as he was, he would sit outside many rooms, even until the end of his life.

I t was during this period of Carver's greatest renown that he had some contacts and conflicts with Henry A. Wallace, with whom he had a long acquaintance. Wallace's father, Henry Cantwell Wallace, Carver's old professor, had been a wonderful friend in earlier years. Henry C. Wallace served as U.S. Secretary of Agriculture under Presidents Harding and Coolidge and died in office in 1924. Carver bred a hybrid amaryllis and named it after him. The son, Henry Agard Wallace, was only about six when Carver was a graduate student at Iowa. Carver spent a great deal of time with the Wallace family and took the little boy hiking with him a time or two, explaining some of the rudiments of botany as they ambled in the woods.

When the younger Wallace grew up, he, like his father, was appointed U.S. Secretary of Agriculture; he later became Franklin Roosevelt's vice president. Carver was an enthusiastic supporter of FDR, but his relations with Henry A. Wallace became increasingly strained. As Agriculture Secretary, Wallace visited Tuskegee in 1933 at Carver's invitation. The country was in the trough of the Depression. Addressing the student body, Wallace credited Carver with inculcating him with an early love of plants; then he made some general comments about the administration's plans to restore the economy and balance production on the farms. Carver in his turn spoke only a few words. "I haven't any good excuse for being here, except that I was ordered to come," he said ambiguously. He quoted a biblical passage suggesting that Wallace was "diligent in business" and sat down.

The policy that Wallace initiated to "balance production" was one of the most unpopular measures of Roosevelt's presidency. The Agricultural Adjustment Act was a strategy for preventing surpluses and driving up prices for certain farm commodities. It required cotton farmers to plow under 30 percent of their growing crop—ten million acres—and to slaughter 6 million pigs. The farmers who complied were given benefit payments. But at a time when families all over the country were going hungry, the radical policy of destroying food and creating artificial scarcity seemed outrageous. The Depression had blighted every farm in the land. Each Christmas, as he had done for several years, Carver took time to ask his friends not to send him gifts—to use the money to relieve the many who were "really suffering . . . I get my three meals per day, have a comfortable place to sleep and have a job. There are thousands who cannot boast of a single one of these comforts," he wrote. Carver, whose life had been spent teaching people to use every conceivable material resource to relieve their privation, could not have supported these sacrifices of cotton, pigs, and corn; it was almost certainly this farm policy of Wallace, and not any personal affront, that caused Carver's barely suppressed anger. However, he had made a point of never engaging in political arguments, so he kept his peace, sullenly.

Wallace visited Tuskegee again in 1936, and this time relations between the two were obviously tense. "The President [Patterson] had called all of the students into Logan Hall, the gymnasium," a contemporary recalled, "and it was packed, even the balcony. Wallace looked out and said, 'Where's Dr. Carver? Go get Carver and tell him to come on up here.' It was Saturday. Finally Dr. Carver showed up and he was not pleased at having to stop what he was doing and put on a tie and coat. He got up and made his remarks. He recited a poem by Edgar Guest. He didn't say a word about Wallace, and then left at once, right out the side door." Austin Curtis recalled that Wallace did not address the older man quite respectfully. His tone toward Carver had become noticeably more patronizing.

Yet two years later, the rift appears to have been healing. Wallace encouraged President Roosevelt to issue a Carver postage stamp. Carver's perennial biographer Raleigh Merritt requested and received a tribute to Carver for the dust jacket of a new edition of his book. As usual, Wallace emphasized Carver's great soul, not his great science. Wallace then asked Carver to write an article about their friendship so that he could advertise his position on the race issue in his campaign. Carver demurred. "I have refrained from any political writing of this kind," he wrote.

On several occasions Wallace conceded that Carver was "a great scientist." Yet Wallace, writing to a friend after Carver's death, is reported to have remarked, "Between you and me, I am inclined to think that his ability as a chemist has been somewhat overrated. I have been in his chem. Lab at Tuskegee but frankly I doubt if much of practical value came out." If Wallace did have reservations about Carver's scientific accomplishments, it is not surprising. Wallace had been born into a world of the finest resources available for agricultural research. He had access to the most advanced laboratories in the country, and regularly communicated with the best scientific minds in government and academia, people who were flattered by his attention and eager to give him information. Carver's access to any lab worthy of the name began when he entered Iowa State and ended when he left for Alabama four years later. Throughout his entire career at Tuskegee, he could not procure a measly piece of ten-dollar apparatus without having to appeal to the president of the institution. Wallace had seen Carver's lab, but he had no conception of what it was like to be full of ideas and destitute of resources to investigate them.

Handsome, spoiled, and mercurial, Wallace was an interesting man. It is rather a pity that he and Carver did not have better rapport, since both of them might have profited by a real friendship. At the least, Carver would have steered Wallace away from his disastrous idea for bringing up the price of farm commodities. Wallace resigned as Secretary of Agriculture in 1940 to become FDR's running mate. As vice president in 1944, he was a credulous visitor to the Soviet Union where the NKVD, Stalin's secret police, took him on a tour of two Potemkin slave labor camps in Siberia—that is, completely phony villages worked by happy "volunteers" who supposedly enjoyed all the benefits of democracy. Wallace duly came home chirping about the utopian labor conditions and rational agricultural system under Stalin. At that time, Stalin had already had two waves of purge trials, had inflicted a state-ordered famine in the Ukraine, and had in one mode or another murdered about 20 million of the many millions of Soviet civilians who were to perish during his regime. To Westerners who bothered to read the information coming out of the country, the facts about Stalinism were known, but not to Wallace. Even Carver had become wise to Stalin's "Utopia," despite his initial interest in an alternative economic system. In the 1944 election, Roosevelt replaced Wallace with Truman as his running mate but placated Wallace by appointing him Secretary of Commerce. Truman fired Wallace from that post a year after succeeding to the presidency. Wallace then became the editor of *The New Republic* and a harsh critic of Truman's foreign policy and the country's descent into the Cold War. He correctly predicted that the Truman Doctrine, announced in 1947, would mark the beginning of "a century of fear." At about the same time, newspapers published a series of letters dating from the 1930s written by Wallace to one Nicholas Roerich, a Russian artist and archeologist. An active and committed Communist, Roerich had started a wide-reaching peace movement in the 1920s which Wallace had ardently supported. During the period of their correspondence, when Wallace was in his forties, Roerich had taken up Indian philosophy. Wallace thus addressed Roerich as "Dear Guru;" wrote of anticipating the "New Day," when the people of "Northern Shambhalla"—a Buddhist term for the kingdom of happiness—would enjoy a time of peace and prosperity; and signed himself "G," for Galahad, the name Roerich had given him. It made people queasy to realize that the author of the jejune letters had been vice president to a very sick FDR and missed being president by a mere eighty-two days.

Having started out as a Republican, Wallace became a New Deal Democrat in order to join Roosevelt and finally, in 1948, left that party to run for the presidency as a Progressive. Wallace was capable of long interludes of clear thinking, and the period of his presidential candidacy was one of them. As a candidate, he advocated friendly relations with the Soviet Union, an end to the Cold War, national government-sponsored health insurance, and complete civil rights for blacks. During his campaign, he rode through the South sitting beside a black aide. That took courage. He refused to appear before segregated audiences or to patronize segregated hotels and restaurants—which meant he could frequent few public places in the South. He was endorsed by the American Communist party and refused to disavow Communist support, so that anti-Communist socialists such as Norman Thomas turned against him. After his stinging defeat in the 1948 election (he received not a single electoral vote in the South) Wallace broke with the Progressive Party, abandoned his lifelong peace activism, reversed his principles, and supported the U.S. intervention in, of all conflicts, the Korean War. Thereafter, he endorsed Republican candidates until his death in 1965 from Lou Gehrig's disease.

A fter the fortieth anniversary celebration, Carver's health took another plunge. In 1937, when the celebration ended, he was about seventy-four. By this time he was suffering from diabetes, serious anemia, arthritis, a failing heart, recurring bouts of influenza, and spells of profound weakness. Nevertheless, he went to Minnesota to give speeches and to visit Glenn Clark, his soul mate who had authored the very popular booklet on his life. Harry Abbott came from Chicago to meet him. Carver returned to Tuskegee depleted and went at once into the hospital. He remained almost bedridden for no less than five months. Carver, who had considered himself moribund since the age of sixty, finally appeared to be coming to the end.

16

MILES TO GO*

B ut not yet. Carver fought off the end as he fought off all failure, by stubbornly refusing to give up. He collapsed on the threshold of death again and again, but managed to push himself back from it each time. It is hard to understand how he held on or why. Sickness such as his tends to create its own world; nothing exists outside it. Ambition, love, pride, independence—all have to wait at the door of the sickroom while the patient addresses his suffering. Anyone as ill as Carver was for the last five years of his life might have wanted to die. Because of his failing heart, he lived with profound, chronic weakness, a feeling of unfocused, all-over misery. But through it all, he looked forward to life. Even in his last days, he had projects he wanted to continue. In all his discussions about God, Carver had never attempted to describe heaven or any sort of afterlife. Possibly he believed that there was nothing beyond the paradise that men could create on earth, if they followed the divine plan. That would explain why he delayed his departure as long as he could. He liked it here and perhaps thought there was no place else to go.

Carver's confidant continued to be Harry O. Abbott. The two reminisced endlessly about their travel experiences. Even after he had been bedridden for two months, Carver wrote, "There is so much I had planned for us to do, and I am very certain that a way will be made for us to do what we have in mind," Carver reported on his "continual improvement" when he found that he could stand a few minutes longer each week. When he could not stand, when he had

*The woods are lovely, dark and deep.
But I have promises to keep,
And miles to go before I sleep,
And miles to go before I sleep.
—Robert Frost, "Stopping by Woods on a Snowy Evening"

what he called a "breakdown," his doctors ordered him to bed, predicted that he would never get up again, and were repeatedly proved wrong.

Though he was no longer young, Abbott was struggling to establish his printing business, the Harrio Stationers. His wife Marge (Marguerite) was a relief worker who suffered from arthritis—and compassion for the poor who were her charges. If Austin Curtis was jealous of Harry, as Carver implied, Harry responded in Carver fashion, by sending kind regards to Austin and the rest of Carver's little family. "Tell them to take good care of you or I will have to fire them all and come take care of you myself. I can at least beat them all in frying salt meat." In his spare time, Harry was working on a formula for growing hair ("Castor has been used since the beginning of time," Carver advised him; "almost all hair growers have a little castor in them,") and on a formula for perfume. (Carver reminded him that some of the finest perfumes contained polecat musk.) Abbott won a friendly bet that he could stump Carver— a standing bet that Carver maintained with botanists all over the country: he sent Carver some beans that the scientist could not identify. "You have put one over on me. I didn't think you could do it, but you certainly did." Abbott described what he was planting on his little patch of Chicago. "I wouldn't be surprised if you turned into a real dirt farmer," Carver wrote from his bed. The two never ran out of things to share. Carver revealed irritations to "My beloved friend, Mr. Abbott," as to no one else. "The Booker Washington stamp is assuming absolute enormous proportions and where it is going to end I do not know." He discussed Booker II, the great Booker's grandnephew, who was apparently in a drying-out program in Chicago. "If he would just brace up and stop putting that vile stuff into his stomach," Carver lamented. "I doubt if it is generally known here what is being done for him. A few know it. Something of a similar nature is being done for Portia [Booker T. Washington's daughter]. But she has a good size music class and is doing much to help herself."

When Carver did not hear from Abbott for a few weeks, he fretted like a father. "I was almost frantic," Carver complained. "I had all sorts of misgivings. In fact, I dreamed one night that your mother was dead and that was the reason you did not write. However, please don't let this happen any more. Just drop me a card saying that all is well if you don't have time for more." The telephone was of course in widespread use and Abbott, living in a huge city, probably had one but could not afford the luxury of long distance calls.

Telegraphing was fairly common, though not between Carver and Abbott. The telegraph companies featured specially decorated greetings for holidays, such as the telegram Clarence Hart sent on Carver's last Father's Day.

After five harrowing months of needles, bedpans, catheters, noise, helplessness, and boredom, Carver was finally released from the hospital in October 1938. "It is like emerging to a new world," he said. Some things were indeed new. His feebleness forced him to move from his longtime home in Rockefeller to Dorothy Hall, a few yards from his office. Because of his massive collection of art objects and trash, moving was an enormous undertaking. In his new apartment, he again installed his mother's little spinning wheel just inside his front door. Each time he came home, he reached out and gently touched his only memento of her. His meals could be brought to him because his new rooms were right over the dormitory kitchen. Until Henry Ford paid for an elevator to be installed, a full three years after Carver had transferred to Dorothy Hall, Carver could only leave his apartment on the random days when he felt strong enough to go down the nineteen steps to the building's front door. Those were the years when he developed a reputation for never answering his door and not allowing interruptions. As he was forced to explain, his bedroom was at the very back of the apartment and he often did not hear the door. Sometimes he confused the knock with all the other racket of an undergraduate male dormitory. The windows rattled, the door rattled, and the doors to the kitchen downstairs sounded just like his door.

But the move to Dorothy Hall had advantages. The matron, Mrs. Martin, middle-aged and protective, looked after him attentively. The student who brought his meals was allowed to open the door without knocking and set the food on a nearby table. The tray contained a teapot, hot water, teabag, his napkin, a vase with a flower in it, and his meal, which of course remained untouched if it arrived after the campus clock had stopped chiming the hour. Carver noticed that one delivery boy had a large scar on his throat; he massaged it with peanut oil for several weeks until the scar diminished. When he was housebound, Carver entertained himself with books and with three daily newspapers: the *Montgomery Advertiser*, the *Birmingham News*, and *The Atlanta Constitution*, along with *Time* and *U.S. News and World Report*.

For nine years he had the same paperboy, Frank Godden. When a senator from Illinois came to spend the day with Carver, Godden took the visitor around the campus, after which Mrs. Martin prepared an impromptu lunch of sandwiches and lemonade. The senator showed his appreciation by sending young Godden a large package—underwear, a shirt, things he thought the boy could use, and a money order for five or ten dollars. "Now I want you to write a letter of thanks," Carver instructed him, "and I want to see it before you mail it." If, after his death, Carver did arrive in some sort of afterlife, he no doubt looked for a way to send his thanks to the pallbearers and gravediggers who had helped him relocate. In Dorothy Hall, a second paperboy, Edward Braye, brought him the *Alabama Journal*. He was often invited inside Carver's cluttered nest. Though the lining of Carver's hat was mended with safety pins, Braye observed that Carver was always sewing something, "stitching up this or patching up that . . . His sweaters were generally in pretty good shape, but his pants were always beat up . . . He couldn't stand it if he missed one of his papers." Not surprisingly, Carver's little apartment was the repository of years and years of old news.

Carver continued to spend some nights in the hospital for the rest of the year, but very slowly he began walking, if only a few steps outside his building. The next year, 1939, he was still too unsteady at Easter to attend services—he was taken to the dining room in Dorothy Hall where he could see the students parading to the chapel. Yet he was planning to go to Minnesota to give another lecture. Invitations from outside the South afforded singular opportunities to publicize Tuskegee; at one time, he had been under some pressure to accept them, but now he traveled because he wanted to. He wrote to Harry Abbott, "My heart was tested night before last and while they want to make me feel good, I can tell that they are not satisfied with its action. In fact, I know that as well as they do . . . rest assured that if I can make the trip at all it will be very largely to see you." Sure enough, a few weeks later Carver and his unsatisfactory heart were on a train for the long trip. Once back home, it took the entire summer before he was again strong enough to walk the block to the post office. But then in the fall he crisscrossed the country by train on a junket of two months that would have exhausted a person in the bloom of health—first to the 1939 World's Fair in New York, and then back and forth between Chicago, New York, Tuskegee and Minneapolis, to give lectures, appear on radio shows, and see the Abbotts. That became the pattern of Carver's last years—a long trip and lectures, then months in bed recuperating, then off again for another killer journey to accept the honors that washed over him. The little life left to Carver was largely eaten up with the obligations—and pleasures—of fame.

During the World's Fair trip, the New Yorker hotel declined to honor Carver's reservations and shunted Carver and Curtis into a corridor. Curtis called in the press and a representative of Doubleday, the publisher of Rackham Holt's biography of Carver. The publisher threatened a lawsuit, whereupon Carver was finally given a room, six hours after he first appeared at the desk. Instead of leaving, he had sat his ground (Curtis asked the hotel for a chair) in a hall. The incident was widely publicized, even as Carver was on the air talking about his work with plants.

Radio in those days was not pervaded by news analysis as television is today. The most popular programs offered human-interest stories that gave unsophisticated people a glimpse of the variety of the world outside their own towns. People loved programs about ordinary individuals accomplishing something extraordinary. Since there were yet no public stations, it behooved the major networks to provide educational material. Carver, well spoken and articulate, was an ideal radio subject. In his last years, he was invited to appear on at least a dozen national shows: Edgar Guest's *It Can Be Done, Inside Story, Ripley's Believe It or Not,* and many regional broadcasts such as *General Electric's Science Forum.* People who never read anything thus knew all about George Washington Carver.

The program *Strange As It Seems,* sponsored by Ex-Lax, was aired coast-to-coast from New York on Thursday night at 7:30, between two other "big" shows, *Amos n' Andy* at 6:15 and the musical program *Major Bowe's Hour* at 9:00. *Strange As It Seems* featured examples of true scientific and historical phenomena. A program might showcase a child math wonder or describe how Russia's Peter the Great made wearing a beard a criminal offense in the seventeenth century. Carver, with his amazing peanut products—washing powder, shoe polish, gasoline, alcohol, paper, insecticide, wallboard, and all the rest—could have kept the nation listening for much longer than the program's twenty-five minutes.

On *We the People,* broadcast from Chicago, individuals of all sorts told their unusual human-interest stories. The producers went to great lengths to verify that the stories were true. The narrators used their own words; listeners across the country could hear a Boston inflection one week, a Florida drawl the next.

Sponsored by Sanka coffee and enormously popular, *We the People* featured such attractions as the "mentalist" Dunninger describing the case of a dead man's guitar that mysteriously strummed every night, a petty criminal who solved a murder he was accused of committing, and a scientist with a peculiar voice who explained that he had produced hundreds of useful items from peanuts, sweet potatoes, persimmons, and beans.

At the end of 1939, Carver was back in New York to receive the Theodore Roosevelt Medal for "outstanding contribution to southern agriculture." The medal was no ordinary award, and Carver was ecstatic. But he managed to stand, sit, wait, and walk only by sheer force of will. The train trip to New York took twenty-two hours. Traveling within New York is never easy, even now, even for people who are not elderly and ill. The same week as the Roosevelt award, he addressed the *New York Herald-Tribune* Forum. "Nobody realized how very sick I was," he later wrote. "When I arrived, I did not expect to get back to Tuskegee alive." Nevertheless, from New York he went directly to Michigan to visit Henry Ford, another long trip, but one he would not have passed up for all the magnolias in Montgomery County.

C arver ardently admired Ford who, he declared, had the most remarkable mind he had ever encountered. Their conversations continued to inspire Carver even after Ford began descending into paranoia. Carver the agricultural chemist could understand someone who had tried to build steam tractors before he built automobiles and who wanted to build machines that would end farm drudgery. Ford deeply loved the land and nature. Though not a rounded biologist like Carver, he was intensely interested in certain topics, such as birds; his farm had five hundred birdcages. Carver was especially fascinated by Ford's assertion that solutions to engineering problems "just came to me, plucked out of the air." That was the way Carver, too, got his best ideas. For his part, Ford made many gestures to show he was sincere when he pronounced Carver America's greatest living scientist. Ford's historical museum in Deerfield Park contained a full-size replica of the cabin where Carver was born. He contributed money to Carver's projects, added to Carver's equipment at Tuskegee, built George Washington Carver schools in Michigan, Georgia, and Florida, and finally offered Carver a place at River Rouge, where he established the George Washington Carver Laboratory.

They tried to see each other once or twice a year, either at Tuskegee, at Dearborn, Michigan, or at the Fords' plantation in Ways, Georgia. Like Carver, Ford had built his first little house with his own hands, a dwelling of twenty-one square feet. But that was fifty years before he became rich. At "Fairlane," Ford's fifty-six-room house on the Rouge River, the scientist who liked being mistaken for a hobo was the guest of a billionaire who liked to pose as a plebian. An army of servants kept the place clean; Clara Ford made them buy their own uniforms. The mansion contained a bowling alley, pipe organ, indoor swimming pool, and bathrooms equipped with circular fixtures that sprayed the bather from all sides simultaneously. At home, Ford wore a coat and tie; his wife wore cocktail dresses. Ford, "the common man's genius," had learned how to enjoy both private luxury and public simplicity. At very little inconvenience, Ford kept rooms always ready for Carver and Curtis, both in Dearborn and at his 75,000 acre estate in Georgia, in case Carver was able to stop in on the way to some lecture.

In November 1939, Carver came home from Dearborn prepared to die. He made out a will and nailed down the legal details of two projects he had been working on for some time—completing the George Washington Carver Museum and Creative Research Laboratory at Tuskegee and setting up the Carver Foundation as an endowment for the museum and a scholarship fund. He remained bedridden for two months. But while reading and rereading his rather complicated will, Carver realized that he could not die immediately. The Carver Museum was not firmly established. Without his impetus behind it, the whole project might fade away, half formed. He would have to put off his life's ultimate ceremony.

His recovery was not quick, but it was steady. It took him three months to be able to bend his knee. Because of his weak heart, fluids collected in his body and left him swollen, especially his hands, feet, and knees. His movements were limited to places on campus where he was unlikely to meet people who would require him to talk, since he was short of breath. "I walked as far as James Hall," he reported in April 1940, "and had to come back on account of an audience of girls who saw me and here they came, so naturally I didn't feel strong enough to be bothered with them so I just turned around and came on back." Chatting with people was tiring. "They don't realize that, of course, and they haven't seen me in weeks and they want to talk." He still could not write. "First my right hand gave way, then the left one . . . sometimes I cannot even sign my name so that it is legible. This depends on how the heart is working." His appetite gradually improved, however, and he began pestering Abbott to find him foods he could not get in Alabama. "Send me a little package and let the bill accompany the package," he asked. Sometimes it was beans he wanted ("I hope you can find those big butter beans as I feel like I would enjoy a good mess of them"), sometimes pigs' feet or fried apples. He was convinced that pigs' feet with their gelatin contributed greatly to his restoration; he ate what he called "large quantities"—three per day. Food worked its way into nearly every letter, if only when Carver reported to Abbott what others had sent him—breads and cream cheese from Dr. Ross, figs from the second Mrs. Logan, Chinese cabbage, soybeans, chickens galore, and even homemade blackberry wine—he stirred a teaspoon into a glass of milk twice a day. Years earlier Carver had made wine from dandelions, the only one of his concoctions that he did not urge on his hapless students. Austin's wife introduced him to store-bought fried pork rinds, which he devoured. When his dinner was late, Carver could retaliate by ignoring it and eating his own soybean soup.

From time to time, Abbott scraped up the money to visit, and news that he was coming always energized Carver. "I cannot contain myself until you get here." In March 1940, he wrote, "I will arrange to break all the rules and save my strength for your coming as there is so much I want to talk to you about, and it is not at all improbable that we may get out to Oklahoma in the near future if I can gather strength enough and the way that I am going now, it does seem so." Carver never gave up his wistful hope that he and Abbott could make one more trip. It took four more months before Carver could report that the swelling and stiffness in his ankles were gradually leaving. "I can pick up my feet without staggering so much." Oklahoma seemed closer. By September, he was able to walk unaided down the steps of Dorothy Hall. "They said I would never walk any more if I survived this last attack. It is something to be proud of." The first place he walked was to his new museum.

* * *

The George Washington Carver Museum, housed in the Institute's remodeled laundry building, was substantially financed by Henry Ford. There was quite a bit of opposition to the museum—"sour grapes," Carver called it—from people in the college who hoped the whole project "would die in the borning." Some faculty members resented him, resented the fuss the public made over him, and objected to the expenditures for the building. Carver was enormously proud of the museum as he saw it taking shape. Regarding its opening, he wrote to Harry Abbott, "Whenever I think, and that is quite often, about your not being here at this time and will not be here, it makes me kind of sick at heart."

The museum gathered together Carver's huge collection of native plants and his collections of minerals, birds, and clays. The hundreds of products he developed from peanuts, sweet potatoes, and native clays were represented. The Carver exhibits of fibers, paints, building materials, cosmetics, and all the rest had traveled widely; thousands of people all over the country had seen them. But at home, they had stayed locked away in the agriculture building. The museum dedication was the first time many Tuskegee trustees had seen any of the displays that documented his life's work. One friend, noting the range of his genius, declared that Carver would eventually succeed in isolating food from rocks. (Someone had already done it; the food was called "salt.")

Dozens of Carver's paintings were displayed, along with his "textile art," that is, examples of his crochet, embroidery, beadwork, and needlepoint, exhibited in unstained bare wood frames. Carver thought so much of his paintings that he wanted one entire room set aside for them—an art gallery attached to the main museum. It was a historical museum of food chemistry and of Tuskegee. Carver's first laboratory classroom was on display, along with a replica of the first Jesup Wagon and photographs through the years. Carver was not alive to see almost all of his paintings destroyed by a fire in the museum on November 24, 1947, while the school was celebrating Thanksgiving. All but three of his paintings were lost, and those three were badly damaged, so that it is not possible now to judge Carver's talent as an artist.

The exhibits were not complete when the museum opened, and Carver worried incessantly that "they"—the trustees, who were local Tuskegee officials—"would not have the vision" to develop the project. "I do not want any third rate collection in this museum," he frankly declared to Patterson. "My greatest ambition is that it shall be a credit to all the people, Tuskegee Institute, and our race." Harry Abbott was skeptical that the museum would ever be the splendid place its creator envisioned; he regularly worked himself into a temper because the school had never discharged "its full duty toward you." "As you know," Carver answered, "I cannot write and therefore have to reserve my personal comments until I can see you or can write . . . I sometimes wonder myself just what the future will bring forth [regarding the museum]. We will see just what takes place, that is, you will see, not myself." Carver confided his hurt when the film *The March of Time*, in which he was featured, was shown in the auditorium at Tuskegee. "Unfortunately, I did not know anything about it, and did not get to see it . . . Those in charge did not think of me."

The exhibits were mounted slowly, with one situation after another intervening. When the exhibit of his 1896 laboratory was put up, the first visitors stole the objects off the desk. For seven months, Carver asked President Patterson for cases so that the displays he had prepared could be protected. When a few cases finally arrived, there were no locks; irreplaceable objects were vandalized almost as if they had not been behind glass. Month after month in 1940, Carver wrote nearly identical letters to Patterson, pleading for locks. "The stealing continues . . . this morning I went to get some things and they had disappeared." The world was full of collectors of stamps, envelopes, handkerchiefs, and all sorts of souvenirs, he wrote. "When they get a chance to enrich their collections, they do it . . . I am holding back certain things that I am afraid to put out because they cannot be duplicated if they disappear." Since the building's windows were not secured, there were a series of break-ins by burglars who were after the donations box. Carver repeatedly asked that a guard be assigned to the museum, "as I often find people wandering around without anybody to look after them."

Carver knew that he was racing against time in the matter of the museum. "This museum," he said, "is what has kept my old heart alive." And indeed, it was the project above all others that obsessed him in his final years. On the face of it, Patterson seems to have been negligent in protecting the collection—allowing roof leaks to go untended, for example, until two paintings were damaged by water. "A pastel painting," Carver admonished him, "—if water falls on it, that is the end of it." But Patterson's letters and attentions to Carver were effusive during the period when the museum was being developed: "The new art exhibit beggars description," Patterson wrote. "Many of those who witnessed it yesterday experienced a mingled emotion of pride and soul lifting ... This is a priceless gift to Tuskegee Institute."

Despite such warm words, Carver had every reason to worry about his collections. The high-sounding Carver Creative Research Laboratory beggared description, too. In 1939 two former students were instructed to set it up—in an old room attached to the museum building. The room still contained a large boiler with its accessories, and no lights. The entire equipment consisted of one gas jet, one water faucet, a fruit jar, containers, and other makeshift pieces—exactly like the "laboratory" that had confronted Carver when he first arrived at Tuskegee in 1896. Tuskegee Institute eventually removed the boiler, leaving a pile of dirt that required the labor of three boys to remove. The school assigned masons to cement the exposed floor but declined to provide the fifteen dollars' worth of paint needed for the walls. Carver explained how to mix calcimine clay paint. Meanwhile, Tuskegee continued to solicit donations for the various Carver projects from people who had no notion of the "Carver Creative Research Laboratory" except its name, which was itself an example of creative imagination.

Carver's museum was not the only project Patterson was trying to get off the ground, nor was it the largest. Since black patients were excluded from the Georgia Warm Springs Foundation, the National Foundation for Infantile Paralysis in 1939 granted $161,250 to Tuskegee for the establishment of a crippled children's clinic. It was not under Carver's direction or administration but under the control of a physician, John W. Chenault, an orthopedist. Chenault respected Carver, who was very pleased with the new hospital, even though he was not consulted about it and had no part in its services. "It is really an enormous thing, as it calls in specialists from all over the country and patients literally swarm in for treatment," he wrote. As for himself, he intended to continue his own work in massage. He maintained an affectionate relationship with Dr. Chenault, whom he liked, and therefore teased. "My dear Dr. Chenault," he once wrote: "This is to extend to you greetings and to say that the next time I come to your office to see you that you will be in and stay in. If you would do right, you wouldn't have to run every time you look out and see me coming. This is to notify you that I am going to get my hands on you so you had just as well figure out what is going to happen." Chenault replied with a warm letter of apology. Clearly, no animosity there.

A month after making his will, Carver got "better." He was again sick in March 1940, when he went to the quiet dedication of the Carver Industrial School in Ways, Georgia, but he was rewarded for his effort by being able to spend a whole, blissful day with Ford. "He did not leave my side for ten minutes. He rode beside me in the car, helped me over rough places, wouldn't let me walk anywhere, and kept people away from me." Ford and Carver were both in their mid-seventies. Ford was physically stronger and more agile than his charge, but Carver, at least, never lost his mental acumen or his lifelong, congenial sanity. Ford kept everyone away as a matter of course, convinced that myriad assassins were stalking him and his family, particularly his grandchildren. He followed a deliberately erratic schedule so that no one could predict where he would be at any given time. Even the principal of the industrial school had no idea when Ford would show up for the dedication which, it turned out, was a spur-of-the-moment affair, attended only by the students, a few school officials, and Ford's inevitable bodyguards. Carver, surprised at the timing, did not have his notes with him and had to leave off the pretty speech he had prepared.

When he came back, Carver was sent to bed, according to the usual pattern of his fluctuations—a few weeks up; several months down. He was still receiving some thirty letters a day about his massage oil treatment, which he answered by dictating from his sickbed. Physicians were now writing to him fairly often, including one surgeon in Mexico who had been practicing medicine for forty years and was profoundly moved by the cases he saw daily of paralysis in children. In New Orleans a physician in Charity Hospital acknowledged that Carver had cured dermatitis on the doctor's hand with applications of potassium iodide. "I feel sure that had I been able to stay in Tuskegee another two weeks under your care and observation, the irritation would have been healed long ago. The area that healed during your treatment has stayed well." There was enough encouragement from medical men to keep Carver hopeful that his program of massage therapy would one day get a fair trial, but there was not enough solid professional endorsement to let him expect government funding for such a test during his lifetime. Pathetic letters came as always from people trying to avoid surgery, such as a Michigan woman who feared ovarian surgery because her husband would leave her if she could not have children. "Help me, for God's sake," she wrote. "I need you. Please don't turn me down. I won't always be troubling you to do anything else. Please help me." Some of his old patients sent news that they were improving. Others, strangers, knew their cases were beyond the help of any therapy Carver could offer; they just wanted his prayers, since they believed God listened to him. By 1940, the number of inquiries about the oil treatment had risen to some 6,000.

Carver's champions still believed he had found an effective treatment for infantile paralysis long after he himself had recognized the limits of oil massage. Now and then he had to rein them in, bluntly. "My dear Mr. Porter," he wrote one of his indefatigable advocates. "You are classifying me, whether you mean to do it or not, as an M.D., which I am not . . . My work in connection with infantile paralysis comes in the atrophied muscle group. After the disease has done its work, then if it has left any muscular atrophy or dystrophy, I see what I can do towards the building up and restoring such muscles." Carver explained that he hoped the treatment could meliorate damage caused by many diseases, not only infantile paralysis. "I have said to you before that an investigator never gives out definite information until its effectiveness has been proven many, many times . . . An investigator does not want to be bothered with statements purporting to what he has found, as he doesn't know whether he has found it or not." Nevertheless, Porter did not stop touting the "cure" for polio; he became a well-intentioned nuisance to Carver, who was afraid his groupie would wind up antagonizing the entire medical profession. "My Esteemed Friend Mr. Porter: May I most strongly suggest that you let the doctors alone, that is, the medical doctors, let them alone unless you run up against them face to face." It was not only Carver's scientific accomplishments that were exaggerated by his admirers. One man wrote to confirm information he had read in the press: "It was stated that Dr. Carver's paintings of flowers were to hang in the Louvre gallery. Is this true? And did Dr. Carver tour the Middle East as a concert pianist?"

Carver, certain that the potential of the peanut had not been fully ex-
plored, never set it aside. He went back to studying its enzyme composition.
He longed to follow up on Kellogg's work on its vitamin and riboflavin content, especially Vitamin B1 to prevent pellagra; but such research would require "extensive feeding experiments with rats, guinea pigs, and other animals,
and we have not funds, of course, for such work." He was experimenting with
peanut butter bread, investigating the possibility of deriving antifreeze from
peanut oil, and testing peanut shells as a root stimulant for flowering plants. A
U.S. senator wondered if peanut oil could be substituted for coconut oil in the
manufacture of soap and asked Carver to provide a comparative analysis of the
acids. Carver had promoted peanut oil for soap-making forty years previously,
but the notion was just catching on.

Many of Carver's old ideas were being revived as America prepared to enter
the Second World War. Newspapers were running articles about the food and
fodder value of the sweet potato thirty-one years after Carver had published a
bulletin describing the root's nutritive properties and giving twenty-five recipes. The U.S. Department of Agriculture sought his help in preparing a publication on how to dry sweet potatoes. He sent a bulletin he had written on the
subject decades earlier and remarked that he possessed some of the potatoes
he had dried in 1910 which were still in fine condition for cooking. At that
time, Carver noted, his work with the sweet potato "aroused no special interest," so it had been dropped "for matters of greater importance."

The *Dallas Morning News* began giving some attention to the shortage of
drug crops in the United States during wartime. Carver sent his friend the
editor a little something he had published twenty-two years previously when
he was trying to promote the raising of medicinal herbs in the South—a list
of 115 plants found in Macon County, Alabama, alone, "recognized by the U.S.
Pharmacopeia, along with their technical and common names, and the parts
used." Even Carver's famous banquet of 1911 featuring nothing but transmog-
rified peanuts was rewarmed in a magazine article. Carver sent the menu and
the recipes for mock chicken, peanut ice cream, peanut coffee, and the rest.
He reminded the writer that the peanut shells could be made into elegant stationery on which to write the invitations.

With one swollen foot in the grave, Carver was still full of enthusiasm for
research. He looked into the feasibility of using crude oil as a component of

paint. He wanted to do something with defibrinated pinecones—there were many more pinecones than brains around Tuskegee, he observed. Ford got Carver interested in soybean plastics, and Carver interested himself in growing soybeans for food, a project he had started many years before. It was still impossible to get soybeans in Alabama, and practically nothing was known about them. Carver wanted to work out recipes and try to popularize the soil-enhancing soybean, even though in his day no one could imagine housewives accepting anything so odd as soy milk, soy sauce, bean curd, or glass noodles. He was exploring medicinal uses for the persimmon, another common Alabama plant. For two years a Tuskegee dentist had been using a persimmon astringent prepared by Carver for curing pyorrhea. Carver now discovered that a modified form of the astringent was effective in curing athlete's foot.

Paul Miller, a scientist from the Bureau of Plant Pathology of the USDA, came to stay at Tuskegee for a time in order to do a major study of Carver's extraordinary fungus collection. Nobody at Tuskegee knew enough about mycology to appreciate the value of Carver's specimens. The idea that the federal government would send one of its scholars to the southern hinterland to work under the guidance of a black taxonomist—even a famous one—was deeply gratifying to Carver. He had believed that his prodigious knowledge of fungi would die with him and that his unremarked collection might be lost, misplaced, or ruined through negligence.

Thus, Carver's research resumed as usual, but his tenancy in normal life was a month-to-month lease with no certainty of renewal. He described getting up at a ceremony to accept a dedication. "I turned absolutely blind twice, so that I could not even see the lines of the paper." In 1940, he got a new set of false teeth, made for him by a dental surgeon who spent some time working in the Infantile Paralysis Clinic. For the first time in five years, he could leave his teeth in even when eating. "In all my experience," Carver wrote, "I have never gotten such comfort . . . What a real joy it is to see a man as skillful as yourself." He was no longer the zealous workhorse he had been for most of his career, but he worked hard when he could work at all. "When the heart gets to functioning well, I manage to get to the office from 6:30 a.m. to about 10:00 a.m. then I go in to rest. I am back again from 1:30 to 3:00 p.m., when I go back again." At times he was obliged to remain in the rest of the day because by afternoon he had no more energy for the stairs. In August 1940, he wrote to

Lucy Crisp that he had to be extremely careful on his feet. "I have no power to catch myself if I start to fall, and many times have to fall and roll over one or two times before I can catch myself."

One can only imagine the frail, courageous man falling and rolling over "one or two times" in order to get to his laboratory. It seemed that only a resilient, fine wire connected him to active life. Nevertheless, in September 1940, just as it was time for him to go into his autumnal dying mode, he astonished everyone by starting to give massages and to instruct others in his technique. The hands that for sixty years had been able to do anything and everything were now useless for drawing, painting, penmanship, artistic needlework, fixing machinery, or playing musical instruments, but they could still relieve pain. Soon he was back to giving out tonics and illegally prescribing medicaments, to the dismay of his physician friends. Five motherless kittens adopted him, trailing him in a line from his dormitory to the museum, appropriating his office, and counting on him for breakfast and dinner. For fun, he was making some experiments with hydroponic gardening and breeding amaryllis, which he had been fiddling with for years. In the last months of his life, he succeeded in crossing the amaryllis with the Easter lily to get "a pure white flower with some green down the center." Carver's favorite blossom, at least at this point in his lifelong love affair with flowers, was the japonica.

Through most of 1941 he worked every day behind the glass door of his lab, always wearing a big white lab apron. Despite his diabetes, anemia, heart failure, and who knew what else, he had resumed identifying fungi samples and filing reports for the USDA. He was trying to see if the fiber of southern okra could be used in sandbags as a replacement for jute, an import. He continued to work with his old friend, the chinaberry, with fibers of the catalpa tree, and with a vine from a plant called the "dish rag gourd." He still could not write, and Tuskegee was still reluctant to give him stenographic help. He had the services of a secretary only half of each working day, Mrs. Jessie Abbott, a relative of Harry. In his office, his microscope sat on a chair to the right of his desk. On the wall, the portraits of his three heroes looked at him as he worked: Thomas Edison, Henry Ford, and Luther Burbank. Behind his desk was a Maxfield Parrish calendar painting in the strong blues that he loved. When he was up to chatting, Carver came out to greet visitors to his museum—Marian Anderson, Lena Horne, Joe Louis, and average people, too. Eliot Battle used to pass by the museum every morning on his way to work. Meeting Carver "was one of the most exciting experiences I have ever had in my life . . . the respect that he showed a young, sixteen-year-old boy I think was the reason for my real success . . . He encouraged me each time I stopped, not just the first day, but every time I would pass. Invariably, Dr. Carver would either be cutting flowers or cutting shrubbery or working around his area there outside the museum in the early morning hours."

The letters he received from ordinary people let him survey the human condition, lest he become too concerned about his own. One man begged him to create an odorless, tasteless drug that he could put into his son's drinks to cure his alcoholism, even while another was wondering why Carver didn't try to make a whiskey from peanuts that would be "of great medicinal value to humanity." A lady asked for Carver's suggestions for books for her son, whose picture she sent along. "*The Harvester, The Girl of the Limberlost,* and *Laddie,* all by Gene Stratton Porter," he answered. One man wrote, with a blunt pencil, to ask how he could exploit his patent for something or other. For starters, Carver suggested amiably, he could buy a pen. Others announced their cures for cancer. Carver received an interesting letter from the Oklahoma State Hospital for the Negro Insane asking if there were practical uses for human hair and whether "Negro hair" or "Nordic hair" would be more valuable. The writer was inspired to communicate with Carver after watching one inmate give another one a haircut. The requests from strangers for loans had not diminished. One poor man had what he thought was his own cure for pyorrhea; he sent off for a patent application but found he did not have the forty dollars required to file. "I had Are white man want to back me up but I Am Are Fraid of him . . . Mister Carver I Dont beleave you would Beat Me out of it. Your Truly. God Bless us All."

One of the most arresting letters Carver received came from a man in prison in Mexico for "bankruptcy," who happened to be in charge of the prison school. He wrote that he had $285,000 hidden in a trunk in the U.S. Customs House. He offered Carver a third of the loot if Carver would come to Mexico and pay the expenses incurred at his trial so that the embargo on the trunk could be lifted. Carver was instructed to reply through a third party who would deliver his response personally. "I beg you to treat this matter with the most absolute reserve and discretion," he wrote. Everybody without exception, it seemed, trusted George Carver.

Carver was not one of those prodigies who was unrecognized and unappreciated in his lifetime—except at certain moments by Tuskegee. The longer he lived, the more prizes and praises he collected—a dazzling number of medals, trophies, plaques, certificates, and awards—even a gavel made of wood from the stairway of Abraham Lincoln's home. He was named to distinguished committees, such as the birthday committee of the Thomas Edison Foundation, alongside Harold Urey, Albert Einstein, Herbert Hoover, and a slew of university presidents. He declined many honors that required travel, or he sent Curtis in his place with an acceptance speech. By the beginning of the 1940s, Carver's name was everywhere—in the press, on the radio, in movies and newsreels. "I cannot begin to tell you," Abbott wrote, "how many people, many of them whites, who have told me of hearing your radio talks. Sometimes I have to talk and talk about you." Harry and Carver would compare notes about the films featuring him—Harry saw them at the Metropolitan Theater in Chicago, and Carver saw them, when he could, in Tuskegee.

Despite his crippled hands, Carver was asked by his fans to autograph everything from graduation caps to Booker T. Washington stamps which Tuskegee was selling. The kingbreaker Wallace Simpson wanted him to sign several large blocks of the stamps. Groups that wanted permission to name buildings after him—there were dozens—were gently informed ("I regret so much . . .") that his name had been copyrighted by the Carver Foundation and he was no longer at liberty to authorize its use. Naturally, the Carver schools, institutes, and libraries sprang up anyway. The people who wanted to write, record, or film accounts of his life could have filled Wyoming. The president of a Texas teachers' college gave a speech about Carver and distributed a huge quantity—10,000 copies—to high school students so that by the time of Carver's death the following year, probably no youngster in Texas had escaped learning about him. Carver discouraged biographers, since such projects necessitated his sending written information or submitting to tiring interviews. The writers refused to be discouraged: "It is possible that you have no idea of how much I have worked on your life . . . I have had to take so much from thin air." For special organizations, Carver took the trouble to be honored: he was "deeply grateful" to the black kids at the Arkansas School for the Deaf who wanted to name their first literary club after him.

Those who did not want his life in brief wanted "a brief outline of your philosophy of life." They received copies of what he called "Slogans"—inspirational statements similar to those being popularized by radio counselors of the day. Tuskegee published a wall calendar using one of his slogans for each month. "How far you go in life depends upon your being tender with the young, compassionate with the aged, sympathetic with the striving, and tolerant of the weak and the strong. Because someday in life you will have been all of these." Bits of scientific observations would show up among the slogans: "Candy may be made from wood by separating the cellulose from the other constituents, dissolving it in sulfuric acid, diluting, boiling, and neutralizing the solution." "A high grade of button may be made from casein and formaldehyde"—as if anyone but Carver would attempt to make wood candy or manufacture his own buttons.

To religious groups that clamored for his counsel, he sent biblical quotations. For Harry Abbott, he wrote out in his own shaky hand a comment that has become part of Carver lore: "One of the things that has helped me as much as any other is not knowing how long I am going to live, but how much I can do while living." He advised parents to let children handle "natural objects and real things," so that they might hail the first warm days of spring as "the opening of the mud pie and doughnut season." The life of the butterfly, he thought, presented a striking analogy to the life of the human soul; perhaps it was for that reason that the ancient Greeks, "with their imperfect knowledge of insects," gave the same name "Psyche" both to the spirit of life and to the butterfly. Notwithstanding the prayer sessions he held with Hardwick and, more recently, with Glenn Clark, Carver described his form of prayer as "more of an attitude than anything else. I indulge in very little lip service." In a kind of meditation he carried on many times a day, he contemplated the animal, vegetable, and mineral kingdoms, "their relations to each other, to us, our relations to them, and the Great God who made all of us."

Henry Ford came to Tuskegee in March 1941 for the dedication of the George W. Carver Museum, together with the squadron of bodyguards that shadowed him everywhere. As usual, he declined to give advance notice of his arrival and would have no outsiders witness the speechless and almost wordless ceremony. Ford and his wife inserted some soybean plastics and fibers into a cement slab, inscribed their names into the soft cement and, doubtless to Carver's disappointment, "that was it." However, Ford went to Carver's room afterward and shut out his guards so that the two spent a long, private hour discussing their plans for nutrition research.

The Variety Clubs of America, an organization of entertainers, gave Carver its Humanitarian Award in 1941 in a widely publicized ceremony in Atlantic City, New Jersey. The organization donated $1,000 to the Carver Foundation. Carver was under some pressure to make the trip to accept what was then a princely gift. The Variety Clubs were so insistent on his receiving the award in person that they offered to pay for his physician and a nurse to accompany him. He received a standing ovation from the audience of 1,200. Carver described it as "the most colossal, spectacular, educational, and dignified occasion that I have witnessed." As usual, he wasn't sure "why I should be singled out to receive such a signal honor." A writer for *The Atlanta Constitution* remarked, "Any man who is puzzled to know why . . . is alone in his bewilderment."

Simpson College in Iowa, which had awarded him an honorary doctorate in 1928, invited him to give a baccalaureate address in 1941. The trip allowed him to return to the Indianola of his youth where he had been so poor and yet so happy. Though much had changed, he saw "the very spot where I had a little laundry and the man who operated the store where I had bought five cents' worth of meal and five cents' worth of beef suet . . . You can imagine how thrilling it was." Simpson began a fund-raising drive for a new science building to be named after Carver. When he tried to deliver the address, he became very weak at the podium, but with the aid of an official providing some remarks he got through the talk. The audience of two thousand was not aware that for a few moments he was near collapse.

He was too ill to go to New York to receive one of the grandest awards of his life, the honorary degree of Doctor of Science from the University of Rochester. The president of the university took the unprecedented step of coming to Tuskegee on June 18, 1941, to confer the degree. In 1942, Selma University in Alabama awarded Carver another honorary Doctor of Science degree. The same year, he received the honor that perhaps as much as any other brought him into the homes of the people he had spent his life trying to help. *The Progressive Farmer,* a literate and thoughtful magazine that had been read by farmers since 1886, named Carver Man of the Year. Nearly every southern farmer who read anything read *The Progressive Farmer.* "Instead of a fiction story," the introduction stated, "we are presenting the true story of one man's life that is indeed stranger than fiction."

With each new honor, there came greetings from fellow celebrities, including a sly offer from W. C. Handy to sign his autobiography, *Father of the Blues,* in which Carver was mentioned (if Carver chose to order the book for the price of three dollars.) For each luminary who wrote to him, he received 100 letters from ordinary people and responded to all. He sent one man in Indiana a recipe for grass tea. He explained to another in Virginia why kudzu would not make a good textile. He advised some horticultural researchers in Boston that ragweed tea was a sure-fire remedy for stomach upset and sent the recipe. Foreigners wrote to him for guidance on spraying leaves for insects. "The general rule," Carver advised, "is to ascertain whether the insect chews his food or sucks it. If he sucks his food there is no need to poison the leaves as you must get what is known as a contact poison, that is, something which is put on his body that will kill him." For chewing insects, the plant had to be sprayed so that when the insect ate the leaves he would be poisoned. He thought it was elementary information, but they welcomed it in Costa Rica.

Students from these years distinctly remember Carver pulling up some grass in the yard, bringing it into a home economics class, and helping the girls make a salad of it with onions and eggs. Will Rogers gave a presentation in Tuskegee's chapel in 1942. Meeting Carver, he said, letting his voice rise in an uncanny imitation of him, was "the first time I ever met a man with a tenor voice who amounted to anything." Carver, in the front pew, laughed uproariously, along with everyone else. A recording of Carver's "tenor" voice may be found in the George Washington Carver National Monument in Diamond, Missouri—the occasion was his 1942 commencement speech at Selma University. His voice is strong, considering that he had little more than six months to live, and his accent clipped, like a faster-talking and squeaky FDR. The speech is notable mainly for the contrast it offers between the folksy vernacular of Carver's letters and the precise diction of his actual talk. His speech reflected no southern drawl whatever and no regionalisms—it was altogether a professorial delivery.

Carver remained connected to Lucy Cherry Crisp through the common thread of their resilient, rarely mentioned, interest in Jim. Hardwick by this time had left the Y.M.C.A.; he and his wife were running a bookstore and publishing house in Birmingham. He did not write to Carver. "Wherever he is," Carver wrote to Crisp, "I trust he is doing well. I regret that I am not in touch with him, as you know what we both think of him." From time to time, Crisp sent Carver generous packets of her doggerel (which she herself admitted was not "real" poetry), her clay sculptures, and her paintings. When she worked for the Y.M.C.A. in Macon, Georgia, from 1938 to 1940, she would drive down to see him in her Ford. The 120-mile trip took four and half hours—when the dirt roads were not morasses of hub-deep mud—at twenty-seven miles per hour. Although she was only in her early forties, Crisp, like Carver, had had a couple of bad falls, suffered debilitating bouts of flu, and suffered even more severe bouts of "general depression" that kept her from working on the Carver biography. "I recall that you once told me you did not believe in this business of pretending to laugh when there was no laughter within you, or to sing when there was no real song in your spirit," she wrote. By this time Doubleday had contracted with Rackham Holt to write a biography. Since it seemed even then that Crisp might not finish her manuscript, she unselfishly offered to turn over all her material to Holt, just as Mrs. Milholland's daughter had turned over her late mother's manuscript to Crisp. Carver advised her to wait for the publication of all the other biographies about him that were then under construction and then to finish hers, which he believed would have information that could be found in none of the others because of their long friendship and because she would have the advantage of being able to write about the end of his life. She decided to keep working on it, but in fact, she never finished it. On Christmas Eve, 1942, a few days before Carver's death, Crisp sent President Patterson her bust of Carver that was cast in plaster, a gift to Tuskegee "with no strings whatever attached" but with the hope that if Tuskegee saw fit to display it, she might sell copies to other schools and libraries for ten dollars and remit a two-dollar royalty to the Carver Foundation. Crisp was a kind, humble woman with some talents. It is easy to see why Carver was fond of her. It was not Crisp, however, but Rackham Holt who, just as Carver died, came out with what for many years was considered his definitive biography.

A ustin Curtis put out the story that when Holt came to interview Carver, he took a dislike to her and refused to have any dealings with her. After Curtis's intercession, the story went, Carver agreed to answer specific questions in writing if she would submit them in writing—with Curtis serving as the intermediary. Curtis's reason for concocting this ridiculous tale was that after Carver's death, the Tuskegee administration objected to Curtis's collecting half the royalties from Holt's book. Tuskegee considered that whatever help Curtis rendered to Holt fell under his obligation as Carver's assistant who was being paid by the school. When Curtis refused to give up a share of the royalties, Tuskegee fired him. Consequently, he tried to justify his stance by posing as an essential participant in the writing. Holt, he averred, had only seen Carver in person on two occasions.

In the first place, Carver could not write or type at the time and would not have cooperated in any project that added to his oppressive paperwork. In the second place, his dictated letters to Holt—over twenty-five—and photographs taken with her indicate that they were on quite friendly terms and that he liked her just fine. Holt did irk Henry Wallace by importuning him for information about Carver's life in Iowa, but nothing in Carver's letters to her indicates that she got under his skin. In the third place, Holt stated many times, even in testimony before the U.S. Congress (during the deliberations for establishing a Carver Monument) that she spent five months at Tuskegee during which she saw Carver every day for several hours. During that time she lived in Dorothy Hall and was quite friendly with Mrs. Martin, who tended Carver very closely. Carver's letters show that Austin Curtis's contribution to the biography consisted in gathering documents about events in Carver's youth which he could not recall, such as his exact itinerary when he was moving around Kansas. Carver and Curtis recommended that Holt look at other publications about Carver that were coming out across the country, since some of these writers had access to primary records about his early life. For his help in gathering already-published materials, Curtis, who was ever alert to the fragrance of cash, somehow talked Holt into sharing her profits from the book. Anyone reading Holt's well-written biography can recognize that it reflects intimate personal knowledge of Carver and his quirks and could not have been patched together from a compendium of questionnaires.

Curtis did his level best to step into Carver's shoes even before Carver no longer had need of them, and in later years capitalized wherever possible on having been Carver's assistant. In trying to raise funds to establish the Carver Creative Research Laboratories in 1937, Curtis sent out tens of letters that began thus: "Dear Mr. So-and-So: I am assistant to Dr. G. W. Carver, and the first person he has ever permitted to work with him. All these years he has preferred to work alone with no assurance of his work being carried on rather than select an individual who did not meet with his qualifications. It was my good fortune two years ago to be selected by Dr. Carver as the one having the qualifications he felt his assistant should possess, and it is for me to see that his valuable work is preserved." These were interesting claims, considering that Carver had nothing to do with Curtis's "selection." However, Curtis was right that it fell to him to see that Carver's work was preserved; nobody else was as deeply and consistently concerned about it. Carver made him secretary of the foundation and expected Curtis to succeed him as director of the experiment station after his death.

Because of Carver's physical frailty, Curtis accompanied the elder man everywhere and usually remained close at hand even when friends visited. Often he was useful in keeping people away from Carver, but sometimes he went too far in exercising that authority. On one occasion Carver had to make apologies when Curtis apparently declined to let Carver's secretary Jessie Abbott see Carver. She was leaving Tuskegee for a time and wanted to bid Carver goodbye. Carver wrote, "I am very certain that Mr. Curtis was pretty well taxed as so many people were demanding him to put them in touch with me, and then he had his own family to look after." Carver was very happy that, when he failed to answer her knock, Mrs. Abbott let herself into his apartment ("She knows how to do it, and there is no need for ceremony between us"). But she apparently found him asleep and did not disturb his rest.

Curtis was usually present when biographers and journalists came for interviews, and he made sure they appreciated Carver's dependence on him. When Carver was sick, he could not venture out of doors without Curtis at his side, and when he was well, any stroll farther away then his office had to be taken on Curtis's arm. In 1940, Carver wrote to Curtis's wife, "I am feeling just a little lonesome this morning, as Baby has gone to New York City . . . I miss the dear boy so very much although I try not to notice it as best I can, but for some reason I cannot help but miss him. He has gone to New York to receive the testimonial to be presented to me . . . It seems so very interesting to me that I have never looked upon him as simply an assistant, but rather as a great big son that I was at liberty to play with and have a good time generally. He is certainly a very dear boy." And a boy he remained in Carver's eyes throughout their eight years together. Unlike Abbott, Curtis did not take his meals with Carver except occasionally, and his wife did not regularly have Carver over for what he called "real" dinners, a respite from the dining hall food.

When Curtis left Tuskegee after Carver's death, he went to Detroit to set up a business selling peanut products. "The first product I started with was our rubbing oil from the peanut for the relief of pains of arthritis and rheumatism." Was it Dr. Carver's formula? "Well, it's one we worked on together," he said. When he arrived in Detroit, he advertised his company by giving a banquet in which all the dishes were derived from peanuts. Curtis acquired two patents: a sanitary toilet seat cover for public restrooms (which he patented in 1940, before he had left Tuskegee), and something he patented with another man, a "less irritating shaving material" made with olive oil, such as Carver had developed years before. Carver had even gone further, having developed an aftershave from the Chinaberry plant which he, of course, never tried to patent. Far from spreading Carver's fame after the scientist's death, Curtis refused to cooperate with any memorial project unless there was something in it for him. When the effort was underway to furnish the George Washington Carver National Monument, Curtis declined to be interviewed unless he received a fee, although dozens of others gladly and freely volunteered their reminiscences. Carver never in his life accepted a fee for exhibitions of his work. But Curtis, asked by the monument officials for specimens of products Carver had developed, demanded payment; moreover, he resented that the monument was turning into a splendid memorial without him. "I . . . know more about his work and the man than any other individual," he wrote. "It is too bad that the services of one so qualified and versed on Dr. Carver's life and work has not been utilized in the development of this memorial." In later years, Curtis branched out beyond science. He ran for Congress in 1958 and lost.

In the years when the old scientist depended on Curtis to escort him outdoors, his letters to the younger man contain the bantering that Carver used with his boys. At some point, Curtis sent his wife a list of what Carver called "don'ts and dos." "You had better not send one of those lists to me, I can tell you that now," Carver wrote. "I think that possibly the fact that Buster was wished off on me has caused me to slump because to have both of you on my hands is just absolutely too much, as you well know that you are no improvement over Buster whatever."

C arver's ongoing jest with all his assistants was that they needed discipline. Frank Steele, who had earned a doctorate, was taken to task for his poor penmanship. "You need not come with any back talk and tell me that I ought to learn to read writing, because this is not writing . . . I know that day when you left you needed to be all beat up . . . Of course I hate to do it because it is against my sweet disposition." In another letter to Steele: "Austin, you and Buster Cooper all belong in the same class . . . I have to beat up Austin; it is an everyday affair with me." The ladies who served as his secretaries were cohorts in Carver's little fiction of keeping the boys in line. He claimed Mrs. Abbott loved to beat up the boys, "and it saves me a very great deal." Mrs. Watkins was appointed his official assistant disciplinarian: "I had to beat up Ralph [Williams] this morning just like I was beating a horse to get a coat on him, and I know that you can be of great service." When he wanted to invite a Reverend Richardson to visit him, he wrote, "The last time I gave you a good peeling, the day or two afterward I saw you and I felt that I could see a hint of a tint of a shade of improvement. Now if you could have these peelings every few days I believe I could put you into a sort of respectable condition, so do come over as soon as you can." Carver was at the time "getting so that I can walk a little bit and not get absolutely exhausted."

It is evident that whatever reserve had existed between Carver and Patterson at the beginning of the president's tenure had dissolved by the later years. Patterson brought his family to visit Carver—his sisters, parents, children, and grandchildren. Carver at long last even began to tease his boss. He wrote to

Mrs. Patterson, "I had such a delightful trip to Chicago with your husband . . . I was sorry, however, to have to whip him two or three times, but I think that you will be better when he comes back." More seriously, he continued, "I was so sorry to have to leave him." (Carver continued on to Detroit to visit Ford.)

Patterson was a kindly man. At one point, Carver was well enough to give a short talk to some girls who had completed one of Tuskegee's certificate programs. Patterson wrote to thank him: "I understand that one of the young women stayed up until after twelve o'clock just holding her little certificate and calling people into her room to show it to them, and her expression was that 'I was never so happy in all my life.' They wonder if you would sign these little certificates? It would indeed make them very happy, but don't do it if it would not be in good form to do so, as the exercises were intended to be just simple and a sort of little family affair. Your speech was most encouraging and inspiring as it always is." It is hard not to like a president of a big school, which Tuskegee was by then, who takes time to make a request on behalf of a group of young girls, even if he keeps forgetting that Carver can't write.

On Christmas Day, 1941, Patterson and his wife braved bad weather to bring Carver an elegant dinner, on gold-trimmed dishes with utensils to match, and a hand-embroidered napkin—details that Carver noted with his usual boundless gratitude. "When you came in through the rain bringing the dinner, I confess I filled up at once," he wrote, "because you brought with you that metaphysical something that spoke in no uncertain terms the vision of a great movement destined to bring a new light to the educational world, and that light is going to begin shining right here at Tuskegee Institute." One of Patterson's Christmas gifts to Carver was a bronze cast of his little grandson's hand, since, like all grandparents, he believed everyone was as infatuated with his little one as he was.

The chef at Dorothy Hall, aptly named Mr. Spicely, took a particular interest in Carver's diet and sometimes even ate with him. After Spicely left Tuskegee, Carver thanked him in a long and interesting letter:

> I was deeply touched yesterday when I read your note, as I am very certain that you know how much I appreciate you and the work that you are doing. You have a type of work that heretofore has been regarded as manned by rough individuals. I can recall as a child my first impression of

men cooks. They were running on steamboats and they were called "steamboat roustabouts." When on duty they had just a fair degree of decency that was very strained, but just as soon as they got out of the kitchen and to themselves, they were true representatives of old Satan himself, and it wasn't at all unusual for them to return to their work all cut up, bruised, black-eyed, and in a general ragged condition after a night of carousal.

I think of you in this connection very much as I think of Joe Louis. Joe Louis has come in and absolutely dignified the profession of boxing because he is perfectly decent, wholesome, and a fine representative . . . My feeling is and always has been that the preparation of foods with all of its intricate ramifications requires the highest type of intelligence.

Spicely went on to become a chef at the Waldorf Astoria in New York. Tuskegee's cooking declined, apparently, after he left. The poor quality of the victuals was one of the causes of a massive student strike that occurred in 1941.

The Depression was officially over; U.S. agriculture and manufactures had been hugely stimulated by war orders. Yet there was aching poverty, as Carver noted to one person who sent him castoffs to distribute: "If you could only be here two or three days and go around and see the suffering and the needs." Carver described how a week before "a poor old man who is now away up in the seventies, if not older, came tottering into my office. He brought a little, tiny bag of peanuts that he had raised on his little farm and wanted me to buy them, with the plea that he had nothing to eat. He evidently had walked about seven miles from the country. His hair is perfectly white and he is so feeble. I think that I shall give him some of the things you sent, and we have so many here, women and men, who literally live out of the garbage receptacles."

Despite commiserating about hunger in his letters, Carver was rather tough-hearted toward the scavengers. Seeing a familiar face at the trash can, Carver once remarked to a student, "Now I'm a believer that germs and things don't necessarily kill anybody. Look at him, how stout he is, and he's eating out of the trash can." That was bad enough. But at Christmas time, he wrote to Jack Sutton's parents:

I am telling my friends as far as I can not to send me a lot of stuff because I can't use it and never will, and there are so many people that really need it. Every morning I stand in my room and have done so for a year or so, and see a man come just as regularly as morning comes, about four or five o'clock, and gets his breakfast out of the garbage can. Sometimes he stands right there and eats it with his children—I think he has five. I save up such little things that they bring me that I don't eat, such as rolls, bits of bacon, and things of that kind, wrap them up in a little bag and throw them down to him.

It would seem that Carver could have done better. There were those few meals he allowed to be thrown away untouched because they arrived thirty seconds too late; he might have simply set them aside until the next morning. There were meals he could have prepared from his pantry for the scavenging family. There was food he could have requested from the cafeteria and set aside for them. Considering that a few dollars a week could feed a family in those days, he could even have thrown down grocery money. Carver himself regularly examined garbage to find items he could use in his laboratory. He was as happy sorting trash as a shopper in a thrift store, for he considered that everything he handled was reusable, even if he himself could not reuse it immediately. Perhaps the idea of second-hand food was not as repugnant to him as to most people.

Holed up in his apartment, Carver nevertheless learned a great deal about the war and not only from his long, daily bath of newsprint. A missionary friend wrote him a horrific tale of crossing the Atlantic in a German ship headed for Angola, carrying escaped Jews among the passengers. The captain had the colors of the ship painted out, ran at night without lights, and entered darkened ports for refueling, trying to find a neutral port that would neither scuttle the ship as being that of an enemy nor send the Jews back to Germany.

The last year of Carver's life started out badly with a severe attack of his yearly nemesis, influenza. When he returned to work after two months, government agencies were beseeching him for substitutes for scarce products—the War Production Board was particularly anxious to produce synthetic rubber. In March 1942, he wrote his last bulletin, which turned out to be the most popular of his career: "Nature's Garden for Victory and Peace," about edible wild plants. It led to feature articles in *Pathfinder* and *The Saturday Evening Post* and to a downpour of mail from people wanting information about "eating weeds." Henry Ford visited him—Carver was strong enough for that.

Some years earlier, Carver had decided to end all the speculation about his birth date and settled on "some time in July" of an unspecified year. Usually, Abbott was the only one of his friends who remembered the fictional birthday, as Carver himself generally forgot it. But by the 1940s, one of his admirers, Richard Pliant, was lobbying Washington to create a national monument at Carver's birthplace, Moses Carver's old farm. Carver was naturally interested in the facts Pliant was able to establish concerning his early years as he interviewed the oldest settlers of Diamond to see if someone could fix the exact day. Carver warned Abbott not to talk up the birthday. "Nothing definite can be found," Carver wrote, "except it was some time in July, and now at this late date it is just as well not to stir up anything that will give me as much trouble as the establishing of a birthday."

He could no longer play the violin in church, as he had even a few years earlier. But when he could get over to the chapel, he participated in services, as when he recited William Cullen Bryant's "Thanatopsis," one of the poems he loved best. But in June, Carver wrote to Abbott that he had so little strength, he wasn't sure what might happen at any moment. He was too sick to walk or even, at times, to sit up. In July he was even worse, and his doctor thought the end was close. Henry Ford, meanwhile, was eagerly waiting for him to be well enough to come and dedicate the laboratory he had established in Carver's honor. So, as he had done before, Carver astonished everyone by getting up unsteadily one day, packing up some compounds he had recently developed, and boarding a train for Michigan.

Although many of Ford's theories concerning food and health were daft notions that Carver could hardly have subscribed to, Ford enthusiastically endorsed all of Carver's nutritional ideas. They both agreed that in order for farmers to prosper, they had to produce on their land not only food but plants and minerals that could supply industry—such things as plastics, purifiers, fuel alcohol. Carver had promulgated these ideas since 1900. In Ford, Carver had a friend with whom he could seriously discuss conservation, recycling, ecology, hydroponics, and the dangers of excessive chemicals in the air and food.

Ford revived Carver's interest in soybeans, despite the unavailability of research-quality beans in Alabama. Based on Carver's venerable peanut menu, Ford wanted to create a soybean dinner menu. Their mutual interest in the properties of plants gave Ford the idea for a Carver Nutritional Laboratory in Dearborn, a project that grew over several years. Carver sent duplicates of his vegetable and fruit exhibits and, throughout 1940 and 1941, steadily provided samples of his renewed chemurgic research. There is no doubt that Carver's contacts with Ford, whom he called "my great inspiring friend," were richly stimulating, especially during the development of "what Mr. Ford insists upon calling *my* nutritional laboratory" in Dearborn. "Just to think," Carver wrote, "it has already cost $100,00 and he will put there whatever I want, regardless of what it costs. Can you imagine my being in possession of such a thing?" It was the dedication of this laboratory that caused Carver to crawl out of his sickbed in July 1942 to go to Dearborn for "an indefinite stay."

So it finally came to him, a real laboratory where he could do any kind of advanced research that he cared to. What throbbing he must have felt when he realized, almost as soon as he arrived in Dearborn, that the marvelous gift had come too late. He was already too old, though he would not yet admit it. He returned home a mere two weeks later only half alive. He had wanted to work longer in "his" lab, but he felt himself getting steadily weaker as he tried to keep up with the dynamic Ford, until he was almost at the point of being too sick to leave. His mind, however, was more than alive with plans and projects. He was eager to prove that soybeans, like peanuts, could yield extraordinary products. Now that he had a modern laboratory and a knowledgeable staff, all he needed was time and tenacity. "By the Healing Power of the Great Spirit, along with the doctor's directions," he wrote to Glenn Clark, "I am still holding on."

17

A MILLION THANKS

Tuskegee rarely gave holidays to its students; even on Sundays they had to march to chapel in the morning and evening and sit in assigned seats. The youngsters would speculate about who was likely to die so that they might have a holiday. Carver's name came up first, as he was so often in extremis, but he always disappointed them. Likewise, any time Carver's friends made travel plans to see him "one last time," he rallied, so that after a time they were obliged to make another "last" visit.

Most often in his final years, he rose from what should have been his deathbed because he wanted to see Henry Ford. Even in the deep winter of their lives they continued to be kindred spirits, alike in many—but not all—ways. They were both ardent pacifists. They were self-made men celebrated in an era when the public respected successful common men and valued native wit over formal training. Their hatred of waste—neither could bear to throw anything away—caused them to be creative. Their minds did not follow worn paths. When asked how he would make journalism better, Ford answered that he would find a way to extract the ink in old newspapers so that both the ink and the paper could be reused. Both he and Carver were original, always preoccupied with such futuristic projects as finding a fuel alternative to gasoline in sugar cane, potatoes, or grain. They were ecologists at a time when ecology was a recondite word.

When Carver spoke at the National Farm Chemurgic Council meeting in Dearborn in 1937, Ford followed him on the platform with a succinct speech: "I agree with everything he thinks and he thinks the same way I do." But the reverse was not always true; that is, Carver did not agree with all of Ford's views except in the area of chemurgy. Ford, like Carver, had left home and farm at an early age. But whereas Carver spent decades struggling desperately to get an education, Ford quit school at fourteen and forever after scoffed at books, experts in any field, and erudition. His refusal to speak or even read in public was due less to his purported shyness than to his awareness that his reading, writing, and formal command of English were no better than that of a third grader. He wrote nothing, not even personal letters, and dictated nothing, relying instead on informal verbal instructions to his secretaries, who composed his letters and signed their own names—"Mr. Ford thanks you sincerely for . . ." Hence, the monthly letters Ford and Carver exchanged in Carver's last years passed through the literate filter of Ford's secretary Frank Campsall. The industrial magnate had no use for religion and was a fanatical Jew-hater who in 1938 accepted the Grand Cross of the German Eagle from Hitler. He loathed Communists. Music meant nothing to him except for simple fiddle tunes that could accompany square dancing. He was reputed to have said that he "wouldn't give five cents for all the great art in the world." Poetry to Ford was a foreign language—meaningless. His ignorance of any subject did not distress him for, as he astutely commented, "I can find a man in five minutes who can tell me everything about it."

Carver, for all his lack of pretension, was a cultivated man who loved classical music, opera, and every form of art, was steeped in literature and poetry, was a devout believer, sympathized with Jews, and respected learning and learners. Unlike the wily and skeptical Ford, Carver was so trusting that he could be duped by anyone who possessed even an ounce of business acumen. Ford was hostile to everything that represented city sophistication—high finance, high society, higher education. Above all, he took the measure of anything according to its utilitarian worth. Carver was hostile only to war. Despite his lifetime of putting waste products to use, he would have understood completely the line of poetry by A. R. Ammons: "Nothing useful is of lasting value."

In his early years, Henry Ford was certainly the best-known and possibly the most admired public figure in America. People loved him because they loved the Model T that he had given them, the machine that ended the isolation of village and farm and revolutionized life everywhere in the United States. Even though every customer who bought one of the first Model Ts had to be taught to drive, Ford had the vision to see what few others could imagine when the cars first appeared—that the horse, which had been the major means of land transportation through all of history, would disappear from streets and roads in less than a generation. Wagons, blacksmith shops, stables, and all the rest were replaced by a machine, the Model T, that garnered more affection than if it had been a living creature consuming oats and sugar cubes instead of petroleum.

For a long time, Ford was a genuine hero, a true reformer, with a list of exemplary projects—English schools for immigrants, hiring programs for the disabled, a model hospital, prison reform, a trade school for orphans, and many others. But Ford's idealism was damaged after sustained press campaigns against him. Why the hostility? Because of his passionate opposition to the First World War, a war that nearly everyone today regards as an example of futile carnage and international insanity. Several trials, especially the *Chicago Tribune* trial of 1919, subjected him to a long barrage of public mockery and left him disillusioned and embittered. "The cruel ridicule of his altruism," one writer explained, " . . . came always from educated, highly literate city dwellers." The derision did not diminish Ford's hero status in middle America, but it changed his character. Embattled and hurt, he became callous, anti-intellectual, anti-urban, and withdrawn from society. More and more, he relied on a succession of ruthless managers to run his businesses.

By 1922, Ford was the richest man in America with an estimated *daily* income of $264,000. Unlike other capitalists, he was not resented. He represented the virtues and prejudices of small town and rural America: hard physical work, thrift, sobriety (he was fiercely opposed to drinking and smoking), practicality, ordinary speech, and simple habits. He crafted his down-home image. In the small notebooks that he carried with him to jot down ideas (notebooks that are preserved in the Ford archives), we can see his trial-and-error attempts to formulate pithy maxims that he could repeat to the press: "No one can hurt nature"; "i expect to have all the money i can use as long as i live and so will every one else if they use it for the benefit of others." His loudly publicized move to pay his workers five dollars a day endeared him to all of labor, while only the workers in his plants found out that the princely wage was in practice ringed with qualifications and reductions. A Ford-for-President movement swept the country in the early 1920s, fed by Ford's steady distribution of folksy propaganda. He had come to hate what little people hated: banks, speculators in land, the stock market, financiers, aristocrats, heirs to great fortunes. He said things every debtor agreed with.

Ford's popularity temporarily plummeted during the Depression that destroyed so many American illusions. In Detroit, the country's fourth largest city, 5,000 families a month were being evicted in 1932, sent to wander the frigid streets with their possessions on their backs or to huddle in huge tent cities. Seventy percent of the unemployed in Detroit were workers who had been laid off by the Ford company. Four thousand children were standing in bread lines every day. And yet Ford would take no responsibility for them. When people turned to him for solutions to the crisis, he uttered inanities: "If we could only realize it, these are the best times we've ever had." Factory layoffs, he said, gave people the opportunity to go back to the farm—as if the unemployed had farms to go back to. In the depths of the Depression, Ford denounced all charity, free food, and free housing. He said that agencies such as the Community Chest, a precursor of the United Way, should be condemned. Meanwhile in the state of Washington, forest fires raged because unemployed lumberjacks and farmers had set them in hopes of getting work as firefighters.

The Depression shattered the public's implicit faith that businessmen like Ford could manage the country's economic welfare. Several thousand people joined a Communist hunger march on Ford's River Rouge plant in 1932, wanting to present a petition to the management for jobs and relief assistance. Ford's private force of ruffians attacked them, killing four and wounding twenty. The event shocked people who had thought that Ford was one of them. When he opposed the New Deal, the only relief offered to the desperate millions, his worshippers abandoned him. In 1937, Ford's goon squad brutally beat some union organizers in another bloody melee. All the major magazines and newspapers blazed with photographs of Ford's "servicemen" clubbing employees and union organizers into unconsciousness. It is no surprise that the manager of Ford's River Rouge plant saw fit to have his mansion patrolled by dogs and guarded by armed men in a gun tower on the roof, not to mention the real lions and tigers he kept in his den. The well-publicized innovations in Ford's plants actually made life worse for his workers. When he reduced the workweek, the assembly line was speeded up to produce as many cars in four days as it had turned out previously in five. When he increased wages, the workload was increased and the men's hours were cut. A network of spies rooted out union sympathizers, and 800 full-time thugs cruised his Dearborn plant, enforcing a rough discipline. By the late 1930s, Ford had the worst record of labor relations in an industry whose standards for worker well-being were none too high. His workers, it was said, cursed him in sixteen languages. Ford's priorities, however, had shifted from his plants to his other projects.

His solution to the Depression was an undertaking he called "Back to the Land." Within twenty miles of Dearborn, which was itself a suburb of Detroit, Ford built a cluster of small factories and created villages to serve them. The workers farmed part time and worked in the plants during the growing season— an attempt to combine farming and industry. In their planned communities, all smoking and drinking were prohibited and backyard gardens were compulsory. Ford, the man who led the country into the modern age and allowed millions to escape the ignorance of provincial communities, was spending fortunes to reverse the urbanization that he himself created. Despite his pieties about the benefits of agrarian life, the villages could not survive without his direct investment; therefore the movement did not spread. No one had the money to buy a farm and start raising his own food. Those who were already farmers when the Depression started had now been forced off their land by foreclosures. They could be seen trudging along railroad tracks and huddled beside campfires all over the country.

Ford's "Back to the Farm" idea failed. The Depression finally ended as Europe prepared for the Second World War and the U.S. government made massive investment in war materiel. By that time Ford was immersed in another idea, his grandest and in some ways most successful project, Greenfield Village, an attraction still visited by over a million tourists a year. Ford wanted to set up a museum that would show the lives of ordinary people. He had been ridiculed for his famous comment, "History is bunk. Why, it isn't even true." Historians described conquests and battles and detailed the nation's political changes, he said. But they never described such things as how the land was harrowed for cultivation. Historians knew nothing about harrows, Ford exclaimed, "yet our country depended more on harrows than on guns or speeches. I thought history that excluded harrows and all the rest of our daily life was bunk. And I think so yet." In this, as in much else, Ford was correct.

Greenfield Village was designed as a huge complex of restored buildings and streets from the past, ranged around a central museum. The village contained the cabin where Ford's hero William McGuffey was born, complete with contemporary household and yard items, the bridge McGuffey walked on as a boy, and a set of McGuffey readers. The houses of Edgar Allan Poe, Walt Whitman, Patrick Henry, and the house Ford thought was Stephen Foster's were transplanted to the village, along with many others. The original Menlo Park laboratory of Thomas Edison was reassembled, together with some of his other laboratories, their gardens, walkways, and shrubbery. For twenty years prior to the museum's opening, trainloads of antiques arrived in Dearborn so that the amazing Greenfield Village might have each kind of article used in America since 1607. Ford possessed one example of every type of shoe or boot ever worn, along with carloads of outdated equipment that no one knew how to operate. Greenfield Village had five active schools purchased by Ford and reconstructed in every detail, along with a steamboat, railroad station, steam locomotive, boarding house, and Cape Cod windmill—all so that people could visualize the past. In 1942, he installed a replica of the slave cabin where George Washington Carver was born.

Dazzled by Greenfield Village, which he thought was a brilliant undertaking in mass education, Carver gushed with admiration for Ford. He closely attended another part of Ford's restoration project, a private school system. Ford insisted that if the country could afford wars costing billions, it could afford education. Carver wholeheartedly concurred. As with everything, Ford's ideas about educational methods were adamant. He had built his first, highly successful trade school in 1916, with one teacher, six boys, and six machines. In the 1930s, he built or supported a number of schools. The five in Greenfield Village were mostly one-room affairs with texts and methods imitating rural education of the nineteenth century.

In 1939 and 1940, Ford named his farm school project in Florida after Carver and built two new George Washington Carver schools, one for black children in Greenfield Park, and one in Ways Station, Georgia, fifteen miles south of Savannah. Ford established a colony—a social experiment—in the impoverished rice country. From a deprived backwater, Ways was turned into a thriving community with two free clinics, a community house with twenty guest rooms, a factory, sawmill, and renovated residences, all funded by Ford. The county built a school for whites; Ford donated school buses, free medical and dental care for the students, and free lunches. Then, consolidating several one-room black schools in the area, he built the George Washington Carver industrial school for blacks and paid all its expenses. Ford's schools were based on the work-study model that Tuskegee and many of the black colleges used. The schools regulated every detail of the students' lives.

Ford's rules for hiring teachers were not unusual requirements for the time. Teachers had to be single women of puritanical habits. During the simple dedication of the Carver school, Carver saw one of the teachers, Gwendolyn Woods, and recognized her as the daughter of Booker T. Washington's one-time chauffeur. "Hey, Little Woodsy," Carver called out, dropping out of a line to go over and hug her. "Woodsy" was reprimanded for messing up the orderly procession of students into the school. Teachers were obligated to attend church on Sunday and to participate in a family-style breakfast every morning. During his visit, Carver particularly enjoyed the breakfast—the first buckwheat cakes he had tasted since childhood. Ford's strong preference was toward vocational schooling that fitted academic learning, what there was of it, into manual training. The students learned by doing. If water was needed, they learned how to dig a well; if the tractor broke, they overhauled it. This was exactly the method taken by Booker T. Washington two generations earlier. Despite his scorn for theories, Ford's educational program was one that worked in theory only, being too haphazard in practice. However, it should be noted that the 200 black children in the Carver school were receiving the best education available to them in Ways Station, Georgia, at that time. Ford even financed evening classes for illiterate adults. Like nearly everyone who saw Ford's resplendent example of social planning in Ways, Carver was wonderstruck. He sometimes addressed Ford as "My Prince of Educators." It would take some time before observers realized that Ford's town could not survive without Ford's money: it was simply another museum of sorts that had to be permanently subsidized.

Ford liked theater, and he loved country dancing. Beginning in 1924 and lasting until 1943, he and his wife hosted Friday night dance parties at which his high-level employees were expected to appear, formally dressed. Only tap water was served as the guests danced to "Aunt Dinah's Quilting Party" and Virginia reels. The parties ended at midnight with an offering of nonalcoholic drinks and cookies. Ford hired instructors to teach dancing first to his own executives, then to the children of Dearborn, and then to college students around the country, so that through his efforts, many thousands were exposed to square dancing, Ford's alternative to the Charleston and jitterbug.

Ford had once predicted that his cars would make horses obsolete. Twenty years later, he decided the time had come to get rid of cows, although here the animals eventually prevailed. Cows were unsanitary, expensive, and demanding, he said; Carver agreed with him. Ford prescribed substituting soy and peanut milk for dairy and, during the Depression, spent over a million dollars in soybean research. The work he sponsored with soy paralleled Carver's work with peanuts and other plants. At the Chicago World's Fair in 1933, the Ford exhibits showed plastics, soap, paint, linoleum, margarine, and fodder made from soybeans, just as Carver, at the same fair, was exhibiting some of the same products made from peanuts. At the 1939 New York World's Fair, Ford was showing textiles made from soybeans while Carver was developing synthetic silk from sweet potatoes. While Ford's interest in soy milk was at its height in the 1940s, Carver's formula for peanut milk was continuing to save lives in Africa. In Ford's modern, mechanized laboratory, his chemists made paint enamel and shock absorber fluid from soybean oil and used soybean meal to mold distributor cases, electrical switch assemblies, and other auto parts.

Ford's theory that people could live entirely from products from the soil, without petroleum, mined minerals, or farm animals, stimulated Carver to test the potential of numerous plants during the last two years of his life. Carver developed various sample by-products from okra, cotton stalks, yucca, palm fibers, white oleander, white mulberry, rattan, sida, milkweed, ramie, Georgia clays, jute, and sumac berries—an enormous amount of experimentation for a man who could only walk over to his microscope on "good" days. Ford sent him some soybeans to work with at Tuskegee; Carver sent back some protein-rich soy gravy to use as a meat substitute. The back-and-forthing between him and Ford, as much as anything else, made Carver want to live and work. Aside from his conviction that Carver was a great scientist, Ford liked Carver precisely because he was outside the scientific establishment, excluded from the circle of academic and corporate elites whom Ford detested.

Ford, like Carver, was absorbed in other projects besides chemical research. In his hospital in Dearborn, Ford tried out several unconventional ideas, such as putting patients on a kind of conveyor belt that passed them through a line of specialists. Each physician focused on a specific organ or organ system. The doctors would arrive at a diagnosis and treatment plan in a matter of minutes while the bewildered patient rolled on to his room. It was not a popular plan. According to one biographer, Ford sometimes visited heart patients in their rooms and instructed them to ignore their doctors' orders, eat raw vegetables (he was fond of alfalfa), and lie on the floor. Ford's theories about health and disease were largely faddish dictums; he believed, for example, that meats, vegetables, fruits, and starches should not be eaten together in the same meal. He made simplistic pronouncements, as when he told *The Detroit News* that all sickness was due to "wrong acts' and to "bad mixtures in the stomach." Despite Ford's failures and the paradoxes of his personality, his funeral in 1947 tied up traffic in Dearborn for miles, as thousands of weeping mourners from all parts of the country and all walks of life lined the route of his procession and tried to touch his casket.

It is hard to know how much of Ford's aberrant thinking Carver was aware of, since he had no part in the hospital project that most clearly exposed Ford's lunatic side. It is certain that he appreciated Ford's forward-looking innovations, of which there were many, and ignored the propositions he did not agree with, also numerous. He gave Ford credit for espousing practices that he himself had been promoting for forty years, such as organic gardening. He usually addressed his letters to "My Beloved Friend," but often he called Ford "My great prophetic friend." Carver's 1937 visit to Dearborn coincided with Ford's union troubles. He could not have missed knowing about Ford's ruthlessness, and Carver was undoubtedly aware of Ford's scalding attacks on his idol, Franklin D. Roosevelt, which were all over the newspapers and radio. However, Ford's attitudes about government or politics did not seem to ruffle Carver any more than anyone else's opinions. It was Ford's initiatives in botany research that Carver esteemed, and in these, there was little to criticize and everything to praise.

The dean of Tuskegee's school of agriculture, Dr. Walter Hill, remarked in 2004 that at work Carver was "the connector, all by himself." "He was the person in the lab doing the basic research thinking, the applied research thinking, tying it to the land, trying to tie it to business, and he had very few people around him to interact with him as he did this. People would come in sporadically, come and go, come and go." That observation about Carver goes far in explaining his attraction to Ford. Before their friendship, Carver was isolated in the loneliness of genius. Ford was the first person who shared his vision of the potential benefits of agricultural diversity, the principle Carver had promulgated through his entire career. Ford had the prestige, money, power and, most of all, the will to demonstrate that the way out of rural poverty was for farmers to supply the needs of industry—farmers, not oil or mining companies. Each time Carver talked with the industrialist, he came away feeling that his own work with plants was vital and that he had to go on with it. No wonder he left his bed repeatedly to visit Henry Ford.

C arver's heaviest burden—his correspondence—was also what kept him connected to the world. Carver's deep friendships were carried on in letters throughout his life, and this was especially true in his last years, during the isolation of prolonged illnesses. Each of his close friends fitted into a particular socket of Carver's mind. Carver did not reflect on Supreme Beings with Henry Ford or discuss plant chemistry with Glenn Clark or hybrid flowers with Lucy Crisp. To illuminate all of his interests, he needed a number of relationships, and he had them.

He was no longer obsessed with the Creator as in the Hardwick years, when any observation about nature could set him trembling with religious intensity. Nor did he still receive interminable letters from backwoods theologians. But he remained engaged with God and in the period just before his death, maintained a frequent correspondence with three individuals whose primary interest in him was as an ardent believer.

Gloria Dare was a self-styled "mystic" from Hollywood, a feminist, who sent Carver glamorous pictures of herself and large excerpts from dozens of self-published essays—on reincarnation, the brotherhood of humanity, advice on life, etc.—all tediously overwritten. Carver did not engage in long exchanges with her, but he addressed her as "My beloved friend, Miss Dare," and answered her letters genially until her death late in 1942 from a stroke. In his letter of condolence to her husband, he wrote that Dare had a remarkable mind; it *was* remarkable for its egotism. "My heart goes out to you in a way that you cannot fully realize." Because he was such a sincere man and sincere writer, Carver was an expert at that most difficult missive, the letter of condolence, and produced many masterpieces as his comrades died off.

Carver wrote fairly often to Dr. Fred Chenault, a Birmingham pastor (not to be confused with the Head of the Tuskegee Crippled Children's Clinic). Their communications were those of two intelligent believers, with none of the heat of evangelism. Both Chenault and Harvey Hill, another of Carver's enlightened brothers in Christ, wrote articles about him for various publications.

The most regular and fervid of Carver's religious correspondents was Glenn Clark, who taught creative writing at Macalester College in St. Paul, Minnesota. Clark brought Carver's name before the general public with "The Man Who Talks with Flowers," a little work that, thanks to its low price, enjoyed a wider circulation than the full-length biographies that were published then and later. Clark had been among the people Carver influenced on his first "crusade" in 1922, when he also met Jim Hardwick. Even after decades, Clark and Carver continued to believe that their message of brotherhood would spread out from their little group to the whole country. Clark repeatedly expressed his sense that Carver was his, always with him, helping him, along with "my dear wife in the other world . . . helping me every day, too." Carver wrote that it was "impossible for me to undertake a project without your being right along with me, one and inseparable," notwithstanding their physical distance. "You continue to walk by my side daily, especially when I am doing creative things," Carver wrote. Clark sent Carver many examples of his bad poems and texts of broadcasts he was making over the radio, along with large collections of vapid preachments for the aching soul. Carver, whose soul never appeared to be under the weather, irrespective of his physical well-being, nevertheless perused the writing and responded warmly. Carver still felt constrained when dictating letters and lamented that he could not write (that is, by hand) his most personal feelings to Clark. "I have never been able to feel your presence in a very strong personal way as I have been able to do this summer," he wrote in 1941. "Oh, I have so much to tell you, so much that seems too sacred to write. If I could write myself I would do it, but nevertheless, when I see you we will go over these marvelous things."

In one long missive during the war in Europe, Clark described how his radio broadcasts had influenced Hitler: the voice of God spoke through his lips in a message of love that persuaded Hitler, according to Clark, to offer a peace treaty to England and France. Mussolini, hearing Clark's message, was moved to pray on his knees for some agreement with the Allies that would end the war. God answered his prayer immediately, Clark wrote, by inflicting on him the Greek campaign, which brought "death and destruction to Italians and the greatest humiliation of the Duce in the entire war." Stalin remained impervious to the Love broadcasts until the Voice spoke through Clark and advised that Russia (which was then an ally of Hitler) would enter the war "in a surprising and unexpected way." Clark did not acknowledge that it might have been the German invasion of the Soviet Union, and not Clark's forecast, that caused Stalin's about-face. Clark was sending these disclosures about the power of love, he averred, only to "a very few persons who have sufficient purity of heart and freedom from condemnation to receive them."

It is not surprising that delusional "seers" and people who purported to be the mouthpieces of God should write to Carver. What does seem strange is that Carver, who was no longer in the throes of fanaticism, would consider Clark his constant ghost companion and squander his diminishing time and energy responding to Clark's flummery. Clark was not the most vacuous of the many mediocrities who sent their tomes to Carver, but he was the one Carver took seriously. He was prolix, semieducated, and presumptuous, especially in his conviction that God could not speak for himself and needed Clark's embassy to the dictators. Carver not only welcomed Clark's expatiations, he claimed that they were necessary to him. When writing to Clark, Carver often fell into the soldierly idiom of the evangelicals, assuring him that "we are going to win out" in the "crusade."

If Carver suffered Clark gladly, it was not because he had no better correspondents. From 1939 to 1943, he received several personal letters from Henry A. Wallace and Franklin D. Roosevelt. All of these admired Carver, but none had time to maintain a deep friendship with him. But other serious-minded individuals had both the time and tendency to share their private thoughts. Several journalists had become personal friends over the years, especially those writers who had enjoyed long interviews with Carver while putting together brochures about him. Being writers anyway, they loved opening up to him, and he responded, unfailingly. Some were religious people who shared his predicatory impulses. But none of them fascinated Carver. None except Glenn Clark held him in the thrall of a bond that he believed existed between himself, Clark, and God. It was the same mystical sense of triangular presence he had felt years before with Jim Hardwick, but this time the passion that kept it going was neither as strong, one-sided, or erotic.

As for Carver's other friends, there was Ross in Kansas. Mrs. Ross was somehow able to ship an endless number of "birds" to Carver, so that he and Dr. Ross exchanged elegies about great meals they had shared through the offices of the U.S. postal service. Carver could no longer send hand-painted Christmas cards, but in 1939 he had a photograph taken of himself standing next to one of his paintings in the art gallery, and that became his yearly Christmas greeting.

Mrs. Milholland died in 1935 at the age of eighty-five, but Carver felt a connection to her daughter—he had babysat for her when she was an infant—and maintained a correspondence with her. He reported having strange dreams in which he was back in the Milholland home. "As you know, your home was my home at Winterset." When Carver had first exchanged letters with the Milhollands in 1896, and for a number of years afterward, it was still possible to mail a letter to "Dr. Milholland, Winterset, Iowa," and have it arrive. Carver advised the Milhollands to hold on to any handwritten letters of his, as one day they might become valuable.

Carver never spoke out on political topics even to his friends, except for general comments, although he let it be known that he was strongly pacifistic. Much as he liked Franklin Roosevelt, he deplored America's entry into the Second World War. Otherwise, his ideas on foreign affairs were hardly ideas at all—more like half-formed impressions confused by his belief that God must be behind war as He was behind everything. "I really think that man Hitler is difficult to understand," he wrote in 1940. "Well, I suppose it was difficult to understand Judas and yet Judas was no doubt raised up to do the terrible thing that he did. That sounds a little like the doctrine of foreordination, however, I did not mean it just in that light."

In Ghana, people were having trouble growing grass and called on Carver for help. He sent a powder that helped revive the grass, and the government honored him with a Carver postage stamp. Carver's former students married and developed paunches but wrote to him still as their beloved father, just like his young white friends Dana and Cecil Johnson, who were still white, but no longer young. Dana Johnson finally wed in middle age, but Carver could not attend the ceremony because he was, as he explained it, about to die, an event that was somehow cancelled at the last minute. Clarence Hart, now gray-haired, continued to write to "Dear Dad." Carver asked him if he had any hand-painted Christmas cards or pictures that he would care to sell to the Carver Art Gallery. Clarence responded indignantly that he had a number of small paintings but he would no more sell them than he would sell Carver's friendship. Charles Albert, a doctor now, sent his sons to visit, looking exactly as their father looked when Carver first met him. To these, his special boys, Carver wrote what loving parents often feel: "It is absolutely impossible for you to know what the lives of you dear boys have meant to me, and what they mean yet."

Jack Sutton kept in touch and tried to send food. Carver advised him to give it to people who needed it more than he did, except perhaps for some pinto beans that he had been craving. The Blue Ridge boys wrote to him; they were now the rusting heads of companies and families. On his 1940 Christmas card, Wilson Newman wrote in his familiar scrawl, "I think of you much more often than my letters would indicate. I hope your health is better. You have been an inspiration to many—including . . . Wilson."

One by one Carver's friends died: Olin H. Stevenson, his colleague in mycology, Robert Moton, and Moton's wife, along with dozens of other friends and enemies who had shared his life in the little community of Tuskegee Institute. Emmett Scott was still thriving in Washington and still promoting the memory of Booker even as he congratulated Carver on his honors: "Your modest bearing reminds me so greatly of our late beloved friend, Mr. Washington." In other years, Scott told people that there were two saints at Tuskegee, Booker T. Washington and George Carver. Tom Huston, still of sound mind, took it to Miami where he was enjoying life, according to the man who pushed him out of his company. The possible mental breakdown that Austin Curtis mentioned must have occurred after Carver's death.

It is said that Tuskegee Archives holds a document, an affidavit signed by Jessie Guzman, the archivist and friend of Carver, attesting that the old scientist kept company with a Tuskegee lady right up to his death. There seems to be only one explanation for such a bizarre oath: to gainsay rumors about Carver's private life. Considering Carver's poor health in his last years, the affidavit hardly settles any questions about his sexuality. We can be sure, however, that despite having other companions, Carver never forgot his Jimmie.

Everyone in the country knew when Carver fell ill, since it was reported in detail in the newspapers. Jim Hardwick must have also known. When Carver wrote to the Blue Ridge family, he usually found a way to mention "the boy," that is, the most important of all his boys. "I certainly think very often about the wonderful days we spent together. I have not heard from dear Jim Hardwick in a long time. I do not even know just where he is." Occasionally he wrote to Jim's mother, needing somehow to pass a message to Jim. "I am especially happy to learn that Mr. Hardwick has not forgotten me as under no circumstances do I want to lose track of him, his prayers and his interest." He closed the letter: "I hope Mr. Hardwick will write to me. I do not know his address." It seems that Mrs. Hardwick was careful not to give Jim's address to Carver. While Carver was in bed with the flu in 1942, he sent her New Year's greetings and a plaintive note: "I hope that dear Jimmie is well and that all is going well with him. I have not heard from him now in something more than two years." At that time, Carver had exactly a year left to live—without any word from Jim.

If Carver ached for Jim right up to the end of his life, Birdie Howard during those last years was likewise feeling the chafe of unrequited love for the man she called "the angel of earth" and "the greatest scientist ever known." Hers, however, was a cheerful and undemanding devotion. Addressing him as "Darling Friend" and, most often, "Dearest Dr. Carver," she followed the milestones in his career and related her thoughts—about him and about her own modest life. She was infuriated by the Hotel New Yorker incident but proud of Carver's "silent courage that won the victory only to color anew that personality of yours lifting us higher and even higher. You came away towering over them like an elm. Remember? You looked at one—I saw the photo in the paper— and you are tall and splendid to look at." Birdie apparently had frequent contact with children and from time to time described the woes of certain youngsters. "I wish I could take him," "I wish I could take her," she sometimes wrote of loveless little ones. She did take them home intermittently to care for them.

One of "her" children was convinced that Carver was her grandfather who lived far away.

Carver was indifferent to money because, having his food, lodging, and medical care paid for, and being unable to go very far away from his circumscribed little area, he had no need of cash. He might, however, have left a small legacy to such cash-strapped friends as Harry Abbott, Clarence Hart, Emile Hooker, and of course, Birdie. Birdie wrote of wishing for a position where she could make "a reasonable living." "I keep my expenses down to the bare bones, and cut every cuttable corner," she wrote. Just a thousand to Birdie of the sixty thousand that Carver eventually bequeathed to Tuskegee would have made the difference between comfort and penury, but it was not to be.

Nevertheless, when Birdie read that Carver had donated his entire savings to the Carver Foundation, she was overjoyed. "Words fail me for an expression of your generous gift . . . It is more blessed to give and I hope and pray that you'll reap the full measure of your big, generous heart. Many people think you did wrong or those younger men influenced you to take such a step. Thus you see people look for the green-eyed monster at all times in all things. I know you are the brain of the whole thing." Birdie was a giver, not a taker. She would have given Carver anything she had or hoped to have. Hearing him mention his probable age on the radio, she wrote, "Seventy-eight is young. I hope you get to be more than a hundred. Many get to be that age. The Bible says so. I do not believe I will get to that age, and since I heard you say that, I prayed and asked God to give you the years that should come to me." She was always concerned about his health, although she herself was sometimes quite ill. "I am sitting up now," she once reported after some severe malady. "I can sew. I wish you'd tell me something to make for you as I would like to leave you something." Presumably, she meant she wanted him to have a memento in case God took her up on her offer to transfer some of her time on earth to Carver's account.

Carver's letters to "My esteemed friend, Miss Howard," were appreciative but not more emotional than letters he wrote to dozens of friends. Sometimes he wrote about his cherished museum: "This is the first time that anything of the kind has been done by our people for our people, and I am hoping that they will take care of it and appreciate its meaning and develop it . . . a credit not only to our people but to all people." Birdie was under the impression that the infantile paralysis center at Tuskegee would be under Carver's aegis. She had dreams foretelling the groundbreaking and averred that the polio center "will be a monument to you until the end of time." "To you all the credit is due and I feel like God will spare you to see this great work carried out." She added, "You grow sweeter as the years go by."

"I did not hear you on the air," she wrote another time, "but I heard that you said you were an old man with white hair. I think white hair is beautiful and lends dignity to you." Birdie never described her own appearance, but we know that she was a very light-skinned Negro, since she complained in one letter about having acquired a deep tan and wanting some of Carver's "tan-remover" to make it fade.

Birdie was constantly having what she thought were predictive dreams about Carver or his friends. A dream about flags flying at half-mast at Tuskegee, for example, she understood as an omen of Mr. Moton's death. Carver responded that he thought she was psychic and that all her dreams had a definite meaning. "If you feel a sense of satisfaction after you know what has happened, it is a good indication that the dream was interpreted correctly." Birdie was keenly disappointed when Carver came within a few miles of her at Ways Station, Georgia, and did not see her (she lived in Waycross.) He explained that he was accompanied every minute by Henry Ford, President Patterson, and Austin Curtis, that all arrangements were made for him ahead of time, and that in any case he was so exhausted by the trip that he was unable afterward to walk without support. Even before receiving his explanation, Birdie had excused him. "I'm dreaming about you again. It won't matter how you come to me as long as you do come. If you don't come, I'll still wait. Your letters have made you more real and more close to my heart than anybody else can ever be."

In 1941 Birdie's Christmas present to Carver was a pair of hand-embroidered pillowcases. She substituted his initials for the "Mr. and Mrs." and "His and Hers" patterns, "as no Hers or Mrs. was at your house." "I do not know just what is correct to make a gentleman for a present," Birdie confessed, "so just smile if I'm wrong." Unlike many men of his generation, Carver appreciated the artistry of beautiful handiwork. His own crochet work was featured in McCall's magazine that year.

In her letters, Birdie often digressed into a stream-of-consciousness narrative that was ungrammatical, heartfelt, and authentic. Sometimes she all but proposed to Carver. "You said in your letter that you hope the New Year would bring many additional joys and successes that I have not experienced before. Dare I hope your wish come true. I have reached the point where I realize that the only supreme joy a woman could have would be a husband. I look at life in horror when I think I may be alone always. Your Sec often address my letter as Mrs. I thought you knew I was never married. In fact I have no beau . . . I have much to be thankful for. You are getting well and my brother will walk. A million thanks for everything."

Carver wrote a long, warm thank-you letter for the "exquisite" pillowcases. "They are indeed treasures and coming from you makes them all the more valuable when I know that you did this with your own hands." He remarked that he was not able to attend the dedication of the Infantile Paralysis Center as he still could only walk a few steps around his room. Other letters followed on both sides. Birdie never quoted verse after verse of Scripture to Carver; she seemed more sincere in her piety than many of his friends who did. Deaths occurred in her family, and she herself had trying times, but her letters were all about Carver. "Darling Big Chief," she wrote after his trip to Simpson College and to Dearborn.

> Love, Congratulations, and Thanks for everything. I don't know just where to start this letter . . . I recognized you in the clippings about Mr. Ford. I only wish I could talk with you. No I do not. I could not take Mr. Ford's place with you for one second for I know what you are doing will be of benefit as century after century goes by. I rejoice as you have seen the Infantile Paralysis Center and go to the woods you like so and all that money in one lump didn't frighten you. Your many little kindnesses and your generous impulses, the lovely, lovable qualities that few possess makes you our outstanding humanitarian of all times.

She quoted a dedication to him: "'Out of undreamed of resources in the human soul with no personal consideration or selfish interest you brought new life, new hope to a tired, defeated, and hopeless people.'" Birdie wondered why Carver did not travel in a trailer. "It's wonderful to go about in them. This year is bringing you the successes you wished for me. To read about you is like walking in a flower garden, all beauty. My one regret I did not hear your voice. You'd like to go somewhere else. I'm praying that god may give you the strength to make the trip." Birdie could write correctly when she tried to, but she let her words to Carver spill onto the page in a deluge of emotion undammed by punctuation.

Birdie worked with someone who had formerly been at Tuskegee and made frequent, vexing remarks about Birdie's friendship with Carver. The woman once called Birdie on the phone to "tease'" her. "Guess what happened?" she asked Birdie. "Old fess Carver is dead." When she discovered the prank, Birdie angrily asked the woman why she took so much of her time "saying unkind things to me." "I do hope you will live for years and years," she concluded. "With a heart full of love for you, Yours, Birdie J. Howard."

"The person who thought that they were annoying you somewhat is most interesting and laughable from several angles," Carver wrote back. He was glad she was not letting it bother her, he wrote, as if he did not know quite well that she was seething. In July 1941, she sent only a birthday card, and he sent only a short acknowledgement. But in the autumn, the long letters resumed and continued through the next year. As if she knew time was running out, Birdie wanted to get everything said. "You were in an excellent mood when you wrote last," she began. "I hope you are still fine." He had written to her about a new product he had created. "It's extraordinary!" she wrote. "I don't see how you do it—making cloth out of skimmed milk. Such a sweetheart! I hope I will someday see it." She lamented that he still came in for unfair criticism. "My heart is beating in a paean of thanksgiving always for your success."

With her usual flowing from one topic to the next, she wrote, "I know the emotions that play bob with us are the ones we push down under and refuse to recognize. I cannot make the modern grade," she admitted. "No matter the air of gay cynicism that makes virtue a thing to laugh at. The loss of it marks a milestone in a girl's life and she will know down deep inside that she has lost something precious she can never regain. In this new generation they drink too much, swear too much, pet too much, some too crazy for thrills to wait, some too crazy in love to care . . . Well, I do not belong in the air of reckless philosophy, 'Live today for tomorrow may never come.'" She had good news, too. She had cleaned up the prizes for canned fruits at the fall fair: four blue ribbons, two red, and one white.

"I love you. Take care of yourself because of this love that will last and hold us both until there is another time somewhere, somehow. Wherever the somewhere is, I'll hear it in your heart."

For Carver's birthday the next July, Birdie sent him a cross-stitched "Home Sweet Home" sampler and some candy, for which, of course, he thanked her. "Yes, the candy was delicious," she wrote back, "because that was your own recipe taken from *Service* magazine." As for the sampler, "All my life I have wanted a home with the flowers everywhere . . . I often wonder why you never had a 'Home Sweet Home.'"

It was Carver's last birthday. His last recorded letter to her is dated August 18, 1942, just as he returned exhausted from his trip to Dearborn. It's a perfunctory letter, even in comparison with the guarded tone of most of his missives. He mentions that he has "piles and piles of letters and packages awaiting me; just when I will get to them I cannot say. At this time my strength is pretty well used up." It is likely that a few more letters were exchanged in the four months before his death but not many, since he was in pain after October. Birdie's prayer was not heeded. She was not allowed to die before him.

He was struck in late October with an acute attack of what the doctors identified as "indigestion," one of the symptoms of heart failure. He never really recovered from that attack. In November and December he was suffering, even as thousands more Americans were getting to know him through a *Reader's Digest* article about him, "No Greener Pastures."

Around Christmas Day, 1942, Carver had a bad fall because, according to his secretary, "he is so independent that he simply would not let Mr. Curtis or any of the boys walk to and from his room with him. We have each and every one pleaded with him, but he won't let them walk over by his side, let alone help him." He fell trying to get into the door of his museum but insisted on answering his mail that day and for the next two days before he was forced by his weakness to stay in his rooms. "He is very thin and feeble," Mrs. Abbott wrote to Harry three days before his death, "and I wanted you to know the truth." The day after Mrs. Abbott's letter, Carver declined still more, and his condition was given out as "critical." He died on January 5, 1943, in the evening. His probable age was eighty or eighty-one. The morning of his death, Austin Curtis sent out several letters in his name, including one to Mexico giving instructions for making a cheap paint from used motor oil and clay. Some students held a candlelight vigil for him all day and throughout the rainy night of his death. Others went on about their activities. One of Carver's young disciples was returning from band practice with some friends. They were letting off steam after a long rehearsal, yelling and being silly, when the head matron emerged from the dormitories. "Boys, cut that noise out. Dr. Carver just passed."

A ll of the students were asked to attend the afternoon funeral in the chapel. It was crowded to overflowing and included a number of sudden relatives who claimed to be Carver's sister, brother, or cousin. Carver's coffin, under a blanket of flowers sent by Henry Ford, was carried around the campus by pallbearers from a student fraternity. Students marched behind the casket into the chapel. Carver had loved flowers, and almost the entire chapel was covered with them. Seating was segregated, except for the white friends who insisted on sitting on the colored side. All around the country, schools and libraries named after Carver held their own funeral services.

Carver would have enjoyed his funeral at Tuskegee. The program reprinted a Tennyson poem he often recited: "Flower in the crannied wall / I pluck you out of the crannies, / I hold you here, root and all, in my hand, Little flower— but if I could understand / What you are, root and all, and all in all, I should know what God and man is." In the program were some of his favorite biblical quotations: "In all thy ways acknowledge Him and He will direct thy paths;" "Go forth under the open sky and list to nature's teachings;" "I will lift up mine eyes unto the hills from whence cometh my help;" "And God said, Behold, I have given you every herb bearing seed, which is upon the face of all the earth, and every tree, in which is the fruit of a tree yielding seed; to you it shall be for meat." The hymns included "There is a Balm In Gilead," "The Old Rugged Cross," "My Faith Looks Up to Thee," and a solo sung by Carver's old friend Thomas Campbell, "One Sweetly Solemn Thought." The organ played one of Carver's favorite classical pieces, Handel's "Largo." Telegrams were read from President Roosevelt, Vice President Wallace, and other dignitaries. President Patterson gave a moving tribute, not too long. The sermon paid homage to "this humble Negro genius who asked nothing for his labors, but gave his discoveries to the world." Carver was interred in the Tuskegee campus cemetery. His tombstone read, "He could have added fortune to fame, but caring for neither, he found happiness and honor in being helpful to the world." With a closing prayer, the service that had been so often postponed had finally taken place. In less than two hours, people were returning to their cars or offices. It had been a nice funeral, not different from others they had attended, but for the most extraordinary man any of them had ever met.

The students who had been willing to sacrifice Carver in order to have a day off were disappointed. Even though "all the radio stations and the whole world was there," as one recalled, everyone went back to class after the service. The students thought, "The greatest man on Earth was dead, and still no holidays."

EPILOGUE

Telegrams of condolence and encomiums from celebrities in every field covered the country for months after Carver's death. Some individuals felt obliged to note his passing because he was black; others respected him in spite of his race. Some honored him as a great scientist—it was still possible in those days to use that term about someone who had published very little in scientific journals. Others called him a great humanist; here the accolade was incontrovertible. All recognized that he was an individual born with no advantages whatever who not only overcame material obstacles but rose above the small-minded conventions of his generation. He fulfilled his dreams and his potential and showed what might be accomplished in the plaintive brevity of a lifetime. He was both a symbol and the very embodiment of what it means to be an American. What's more, he achieved what he set out to do: to have his accomplishments reflected on his race so that all black people would in some sense share in the praise given to him.

And so the acclaim continued. In 1942 the then senator Harry Truman introduced his bill to establish the first federal memorial to a Negro in Diamond, Missouri, a bill endorsed by Albert Einstein, Thomas Mann, Theodore Dreiser, Thomas Hart Benton, Ernest Hemingway, and thirty-seven others. The George Washington Carver National Monument, part of the National Park Service, was established by Congress in July 1943, a beautiful park, museum, and archive on 210 acres that included Moses Carver's original farm and the house he built in 1881. A portrait of Carver gazing at an amaryllis was placed in the Smithsonian Institute in 1944. In 1948 a three-cent stamp was issued with his picture and in 1998 a thirty-two cent stamp. In 1954 the George Washington Carver half-dollar was minted. In 1977 he was inducted into the Hall of Fame for great Americans and in 1990 into the National Inventors Hall of Fame.

Two ships were named in his honor, the Liberty Ship SS *George Washington Carver* and the nuclear submarine USS *George Washington Carver*. In 1994 he was finally awarded an honorary degree from Iowa State University, a Doctor of Humane Letters.

Ralph Johnson Bunche, in dedicating the building named in Carver's honor at Simpson College, called him "the least imposing celebrity the world has ever known." In an interview, Austin Curtis said that Carver wanted to realize the full potential of art and science, "to turn the ugly into the beautiful, the waste into the useful, that even the poorest of God's creatures might be healthier, his home more comfortable, his surroundings more beautiful, his life more significant." Harry Abbott, the man who knew Carver best and loved him most steadfastly, tried when in reflective moods to summarize him. On a New Year's Eve a few years before Carver's death, Abbott wrote to him: "I grant without question all the appraisals of your scientific accomplishment. But all that pales into insignificance when compared with your magnificent stature as a simple, lovable, kind-hearted soul, whose very presence is a benediction and whose interest is a blessing."

Experiment Station Bulletins by George W. Carver

NUMBER	DATE	TITLE
1	1898	Feeding Acorns
2	1898	Experiments with Sweet Potatoes
3	1899	Fertilizer Experiment with Cotton
4	1901	Some Cercospora of Macon County, Alabama
5	1903	Cowpeas
6	1905	Cotton Growing on Upland Sandy Soils
7	1905	How to Build Up Worn-Out Soils
8	1906	Successful Yields of Small Grain
9	1906	The San Jose Scale in Alabama
10	1906	Saving the Sweet Potato Crop
11	1909	Relations of Weather and Soil Conditions to the Fruit Industry of Southeast Alabama
12	1907	Saving the Wild Plum Crop
13	1908	How to Cook Cowpeas
14	1908	How to Make Cotton Growing Pay
15	1909	Increasing the Yield of Corn
16	1909	Some Ornamental Plants of Macon County, Alabama
17	1910	Possibilities of the Sweet Potato in Macon County
18	1911	Nature Study and Gardening for Rural Schools
19	1911	Some Possibilities of the Cowpea in Macon County
20	1911	Cotton Growing for Rural Schools
21	1911	White and Colored Washing with Native Clays from Macon County, Alabama
22	1912	Dairying in Connection With Farming
23	1912	Poultry Raising in Macon County

NUMBER	DATE	TITLE
24	1912	The Pickling and Curing of Meat in Hot Weather
25	1913	A Study of the Soils of Macon County, Alabama, and Their Adaptability to Certain Crops
26	1915	A New and Prolific Variety of Cotton
27	1915	When, What, and How to Can and Preserve Fruits and Vegetables in the Home
28	1915	Smudging an Orchard with Native Material in Alabama
29	1915	Alfalfa, the Kind of All-Fodder Plant Successfully Grown in Macon County
30	1915	Possibilities of the Sweet Potato in Macon County (Revision of #17)
31	1916	How to Grow the Peanut and 105 Ways of Preparing it for Human Consumption
32	1916	Three Delicious Meals Every Day for the Farmer
33	1917	Twelve Ways to Meet the New Economic Conditions Here in the South
34	1917	Forty-three Ways to Save the Wild Plum Crop
35	1917	How to Grow the Cowpea and 40 Ways to Prepare It as a Table Delicacy
36	1918	How to Grow the Tomato and 105 Ways to Prepare It
37	1918	How to Make Sweet Potato Flour, Starch, Bread, Sugar, and Mock Coconut
38	1918	How the Farmer Can Save His Sweet Potatoes
39	1927	How to Make and Save Money on the Farm
40	1935	The Raising of Hogs
41	1936	Can Livestock Be Raised Profitably in Alabama?
42	1936	How to Build Up and Maintain the Virgin Fertility of Our Soils
43	1942	Nature's Garden for Victory and Peace
44	1943	The Peanut
Circular	1912	Canning and Preserving of Fruits and Vegetables at Home
Leaflet	1915	A New and Prolific Variety of Cotton
Leaflet	1915	How to Raise Pigs with Little Money
Leaflet	1916	How to Live Comfortably This Winter
Leaflet	1916	What Shall We Do for Fertilizer This Year?
Leaflet	1931	Some Peanut Diseases
Leaflet	1938	Some Choice Wild Vegetables that Make Fine Foods

Partial List of Carver's Products from Peanuts and Sweet Potatoes (compiled by Carver)

GENERAL PRODUCTS

Axle grease

Charcoal from peanut shells

Cleanser for hands

Coke (from hulls)

Diesel fuel

Fuel briquettes

Gas

Gasoline

Glue

Illuminating oil

Insecticide

Eighteen types of insulating boards

Linoleum

Lubricating oil

Nitroglycerine

Colored paper from skins

Craft paper from vines

White paper from vines

Printer's ink

Plastics

Rubber

Shoe and leather blacking

Sizing for walls

Soap stock

Soil conditioner

Eleven kinds of wall boards from hulls

Washing powder

Wood filler

Laundry soap

Sweeping compound

COSMETICS

All-purpose cream

Antiseptic soap

Baby massage cream

Face bleach and tan remover

Face cream

Face lotion

Face ointment

Fat-producing cream

Glycerin

Hand lotion

Oil for hair and scalp

Peanut oil shampoo

Pomade for scalp

Pomade for skin

Shampoo

Shaving cream

Tetter and dandruff cure

Toilet soap
Vanishing cream

FOODS
Bar candy
Five breakfast foods
Bisque powder
Buttermilk
Butter from peanut milk
Caramel
Cream cheese
Nut sage cheese
Pimento cheese
Sandwich cheese
Tutti-Frutti cheese
Chili sauce
Chocolate-coated peanuts
Chop Suey sauce
Cocoa
Cooking oil
Cream candy
Cream from milk
Crystallized peanuts
Curds
Dehydrated milk flakes
Dry coffee
Evaporated milk
Flavoring paste
Golden nuts
Instant coffee
Lard compound
Malted substitutes
Mayonnaise
Meat substitutes
32 kinds of milk
Mock goose
Mock chicken

Mock beef
Mock oyster
Mock veal cutlet
Oleomargarine
Pancake flour
Peanut bar #2
Peanut bisque flour
Peanut brittle
Three kinds of peanut butter
Peanut cake
Peanut chocolate fudge
Peanut dainties
Peanut flakes
Eleven kinds of peanut flour
Peanut hearts
Peanut kisses
Brown peanut meal
Peanut meat loaf
Peanut and popcorn bars
Two kinds of peanut relish
Peanut sausage
Peanut surprise
Peanut tofu sauce
Peanut wafers
Pickle, plain
Salad oil
Salted peanuts
Shredded peanuts
Substitute asparagus
Sweet pickle
Vinegar
White pepper from peanut vines
Worcestershire sauce

BEVERAGES
Beverage for ice cream
Blackberry punch

Evaporated peanut beverage
Cherry punch
Normal peanut beverage
Peanut beverage flakes
Peanut lemon punch
Peanut Koumiss beverage
Peanut orange punch #1
Peanut orange punch #2
Plum punch

STOCK FOODS

Hen food for laying (peanut hearts)
Molasses feed
Peanut hay meal
Peanut hull bran
Peanut hull meal
Peanut hull stock food
Peanut meal
Three varieties of peanut stock food

MEDICINES

Castoria substitute
Emulsion for bronchitis
Goiter treatment
Iron toxic
Laxatives
Medicine similar to castor oil
Oils emulsified with mercury for treat-
    ment of venereal disease (two
    kinds)
Rubbing oil
Tannic acid
Quinine

LIST OF PRODUCTS MADE
FROM SWEET POTATOES BY
GEORGE W. CARVER

General

Alcohol
Seventy-three types of dyes
Fourteen types of wood fillers
Five types of library paste
Medicine
Paints
Paper from vines
Rubber compound
Shoe blacking
Stains
Synthetic cotton
Synthetic silk
Writing ink

Stock foods

Hog feed
Three types of stock feed meal

Foods

Three types of after dinner mints
Bisque powder
Five types of breakfast food
Fourteen types of candy
Chocolate
Coffee, dry
Two types of dried potatoes
Dry paste
Egg yolk substitute
Four types of flour
Granulated potatoes
Instant coffee
Lemon drops

Four types of meal

Mock coconut

Three types of molasses

Orange drops

Potato nibs

Sauce

Spiced vinegar

Starch

Sugar

Synthetic ginger

Tapioca

Vinegar

Yeast

APPENDIX 3

Dr. Joseph Kenney's Letter to Booker T. Washington and the
Executive Council Concerning Unsanitary Conditions
at Tuskegee, March 26, 1903

To the Executive Council: Esteemed Body: I wish to invite your attention to the general sanitary condition of the institution. I would say that the health and welfare of this large community of persons is in a rather bad state. On the highways where everyone walks and sees, conditions are more favorable, but in many instances, down in the secluded places, where germs hatch and multiply and diseases propagate, the spectacle is all but favorable . . . I want to speak of the grounds in the woods behind that building [Rockefeller Hall] . . . The whole place is one general toilet and the odors which arise at times are fierce. One has only to step through the fence near the new bathhouse to have his esthetic senses shocked . . . As a further topic of consideration I'd mention the toilets . . . Earth closets never have and never will be successfully used by 1400 people in small areas. For drainage or sewage we have no convenient outlet. Some of the toilets are frightful. I'd mention two especially. The large general toilet below Cassidy is fearful. The stench meets one several yards away. Water from the bathroom runs through underneath the house and stands in a very unsightly pool below and then seeps away down into . . . mosquito breeding swamps, where it stands and pollutes the air with its malodorous stench. I know it is much easier to criticize these ills than to offer the remedy. Still, I'd suggest thorough drainage by ditching that entire swamp, collect all this water in pipes, and lead it some distance down the stream. That I am sure would help some. Next, I'd suggest more care about the toilet. Every particle of excrement should be collected in the pails and more lime or simple dry earth mixed and then hauled away. One of the best and simplest deodorants is dry earth. A barrel of it should be in each closet and a man should be appointed whose duty it is to keep them in proper condition and see to it that this earth or lime, or both, are freely used quite frequently during the day. The toilet behind the barracks ought to be attended or condemned. The boys have made that whole field, . . . the fence sides and the field behind, a veritable toilet, and I can't blame them, for what human being can voluntarily consent to use this place that stands for the toilet? The toilet is nearly filled, a large heap of excrement is behind it, and the urine seeps or trickles down in the sand from the urinos with no provision for its removal. The sight and stench are revolting . . . I was surprised to see that the night soil from the toilet in Dorothy Hall was pulled out and banked instead of every particle being hauled away . . . There is one other nuisance of which I am forced to speak. It is the slaughter house. Yesterday and today the odor from that place was sufficient to nauseate a delicate stomach . . . I think I saw the cause of the bad odor. I was out quite early and watched the buzzards gathering, apparently, for their morning meal. I went to the spot and there seemed about fifty. The object of this attention was a pen into which was thrown all the offal and refuse from the slaughterhouse and here the buzzards feed.

The night soil cart stood near. A more repulsive object you need not wish to see. I'll not disgust you by description. I no longer wondered why it smells badly when passing at night, nor did I blame the horse I was riding for being frightened. Suffice it to say, a new one is much needed, one that is made and lined with zinc or sheet iron and will not leak. (I again urge here that more lime, but especially an abundance of dry earth be used in these earth closets. Farther down the hill seems to be or to have been at some time a dumping ground for this night soil cart . . . I urge that the slaughter house be moved, that the general rubbish or garbage be burned, that the dumping place be moved, that night soil be thoroughly mixed with dry earth on poor land some distance away from any kind of building. Most persistently I urge that some step be taken at once to prevent the odor molesting people at the hospital, road, and barn . . .

I don't try to be an alarmist and know that I am not a pessimist, but some communicable or zymotic disease will gain a foothold among us, the conditions are ripe for a widespread epidemic, and I know that on investigation by experts we should be condemned and severely criticized. . . . With great respect I beg to subscribe myself humbly—Joseph A. Kenney

—Kenney to the Executive Committee, March 26, 1903
GWC Papers, Tuskegee Institute Archives

CHAPTER ONE. "Carver's George"

1   **prowling the vicinity:** Robert P. Fuller, "Report on Project #4, 'Moses Carver and his Family,' Interview with Mary Hardin," Dec. 4, 1952, U.S. Department of the Interior National Park Service, n.d., George Washington Carver National Monument Archives, Diamond, MO.

1   **birth is undetermined:** The abduction is described in George's brief memoirs written in 1897, 1922, and 1927, and in interviews with journalists. Manuscripts, George Washington Carver Papers, Tuskegee Institute Archives. Bentley's rescue is described in Fuller, "Moses Carver and his Family," Interview with Mary Hardin." George recalled being about ten when he arrived at the Neosho School for Colored Children, which had just opened. The school was established in 1872; therefore, George must have been born about 1862.

2   **backbreaking labor:** One of the graves in the family cemetery is that of Charity Dunn, who died October 10, 1838. She was the mother-in-law of Moses's brother George. Diamond Grove is now called Diamond and is located fifteen miles from Joplin, which came into being around 1870. Anna Coxe Toogood, "Historic Resource Study and Administrative History, George Washington Carver National Monument, Diamond Missouri," U.S. Department of the Interior, National Park Service, Denver, CO, July 1973.

2   **overwork a way of life:** Carver bought eighty more acres in 1842–44, some from his brother Richard. U.S. Patent Office Certificate 7011, v. 11, p. 240, in GWC Monument Archives; Agricultural Census of Federal Census Records, 1850. In 1853, Carver received patents for other parcels of land that the government awarded free, with the major requirement that the grantee had to cultivate a portion of the land in crops or timber.

3   **The Carver brothers . . . wilderness farther west:** Moses Carver's ancestors were English and had lived in Pennsylvania since before the American Revolution. George Carver's comment regarding German origin is in "A Brief Sketch of My Life," c. 1927, GWC Papers, Tuskegee Institute Archives.

3   **Lincoln . . . played as children:** Carver remarked that Moses had told him many interesting stories about the Lincolns. George W. Carver deeply revered Lincoln. Carver to Lyman Ward, Mar. 3, 1941, GWC Papers, Tuskegee Archives.

3   **sticks and clay from there up:** Anna Coxe Toogood, "Historic Resource Study," 34. Toogood described the cabin in which George was born. It seems that the "big" cabin where he grew up after the kidnapping was identical to it except in size, according to

Moses Carver's grandnephew Tom Williams. Paul Beaubien and Merrill J. Mattes, "The Archeological Search for George Washington Carver's Birthplace," *Negro History Bulletin* (Nov. 1954): 33–38.

3   **spread out:** Quoted in Toogood, "Historic Resource Study," p. 24.

3   **children moved out:** The boys moved away; the girl, Susan or Sarah Jane, married a neighbor, Williams, who built a house on the property. Moses deeded all the property to them and another nephew. "Warranty Deed," Cherokee County Kansas, Oct. 22, 1901, GWC Monument Archives.

4   **help with heavy chores:** "Received of Moses Carver Seven Hundred Dollars in full consideration for a Negro girl named Mary age about Thirteen years who I warrant to be sound in body and mind and a Slave for life. . . . Oct. 9, 1835." Notarized Bill of Sale from Colonel Grant, GWC Monument Archives.

4   **Jim's father:** In another census record, the man is named as "Jackson Carroll." "Free Inhabitants in Marion Township in the County of Newton," U.S. Census, State of Missouri, July 12, 1860.

4   **rescued from the raiders in Arkansas:** James Saxon Childers, "A Boy Who Was Traded for a Horse," *American Magazine*, Oct. 1932, 24–25; *Reader's Digest*, Feb. 1937, 5–9.

5   **even basic information:** See the letter Carver wrote a few months before his death to Richard Pliant, who was trying to establish the George Washington Carver Monument: "I have absolutely no way of furnishing the information you wish, as an orphan child struggling for existence did not have much time to work out details of the kind of cabin and things of that kind . . . You will have to depend upon the old residents who may remember certain facts." Carver to Pliant, Aug. 15, 1942, GWC Papers, Tuskegee Archives.

5   **Carver birth . . . between 1861 and 1863:** The 1870 census lists him and his brother Jim as being "about 10 and 12." For Jim, who was born in 1859, that seems nearly right—he was eleven. George was a tiny little runt of a boy. No one was likely to overestimate his age. Thus he was probably nine or ten at the time of the 1870 census. If he were born in 1865, the year given in several biographies, that would mean that a census taker had estimated him to be ten years old when he was actually only five. Moreover, the 1865 birth date makes Jim older by six years, which is unlikely, considering that he and George were constant playmates, and contemporaries remembered them as being about two years apart in age. For a long time, 1860 was the accepted birth date of Carver. That was because the National Park Service, according to its correspondence, wanted to hold an impressive dedication of the visitor center of the George Washington Carver National Monument on the supposed centennial of his birth, 1960. Park Service historian H. Raymond Gregg has written, "Unfortunately, after several years of intensive analysis of the problem by various historians of the Service, no general agreement has been reached as to an actual verifiable date, or even a strongly probable theoretical date. Nevertheless . . . we recommend recognition of July 12, 1860 as the 'traditional birthdate,' even though it is not subject to documented confirmation." Quoted by Anna Coxe Toogood, "Historic Resource Study," 8, GWC Monument Archives.

6   **poor white trash:** The mutilation occurred on May 24, 1856, at Pottawatomie Creek, Missouri, in reprisal for the burning of Lawrence, Kansas, by Quantrill's gang on May 21.

William C. Quantrill, with a band of 500 southern irregulars, attacked Lawrence, deep in Union territory, murdering civilians and burning the town before retreating into the Missouri woods. See Bruce Nichols, *Guerilla Warfare in Civil War Missouri, 1862* (Jefferson, NC, 2004).

6 **plundering and destroying:** To get rid of Confederate sympathizers in the occupied territory of southwest Missouri, a Union officer evacuated four counties (Jackson, Cass, Bates, and part of Vernon) near Newton. Hundreds were forced from their homes, their property plundered and destroyed. Soldiers and bands of robbers—bushwhackers—roamed over the blighted district throughout the war. Afterward, people came back to a devastated land. Missouri artist George Caleb Bingham painted *Order Number Eleven*, showing the hardships of those forced out of the border counties of Missouri.

6 **Jesse James . . . Missouri border:** James's first raids were in retaliation for an attack on his home by a Unionist gang in Clay County.

6 **broke down completely:** A Union victory in March 1862 at nearby Pea Ridge in Arkansas was said to have ended the Civil War in Missouri. But after that victory, thirty-five skirmishes were reported in Neosho and one in Diamond Grove itself. The most authoritative source for the chaotic situation is Michael Fellman's splendid *Inside War: The Guerilla Conflict in Missouri During the American Civil War* (New York, 1989).

7 **sickly and puny for years:** George Washington Carver to Dr. and Mrs. Milholland, Ames, Apr. 1891, GWC Monument Archives; "Biographical Sketch," 1897, GWC Papers, Tuskegee Archives. "My body was very feeble," he wrote of his childhood, "and it was a constant warfare between life and death."

8 **persimmons . . . awful good:** Miscellaneous Quotations, GWC Monument Archives.

8 **fashion, even in the sticks:** Robert P. Fuller, "Report on Moses Carver and his Family," interview with Forbes Brown, U.S. Department of the Interior National Park Service, n.d., GWC Monument Archives.

9 **workaday lives with color:** Robert P. Fuller and Merrill J. Mattes, "The Early Life of George Washington Carver," Chapter 4, 1957, GWC Monument Archives.

9 **couldn't do with mine:** George Washington Carver, "Miscellaneous Quotations, GWC Monument Archives.

9 **instrument he couldn't play:** Thomas Williams, quoted by Toogood, "Historic Resource Study," 25; Fuller and Mattes, "Early Life of GWC."

9 **if not Aunt Sue?:** In one narrative prepared by the National Park Service prior to dedicating the GWC Monument, there is a reference to the sketch having been made for Carver's biographer, Rackham Holt, in the 1930s. This is obviously incorrect, as the sketch is a childish drawing unlike his adult work.

9 **liked raising things:** He planted apple orchards, wild and cultivated plane trees, oak, walnut, ash, sassafras, wild cherry, and more than 500 Dutch elm. Crops included wheat, flax, and rye—a mixed farm, typical of the area. Agricultural Schedules of Federal Census Records, 1850–1880; Merrill Mattes, "Report on George Washington Carver's Boyhood Surroundings," p. 43, National Park Service, GWC Monument Archives.

10 **Monday lunch and supper:** "Reminiscences" (of George's contemporaries, gathered after his death), Miscellaneous Documents, GWC Monument Archives.

10 **planters for his flowers:** Robert P. Fuller, "Moses Carver and his Family," interview with Eliza Winter, July 25, 1955, U.S. Department of the Interior National Park Service, n.d.

10 **reused . . . some time:** Fuller, "Moses Carver and his Family," p. 4.

11 **attend their funerals:** Fuller, interview with Eliza Winter, p. 40.

11 **loved children, however:** Merrill Mattes, "Carver's Boyhood Surroundings," p. 31.

12 **mean to his wife:** Carver to Martha Lupton, Aug. 26, 1941, GWC Papers, Tuskegee Archives.

12 **member of the Masons:** Merrill Mattes, "Carver's Boyhood Surroundings," p. 31n.

12 **trading and shopping:** "Moses Carver's Livestock, 1850–1880," Miscellaneous Documents, GWC Monument Archives.

12 **half gallon of coal oil:** Grocery receipt from G. H. Martling & Co., Martling MO, 187?, Miscellaneous Documents, GWC Monument Archives.

13 **traded for store-bought items:** Miscellaneous Documents, GWC Monument Archives.

14 **"croup" as the next one struck:** Thomas Williams, quoted by Toogood, "Historic Resource Study," p. 25.

14 **help his eyesight:** Interview with John Harris, 1948, Toogood, "Historic Resource Study," p. 24.

14 **bronchitis:** Penicillin was discovered in 1928 but did not come into general use in country towns until later.

15 **what he was trying to say:** Miscellaneous Documents, GWC Monument Archives.

15 **"very slowly":** Carver to Howard Faulk, Apr. 19, 1940, GWC Papers, Tuskegee Archives.

15 **real deformity:** Writing apparently on the basis of information told to her by Carver, Lucy Cherry Crisp avers that he cured the hump by forcing himself to walk around with a stick reaching across his back and under his arms. See "Diamond Grove" in "Carver," manuscript, Lucy Cherry Crisp Papers, Special Collections, Joyner Library, East Carolina University, Greenville, NC.

15 **to suffer the same fate:** Carver's memoir of 1897. The foregoing quotations of Carver are all taken from the same narrative. Manuscripts, GWC Papers, Tuskegee Archives.

15 **played with plants:** George's favorite game was marbles. Ibid.

16 **three feet by six feet:** Ibid.

16 **access to a brush:** Aunt Sue had used pokeberries for coloring butter and cakes and for dying clothes. She boiled oak bark to make black dye, hickory for yellow, and chestnut for brown.

17 **served as the post office:** Merrill Mattes, "Carver's Boyhood Surroundings," p. 27.

17 **contented ignorance:** See online Free Public Records Directory, Neosho County, Kansas; Deed Books, Newton County Courthouse, Neosho, MO; Abstract of Wills and Administrations, 1838–39, Newton County Library, Neosho. Interviews were recorded with old-timers of very advanced years by Peter Duncan Burchard, Carver Oral History Project, 2004, GWC Monument Archives.

17 **among us in the front row:** Forbes H. Brown, memoir written for National Park Service, 1952, quoted in Fuller and Mattes, "The Early Life of George Washington Carver, Part I."

18 **"Spit and Step in it":** Fuller, "Report on Moses Carver and his Family," interview with Forbes Brown, p. 21.

18 **colored school . . . in Neosho:** Interview with Mary Lou Hardin in Toogood, "Historic Resource Study," p. 25n.

18 **not permitted to enter it:** According to Forbes Brown, the Sunday school teacher, Flora Abbott, took an interest in George. It may have been at her urging that he was allowed to attend the regular school briefly.

19 **in the Alcott mode:** Carver related the story of the novel-writing to Rackham Holt, who repeated it in her testimony before the U.S. Senate Committee on Public Lands and Surveys and the House of Representatives Committee on Public Lands, Washington, DC, Feb. 5, 1943.

19 **could get an education:** Fuller, "Report on Moses Carver and his Family," interview with Harold A. Slane (son of the teacher), 1956, p. 26.

19 **School for Colored Children:** Harvest Bank donated the school building to the George Washington Carver Birthplace Association in 2004. Peter Duncan Burchard, interview with Supt. Scott Bentley, Diamond, MO, Nov. 1, 2004, Carver Oral History Project, GWC Monument Archives.

19 **turned his back on the school:** In his 1897 sketch of his life, George Carver wrote that his brother left to go to Fayetteville, Arkansas, at age nineteen and shortly afterward he, George, struck out alone for Neosho. That is obviously wrong, since census records show that Jim was not nine years older than George. At some point, George Carver remarked that Jim had gone off for a time to learn the plasterer's trade.

20 **Watkins house next door:** As a slave state, Missouri outlawed education for Negroes in 1847. The new state constitution of 1865 permitted black elementary schools, but the law was not mandated for seven years. Neosho was ahead of the rest of the state in constructing what came to be known as the Lincoln School. Burchard interview with Scott Bentley.

20 **insisted on writing:** The white woman who had been the instructor was replaced by order of the Reconstruction government by a young black man whom George regarded as ignorant.

20 **middle-class people:** Application to Continental Insurance Company of New York, Sept. 22, 1884; promissory note to American Harrow Company, Oct. 1, 1893, in GWC Monument Archives.

21 **"such a good man":** Quoted by Rackham Holt, *George Washington Carver* (New York, 1948), p. 25.

21 **queenly, snappish, and venerable:** See Mariah Watkins's letters to Cal Jefferson, Neosho, 1905–1925, and the letters of the Neosho Bank to Jefferson concerning "Aunt Mariah" in GWC Monument Archives.

21 **confess to journalists:** The story was repeated in many articles about Carver, and in Rackham Holt, p. 19.

21 **his Sunday best:** See, e.g., "Diamond Grove" in "Carver," Lucy Cherry Crisp Papers.

CHAPTER TWO. "Drifting Toward Life"

24 **with drawn revolvers:** *Fort Scott Daily Monitor,* Mar. 28, 1879.

25 **dashed . . . onto the sidewalk:** Quoted in Robert P. Fuller and Merrill J. Mattes, "The Early Life of George Washington Carver, Part I," report for the National Park Service, George Washington Carver National Monument Archives, Diamond, MO, 1957, p. 16;

Fort Scott Daily Monitor, Mar. 28, 1879. The newspaper reported only the lynching and the events following it; Carver described the head bashing. See also Carver's account as told to Rackham Holt, *George Washington Carver* (New York, 1948), p. 32. Whereas Holt recorded many inaccuracies in her biography because of Carver's inability to remember clearly the events of his early life, this incident no doubt was recalled in stark detail. Carver's eyewitness account may have been more nearly correct than that of the newspaper writer, who was not on the scene.

25   **display of crowd hysteria:** The statistics given are actually for the year 1882, the first year for which approximate records are available on lynching. The Fort Scott incident took place in 1879. George Washington Carver Papers, Tuskegee Institute Archives.

27   **accordionist for school assemblies:** Often Carver's written responses to questions about his youth are at variance with what he told interviewers and at variance with certain known dates. He once estimated that he attended high school in Minneapolis, Kansas, for about seven years, which would have meant that he graduated in 1887. Actually, he was by then far away from Minneapolis, where the most likely estimate of his attendance is two years, 1883 and 1884. Microfilm Reel 1, ibid.

27   **science or classics track:** "Manual of the Public Schools of Minneapolis," 1887, GWC Monument Archives.

28   **Jim's Seneca tombstone:** George Carver mistakenly wrote in 1927 that Jim died in Fayetteville, Arkansas, fifty miles away; details of Jim's death in Peter Duncan Burchard, Oral History Project, U.S. Department of the Interior National Park Service, n.d., GWC Monument Archives.

29   **selling them for $500:** Fuller and Mattes, "Early Life of GWC," p. 62.

29   **Chester recalled:** "The Better Way," church bulletin, Sept. 9, 1943, in the GWC Monument Archives.

30   **on the Missouri border:** In an 1897 essay, George Carver's memory located it in Iowa, but he seems to have been mistaken.

30   **hardly more than a village:** "Fort Scott and Minneapolis," in "Carver," Lucy Cherry Crisp Papers, Special Collections, Joyner Library, East Carolina University, Greenville, NC. Crisp gives the number of students as 150 and the town population as 600. The college's statistics are used here.

30   **never arrived:** When Nebraska Center was named county seat of Buffalo County, it consisted of a house, a store building, and a warehouse. A partial list of ghost towns in Kansas (1859–1912) reflects the grand hopes and grand names attached to them: Alexandria, Athens, Berlin, Calcutta, Chicago (three towns), Cincinnati, Cleveland, London (two towns), Moscow, Oxford, Paris, Pittsburgh (two towns), Rome (two towns), Sparta, and St. Louis. Daniel Boorstin, *The Americans* (New York, 1965), pp. 165, 298.

30   **Cal recalled:** Peter Duncan Burchard, *Carver: A Great Soul* (Fairfax, CA, 1998), p. 6.

31   **protect you and yours:** Fuller and Mattes, "Early Life of GWC," p. 37.

31   **book learning:** Rev. Russell Conwell of Philadelphia was widely celebrated for a speech he gave thousands of times, "Acres of Diamonds," in which he said, "There is not a poor person in the United States who was not made poor by his own shortcomings." Quoted in David M. Kennedy, Lizabeth Cohen, and Thomas A. Bailey, *The American Pageant*, 13th

ed. (New York, 2006), pp. 497–98. See also Samuel P. Hays, *The Response to Industrialism, 1885–1914* (Chicago, 1957), and John A. Garraty, *The New Commonwealth* (New York, 1968).

32 **rejected George Washington Carver:** Toby Fishbein, interview with Austin W. Curtis, Detroit, Mar. 3, 1979, Carver Oral History Project, GWC Monument Archives.

32 **lands . . . reopened by the government:** In 1887, President Grover Cleveland threw open to settlement the still unclaimed public portions of the land-grant areas that had been reserved for the optional use of railroads.

33 **claim on 160 acres:** The founder of the town is recorded as Elmer Beeler, but Carver always referred to the man he followed as "J. F." or "Frank." Carver's plot was near Beeler, seventeen miles from Dighton and fifty miles north of Dodge, near the Santa Fe railroad and Walnut Creek. Carver to Harry Abbott, Aug. 26, 1937, GWC Monument Archives.

34 **Indians, Negroes, and women:** The Homestead Act of 1862 took effect at the same time as the Emancipation Proclamation. Anyone who did not want to wait out the five years for a free title could acquire it at once by paying $1.25 an acre. He could also add to his original 160 acres by buying more land at the $1.25 price, just as Moses Carver had done in Diamond Grove. Farming in the waterless plains required expensive plows to break the tough sod and expensive equipment to dig deep wells. Many homesteaders finally gave up and returned to the East, but many others carved out new homes and new lives because of the act. Homestead application by George Carver, Oct. 20, 1886; Affidavit of improvements, Kansas, U.S. Land Official Certificate, June 21, 1888, both in GWC Papers, Iowa State University Archives.

34 **an easier supply:** According to the valuation on his homestead application, the trees were worth $350 and the land, after improvements, worth $1,600. The document includes an enumeration of George's furniture and the statements of his residency and improvements. Deed and homestead application, GWC Papers, Iowa State Archives.

35 **keep himself from laughing too:** Rackham Holt, p. 46.

36 **cave-dark:** The soddie was at least more comfortable than the dugout houses some people made, caves in the sides of hills that offered no protection from the rain. When water got in a dugout, the people bailed it out as best they could and waded around in the mud until the floor dried out on its own.

36 **buffalo droppings . . . stippled the prairie:** In 1868, a train on the Kansas Pacific railroad once waited eight hours for a herd of buffalo numbering a few hundred to amble across the tracks. With the building of the railroads, the herds were quickly massacred for buffalo robes, for steaks, or for sheer sport. The killers, some of them shooting from moving trains, certainly never picked up the remains of their prey. By 1888, the carcasses had been picked by vultures.

36 **touched the food again:** "Here is the rundown of the operations that mother went through when making baking powder biscuits . . . Stoke the stove, get out the flour sack, stoke the stove, wash your hands, mix the biscuit dough, stoke the stove, wash your hands, cut out the biscuits with the top of a baking powder can, stoke the stove, wash your hands, put the pan of biscuits in the oven, keep on stoking the stove until the biscuits are done (not forgetting to wash the hands before taking up the biscuits)." Charley O'Kieffe, *Western Story: The Recollections of Charley O'Kieffe, 1884–1898* (Lincoln, NE, 1960), p. 32.

36 **emigrated to milder conditions:** Kennedy, Cohen, and Bailey, *The American Pageant*, p. 539. To this day, the federal government, which owns about a fourth of all U.S. land, has many millions of acres that may be homesteaded, but they are mostly grazing lands unsuitable for farming.

37 **or the accordion:** Frank Beeler, *The Highland Vidette*, Mar. 27, 1938, quoted in "Fort Scott and Minneapolis" in "Carver," Lucy Cherry Crisp Papers.

37 **literary society in 1887:** *Ness City Times*, Dec. 15, 1887.

38 **other valuable considerations:** The banker's name was George Borthwick. By 1937, one of Borthwick's associates was writing Carver that oil had been discovered on the property and was producing 900 barrels a day. Nevertheless, the company that developed the wells decided to explore what they thought would be a heavier supply southward. O. L. Lennen to Carver, Ness City, KS, Mar. 4, 1937, GWC Monument Archives.

38 **"splendid residence":** "Biographical Sketch, 1897, Reel 1, GWC Papers, Tuskegee Archives.

38 **introduction to Mrs. Milholland:** "Only the other day the thought came vividly to my mind how I heard your beautiful voice in the choir and what a profound impression it made upon me." Carver to the Milhollands, Tuskegee, Feb. 28, 1905, GWC Monument Archives.

39 **"as no one else does":** Mrs. Milholland's memoir of George, written several years before her death but never published, quoted at length in "Fort Scott and Minneapolis" in "Carver," Lucy Cherry Crisp Papers; Carver to Mrs. Milholland, Tuskegee, Feb. 25, 1928, GWC Monument Archives. Mrs. Milholland died in 1935; correspondence with George was then taken up by her daughter, Mrs. Closson.

39 **he was not rejected:** In a letter to Mrs. Milholland nearly thirty years after he entered Simpson College, Carver wrote, "You know of course that it was due to yourself more than to anyone else that I started to college. I think I told you the story of my deciding to go— how it troubled me for many weeks. You possibly recall that it was your custom to have me report to your house every day for a recital of what I had done during the day. I missed several days. You sent one of the girls down to the house where I was 'batching' to see what was the matter. I went up to your house, and you catechized me very strongly as to why I had not been up. I didn't tell you the whole truth, and you knew it very well. It was my decision with reference to college that was troubling me. You had put it into my head, and I didn't see any way to do it, as I saw no way of getting the means; but when I decided to do it, everything seemed to clear away. You recall I presume that I told you I was ironing a short bosom, feeling very depressed, when a voice seemed to say to me, 'Why don't you decide to go to college?' I had begun an argument with this voice to the effect that I had no money, was already in debt, it was only two months before school opened, and I just could not do it. I grew more perturbed all the time, and finally the voice appeared again and said, 'George, why don't you go to college?' I left the iron sitting on the shirt bosom, forgetting really what I was doing, turned entirely around and said to this voice, 'I will.' From that very moment I seemed to come to myself, and was the best person you ever saw, as I had made a decision." Carver to Mrs. H. M. Milholland, Tuskegee, Aug. 18, 1918, GWC Monument Archives.

CHAPTER THREE. "A Real Human Being"

40   **real human being:** Quoted by John G. Gross (former president of Simpson College), "A Truly Great American," *Virginia Methodist Advocate*, n.d., George Washington Carver National Monument Archives, Diamond, MO.

40   **steam heat and skylights:** Catalogue for Simpson College, Indianola, Iowa, 1891–1892, ibid. In 1956, the building in which the art studio was housed was renamed the Carver Science Building.

41   **famished month:** In response to requests, Carver wrote three autobiographical essays in, 1897, 1922, and 1927. George Washington Carver Papers, Tuskegee Institute Archives.

41   **George was destitute:** Quoted in "Fort Scott and Minneapolis" in "Carver," unpublished manuscript, Lucy Cherry Crisp Papers, Special Collections, Joyner Library, East Carolina University, Greenville, NC; Rackham Holt, *George Washington Carver* (New York, 1948), p. 64.

41   **mobilized . . . to give him work:** George mentioned the W. A. Liston family (whose first initials may have been A. W.) and the family of Reverend A. D. Field as being tremendously helpful to him; see "Brief Sketch of My Life" (1927).

42   **insight . . . into his fellow beings:** P. T. Morley, quoted in Robert P. Fuller and Merrill J. Mattes, "The Early Life of George Washington Carver, Part I," p. 32, report for National Park Service, GWC Monument Archives.

42   **opened its white arms to him:** The town had a population of about 2,400 and boasted two railroads running though it.

42   **Mrs. Liston wrote:** Quoted in "College Years." In "Carver," Lucy Cherry Crisp Papers.

42   **stoutly denied it:** George Carver to Mrs. Milholland, Indianola, Mar. 1891, GWC Monument Archives.

43   **His voice was very peculiar:** Mrs. J. M. Robbins, quoted in "College Years" in "Carver," Lucy Cherry Crisp Papers.

43   **when she wasn't around:** Interview with Pauline Townsend, n.d., Misc. Papers, GWC Papers, Tuskegee Archives.

43   **cultural event he could afford:** *Virginia Methodist Advocate*; Simpson College transcript, GWC Monument Archives.

43   **three octaves below:** Carver to Mr. and Mrs. Milholland and Frances, Indianola, Apr. 1891, GWC Monument Archives.

43   **borrowed shed:** "My roses are just beginning to grow again. I want to try to root one of each for you if I can." Carver to Mr. and Mrs. Milholland, Indianola, Apr. 1891, ibid.

44   **humble servant in God:** "I beseech you, Doctor, to wait until I come up, and I will tell you the joke I have on you; it is very good indeed, so much better than the key," a reference to an arithmetic key that was supposed to help George bring up his one poor math grade. Ibid.

44   **"but the home folks":** Carver to Mr. and Mrs. Milholland, Ames (n.d.), ibid.

45   **art school the next year:** "Memorabilia," GWC Papers, Tuskegee Archives.

45   **yearning for his classmates:** Simpson's president, quoted in the *Virginia Methodist Advocate*.

45   **rehabilitating wayward youth:** www.rofflehaus.com/wiki/Etta_Budd.

46   **growing anything but corn and hogs:** The first graduating class in 1872 consisted of 28 students; in 1914, the number was 3,500. Most of the land-grant colleges became state universities. Office of Institutional Research, Iowa State University.

46   **cavalry in any numbers:** Continuous warfare with the Indian raged in the West from 1868 to about 1890; about one-fifth of all soldiers assigned to the frontier were black. It is estimated that there were some 5,000   black cowboys, though mainly along the three major cattle trails that intersected the three east-west railroads; see David M. Kennedy et al., *The American Pageant,* 13th ed. (New York, 2005), pp. 532, 537–538; P. Durham and E. I. Jones, *The Negro Cowboys* (Lincoln, NE, 1965).

47   **a place to sleep:** See H. L. Pammel's letter reprinted in *The Ames (IA) Tribune,* n.d., GWC Monument Archives.

47   **transplanted to the South's clay hills:** See "Notebooks," GWC Papers, Tuskegee Archives; Joseph Lancaster Budd Papers, Special Collections, Iowa State University Library.

47   **research in mycology:** See Louis Hermann Pammel Papers, Special Collections, Iowa State University Library.

47   **professor was paid $300:** Iowa's President, Beardshear, earned $3,850. Office of Institutional Research, Iowa State University.

47   **eventually served as U.S. Secretary of Agriculture:** Address at the Waldorf-Astoria Hotel, Feb. 23, 1939, quoted in "College Years" in "Carver," Lucy Cherry Crisp Papers.

48   **advanced degree of practical imagination:** Wilson attended Iowa College, now Grinnell.

49   **forest preservation:** After retirement from the cabinet in 1913, he returned to Tama County and was appointed by the governor to report on agricultural conditions in Great Britain. He died in 1920, age eighty-five, on his own farm, a great figure in American farming. James A. "Tama" Wilson Papers, 1835–1920, Special Collections, Parks Library, Iowa State University.

49   **numbers had almost trebled:** U.S. Federal Census, 1870—1890. See also the interesting chart, "High School and College Graduates 1870—1970" in Kennedy et al., *The American Pageant,* p. 516.

49   **janitor for North Hall:** Fuller and Mattes quoting Carver, "Early Life of GWC," p. 24.

50   **college's landscaper:** C. C. Lewis to Tuskegee Institute (in response to a request for memorials after Carver's death), Carlsbad, NM, n.d., GWC Papers, Tuskegee Archives.

50   **"things went much easier":** Carver to L. H. Pammel, Tuskegee, May 5, 1922, GWC Papers, Tuskegee Archives.

50   **"God has destined for me":** Carver to the Milhollands, Ames, Iowa, Aug. 6, 1891, GWC Monument Archives.

50   **agnosticism . . . at the institution:** Wilson to Carver, Washington, D.C., Feb. 1, 1911, James "Tama" Wilson Papers, Parks Library, Iowa State University.

51   **along Christian lines:** Ibid.

51   **decorating committee . . . student events:** "Memorabilia," Reel 1, GWC Papers, Tuskegee Archives.

51   **Boston Conservatory of Music:** Rackham Holt, p. 76.

52   **"Talking and Working":** "Miscellaneous Papers," GWC Papers, Tuskegee Archives.

52   **worked his way forward:** In 1927, he answered a biographical inquiry with more than his usual slapdash response, describing his college jobs. L. H. Pammel to *The Ames (IA) Tribune*, n.d., in GWC Monument Archives.

52   **"services rendered":** GWC, "A Brief Sketch of My Life," c. 1927, Reel 1, GWC Papers, Tuskegee Archives.

52   **stunts and balancing acts:** *Iowa College Student*, Mar. 6, Aug. 27, Sept. 4, 22, 26, Nov. 13, 1894; May 2, 28, Aug, 15, 1895; Aug 18, Sept. 22, 1896; Iowa State College *The Bomb*, May 1896, passim.

52   **cacti of western Kansas:** The cactus picture won honorable mention in the competition.

53   **"a very fine-looking suit":** Toby Fishbein, interview with Austin Curtis, Detroit, Mar. 3, 1979, Carver Oral History Project, GWC Monument Archives.

53   **"fawn-colored":** Mrs. Liston quoted in "Carver," Lucy Cherry Crisp Papers.

53   **"green with age":** Harry D. Thompson to Mack Shepard, McAllen, Texas, Sept. 20, 1943, GWC Monument Archives.

53   **disgruntled boy had left:** Recollection of John H. Hillman, quoted in Linda O. McMurry, *Carver* (New York, 1982), p. 36.

53   **interested eyes on white women:** 359 black men (and 152 whites) were lynched by mobs in both the North and the South between 1890 and 1892. In some years during the Jim Crow era, the lynching of whites exceeded blacks. Michael S. Pfeifer, *Rough Justice* (Chicago, 2004).

54   **An Iowa classmate, 1945:** McMurry, *Carver*, pp. 36–37.

54   **he did not have to drop out:** C. C. Lewis to Tuskegee Institute, Carlsbad, NM, n.d., GWC Papers, Tuskegee Archives.

54   **he wrote the Milhollands:** Oct. 16, 1894, Ames, GWC Monument Archives.

54   **as an instructional chapter:** Miscellaneous documents, GWC Papers, Tuskegee Archives.

55   **master's degree program:** His undergraduate thesis was "Plants as Modified by Man." With Mrs. Liston and Miss Budd, he sat at the professors' table in the dining hall after the commencement ceremony.

55   **Iowa Experiment Station:** See the biographical sketch in the Iowa State College yearbook (1896), GWC Monument Archives.

55   **George had published papers:** "Grafting Cacti, " Iowa Horticultural Society, 1893, pp. 257–59, GWC Monument Archives.

55   **three on his own:** "Best Ferns for the North and Northwest," Bulletin 27, pp. 150–153, 1894–1895; "Treatment of Currants and Cherries to Prevent Spot Diseases," Bulletin 30, pp. 298–301, 1895–1896; "Our Window Gardens," Bulletin 32, pp. 516–525, 1896–1897; all published by the Iowa Agricultural Experiment Station. See the reference to Carver's work with fungi in "New York Agricultural Experiment Station Report," 1895, and Charles Aldrich to Prof. Charles E. Bessey, n.p., Oct. 6, 1896, Iowa Hist. Society Collection, GWC Monument Archives.

55   **butterfly net in his hand . . . Iowa classmate 1945:** "I was meeting in Des Moines for a day the girl who is still with me after more than 50 happy years. George gave me a shoe box full of sweet peas from his private garden as a gift to her. Neither of us has ever forgotten it." C.C. Lewis, GWC Papers, Tuskegee Archives.

55   **Three girls . . . to their former classmate:** See *West Liberty Index*, Aug. 20, 1896, GWC Monument Archives; bouquets mentioned in "Carver," Lucy Cherry Crisp Papers.

55   **Carver as his authority:** Joseph Budd in Iowa State *Register*, 1899, Rackham Holt, p. 90.

56   **ironclad recommendations:** Quoted in Fuller and Mattes, "Early Life of GWC," p. 49.

57   **With respect, James G. Wilson:** Wilson to Alcorn Agricultural and Mech. College, Dec. 1895, James "Tama" Wilson Papers, Parks Library, Iowa State University.

58   **I expect . . . to go to my people:** Carver to Booker T. Washington, Ames, Apr. 3, 12, 21, 1896, GWC Monument Archives.

58   **"wonderful collector . . . ever known":** L. H. Pammel to *The Ames (IA) Tribune*, n.d., ibid.

CHAPTER FOUR. "Booker"

Two separate microfilm sets of Booker T. Washington Papers are cited here: those in the Tuskegee Institute Archives and those in the Library of Congress in Washington D.C. Two collections of the papers of George Washington Carver are cited: the microfilmed papers at the Tuskegee Institute Archives and the manuscripts in the George Washington Carver Monument Archives in Diamond, Missouri.

60   **An elaborate secret life:** "An elaborate secret life" is the description given by Louis R. Harlan. See Harlan's definitive study, *Booker T. Washington*, 2 vols. (New York, 1972–1983).

61   **plantation in Franklin County, Virginia:** *Up From Slavery* (New York, 1901). Because of the many editions of the book, including paperbacks, chapters rather than page numbers will be cited.

61   **Yule log and singing:** Raymond W. Smock, ed., *Booker T. Washington in Perspective* (Jackson, MS, 1988), p. 10.

63   **Armstrong, a former Union officer:** Armstrong had been a commander of black troops during the Civil War. Together with the American Missionary Association, he established the Hampton Normal and Agricultural Institute, run by the Congregational Church. Its mission was the religious instruction and education of blacks.

64   **plow a field or pick a harvest:** *Up From Slavery*, Chapter 5.

66   **a place for learning:** Ibid. At the behest of Tuskegee citizens who had learned of Hampton Institute, the Alabama legislature appropriated $2,000   a year for establishing the school, but the money could only be spent on teachers' salaries, not on land or buildings.

66   **teachers who could barely read:** Ibid.

66   **forks on a dinner table:** Ibid., Chapter 8.

66   **purchase money . . . except for three individuals:** The money for this initial purchase was lent to Booker by General J. F. B. Marshall, the treasurer of Hampton Institute, who took the money from his personal funds.

69   **his three daughters then attended Tuskegee:** Peter Duncan Burchard interview with Gwendolyn (Woods) Butler, Oct. 17, 2004, Carver Oral History Project, George Washington Carver Monument Archives, Diamond, MO.

69   **or used a toothbrush:** Joseph F. Citro, "Booker T. Washington's Tuskegee Institute," M.A. thesis, University of Rochester, 1972, pp. 533n, 152.

70   **third kiln, which worked:** *Up From Slavery,* Chapter 10.

70   **"religious and spiritual side":** Ibid., Chapter 13.

70   **shifted to repairing fences:** Report by Monroe N. Work; Work to Booker T. Washington, June 11, 1911, Booker T. Washington Papers, Tuskegee Institute Archives.

71   **project . . . should next undertake:** *Up From Slavery,* Chapter 9.

71   **a single personal insult:** Ibid., Chapters 14, 12.

72   **countless demands upon their generosity:** Ibid., Chapter 12.

72   **attend Tuskegee and learn trades:** Booker's daughter Portia attended Wellesley College in Massachusetts for a time. Eventually she acquired a music degree from a white school, Bradford College in New England, and then went to Germany for further piano study. Booker T. Washington Jr. became a real estate broker in Tuskegee. Ernest Davidson Washington worked as a fundraiser for Tuskegee Institute.

73   **advance the body politic:** *Up From Slavery,* speech quoted in Chapter 13.

73   **in the exercise of those rights:** Ibid., Chapter 14.

73   **a racial altercation:** *Atlanta Constitution,* Sept. 19, 1895.

74   **a recent biographer noted:** Raymond W. Smock, *Booker T. Washington* (Chicago, 2009), p. 4.

CHAPTER FIVE. "Dominion of Poverty"

Two different microfilm sets of Booker T. Washington Papers are cited, those in the Tuskegee Archives and the Library of Congress, as well as the two volumes of his published papers edited by Louis R. Harlan and Raymond W. Smock.

75   **Fall over onto the path:** Rackham Holt, *George Washington Carver* (New York, 1948), p. 153. Holt's biography contains no documentation. She interviewed Carver over several months and then submitted questions to which he responded in writing. Her descriptions cannot be verified, but she appears to have had information about Carver that no one else had access to. Carver approved her book before its publication.

75   **some fifty teachers:** Joseph F. Citro, *Booker T. Washington's Tuskegee Institute* (Rochester, NY, 1972), pp. 108–210. Citro tracks the turnover, although he reaches the opposite conclusion, that the faculty was notably stable because Tuskegee kept a steadfast core of teachers who served many years.

76   **lower salary . . . elsewhere:** Louis R. Harlan, *Booker T. Washington,* vol. 2 (New York, 1983), p. 152. Figures given are for 1903.

76   **There were many such cases:** In 1904–1905 alone there were five such cases. See correspondence with James H. Van Sickle, Margaret P. Murrell, L. R. Wormley, and David Houston, Sept. 1904–July 1905, in Louis R. Harlan and Raymond W. Smock, eds., *The Booker T. Washington Papers* (Urbana, IL, 1972).

76   **between $100 and $300 a year:** In 1906, the salary of a black public school teacher might be as little as ten dollars per month; Booker claimed that he had even seen a contract in which a black teacher was paid $1.40 per month.

76   **thumb on every department:** For examples of his instructions, see Citro, pp. 92–97.

77 **"worse than when he is here":** Memo, Executive Council, undated 1912, Oct. 28, 1904, Booker T. Washington Papers, Tuskegee Institute Archives.

77 **"for the sake of education":** Carver to Finance Committee, Nov. 11, 1896, ibid.

77 **consulting his subconscious . . . procedure:** Rackham Holt, p. 147.

78 **students . . . remained at the school:** Anson Phelps Stokes, *Tuskegee Institute: The First Fifty Years* (Tuskegee, AL, 1931), p. 62. See also the educational background of Tuskegee's faculty in Citro, p. 62.

79 **not the plant expert . . . pretended to be:** The incident was recounted by Carver to Rackham Holt, p. 216.

80 **science, literature, history, and art:** Carver to Finance Committee, Nov. 11, 1896, BTW Papers, Tuskegee Archives.

80 **owned nightshirts and toothbrushes:** Lucy Cherry Crisp, "Carver," unpublished manuscript, Section IV, p. 8, Lucy Cherry Crisp Papers, Special Collections, Joyner Library, East Carolina University, Greenville, NC; Emmett J. Scott and Lyman Beecher Stowe, *Booker T. Washington, Builder of a Civilization* (New York, 1917), p. 238.

80 **the beehives; and pastures:** Carver's account, 1903, Booker T. Washington Collection, Library of Congress.

81 **no authority . . . according to his judgment:** BTW to George W. Carver, Nov. 28, 1898. See also J. H. Washington's long letter of complaint to Carver because parts of a harness were found lying in an alley between two buildings. Mar. 20, 1902, GWC Papers, Tuskegee Archives.

82 **whether followed . . . up to J. H.:** Rackham Holt, p. 144; Carver to BTW, Dec. 23, 1902, GWC Papers, Tuskegee Archives.

82 **eating the school's pigs:** Carver to BTW, July 4, Aug. 17, 1898; Carver to Warren Logan, June 23,1897; BTW to Carver Jan. 5, 7, 1901; W. J. Clayton to Carver, Sept. 7, 1899, GWC Papers, Tuskegee Archives; Carver to BTW, Feb. 17, 1902, Minutes of the Executive Council, Dec. 29, 1899, Apr. 13, 1901, BTW Collection, Library of Congress.

82 **back into the milk:** Carver to BTW, Oct. 20, 1900, GWC Papers, Tuskegee Archives; Rackham Holt, p. 141.

82 **continue with the dipping:** Carver to BTW, Feb. 9, 1897; Carver to Logan, Aug. 4, 1898, GWC Papers, Tuskegee Archives; Carver to BTW, Aug. 8, 1898, BTW Collection, Library of Congress. Carver apparently did not bear a grudge against Green because of the incident. Carver referred to him in benevolent terms in later correspondence.

83 **"green grass to walk on":** Quoted in "Black Man's Miracles," excerpt from an undated and untitled journal in George Washington Carver Monument Archives, Diamond, MO.

83 **weather station in Montgomery:** Carver to BTW, Oct. 6, 1899, BTW Collection, Library of Congress.

83 **"odors . . . are fierce":** Kenney to the Executive Committee, Mar. 26, 1903, GWC Papers, Tuskegee Archives.

84 **contents could fertilize plants:** Throughout the period there was a lively competition between earth closets and water closets. In upper-class homes, the waste would fall into water, which could then be piped out to a stream, or the bucket could be emptied by hand at some distance from the house. The water closet won the competition; it proved to be the forerunner of the modern flush toilet.

84 **"sight and stench are revolting":** Kenney to Executive Council, Mar. 26, 1903, GWC Papers, Tuskegee Archives. The correspondence between Kenney and Carver (as the Sanitary Committee), Booker, and the Executive Council over the sewage and drainage situation appears consistently through January 1904 through 1910 and beyond in the Booker T. Washington Collection, Library of Congress. The specific items are detailed by Citro, pp. 283–286. See, esp., report of the Committee on Sanitary Facilities, Apr. 24, 1904; J. A. Kenney to Executive Council, Apr. 6, 1907; Kenney to Executive Council, Jan. 6, 1908; Kenney to Executive Council, Mar. 16, 1908; Kenney to Executive Council, May 18, 1908; Report of Principal, May 29, 1909; Kenney to BTW, May 29, 1909; Kenney to J. H. Washington, Oct. 8, 1909; Kenney to Executive Council, June 3, 1910, BTW Collection, Library of Congress.

85 **water which was used by the dairy:** "This water is not primarily to be drunk, but the majority of students drink it . . . The milkmen use it for washing their hands, the cows' udders, and the milk pails. The creamery men use it for washing their hands, utensils, and for butter making." Kenney to Executive Council, Apr. 6, 1907, BTW Collection, Library of Congress.

86 **"criminal negligence," Kenney exclaimed:** Citro, p. 286.

86 **flies in the school's creamery:** In 1909, Kenney was appalled that a Mr. Ferguson had complained about his toilet "just before he was taken down." Citro, p. 286.

86 **serve black veterans:** Black veterans of World War I could not be treated at white hospitals. Carver and the principal, Robert Moton, went to Washington to argue against the injustice. Moton told Congress and the president, "I have land at Tuskegee. Give us money, and we will build a hospital for black veterans." They did—a 700-bed hospital. Peter Duncan Burchard, interview with Frank Godden, Los Angeles, Nov. 6, 2004, Carver Oral History Project, George Washington Carver Monument Archives. The next issue was staffing the hospital. Dr. Kenney insisted that all employees from the doctors to the ground keepers should be black; Moton finally compromised on that issue.

86 **flowers on the tables:** BTW to L. G. Wheeler, Oct. 19, 1904, BTW Papers, Tuskegee Archives.

86 **correct the broom situation:** BTW to R. C. Bruce, Oct. 19, 1904; to P. C. Parks, E. J. Scott, and C. H. Gibson, Nov. 11, 1904; to E. E. Lane, Oct. 12, 1905; to Mrs. B. T. Washington, Jan. 17, 1907, BTW Papers, Tuskegee Archives.

86 **needed close supervision:** Booker at the time was requiring teachers to sign in at the Academic Building before meeting their classes, a supervision they loudly resented. Citro, p. 240.

86 **walking on the girls' sidewalk:** Julius B. Ramsey to Executive Council, Mar. 6, 1911, BTW Collection, Library of Congress. For examples of boys being disciplined for walking on the girls' sidewalk, see "Carver," VIII, p. 2, Lucy Cherry Crisp Papers.

86 **title plaques for each place:** J. H. Washington to R. R. Taylor, Apr. 28, 1904, BTW Collection, Library of Congress; diagram reproduced in Citro, p. 295–296.

87 **complained lustily about the excessive meetings:** See, e.g., Executive Council Meeting Minutes, Feb. 27, 1899; Nov. 10, 1904; July 17, Sept. 15, 1914; General Faculty Meeting Minutes, Oct. 20, 1903, BTW Papers, Tuskegee Archives.

88 **coached the school's football team:** Citro, pp. 222, 224.

88   **until midnight:** Memo quoted from Emmett Scott, ca. 1904; Harlan, *Booker T. Washington,* vol. 2, p. 155.

88   **a particular task—or not:** Students were paid less than 2½ cents an hour, which sum was applied to their school fees. Harlan, *Booker T. Washington,* p. 146, quoting minutes of the executive council, 1903.

88   **getting a rope . . . ordeal:** Carver to BTW, Sept. 13, 1897; Jan. 21, 1902; Aug. 27, 1898, Carver to BTW, Nov. 4, 1901; Mar. 14, 1902, BTW Collection, Library of Congress; Carver to J. H. Washington, Oct. 30, 1903, Tuskegee, BTW Papers, Tuskegee Archives.

88   **double the number the next year:** *Tenth Annual Report of the Agricultural Experiment Station of the A&M College, Auburn, Alabama* (Montgomery, 1898), pp. 23–25, BTW Collection, Library of Congress.

89   **amazingly accurate:** His collaborators, J. B. Ellis and E. Bartholomew, acknowledged his contributions in three articles in the *Journal of Mycology* in May and June 1902 and October 1903. Carver published his findings in *Some Cercosporae of Macon County, Alabama,* Tuskegee Institute Experiment Station Bulletin 4 (1902), Tuskegee Archives.

89   **compared to the value . . . investigations:** GWC to James Wilson, Aug. 2, 1897, James A. "Tama" Wilson Papers, 1835–1920, Parks Library, Iowa State University.

89   **better than I thought . . . at first:** Mar. 30, 1897, GWC Monument Archives.

89   **a large enrollment:** The rise in enrollment inspired Carver to write a full curriculum for both boys and girls and to draw up syllabi for all the listed courses.

89   **graduate . . . from the farming department:** BTW to George R. Bridgeforth, May 25, Mar. 13, 1910, BTW Papers, Tuskegee Archives.

89   **"about right":** Quoted by the *National Education Association Journal,* 1946, Harry O. Abbott Papers, GWC Monument Archives.

89   **fertilize their barren acres:** "Carver," Lucy Cherry Crisp Papers, p. 156.

89   **every crop . . . in Alabama:** Citro, p. 61.

90   **"the cotton, the cattle, the people":** "Dr. George Washington Carver," Broadcast, U.S. Office of Education. (1940?), GWC Monument Archives.

90   **85 percent . . . was black:** Macon County was 200 sq. miles. Its population in 1910 included 22,000 black people out of 27,000 total. Charles Johnson, *Shadow of the Plantation* (Urbana, 1934), p. 16.

91   **overwhelming majority . . . infected:** In 1902, Charles Wardell Stiles began serious research on the hookworm, the parasite that burrows between the toes of barefoot people when they walk on dirt containing fecal matter. The disease travels through the veins into the heart, lungs, and intestines, eventually causing severe anemia. In 1909, the Rockefeller Sanitary Commission for Eradication of Hookworm Disease was funded. The commission created a carnival atmosphere at their meetings, combining the testing and treatment of people with public testimonials, education, singing, and refreshments. The disease, which had afflicted 40 to 90 percent of counties in the southern states, was virtually eradicated in the South by 1914.

91   **four out of five acres . . . eroded:** "Carver," Lucy Cherry Crisp Papers, p. 125.

92   **seed and equipment to plant:** Owners would sell land to blacks, but they would schedule payments for times when the cotton crop was not ready to be picked so that the pur-

chaser would not have the money to pay his mortgage. According to some contemporaries, whites would agree to lend money on the condition that the blacks would not vote for such reforms as school desegregation. Peter Duncan Burchard, interview with Edward Pryce, Tuskegee, Nov. 23, 2004, Carver Oral History Project, GWC Monument Archives.

93   **vote . . . denied most blacks:** Through his local connections, Booker and many of his Tuskegee faculty were allowed to register and receive lifetime voting certificates. All over Alabama, only blacks who had served in the army or navy were allowed to register. Blacks fought against disenfranchisement, particularly in two cases that reached the U.S. Supreme Court: *Giles v. Harris* (1903) *and Giles v. Teasley* (1904). To his everlasting credit, Booker T. Washington secretly paid Wilford H. Smith, the plaintiff's lawyer who litigated both cases. Harlan, *Booker T. Washington,* vol. 2, pp. 245–246.

93   **black state prison:** Booker tried to get a black reformatory established in the state. BTW to W. S. Reese, Apr. 3, 1904, BTW Papers, Tuskegee Archives.

93   **permitted . . . at the tables:** In opposing train segregation, Washington again exerted strong, secret efforts, at one point even cooperating with his antagonist W. E. B. Du Bois in challenging the Pullman segregation laws in Tennessee and Georgia. Harlan, *Booker T. Washington,* vol. 2, p. 248; for examples of "separate and unequal," see pp. 416, 420, 422.

93   **escaped being lynched:** Carver to BTW, Nov. 28, 1902, GWC Papers, Tuskegee Archives. Johnson's photographs are in the Library of Congress.

94   **school had to be abandoned:** Byrd T. Crawford to Carver, Ruston, 1904; W. E. Glenn to Carver, Ruston Nov. 17, 1904, GWC Papers, Tuskegee Archives. The school was planning an anniversary celebration, which anticipated event sparked the attack.

94   **good will of whites:** Rackham Holt, p. 131.

94   **not antagonistic:** Seth Low to BTW, Dec. 12, 1906, Seth Low Papers, Columbia University. See also *Tuskegee News,* Nov. 1905, passim, and Johnson, *Shadow of the Plantation,* p. 13.

94   **less than $75:** Report by Monroe N. Work; Work to BTW, June 11, 1911, BTW Papers, Tuskegee Archives.

94   **throughout the United States:** In the Black Belt county of Wilcox, Alabama, for example, the yearly expenditure for white teachers' salaries in 1890–91 was $4,397, for a population of 6,545 students. The expenditure for black teachers was $2,482, for a student population of 9,931. Horace Mann Bond, *Negro Education in Alabama: A Study in Cotton and Steel* (New York, 1969), p. 162, table.

95   **deep plowing . . . wash away:** Nelson E. Henry to Tuskegee Institute, Jan. 1894, quoted in Citro, p. 493; Rackham Holt, p. 133.

CHAPTER SIX. "Stand Up for the Stupid and Crazy"

Two different sets of Booker T. Washington's correspondence are cited, those contained in the BTW Collection of the Library of Congress and those in the BTW Papers at Tuskegee Institute, along with the George Washington Carver Papers in Tuskegee Institute Archives.

96   **"Stand Up for the Stupid and Crazy":** "This is what you shall do; Love the earth and sun

and the animals, despise riches, give alms to every one that asks, stand up for the stupid and crazy, devote your income and labor to others, hate tyrants, argue not concerning God, have patience and indulgence toward the people, take off your hat to nothing known or unknown or to any man or number of men, go freely with powerful uneducated persons and with the young . . . dismiss whatever insults your own soul, and your very flesh shall be a great poem . . ." Walt Whitman, Preface to *Leaves of Grass*.

96 **Tuskegee Experiment Station:** The board included the state commissioner of agriculture and several prominent men; in reality, Booker was the one-man control board.

96 **remained at $1,500:** Auburn additionally received state funds, which the Tuskegee station did not.

97 **station got the fertilizer:** Rackham Holt, *George Washington Carver* (New York, 1948), p. 155.

97 **top hat . . . had ever seen:** Ibid., p. 138

97 **Vegetable Pathology, and Dairying:** Lucy Cherry Crisp, "Carver," unpublished manuscript, Section IV, p. 76, Lucy Cherry Crisp Papers, Special Collections, Joyner Library, East Carolina University, Greenville, NC.

98 **cabinet with their wives:** *Montgomery Advertiser*, Dec. 16, 1898. McKinley was scheduled to go to Atlanta in 1898. Booker went to the president before the trip to ask if he would take a 125-mile detour and visit Tuskegee.

98 **including other U.S. presidents:** Theodore Roosevelt, 1905; Calvin Coolidge as vice president, 1923; Franklin D. Roosevelt, 1939.

98 **no black man had ever taken:** Carver to BTW, Ames, Iowa, July 7, 1900, Booker T. Washington Collection, Library of Congress.

98 **losses on the school farm:** Carver to BTW, Jan 17, 1902, ibid.

99 **who knew where?:** BTW to Carver, Carver to BTW, Oct. 29, 1900, ibid.

99 **"does not occur again":** BTW to Carver, Nov. 28, 1898, ibid. GWC to BTW, May 23, June 3, 1908, George Washington Carver Papers, Tuskegee Institute Archives.

99 **incomparably more disgusting:** Booker to George A. Gates, Oct. 29, 1909, Booker T. Washington Papers, Tuskegee Institute Archives. He prohibited his teachers from touching alcohol, although he himself drank moderately, from all reliable reports.

100 **education and self-improvement:** Louis R. Harlan, *Booker T. Washington*, vol. 2 (New York, 1983), p. 170. A small number of graduates in proportion to students who dropped out also characterized Hampton Institute.

101 **generally went to waste:** See his use of peanuts as well; Carver to BTW, Oct. 17, 1904, BTW Papers, Tuskegee Archives.

101 **$75 an acre:** The Institutes usually attracted about seventy-five people. Minutes of Farmers Institute meetings, May 27, 1904, BTW Papers, Tuskegee Archives; Rackham Holt, p. 162. The ten experimental acres were showing a net loss of $16.25 yearly when Carver took them over. After a year, net gain per acre was $4.00. "Carver," VII, p. 11, Lucy Cherry Crisp Papers.

101 **seventy-five dollars was a fortune:** To get an appreciation of the value of four dollars to Carver's farmers: at this time the *Boston Colored Citizen* wrote asking Carver to fulfill his pledge to subscribe. "I am very much in need of the $1.50 to cover your subscription,"

wrote the publisher. Charles Alexander to Carver, Sept. 24, 1904, GWC Papers, Tuskegee Archives.

103 **wearing her new dress:** Rackham Holt, pp. 136, 166, 168.

103 **White House dining table:** Joseph F. Citro, "Booker T. Washington's Tuskegee Institute," M.A. thesis, University of Rochester, 1972, p. 108–210; S. Shields to BTW, Oct. 23, 1901, BTW Collection, Library of Congress; see also the *New Orleans Times-Democrat*, Oct. 1–31, 1901.

103 **delighted by such a show?:** *Montgomery Advertiser*, Mar. 12, 1905. In 1906 came President Charles W. Eliot of Harvard, Julius Rosenwald (who built hundreds of black schools in the South), Secretary of War William Howard Taft, and Andrew Carnegie, who had given the school its handsome library.

103 **not once but many times:** Carver to BTW, Apr. 11, 1906, GWC Papers, Tuskegee Archives.

104 **carrying them . . . to market:** Rackham Holt, pp. 174, 178, 180.

104 **And here is our whitewash!:** Ibid., p. 182.

104 **before going back to Tuskegee:** "Carver," VII, p. 13, Lucy Cherry Crisp Papers.

104 **appointing Bridgeforth to displace him:** Ibid., VIII, p. 2.

105 **understand what you are doing:** Carver to Campbell, Apr. 5, 1926, Dec. 23, 1923; GWC Papers, Tuskegee Archives.

106 **project was abandoned the next year:** See correspondence 1901–1904 between Carver and Alva Fitzpatrick and E. W. Menefee; Fitzpatrick to Peaslee-Gaulvurt Co., Mar. 8, 1902, GWC Papers, Tuskegee Archives.

106 **developed in the region:** E. S. Steele to Carver, Washington, D.C., Apr. 12, 1902, GWC Papers, Tuskegee Archives.

106 **project was never developed:** Carver to BTW, Apr. 10, 1902, BTW Collection, Library of Congress.

106 **shipments of eggs:** Wilson to Carver, Nov. 25, 1901, Carver to Wilson, Apr. 25, 1902, L. O. Howard to Carver, Oct. 30, Nov. 14, 1902, GWC Papers, Tuskegee Archives; Carver to Dr. L. O. Howard, U.S. Department of Agriculture, Nov. 16, 1902, G.S.A. National Archives and Records Services, Washington, DC; Carver to BTW, undated, 1901, BTW Collection, Library of Congress.

106 **for Carver's analysis:** *Feeding Acorns*, Tuskegee Experiment Station Bulletin No. 1 (Tuskegee, 1898). A partial list of substances submitted for Carver's analysis included cowpeas, cottonseed meal, bran, vinegar, ashes (as a medicament for vermin), rape, cane syrup, commercial turpentine, ore, cotton, phosphate, corn sugar, tomatoes, Tepary bean root, crimson clover, hairy vetch, common stone (to assess presence of gold), red beans from China, rose bush roots (infested with Crown Gall bacteria), grass hay, soy beans, castor oil (from an African missionary), crabgrass, pecans, rabbits, Irish potatoes, sweet potatoes, navy beans, pansy seed, velvet beans, and leather. Inventory of letters accompanying samples, 1899, GWC Papers, Tuskegee Archives.

107 **project on soil reclamation:** 1905 Bulletin, Tuskegee Archives; Minutes of the Executive Council, June 10, 1905, Tuskegee Archives.

107 **"would not go out to see it":** Carver to BTW, Nov. 18, 1895, GWC Papers, Tuskegee Archives; Rackham Holt, p. 147.

107 **"crops that we need":** BTW to Carver, Sept. 28, 1900, GWC Papers, Tuskegee Archives.

108 **"industrial, literary and scientific lines":** Carver to BTW, Apr. 8, 1901, GWC Papers, Tuskegee Archives.

108 **warm letter of thanks:** Carver to R. R. Taylor, Nov. 5, 1902, Carver to BTW, Dec. 24, 27, 1902, BTW Collection, Library of Congress.

108 **thirteen varieties of cotton . . . peanuts:** "Carver," VII, p. 25, Lucy Cherry Crisp Papers; Carver to BTW, Oct. 17, 1904, BTW Papers, Tuskegee Archives.

109 **most popular bulletins:** "Carver," VII, p. 17, Lucy Cherry Crisp Papers. Tuskegee Experiment Station Bulletin 6, 1902, Tuskegee Archives.

109 **Booker had to back down:** Rackham Holt, p. 209.

110 **confident . . . I have not used it:** Carver to BTW, Dec. 30, 1909, June 20, 1912, GWC Papers, Tuskegee Archives.

110 **would be printed in house:** One bulletin, "Eighty Birds of Macon County, Alabama, and their Relation to our Prosperity," appears never to have been published. Typescript in GWC Papers, Tuskegee Archives.

110 **"earliest convenience. Booker T. Washington":** Rackham Holt, p. 147.

110 **workers in white uniforms:** Carver to BTW, Dec. 6, 1901, BTW Collection, Library of Congress.

110 **without men and means:** Carver to BTW, Jan. 1902; May 17, 1901, BTW Collection, Library of Congress.

111 **Black Belt farming situation:** "The average Southern farm has but little more to offer than about one-third of a cotton crop, selling at 2 and 3 cents per pound less than it cost to produce it" (1902), Tuskegee Archives.

111 **children on a farm:** *Nature Study Chemistry for Boy Scouts; Progressive and Correlative Nature Study* (for teachers), 1902. He was invited to Knoxville where he conducted a summer nature study course in 1903. His articles appeared in the *Review of Reviews* and *Cornell Countryman,* 1902–1903. The advice column appeared in the *Nature Study Review,* published by Columbia University's Teachers' College.

111 **variety of institutions:** See Carver to BTW, Mar. 3, 1903; Carver to E. J. Scott, Apr. 30, 1903 , BTW Collection, Library of Congress; Byrd T. Crawford to Carver, Oct. 14, 1904; N. E. Henry to Carver, Nov. 17, 1904, GWC Papers, Tuskegee Archives.

111 **took their minds out of Tuskegee:** "It is obvious that the Principal and his colleagues devoted as much time to investigating charges of improper conduct among the members of the faculty as they did violations of school rules by the students. Over and over, Washington was appointing officers of the institution to committees whose purpose was to investigate the reported indiscretions of teachers." Citro, p. 230.

112 **needs of the boarding department:** [Seventeen] Faculty Wives to the Principal, Apr. 4, Sept. 18, 1905; Mrs. E. J. Scott to BTW, Sept. 18, 1905, BTW Papers, Tuskegee Archives.

112 **committee's recommendations:** The first committee's recommendations were exactly those of the faculty wives, but the conditions were not improved. Letters of collective complaint continued coming in. Booker at first tabled them. Finally, in 1909, he appointed a committee and advised it to take plenty of time to study the high cost of goods at the commissary; then a year later he appointed another committee to investigate the same

complaints. Nothing was ever done. BTW to Mrs. H. E. Thomas, Mr. R. R. Taylor, et. al., May, June 21 and 22, July 20, 1909, May 5, 1910, BTW Collection, Library of Congress.

112   **would receive a reprimand:** For examples, see Citro, p. 120–126.

112   **protect the school's reputation:** Citro, pp. 233–239, lays out all the evidence of the case in which it seems certain that Reverend Penney was victimized by an unstable girl after he was required by Booker to lodge her in his home.

112   **chew gum in the offices:** Harlan, *Booker T. Washington,* p. 155.

112   **"improper house" in town:** For instances, see Mr. Cardozo to BTW, May 27, 1907, and an undated memo from Mr. Cardozo, 1907, in which he reports on several teachers violating all these rules. Executive Council Meeting Minutes, Oct. 26, Nov. 27, Dec. 4, 1899, Dec. 26, 1905; BTW to Faculty Members Derelict in Chapel Attendance, undated 1905; BTW to Mr. R. C. Stevens, May 29, 1907; BTW to Several Faculty Members, Dec. 2, 1913, BTW Papers, Tuskegee Archives.

112   **with a male colleague:** BTW to Jane E. Clark, Apr. 21, 1904. Clark volunteered that "Miss Shook is out a good deal with Mr. Chesnutt." Jane E. Clark to BTW, Mar. 19, 1906, BTW Papers, Tuskegee Archives.

112   **"out with gentlemen":** May 18, 1904.

112   **instead of the paths:** E. T. Attwell to BTW, Mr. Yates to R. R. Taylor, Feb. 19, 1907, all in Citro, p. 230.

112   **footsie under a table:** Citro, p. 231.

113   **married clandestinely:** BTW to Tuskegee teachers, Jan. 2, 1914, BTW Papers, Tuskegee Archives.

CHAPTER SEVEN. "Love and Lynch Mobs"

114   **Dreaming about marriage:** Lucy Cherry Crisp, "Carver," unpublished manuscript, Section VII, p. 18, Lucy Cherry Crisp Papers, Special Collections, Joyner Library, East Carolina University, Greenville, NC.

114   **lived . . . into the 1940s:** Toby Fishbein, interview with Austin Curtis, Detroit, Mar. 3, 1979, Carver Oral History Project, George Washington Carver Monument Archives, Diamond, MO.

115   **lady principal:** Adella Hunt, born in Sparta, Georgia, in 1863, attended Sparta's Bass Academy and Atlanta University, a Negro college. Taught at the American Missionary School before joining Tuskegee. Led monthly discussions on women's suffrage at Tuskegee; amassed a large library concerning suffrage. Lectured at conferences of the National Association of Colored Women's Clubs; wrote about women's rights in *The Crisis,* W. E. B. Du Bois's journal. Under Carver's name, she wrote articles for *The Negro Farmer.* See www.spartacus.schoolnet.co.uk/USAnaaacp.htm; H. L. Gates and E. B. Higginbotham, *African American National Biography,* vol. 5 (Oxford, 2008), pp. 293–295.

115   **grits, hot coffee, and fruit were lacking:** Carver to Booker T. Washington, Apr. 16, 1906, George Washington Carver Papers, Tuskegee Institute Archives. Mush is cornmeal pudding—tastier than the name might indicate.

115   **modeled on that of Yale:** Having merged with Clark College, the institution is now known as Clark Atlanta University.

116   **prodding him . . . stress on academic teaching:** Graduates of Tuskegee and Hampton were not considered college graduates; they could not transfer their credits to a higher institution—the Hampton and Tuskegee curricula were designed differently from other schools. To go to college, they had to start over in a regular four-year institution.

116   **"Let them use . . . in talking":** Quoted in Louis Harlan, *Booker T. Washington* (New York, 1983), p. 151.

116   **"his leader, Mr. Washington":** Adele Logan Alexander, "Grandmother, Grandfather, W. E. B. Du Bois, and Booker T. Washington," *The Crisis*, Feb. 1983.

116   **"didn't need to say anything":** "Carver," Section VII, p. 27, Lucy Cherry Crisp Papers. The loan was made in 1902 and repaid in 1907.

117   **from hooks over the flames:** Carver's friend Holtzclaw, the principal of Utica Institute in Mississippi, described the fire tragedies of several mutual friends; Holtzclaw to Carver, Utica (Jan. 10, 1929); [Name illegible], Barbourville, KY (Dec. 16, 1933), all in GWC Papers, Tuskegee Archives.

117   **three ghastly weeks:** Adele Logan Alexander, *Ambiguous Lives* (Fayetteville, AR, 1991), p. 193.

117   **with no one else at Tuskegee:** "Carver," VII, p. 17, Lucy Cherry Crisp Papers; see also Peter Duncan Burchard, interview with Adele Logan Alexander, Oct. 15–Nov. 6, 2004, Carver Oral History Project, GWC Monument Archives.

117   **Adella . . . children joined him there:** "Carver," VII, p. 27, Lucy Cherry Crisp Papers.

117   **he was thirty-seven or thirty-eight:** Burchard, interview with Adele Logan Alexander.

117   **Sarah played Desdemona:** *The Tuskegee Student*, May 5, 1900, Booker T. Washington Collection, Library of Congress, Washington, DC.

118   **threads of silver in his hair:** Carver to Mrs. Milholland, Feb. 28, 1905, GWC Papers, Tuskegee Archives.

118   **"promiscuous mingling . . . each night":** S. H. Porter and S. Ramsey to Exec. Council, Mar. 17, 1910, Booker T. Washington Papers, Tuskegee Institute Archives.

119   **way he was dressed . . . work he was doing:** Toby Fishbein, interview with Austin Curtis, Detroit, Carver Oral History Project, GWC Monument Archives.

119   **mania for presenting . . . perfect:** Peter Duncan Burchard, interview with Henry Deane, Tulsa, Oct. 31, 2004, Carver Oral History Project, GWC Monument Archives.

120   **something else entirely:** In a masterful study of Macon County in 1930, Charles S. Johnson, *Shadow of the Plantation* (Chicago, 1934), p. 148, describes white men living with black women without much fuss being made about it in either the black or white community. He also describes how black men of the area preferred darker women because "Light women want more." The general belief in the area regarding Tuskegee was that it wanted light students and that these more educated students in turn preferred light-complexioned partners.

120   **in both the South and the North:** Burchard, interview with Adele Logan Alexander.

120   **involved in incidents with white women:** *Montgomery Advertiser*, Mar. 7, 1904.

120   **Married . . . 32 years earlier:** Raymond W. Smock, *Booker T. Washington* (Chicago, 1909), p. 190.

121   **play the piano, but not to cook:** Alexander, *Ambiguous Lives*, pp. 128–129.

121   **father never lived with their mother:** *African American National Biography*; Alexander, *Ambiguous Lives*, pp. 156–159.

122   **suggestions . . . ought to be doing:** Booker to Bridgeforth, July 3, 1908, BTW Collection, Library of Congress; *Montgomery Advertiser*, Mar. 7, 1904. Seth Low (1850–1916) was an educator and political figure. He served as mayor of Brooklyn, President of Columbia University, diplomatic representative of the U. S., and Mayor of New York. A leading municipal reformer during the Progressive Era. Chairman of the board, Tuskegee Institute 1907–1916.

122   **"apostle of things as they were":** Raymond W. Smock, ed., *Booker T. Washington in Perspective: Essays of Louis R. Harlan* (Jackson, MS, 1988), p. 4.

123   **Jim Crow . . . height:** Booker's proposition came to be known as the "Atlanta Compromise." Jim Crow was a theater character created by Thomas D. Rice (d. 1860), based on a contemporary song, "Jim Crow." The term refers to laws and customs segregating and suppressing black people.

123   **outright terror:** A grandfather clause meant that a person could not register unless his grandfather had been a registered voter. Since their grandfathers had not been allowed to vote, black people were disqualified from voting.

123   **treated as an exception:** Booker T. Washington, *My Larger Education* (New York, 1911), p. 46.

125   **promoting his leadership dominance:** Joseph Citro, "Booker T. Washington's Tuskegee Institute," M.A. thesis, Univ. of Rochester, 1972, p. 78; Raymond W. Smock, *Booker T. Washington* (Chicago, 2009), p. 146 ff., gives details of Booker's control of the black press.

125   **plentiful and favorable:** Harlan, *Booker T. Washington*, pp. 59, 85, 95, 97, 105.

125   **fierce on both sides:** The Booker-Dubois machinations are detailed in Smock, *Booker T. Washington*, pp. 134–156.

125   **education, pure and simple:** *The Voice of the Negro*, Dec. 1904, quoted by Smock, ibid., p. 148.

125   **dedication to his race:** For a survey of Booker's covert challenges to white rule, see Louis R. Harlan, "The Secret Life of Booker T. Washington," in *Booker T. Washington in Perspective*, pp. 110–132; Smock, *Booker T. Washington*, pp. 134–156.

126   **his exclusive limelight:** For a full discussion of his tactics, see Smock, ibid, pp. 98–152, and Harlan, *Booker T. Washington*, pp. 153–173, 300, 334, 359–378.

126   **not hesitant about using that power:** Harlan, *Booker T. Washington*, "Preface"; see also Chapters 7 and 15, pp. 143–173 and 359–378.

126   **"who is helping the Negro up":** Oswald G. Villard, quoted in Smock, *Booker T. Washington in Perspective*, p. 193.

127   **"every room . . . is wet":** Maude Jackson to BTW, June 22, 1904, BTW Papers, Tuskegee Archives.

127   **soliciting new students:** Executive Council Minutes, Oct. 28, 1904; Oct. 7, Nov. 1, Nov. 18, 1909; Nov. 23, 1910; Jan. 6, 1911, BTW Papers, Tuskegee Archives.

127   **enable them . . . for the term:** BTW to Seth Low, June 18, 1907, Seth Low Papers, Columbia University.

127 **that did not teach them a trade:** M. N. Work et. al., to BTW and the Faculty, Mar. 30, 1914, BTW Collection, Library of Congress; E. T. Attwell to BTW, Feb. 9, 1907, BTW Papers, Tuskegee Archives.

127 **Privately . . . critical . . . administration:** Bruce's father had been a Mississippi senator during Reconstruction; his mother had been the dean of women at Tuskegee.

128 **black colleges of the time:** According to inspections made by the General Education Board of Alabama, work in these classes was equivalent to material covered in the third to fifth grades of the ordinary public school system. "Enrollment of Students in 1903–1904," 1904, BTW Papers, Tuskegee Archives; M. N. Work, "Report of a Study of Tuskegee Students," June 1910, M. N. Work Papers, Tuskegee Institute Archives; W. T. B. Williams, "Tuskegee Institute—Confidential to Members of the General Education Board," May, 1906, Seth Low Papers, Columbia University.

128 **equivalent . . . ninth grade education:** Students coming from schools such as Fisk were not required to take the placement exam because their preparation was "far above the work required here." General Faculty Meeting Minutes, Sept. 10, 1910, BTW Papers, Tuskegee Archives; W. T. B. Williams, Seth Low Papers, Columbia University.

128 **alumni list . . . qualifications:** W. T. B. Williams, ibid.

128 **"or how to trim them":** James R. Broddus to BTW, Feb. 7, 1904, BTW Papers, Tuskegee Archives.

128 **food of any sort was forbidden:** R. C. Bruce to BTW, Dec. 29, 1903, Dec. 30, 1904, BTW Papers, Tuskegee Archives. E. T. Attwell, asked to report on the industrial classes in 1907, found that none of the teachers had any sort of course outline or lesson plan. Nor could they tell him what they were going to teach from week to week. In the architectural drawing class, there were no textbooks. The instructor dictated from a book and the students copied what he said verbatim. That was virtually all that went on in the class. A theory class in brick masonry was totally consumed in figuring out an arithmetic problem. "Not more than 20 per cent of the boys present seemed to show that they even understood the figures or problems, no cost element, no materials to be used, no tools mentioned. Just the calculation of the number of bricks in the wall." E. T. Attwell to BTW, Feb. 9, 1907, BTW Papers, Tuskegee Archives.

128 **plight of the teacher:** Roscoe Conkling Bruce to BTW, n.d., 1904, Apr. 12, 1906, BTW Collection, Library of Congress. Bruce also inveighed against Tuskegee's low salaries, pointing out that they were lower than salaries of black grade school teachers in the North; junior faculty at Tuskegee earned $250–$300 plus board.

129 **defuse his wrath:** Alexander, "Grandmother," *The Crisis.*

CHAPTER EIGHT. "Wrestling with Devils"

130 **settle for discrediting him:** When in a hurry, Carver might misspell "Tuskegee," as well as other common words. But when he had his mind on his writing, Carver wrote correctly and eloquently. Bridgeforth's writing reflected haphazard schooling. J. H.'s was pretty good, overall.

130   **sorehead swept the state:** Sore head, or fowl pox, is characterized by raised, wart-like lesions on unfeathered areas such as the head and legs. The lesions heal but cause a decline in laying. In the wet form of the disease, the chickens develop canker-like lesions in the mouth, throat, and trachea which prevent breathing. The disease is spread by contact and by mosquitoes. In Carver's time, there was yet no vaccination, and farmers were helpless against the disease.

130   **recommendations . . . with copies to Booker:** Bridgeforth to Carver and BTW, Jan. 18, 1904; Bridgeforth to BTW, Feb. 28, 1906; Mar. 30, Apr. 15, 1907, George Washington Carver Papers, Tuskegee Institute Archives.

131   **in proportion to their return:** Carver to BTW, 1902, Carver to BTW, Jan. 17, 1902, Booker T. Washington Collection, Library of Congress.

131   **"shifting priorities":** Carver to BTW, Mar. 7, 1904, ibid.

131   **were passed over his head:** "For reasons which I am wholly unable to discern," he wrote, "many times no attention is paid to my wishes." Carver to BTW, 1902, Booker T. Washington Papers, Tuskegee Institute Archives.

131   **had no such burden:** Carver to Booker, Jan. 20, 1904, GWC Papers, Tuskegee Archives; Carver to Booker, Mar. 7, 1904, BTW Collection, Library of Congress.

131   **Carver's investigative vigil:** Rackham Holt, *George Washington Carver* (New York, 1948), p. 214.

131   **"stay by Mr. Washington":** Wilson to Carver, July 25, 1904, James A. "Tama" Wilson Papers, 1835–1920, Special Collections, Parks Library, Iowa State University.

132   **"he always inspires me":** Carver to Wilson, Aug. 5, 1904, ibid.

132   **dead chickens "all at once":** Minutes of the Executive Council, Oct. 12, 1904, BTW Papers, Tuskegee Archives. Carver had given over a great part of the management to Bridgeforth, but when the poultry yard showed significant losses, he turned to Barrows.

132   **involved in "the deception":** Carver to BTW, Oct. 14, 1904, GWC Papers, Tuskegee Archives; BTW to Carver, Oct. 13, 1904, BTW Collection, Library of Congress.

132   **impressive quantity of eggs and chickens:** Carver to BTW, Oct. 19, 1904, GWC Papers, Tuskegee Archives; BTW to Carver, Oct. 20, 1904, BTW Collection, Library of Congress.

133   **"with the Prin. of the school today":** Bridgeforth to Carver, Nov. 2, 1904, GWC Papers, Tuskegee Archives. Carver's "Short Course in Agriculture," eventually offered free for two weeks to farmers and their wives, proved quite successful. By 1912, over 1,500 were enrolled.

133   **or even reprimand him:** Bridgeforth to Carver, Dec. 6, 1904, E. J. Scott to Carver, Mar. 1, 1905; Bridgeforth to Carver, Mar. 2, 1905; Booker to Carver, May 17, 1906; BTW to Carver, Dec. 14, 1904, GWC Papers, Tuskegee Archives; Minutes of the Executive Council, Apr. 8, 1905, BTW Papers, Tuskegee Archives.

133   **under Bridgeforth's authority:** BTW to J. H. Washington, Oct. 11, 1904, BTW Papers, Tuskegee Archives.

134   **"native to our state":** Carver to BTW, Nov. 8, 1904, BTW Collection, Library of Congress.

134   **decided to stay in Tuskegee:** Carver to Wilson, Nov. 17, 1904, James A. Wilson Collection, National Archives Record Group 5, Washington, DC; Ralph W. McGranahan to Carver, Nov. 6, 22, Dec. 19, 1904, Jan. 26, Feb. 22, 1905; Wilson to Carver, Nov. 21, 1904; Carver to Wilson, Nov. 28, 1904, GWC Papers, Tuskegee Archives.

134 **institution with 83 buildings:** And an endowment of $1.3 million; Lucy Cherry Crisp, "Carver," unpublished manuscript, Section VII, pp. 25–26, Lucy Cherry Crisp Papers, Special Collections, Joyner Library, East Carolina University, Greenville, NC.

134 **making his report too long:** Carver to BTW, Mar. 30, 1906, GWC Papers, Tuskegee Archives.

135 **"It is my intention to give you more":** Carver to BTW, Nov. 14, 1904, BTW Collection, Library of Congress.

135 **to settle the matter himself:** Carver to BTW, Oct. 14, 19, Nov. 8, 19, Dec. 7, 1904; BTW to Carver, Dec. 14, 1904; GWC Papers, Tuskegee Archives.

135 **inflict stings . . . opportunity:** "Mr. Carver: I return the Within drawing. It really means nothing to me. It shows no dimensions, details, or anything upon which I can draw conclusions. You will want to return the Within recommendations at the same time that you return a better drawing." BTW to Carver, June 2, 1905, GWC Papers, Tuskegee Archives. See, also, BTW to Carver, Apr. 6, 1905, ibid.

136 **"should take the other half":** Wilson to Carver, Dec. 20, 1906, GWC Papers, Tuskegee Archives.

136 **were constantly attacked:** Carver to BTW, May 10, 1906, ibid.

136 **Bridgeforth snippily refused:** "It would greatly inconvenience me just now . . . It seems to me from what I have seen of the work that it needs organization." Bridgeforth to Carver, Sept. 7, 1909, GWC Papers, Tuskegee Archives.

136 **to help him clean the yard:** Carver to BTW, Sept. 6, 8, 9, 1909, BTW Collection, Library of Congress, and BTW Papers, Tuskegee Archives.

136 **for throwing out eggs:** BTW to Carver, Apr. 3, May 12, 1909, BTW Collection, Library of Congress.

136 **"Boarding Department at once":** BTW to Carver, May 12, 1909, BTW Papers, Tuskegee Archives.

137 **"help, real help":** Carver to BTW, May 12, 1909, BTW Papers, Tuskegee Archives.

137 **out of the incubators . . . timely fashion:** Carver to BTW, Apr. 26, 1909; BTW to Carver, NY, May 1, 1909, BTW Collection, Library of Congress.

137 **"that you will succeed":** BTW to Carver, May 2, 1909, BTW Papers, Tuskegee Archives.

137 **"regardless of difficulties":** Carver to BTW, May 4, 1909, BTW Collection, Library of Congress.

137 **"doing what you can do":** Wilson to Carver, Apr. 29, 1909, GWC Papers, Tuskegee Archives.

137 **endure Booker's needling:** In a speech Carver gave about substituting carrots for corn, Carver's explanation had been "too complicated": "I am quite sure that if you talk the matter over with Mr. Bridgeforth that you and he can hit upon a scheme that will be much simpler and more practical." BTW to Carver, Sept. 7, 1909, BTW Papers, Tuskegee Archives. Advising Carver to keep in closer touch with his workers in the poultry yard, Booker could not resist mentioning, "You have had some serious lessons in this connection, which I hope you will take advantage of in the future." BTW to Carver, Oct. 2, 1909, ibid.

137 **"December, January, and February":** BTW to Carver, Huntington, Long Island, Aug. 16, 1909, BTW Collection, Library of Congress.

138   **he decided . . . should be grown instead:** Carver to BTW, Feb. 11, 1911, BTW Papers, Tuskegee Archives. See Carver's plans for planting and his closing, "Of course, this is subject to whatever changes you wish to make," Oct. 2, 1909, BTW Papers, Tuskegee Archives.

138   **Carver was working alone:** Minutes, Executive Council, May 12, 17, 1909, Sept. 20, 1909; Carver to BTW, Sept. 6, 1909, BTW Papers, Tuskegee Archives.

138   **a bulletin once in a while:** BTW to Carver, May 12, 1909, GWC Papers, Tuskegee Archives.

138   **giving him back . . . in November:** But in restoring Carver to any position, Booker saw to it that he was deprived of whatever help he needed to succeed. BTW to Carver, Apr. 15, May 1, 2, and 12, 1909, ibid. Booker made it clear that in all disputes, Bridgeforth had the final authority and Carver was his subordinate. J. H. Washington and Bridgeforth to BTW, Oct. 20, 1910; Minutes, Executive Council, Nov. 10, 1910; BTW to Carver and Bridgeforth, Nov. 16, 19, 1910, BTW Collection, Library of Congress.

139   **"manipulate . . . that he has been doing in the past":** BTW to Bridgeforth, Nov. 23, 25, Dec. 3, 9, 1910, New York, BTW Papers, Tuskegee Archives.

139   **"Bridgeforth has the authority to decide":** Committee Report, Nov. 10, 1910; BTW to Bridgeforth, Bridgeforth to BTW, Nov. 16, 1910; BTW to Bridgeforth and Carver, Nov. 16, 1910, ibid.

139   **doing his life's work:** Wilson to Carver, Nov. 27, 1910, James A. Wilson Collection, National Archives, Washington, D.C.; Wilson to Carver, May 15, 1910, James A. "Tama" Wilson Papers, 1835–1920, Parks Library, Iowa State University; Wilson to Carver, June 21, 1901, BTW Papers, Tuskegee Archives.

139   **"fitted up for Professor Carver":** Committee Report to BTW, Nov. 21, 1910; BTW to Carver, Nov. 23, 1910; Carver to BTW, May 4, 1912, in which he complains that hardly any of the promises were kept; BTW to Carver, Sept. 11, 1911; GWC Papers, Tuskegee Archives.

140   **"you may elaborate":** Wilson to Carver, Dec. 10, 1910, GWC Papers, Tuskegee Archives.

140   **congratulations . . . Milhollands:** 1910, GWC Papers, ibid.

140   **"time has come . . . frankness":** BTW to Carver, Feb. 26, 1911, June 1912, BTW Collection, Library of Congress.

141   **might be fitted up "gradually":** BTW to Carver, June 6, 1912, GWC Papers, Tuskegee Archives.

141   **such as precision scales:** "List of Basic Apparatus," Carver to E. J. Scott, Sept. 13, 1911, ibid.

141   **lacked essential connecting pieces:** "I do not think it is fair to deceive ourselves that we have a workable laboratory when we have not." As late as the mid-1930s, according to one account, Carver still did not have an autoclave for sterilizing equipment. Carver to BTW, Sept. 5, 11, 14, 1911, May 4, Dec. 20, 1912; BTW to Carver, Sept. 7, 1911; Carver to E. J. Scott, Sept. 13, 1911; E. T. Attwell to Carver, Oct. 29, 1912; Minutes of the Executive Council, Mar. 29, 1912; BTW to Carver, June 2, 1911; Oct. 12, 1912, BTW Papers, Tuskegee Archives.

141   **out of his own funds:** Carver pleaded with Booker to relieve him of the "constant uncertainty" regarding whether or not he would have a lab. Carver to BTW, Oct. 29, 1912, June 2, 1911, ibid.

141   "1,000 laying hens": Carver to BTW, June 2, 1911, BTW Papers, Tuskegee Archives.

141   **thanks and good wishes:** In preparing to leave, Carver gave an account of conditions in the poultry yard. The Business Committee had ignored his repeated requests for repairs; hence, the yard contained rotting posts, windows without panes, and buildings about to collapse. Carver to BTW, Dec. 28, 1912, GWC Papers, Tuskegee Archives.

141   **civil service examination:** Wilson to Carver, Jan. 2, 1913, James A. Wilson Collection, National Archives.

141   **"a single piece of apparatus":** Carver to BTW, Dec. 13, 1912, GWC Papers, Tuskegee Archives. In 1913, Carver finished the survey, identifying eleven different kinds of soils in Macon County, indicating how each should be cultivated and the best crops for each. Experiment Station Bulletin 25, BTW Papers, Tuskegee Archives.

142   **provoked Booker . . . chide him for his failure:** BTW to Bridgeforth, May 4, 1910, BTW Collection, Library of Congress.

142   **"suggestions of the passers":** BTW to Bridgeforth, Dec. 1910; Bridgeforth to Booker, Dec. 20, 1910, ibid.

142   **usefulness . . . was wearing out:** Inspecting the agricultural building, now under Bridgeforth's exclusive supervision, he found that "everything was dead." BTW to Bridgeforth (copy to the Executive Council), Feb. 26, 1910, ibid; BTW to Carver, Oct. 23, 1909, GWC Papers, Tuskegee Archives.

142   **pickling solution under Carver's direction:** Bridgeforth demurred, prompting irritation from Booker at last. BTW to Bridgeforth, Dec. 9, 13, 1911, BTW Papers, Tuskegee Archives.

142   **"not so vigorous as I am now":** Carver to Milholland, undated, 1911, GWC Monument Archives, Diamond, MO.

143   **The washes were used . . . over the next years:** In 1914 he furnished the school with 48 gallons of paints and stains and 453 gallons of calcimine. Carver to H. E. Thomas, July 2, to J. H. Washington, Aug. 7, to Mr. Fearing, Aug 22, 1912, to E. J. Scott, June 4, 1914; BTW to Carver, Sept. 8, Dec. 10, 1913, Jan. 23, 24, 1914; Bulletin 21, 1911, GWC Papers, Tuskegee Archives.

143   **wood scraps as he could find:** Rackham Holt, pp. 232, 233.

143   **"other sections of the country":** Carver to BTW, Apr. 3, 1911; John H. Washington to Carver, May 27, 1911, BTW Papers, Tuskegee Archives.

143   **bring the school . . . publicity:** Carver to BTW, May 29, 1911, ibid.

143   **"without support to work with":** Carver to BTW, Sept. 11, 1911, ibid.

144   **"it is a home product":** Episcopal church to Carver, Mar. 23, 1912, GWC Papers, Tuskegee Archives.

144   **all such donations:** Rosenwald to Carver, Chicago, Mar. 19, May 5, 1915; Carver to Rosenwald, May 25, 1915, ibid.

144   **"going in" with Scott:** Carver to Scott, Sept. 7, 9, 1911, BTW Papers, Tuskegee Archives.

144   **wanted to manufacture his paints:** Fitzpatrick Drug Co. to Carver, May 20, 31, 1912, GWC Papers, Tuskegee Archives.

145   **"verifying its purity":** E. T. Attwell, Business Agent, to Carver, Oct. 29, 1912, BTW Collection, Library of Congress.

145   **useful item . . . prominent visitors:** Steward to Carver, Sept. 4, 1912, ibid.

145   **mattresses . . . filled with straw:** Carver to E. J. Scott, Mar. 15, 1912; Carver to BTW, May 7, 1912, June 17, 1913, BTW Collection, Library of Congress; Minutes of the Executive Council, June 15, 1915, BTW Papers, Tuskegee Archives.

145   **leaflets . . . rural school houses:** Carver to BTW, Aug. 31, 1912, Nov. 30, 1914, BTW Collection, Library of Congress.

145   **"trash, rubbish, garbage, etc.":** Carver to J. H., June 11, 1915, ibid.; Peter Duncan Burchard, interview with Eliot Battle, Columbia, Missouri, Nov. 1, 2004, Carver Oral History Project, GWC Monument Archives.

145   **fertilizer . . . essential to crop yield:** For cotton and other crops, he used pine straw, oak leaves, and swamp muck. These provided the largest concentration of the three essential elements of plant feed—potash, phosphoric acid, and nitrogen; see Carver to BTW, Aug. 1, 1912, GWC Papers, Tuskegee Archives.

146   **abjured commercial fertilizer:** Carver to J. H. Washington, Apr. 5, 1911; Minutes of the Executive Council, Dec. 1912, BTW Papers, Tuskegee Archives.

146   **research was still in its infancy:** The central role of proteins in living organisms was not fully understood until 1926.

146   **all made from peanuts:** Carver to BTW, Apr. 5, 1911, BTW Papers, Tuskegee Archives; Rackham Holt, p. 224.

146   **quietly disposed . . . had departed:** Oral History Recordings, GWC Monument Exhibit, Diamond, MO.

146   **fifty bolls and squares:** Carver to Wilson, July 2, 1912, James A. Wilson Papers, National Archives.

146   **potatoes and wild plums:** Tuskegee Institute Experiment Station Bulletins 10 and 12, BTW Papers, Tuskegee Archives.

147   **pickled meat preserved by the school:** J. H. Washington to Carver, Jan. 4, 1912, GWC Papers, Tuskegee Archives. Bulletin 24, 1912, was "The Pickling and Curing of Meat in Hot Weather." Bulletin 27 in 1915 gave instructions on home canning fruits and vegetables.

147   **potato laundry starch and syrup:** "Peel and grate the potato. Put the grated food in a cheesecloth bag, dip it in water, and squeeze it. Repeat this dipping and squeezing until no more milky juice comes out. Let the water settle and pour off the clear top liquid. Stir the paste again with more water, let it settle again, and pour it off. The result is starch. If the water washings are boiled down, they yield a good syrup." Rackham Holt, pp. 179–180.

148   **"absolutely beautiful":** Carver to BTW, Jan. 18, 1912, GWC Papers, Tuskegee Archives.

148   **to prepare them for the printer:** Carver to BTW, June 3, 20, 1912, BTW Papers, Tuskegee Archives.

148   **garnered praise from everywhere:** See, among many examples, Carver to BTW, June 20, 1912; the Deputy Commissioner for Education for Massachusetts cited Carver's bulletins as "among the very best." C. A. Prosser to John H. Wilkinson, Mar. 4, 1911, GWC Papers, Tuskegee Archives.

148   **too many postage stamps:** Yale University to Carver, June 4, 1909; Secretary to Carver, Apr. 26, 1911; requests for Carver's bulletins from China, Jan. 12, 1914. Meanwhile, Carver

is asked to put a rubber band around his letters and send a memorandum of the date and destination of each letter so that an accurate "stamp account" could be kept. BTW to Carver, Apr. 13, 1912, GWC Papers, Tuskegee Archives.

148 **funds from the government:** Wilson to Carver, Aug. 17, 1911, James A. Wilson Papers, National Archives.

148 **for staying on Carver's good side:** Carver to BTW, Dec. 25, 1914, BTW Collection, Library of Congress.

148 **"a certain Dr. Brody":** Bridgeforth to Carver, Sept. 11, 1915, GWC Papers, Tuskegee Archives.

149 **harsh feelings . . . their adversaries:** H. B. Bennett to Carver, Stallo, MS, Dec. 18, 1910, ibid.

149 **to get a front row seat:** Carver to BTW, May 28, 1907, BTW Collection, Library of Congress; Carver to Mr. Griffith, July 3, 1916, GWC Papers, Tuskegee Archives; Rackham Holt, p. 198.

150 **who was also somewhat aged:** Robert P. Fuller, "Report on Project #4, Moses Carver and His Family," c. 1951, United States Department of the Interior, National Park Service, George Washington Carver Monument Archives, Diamond, MO.

150 **buried somewhere on his property:** Deposition by Moses Carver in *Carver v. Carver*, Mar. 17, 1902, in GWC Monument Archives.

151 **never bought . . . in his entire life:** "Carver," VIII, p. 2, Lucy Cherry Crisp Papers.

CHAPTER NINE. "Bad Days and Worse"

153 **Across the factional divide:** Adele Logan Alexander, "Grandmother, Grandfather, W. E. B. Du Bois, and Booker T. Washington," *The Crisis* 90, no. 2 (Feb. 1983).

153 **Gossip . . . through the vines of Tuskegee:** "The Logan family travails became the subject of whispers throughout the insular Tuskegee community." Ibid.

154 **"dies by his own hand":** J. H. Kellogg, "Treatment for Self-Abuse . . ." *Plain Facts for Old and Young* (Burlington, Iowa, 1888).

154 **"Watch Your Bowels":** *Montgomery Advertiser,* Sept. 7, 11, 1930, ff.

155 **accompany her to the Sanitarium:** BTW to Warren Logan, Sept, 19, 1915; BTW to John Harvey Kellogg, Oct. 14, 1915; Booker T. Washington Collection, Library of Congress.

155 **She was fifty-two years old:** Various sources give dates ranging from Dec. 10 to Dec. 15.

156 **"dedicate this bulletin":** Bulletin No. 36, Tuskegee Institute Archives.

156 **her cousin, Felix Rogers:** Peter Duncan Burchard, interview with Adele Logan Alexander, Oct. 15–Nov. 6, 2004, Carver Oral History Project, George Washington Carver Monument Archives, Diamond MO.

157 **jailed . . . against the Great War:** "This awful war is beyond my comprehension, but God knows what it is all about and I can trust Him to bring us to the end all right." Carver to Mrs. Milholland, Dec. 16, 1917, GWC Monument Archives, Diamond, MO.

157 **"he gave his life":** Scott to Carver, New York, Jan. 26, 1911; Carver to Scott, Denmark, SC, Feb. 15, 1916; Booker T. Washington Papers, Tuskegee Institute Archives.

CHAPTER TEN. "The Curtain Lifts"

158 **renamed Rio Roosevelt:** "I had to go," Roosevelt wrote. "It was my last chance to be a boy." *New York Times*, Dec. 13, 1915.

158 **"worked, walked nor talked down":** Quoted by Rackham Holt, *George Washington Carver* (New York, 1948), p. 234.

158 **succeed Booker as president:** Probably the *New York Times* paid diligent attention to the issue because Seth Low of Columbia University was chairman of the Tuskegee board. *New York Times*, Nov. 30, Dec. 28, 1915.

159 **R. R. Moton, Principal:** George Washington Carver Papers, Tuskegee Institute Archives.

160 **he . . . repeated no criticism:** Carver to Moton, Apr. 13, 1927, ibid.

160 **sixteen foreign countries:** Carver to Business Committee, Aug. 29, 1927, ibid.

160 **1 million dollars from John D. Rockefeller:** Carver to Moton, Feb. 26, 1925, Apr. 10, 1925; Moton to Carver, Feb. 28, 1925, GWC Papers, Tuskegee Archives.

160 **he . . . was turned down:** Carver wrote to the business committee explaining that he had one grinder that would mill only grains and another only for roots, barks, and herbs. He needed one for stones and abrasives, as he was still examining rocks for farmers and companies. Carver to Mr. Johnston, Dec. 17, 1929, ibid.

160 **personal request to Moton:** Menafee to Carver, Denmark, SC, Mar. 15, 1919; Carver to Moton, Jan. 6, 1930, ibid.

161 **highest and best in life after all:** Carver to Moton, July 18, 1919; Secretary to Carver, July, 25, 1919; Moton to Carver, July 21, 1919; Carver to Moton, Sept. 9, 1919, GWC Papers, Tuskegee Archives. Carver was still petitioning for a full-time secretary in 1922. Carver to Moton, July 18, 1922, ibid. However, he remained very kindly disposed to Moton.

161 **to write . . . and give talks:** E. C. Sage to Carver, New York, NY, Dec. 11, 1916; E. J. Scott to Carver, Dec. 21, 1916; Elizabeth Macdonald to Carver, Boston, Sept. 12, 1917; G. Sheppard to Carver, Banks, Oregon, Oct. 2, 1917; Thompson Kelley Mining Co. to E. J. Scott, Seattle, Nov. 24, 1916; GWC Papers, Tuskegee Archives.

161 **the next day for blacks:** Miscellaneous documents, GWC Papers, Tuskegee Archives.

161 **introduced by Luther Burbank:** A. W. Jacobs to Carver, Los Angeles, Feb. 16, 1916, GWC Papers, Tuskegee Archives. Though he accepted honors from organizations backed by Du Bois, Carver confided to his old friend Lyman Ward that ever since Du Bois had unfairly criticized Abraham Lincoln, he had not felt warm toward him.

161 **I shall never attain . . . Mr. Burbank:** Carver to Moton, Mar. 1, 1910; Oct. 21, 1918, GWC Papers, Tuskegee Archives.

162 **questions from the assemblage:** Lucy Cherry Crisp, "Carver," unpublished manuscript, Section VIII, pp. 7–8, Lucy Cherry Crisp Papers, Special Collections, Joyner Library, East Carolina University, Greenville, NC.

162 **Vendevere's . . . soft drinks:** Miscellaneous documents, GWC Papers, Tuskegee Archives.

162 **he drew out 536 dyes:** Rackham Holt, p. 237.

163 **"Wizard of Tuskegee":** Ibid., p. 248.

163 **took his place . . . Charles Darwin:** *The Economist*, Jan. 9, 2010; H. F. Wood to Carver, London, Nov. 29, 1916, GWC Papers, Tuskegee Archives. The Royal Society celebrated its

350th anniversary in 2010, having been organized in the seventeenth century by followers of Sir Francis Bacon, who convinced the world that ideas should be tested by experiments. The society originated many of the conventions of modern science, such as scientific publishing and peer review, and made English the primary language of scientific discourse. The French Academy of Sciences, founded in 1666, and the American Association for the Advancement of Science, founded in 1848, were similar organizations.

163 **courteously and gratefully declined:** "Carver," IX, 2, Lucy Cherry Crisp Papers; Rackham Holt, p. 248.

163 **offer . . . gracefully resisted:** George Philips to Carver, July 19, 1929, GWC Papers, Tuskegee Archives.

163 **request . . . gently rebuffed:** Lucille Proctor to Carver, Jackson, MS, Feb. 3, Mar. 2, 1922, GWC Papers, Tuskegee Archives.

165 **practical American sense:** Although Tesla accepted an *Edison Medal* later in life, he never got over his bitter experience; *New York Times*, Oct. 19, 1931.

165 **"the credit of whatever I may do":** Quoted by Rackham Holt, p. 248.

165 **plans for international peace:** Clark Howell to Carver, Washington, DC, Feb. 14, 1919, GWC Papers, Tuskegee Archives.

166 **provide for a farmer and his brood:** He produced the corn on two acres. On the other plats, he raised the hay, along with peas, velvet beans, and other food crops.

166 **400 pounds of seed cotton:** Carver to Moton, Sept. 5, 1916, GWC Papers, Tuskegee Archives.

167 **large orders for the military:** Rubber: F. A. Wilson to Carver, Minneapolis, n.d., 1920; mica: A. R. Moseler and Co. to Carver, New York, Feb. 21, 1922, GWC Papers, Tuskegee Archives. Both wanted to form a company with Carver.

167 **Carver to Washington for consultation:** "Carver," IX, p. 3, Lucy Cherry Crisp Papers.

167 **peanut milk . . . commercial interest:** Musker and Co. to Carver, Nov. 26, 1919; Walter Grubbs to Carver, Oct. 1, 1919; Prophytol Manufacturing to Carver, New Orleans, Apr. 17, 1920; American Products to Carver, Los Angeles, Nov. 12, 1921, GWC Papers, Tuskegee Archives.

167 **other Carver Products:** John Carlow to Carver, Philadelphia, Dec. 27, 1921, ibid.

168 **not widely marketed:** By 1855 there were two patented procedures for drying milk. Today, milk is first concentrated to 50 percent volume in an evaporator and then sprayed into a heated chamber, which causes the rest of the liquid to evaporate, leaving fine particles of milk solids. With Carver's limited equipment, he may have spread the concentrated liquid on to a heated surface and then scraped off the dried milk solids. This would probably have yielded milk with a slightly scorched flavor, but doubtless the babies whom it was meant for did not notice. Or alternatively, Carver may have tried freeze-drying the milk, a process that preserves more of its nutrients.

168 **soy milk and soy baby food:** Carver to W. E. Tabb, Feb. 16, 1929; Dr. W. S. Hughlett, Cocoa, FL, to Carver, May 28, 1929; Carver to R. B. Eleazer, Nov. 29, 1930; Baptist Missionary Society to Carver, London, May 6, 1931, GWC Papers, Tuskegee Archives.

168 **patenting his peanut milk:** Carver to Mrs. Milholland, July 27, 1920, ibid.

168 **"not worth such an effort":** Carver to W. H. Crosby, Feb. 13, 1937; Carver to Dr. H. A. Tassell, M.D., July 9, 1941, ibid.

170 **into the hearts of the peanut men:** Rackham Holt, pp. 253–254, quoting the October 1920 issue of the journal.

170 **dirty train car reserved for black passengers:** Carver had recently been in Boston, where he attended church services. The minister recounted the meeting, which occurred a few weeks before his presentation to the congressmen: "A tall, lean, lanky colored man . . . a pure African, who seemed to have no connection with the rather well-dressed group, but wore a shabby suit, dusty boots, and by way of contrast, a delicate flower in his worn button hole. His whole attitude was that of a very plain, unassuming townsman . . . When the service was over and I was shaking hands with the men, this lanky fellow moved up and gave me his hand. 'Good morning, Sir,' he said in a high-pitched voice, 'I'm Professor Carver.'" "Imagine," the minister continued, "Carver, the peanut wizard!" "Carver," IX, p. 5, Lucy Cherry Crisp Papers.

173 **his seat in the separated car:** Carver to George W. Owens, July 10, 1924, "Carver," IX, pp. 28–29, Lucy Cherry Crisp Papers.

173 **industry had ever enjoyed:** Rackham Holt, pp. 256–259; "Carver," IX, p. 8, Lucy Cherry Crisp Papers, quoting Jan. 1921 *Congressional Record*.

173 **dyes, munitions, and other applications:** Carver to Henry C. Wallace, Apr. 15, 1921, Henry A. Wallace Papers, National Archives, Washington, DC. Carver to Moton, Apr. 18, 1921; Tennessee River Improvement Association to Carver, Washington, DC, Apr. 27, 1921, GWC Papers, Tuskegee Archives. The U.S. Department of Agriculture, when receiving requests for information on the nutritional properties of certain fruits and vegetables, especially the peanut, began sending them to Tuskegee for reply. USDA to Moton, Washington, DC, June 10, 1932, GWC Papers Tuskegee Archives.

174 **misleading of mobs searching for another:** *The Tuskegee News*, Jan. 8, 1920, quoting a report by the Department of Records and Research of Tuskegee Institute. An 1896 newspaper account described a lynching in Alabama: "The negro confessed that he was the man who had struck the fatal blow . . . He begged for mercy but there was no mercy in the crowd and they quickly took him to a place in the woods a short distance from the road, with his hands tied, and allowing him a short while in which to pray, leveled their rifles and shotguns at him and sent his soul into eternity in a jiffy." *Montgomery Advertiser*, Oct. 11, 1896.

174 **raising money for Tuskegee:** Carver to J. W. Bergthold (secretary) Oct. 29, 1924. Carver responded graciously as always to Moton's congratulations: "It is my aim to do my little job better and better every day so I can be of real service to you who has the entire burden upon your shoulders." Carver to Moton, Utica, MS, Feb. 11, 21, GWC Papers, Tuskegee Archives.

174 **overflowing appreciation:** Moton to Carver, Dec. 17, 1922, ibid.

174 **"so you can see God in it":** Peter Duncan Burchard, interview with Dr. Sheridan Howard Settler Jr., Tuskegee, Oct. 26, 2004, Carver Oral History Project; Carver to Jim Hardwick, Nov. 7, 1923, GWC National Monument Archives, Diamond, MO.

175 **making himself quite at home:** Burchard, interview with Neutrice Nelson Merritt, Oct. 20, 2004, Clinton, NC, Carver Oral History Project, GWC Monument Archives.

175 **derelict appearance . . . invoked:** "Carver," IX, p. 9, Lucy Cherry Crisp Papers, quoting an unnamed newspaper article. "Every day, farmers, peanut growers, chemists, manufactur-

ers, merchants, and people in all walks of life gathered around Professor Carver's unique exhibit and marveled at the wonderful discoveries of the colored man who has shown the world the wide range of possibilities possessed by the peanut . . . A full-blooded Negro, tall, elderly . . . Professor Carver was rather disappointing in appearance to many . . . Two middle-aged white farmers . . . exclaimed, 'My God, is that him!'"

175 **suitcases full of them:** Burchard, interview with Dr. Benny Mayberry, Oct. 22, 2004, Montgomery, Carver Oral History Project, GWC Monument Archives.

175 **"field of human endeavor":** The committee making the award included Theodore Roosevelt, then Secretary of the Navy, W. E. B. Dubois, and Dorothy Canfield Fischer. "Carver," IX, p. 10, Lucy Cherry Crisp Papers.

175 **"no regret that it came this way":** Carver to Major J. E. Spingarn, Oct. 8, 1925, GWC Papers, Tuskegee Archives.

175 **violence . . . sharply rising:** Carver to Moton, Mississippi, Feb. 11, 1921, ibid.

175 **"taken things by storm here":** Menafee to Carver, Denmark, SC, Feb. 27, 1922, ibid.

176 **huddled inside . . . houses:** R. M. White, "Kenney Memorial Hospital," *Journal of the National Medical Ass.* 91, no. 5 (1999).

176 **acidity . . . in Macon County:** Where lime rock did not exist, the acidity of the soil had to be corrected, he thought, by adding to each acre several tons of caustic lime, agricultural lime and ground limestone, that is, the compound "Mellosoil." Carver to Moton, June 6, 1924, GWC Papers, Tuskegee Archives.

CHAPTER ELEVEN. "Trying to Be Serious"

Unless otherwise noted, correspondence to and from Carver may be found in the George Washington Carver Papers, Tuskegee Institute Archives.

177 **stooped over, and shuffling:** The exception is Lucy Cherry Crisp, who knew him when he was sixty, but whose biography was never published.

178 **"phone" . . . novel abbreviation . . . uneasy:** Carver to B. Lewis, Feb. 26, 1928; Carver to Huston, Oct. 16, 1928, George Washington Carver Papers, Tuskegee Institute Archives.

178 **finally purchased for him:** Carver to [illegible], Dec. 16, 1917, Miscellaneous Documents, George Washington Carver, Monument Archives, Diamond, MO.

178 **"Hello! How are you?" etc.:** Carver to Booker T. Washington, Sept. 13, 1902, Booker T. Washington Collection, Library of Congress.

178 **and he responded:** Peter Duncan Burchard, interview with Carolyn Ford, Tuskegee, Oct. 24–25, 2005, Carver Oral History Project, GWC Monument Archives, Diamond, MO.

178 **"someone else over that mountain":** Burchard, interview with Dr. Frederick Kennedy, San Pedro, CA, Nov. 5, 2004, ibid.

178 **"gives me light and strength":** Carver to Glenn Clark, Feb. 27, 1928.

178 **bedroom, kitchenette, and bathroom:** Lucy Cherry Crisp, "Carver," unpublished manuscript, Section VIII, p. 19, Lucy Cherry Crisp Papers, Special Collections, Joyner Library, East Carolina University, Greenville, NC.

179 **"pig or chicken or something"**: Burchard, interview with Edward T. Braye, n.p., Oct. 26, 2004, GWC Monument Archives.

179 **"no time to clean them"**: Carver to J. H. Washington, Mar. 20, 1906.

179 **"wouldn't have mattered to him"**: Burchard, interview with Robert E. Garrett, Chicago, Nov. 3, 2004; interview with Carolyn Ford, Tuskegee, Oct. 23, 2004; interview with Jeanne Goodwin, Tulsa, Oct. 30, 2004, GWC Monument Archives.

179 **a modern tie**: G. Lake Imes, "I Knew Carver," manuscript, Harry O. Abbott Papers, GWC Monument Archives.

180 **"let's not discuss it"**: Burchard, interview with Robert E. Garrett, GWC Monument Archives.

180 **"missed your appointment"**: Information for the following paragraphs from Burchard, interviews with Dr. Adele McQueen, Silver Spring, MD, Oct. 17, 2004; Dr. Patricia McIntosh-Bell, Tulsa, Oct. 31, 2004; Mildred LaVerne Reed, Tulsa, Oct. 30, 2004; Robert E. Garrett, Chicago, Nov. 3, 2004; Gwendolyn Henderson, Tuskegee, Oct. 22, 2004; Edward Pryce, Tuskegee, Oct. 23, 2004; Elaine Freeman Thomas, Tuskegee, Oct. 24, 2004; GWC Monument Archives. "There was never any meanness about his character at all, but he would concentrate." Interview with Carolyn Ford, Tuskegee, Oct. 29, 2004, ibid.

181 **"Don't ever . . . on the Bible," he said**: Rackham Holt, *George Washington Carver* (New York, 1948), p. 241.

182 **"He has so wonderfully created"**: Carver to Jim Hardwick, Apr. 5, 1924, GWC Monument Archives.

182 **"God's wrath"**: "Carver," VII, p. 21, Lucy Cherry Crisp Papers.

182 **piano . . . their own dorm**: Carver to Moton, Nov. 13, 1924; Rosie Mitchell to Carver, Oct. 22, 1920.

182 **"a married man. SEE!"**: Ambrose Fauvier to Carver, Nashville, Dec. 1, 1917.

182 **people overestimated him**: Huston to Carver, July 20, 1931.

183 **"for your own good"**: Wilson L. Newman to Carver, Nashville, Sept. 18, 1926.

183 **chatting with flowers**: Peter Duncan Burchard, interview with Margaret Washington Clifford, Oct. 21, 2004, Atlanta; Cora Robinson-Lawson, Oct. 23, 2004, George H. Paris, Oct. 27, 2004, Robert L. Judkins, Oct. 27, 2004, Tuskegee, Helen Bratcher, Oct. 28, 2004, Nashville, GWC Monument Archives.

183 **hear more about this dialogue**: Burchard, interview with Arnold Williams, Oct. 30, 2004, Tulsa, GWC Monument Archives.

184 **"fall by the wayside"**: Carver to Mr. Carpenter, Dec. 11, 1927.

185 **"I am not forgotten"**: Carver to Miss. L. Coleman, Apr. 13, 1925: Carver analyzed every detail of the picture and explained why he appreciated it—a task of three pages.

185 **string of kids . . . Agriculture Building**: Burchard, interviews with James J. Lawson, Boyds, MD, Oct. 16, 2004; Edward Pryce, Tuskegee, Oct. 23, 2004; Toby Fishbein, interview with Austin Curtis, Detroit, Feb. 1, 1979; Burchard, interview with Dr. Sheridan Howard Settler Jr., M.D., Tuskegee, Oct. 26, 2004, GWC Monument Archives.

185 **for being in your midst**: Bessie and James Gayle to Carver, 1931. Burchard, interview with Thomas B. Hargrave, Silver Spring, MD, Oct. 5, 2006, GWC Monument Archives.

185 **named his son after Carver**: Walter Nickell to Carver, Detroit, 1931; Nov. 8, 1932. By

the 1930s, Carver had adult "grandsons" who carried his name. George Irwin to Carver, Detroit, Dec. 6, 1932.

185   **"honest and honorable"**: Burchard, interview with Abdul-Salaam Muhammad, Los Angeles, Nov. 6, 2004.

185   **only time . . . to lend money**: For one of dozens of examples, see Albert to Carver, July 7, 1908.

185   **"do something for a white student?"**: Rackham Holt, p. 196; see also J. M. Brown to Carver, Philadelphia, July 8, 1926, GWC Papers, Tuskegee Archives; Carver to W. M. Henry, Nov. 26, 1924, Iowa State University Archives.

185   **white students at Tuskegee**: Carver to Principal Patterson, Feb. 7, 1940.

185   **annual checks**: Noramiller Carver Coar, West Point, GA, Jan. 2, 1926; Carver to Helen Chisholm, Jan. 4, 1926.

186   **Ernest Blanks**: Blanks to Carver, Aug. 17, 1924.

186   **"should have been a better man"**: Carver to Hardwick, Apr. 5, 1924, Tuskegee, GWC Monument Archives.

186   **"Your grandchild"**: Names of former students and young people who wrote to Carver in 1930: Charles Shedd, Ernest J. Frei, Clarence Hart, I. B. Talton, Charles Albert, Charles Harmon, Raymond Lester, Forrest Brown, Clinton Belknap, W. W. Thompson, J. L. Bryant, Wilson Newman, Stephen Brown, Jim Boysell, Paul Guthrie, George Phillips, Arthur Faust, W. P. Nickell, Chester Stevens, Alice Simmons, Ben Pilcher, Dana and Cecil Johnson, Jack E. Boyd, G. W. Jones, Myrtle Williamson, Charles Hyne, Conan Vaughan, and Howard Frazier.

186   **teased him about it**: M. E. Quarez to Carver, Baton Rouge, Jan. 10, 1927; Wilson C. Newman to Carver, Chattanooga, Sept. 8, 1926.

186   **Du Bois, the man of action**: Cricket to Carver, Hartford, Jan. 26, 1919.

186   **to take life seriously**: "Daddy, you don't know what your relation to me means. I am really proud of it and I am going to do all in my power to maintain it." J. M. Brooks to Carver, July 24, 1923.

186   **advice . . . his sister . . . was rude to her**: Charles Hyne to Carver, Boulder, CO, 1925; Apr. 10, 1926.

186   **"'George' first thing you know"**: Richardson to Carver, Ames, IA, Sept. 23, 1917.

187   **disturb Carver's holiday dinner**: Wilson Newman to Carver, Nov. 19, 1928, Nov. 20, 1929.

187   **corny farm humor**: "Postmaster to Farmer: 'Well, are you making any headway courting the widow? Has she given you any encouragement?' Farmer: 'I'll say she has. Yesterday she asked me if I snored.'" Boyd to Carver, 1928.

187   **"Privy Paper"**: Philips to Carver, Chicago, Dec. 19, 1929.

187   **infected with venereal disease**: A. J. Jones to Carver, 1918. One of his most devoted acolytes, Herbert Reiss, reported that he had a spot on his cornea and was told that he would shortly be blind, probably due to "bad blood"—medical slang for syphilis. Herbert thought the doctor meant that he was anemic and begged Carver to let him come to Tuskegee and submit to a nutritional program that Carver would devise. Learning that the trouble was advanced syphilis. Herbert insisted he was a virgin. His doctor deduced that he had contracted it during some mild sexual experimentation with an infected person and restored

his sight with treatments. Reiss to Carver, Austin, TX, July 16, 21, 1926, GWC Papers, Tuskegee Archives.

187 **suppress the Communists:** Frank Liu to Carver, Hankow, China, Feb. 26, Sept. 22, Nov. 3, 1927.

187 **"everything . . . to get his board":** E. S. Burke to Carver, Urbana, IL, Oct. 12, 1925.

187 **school of distinction:** Cyrus A. Morris Jr. to Carver, Chicago, May 10, 1933.

187 **pleaded for his endorsement:** M. M. Simmons to Carver, Winnsboro, LA, Oct. 24, 1925.

187 **greatest living pianist:** Paul N. Guthrie to Carver, New York City, Nov. 5, 1929; Wilson to Carver, May 4, 1929; Dana and Cecil Johnson to Carver, Atlanta, Feb. 2, 1921.

188 **reading for a whole day:** Frei to Carver, May 18, 1929.

188 **fervid letter of thanks:** Carver to Glenn Clark, Feb. 27, 1921; Carver to Mme. Schumann-Heink, date illegible.

188 **scattered to seek their fortune:** J. M. Brown to Carver, Philadelphia, July 8, 1926; J. M. Burke to Carver, Philadelphia, July 16, 1926.

188 **enclosed a book of stamps:** Ben Pilcher to Carver, Austin, Nov. 11, 1926.

188 **junior high school at night:** 1925.

188 **first one . . . had ever penned:** Janice Murphy to Carver, 1925.

188 **death of his father:** Brown to Carver, Sept. 11, 1930. Carver's answers are not known, although the letters of thanks he received indicate that hardly anyone was refused. Carver saved incoming letters but, until he acquired a secretary, he wrote his outgoing letters by hand and did not make carbon copies.

188 **photo . . . to put in his school:** V.P. Holliday to Carver, Atlanta, July 10, 1925.

188 **"75% too high":** Carver to Ross, July 20, 1931, for one of about a hundred examples.

189 **wood on his desk again:** Carver to Dr. Walter Franklin Prince, 1931.

189 **imprisoned . . . wrote about him:** Clifford Mitchell to Carver, Michigan State Prison, Aug. 15, 1931.

189 **"subject you care to write about":** *Peanut Journal* to Carver, Suffolk, VA, Aug. 19, 1924; *Birmingham Reporter* (Oscar Adams) to Carver, Nov. 22, 1924; *American Life* (Moses Jordan) to Carver, Chicago, June 19, 1926.

189 **distributed to 6,000 theaters:** John Hix to Carver, Hollywood, Jan. 24, 1933.

189 **degree . . . was not forthcoming:** Carver to Pammel, Feb. 14, 1923, Iowa State University Archives.

189 **"the work that I am trying to do":** Carver to The Editor, *The State,* Columbia, SC, Oct. 10, 1925.

189 **responding to publicity:** The only teaching he appears to have done at Tuskegee in the mid-1920s was in summer school and guest teaching at other institutions.

189 **Einstein . . . occasion of Carver's death:** "Carver," X, p. 16, Lucy Cherry Crisp Papers; Albert Einstein to Richard Pliant, Princeton, NJ, Dec. 15, 1942, GWC Monument Archives.

190 **isn't worth knowing . . . chemist:** Williamson Candy Company to Carver, Brooklyn, Oct. 6, 1925.

190 **"combination with pecans":** President William P. Bullard, Atlanta, Mar. 21, 1922.

190 **developing their products:** President, Ralston Purina Co. to Carver, St. Louis, Apr. 24, May 5, 1922; Rogers Co. to Carver, Aug. 18, 1922; S. Blodgett to Carver, Boston, Nov. 15,

1922; E. M. de Pencier to Carver, Norfolk, VA, Nov. 29, 1922; T. H. Golden, Edmonton, Canada, 1922, ibid.

190   **profit from them:** Lou Wilk to Carver, Seminary Hill, TX, Feb. 9, 1931.

190   **and twenty-one others:** Carver to Holsey, May 7, 1924.

190   **was a constant request:** [no name] to Carver, Sept. 20, 1931.

191   **straightening kinky hair:** John C. Thomas to Carver, Troy, AL, Mar. 26, 1923.

191   **colony was completely desegregated:** Carver to Mrs. Waterfield (hair growing), Nov. 16, 1922; Carver to Miss E. M. Davis (salve), Nov. 25, 1922; Carver to George F. Pickett (Llano colony), June 6, 9, 1922.

191   **"all you are doing for my people":** George T. Pickett to Carver, Newllano, Apr. 12, 1929; Carver to Pickett, Apr. 19, 1929.

191   **peanuts and other vegetables:** W. P. Burrell to Carver, Newark, Oct. 2, 1919.

192   **paint from crank case oil:** "Carver," VIII, p. 6, Lucy Cherry Crisp Papers.

192   **lasted fifteen years:** Dr. Pammel to *The Ames (IA) Tribune,* n.d., 1928, Miscellaneous Documents, GWC Monument Archives.

192   **raw material . . . that was abundant:** Wade Moss to Tom Huston, Nov. 13, 1925.

192   **dozens of Florida clay samples:** Carver to V. H. Power, Dec. 17, 1925.

192   **"and the citrus fruit growers":** Carver to C. F. Berlow, Aug. 10, 1925.

192   **orange peels . . . what he had done for peanuts:** Wacholder-Lenfestey Glass Co. to Carver, May 4, 1926.

192   **yielded permanent cloth dyes:** Carver to B. R. Clarke, Aug. 6, 15, 1925; Carver to Tubize Co., Oct. 9, 1925.

192   **rich, black paint:** Walter Smith to Carver, Shannon, MS, Sept. 17, 1929; B. Pilcher to Carver, Austin, Sept. 2, 1928; Carver to Mr. Elkins, Aug. 27, 1928.

193   **contribution made by his race:** Carver to J. Thorington, Dec. 19, 1929. That was exactly what happened in 1922 when some of his formulas "were stolen and patented by others," as he vaguely described it to Rackham Holt.

193   **Carver finally gave in:** Carver to E. W. Thompson, Tuskegee, Dec. 19, 1921. Thompson was once a large landowner and the son of a congressman. He and an attorney would make all the patent applications in Carver's name, and Carver would then sell the patents to the company in return for a share of profits.

193   **company . . . formed in 1923:** *Atlanta Constitution,* Aug. 26, 1923.

193   **planned to build a paint plant:** They drew up plans for a $28,000 plant near Cheraw, the location of the nearest train station to Tuskegee. Carver to Pammel, May 22, 1924, Iowa State University Archives. The owner of the property was G. C. Blanks, a white farmer and Carver's close friend.

193   **wanted . . . to market them:** Carver to Henry Overton, *Montgomery Advertiser,* 1921.

193   **time . . . than he had anticipated:** Carver to W. M. Henry, Nov. 26, 1924, Iowa State University Archives.

193   **whatever they asked for:** Capt. E. G. Steis to Carver, Atlanta, Sept. 5, 1924; E. H. Mattes to Carver, Norfolk, Aug. 7, 1925.

193   **without being paid for it:** Carver to Kreami-Krisp Brown Company, Aug. 15, 1924.

CHAPTER TWELVE. "A Real Chemist?"

Unless otherwise indicated, correspondence to and from Carver is located in the George Washington Carver Papers, Tuskegee Institute Archives.

195 **poor southerners:** Lucy Cherry Crisp, "Carver," unpublished manuscript, Section IX, p. 24, Lucy Cherry Crisp Papers, Special Collections, Joyner Library, East Carolina University, Greenville, NC; Rackham Holt, *George Washington Carver* (New York, 1948), p. 265.

195 **"I would be helpless":** "Carver," p. 24, Lucy Cherry Crisp Papers.

196 **"sun went around a flat earth":** *New York Times*, Nov. 20, 1924.

196 **the skepticism of the Times:** Pammel, to whom Carver sent a copy of the letter, saved it; Louis H. Pammel Papers, University Archives, Iowa State University Library.

197 **simply the truth about anything:** John 8–32: "And ye shall know the truth and the truth shall make you free." Carver to Pammel, Nov. 24, 1924, Pammel Papers.

197 **"Aided by Heaven. Inspired by Providence":** Rackham Holt, p. 267.

197 **"theistic evolution" . . . warmly supported:** Theistic evolution held that God is the creator of the universe and all life; biological evolution is a natural process within that creation. Evolution, therefore, is simply a tool that God employed to develop human life.

197 **"but from old-world monkeys":** John T. Scopes, *The World's Most Famous Court Trial . . .* (New York, 1971), pp. 174–178.

199 **a snack for people on the run:** Tom Huston was the son of a Texas peanut farmer. Working out of a shack in Columbus, Georgia, he created a mechanical peanut sheller and a roaster for shelled peanuts. Farmers in need of his machines paid him peanuts, that is, a portion of their crop. In 1926 he designed the little package, patented it with his company's logo, and sold it to independent distributors. Years later, when his peach business failed, his main creditor demanded as collateral his controlling stock in Tom Huston's Peanuts. When the note fell due, control of the peanut company passed into the hands of the affiliate of the financing bank, who ousted Huston. Huston then created Julep Gums but ran afoul of government regulations that favored the monopoly of the Beechnut Company.

199 **a new company manufacturing nuts:** Huston to Carver, Columbus, GA, Oct. 18, 1924, George Washington Carver Papers, Tuskegee Institute Archives.

199 **"where to start . . . have the opportunity":** Barry to Carver, Columbus, June 1, Mar. 15, 1931, Dec. 15, 18, 1930.

200 **same fungus . . . cotton and field peas:** Porter to Barry, Fort Gaines, GA, Dec. 1, 1930; Carver to Grady Porter, Sept. 1, 1930; Carver to Ross, Sept. 15, 1930; Barry to Carver, Sept. 16, 1930, Oct. 15, 1930; G. W. Carver, "Some Peanut Diseases," Feb. 1931.

200 **country by country and state by state:** Tom Huston Company, 1931; Carver to Barry, Mar. 30, 1931.

200 **to disseminate . . . about peanut farming:** Barry to Carver., Columbus, GA, Jan. 23, 1931; Carver to Barry, Sept. 19, 1920, Oct. 15, 1930; Carver to Walter Richards, Jan. 9, 1931.

200 **credentials as a fungus expert:** "Dr. Carver is not a 'mycologist of international fame, neither is he a mycologist of any kind. He is supposed to be a chemist. At any rate, he

knows nothing about fungi . . . every single discussion is wrong." Barry replied with a long letter detailing Carver's credentials (which indeed established him as a full-fledged mycologist), pointing out that Carver had identified some 6,000 fungi specimens. He explained that Carver's report was intended for farmers. Huston to Carver, July 3, 1931.

200 **clannish enough . . . race to which I belong:** Carver to Walter A. Richards, July 1, 1929.

201 **prices . . . having fallen . . . Depression:** Carver to Business Committee, Nov. 20, 1928; Nov. 5, 1930.

201 **dandruff cure made from peanuts:** George Philips to Carver, July 1, 1929.

201 **never . . . got off the ground:** The correspondence for this period has been lost or destroyed in the fire that destroyed many of Carver's records—it is absent from the archive. In 1930, with the Depression casting a cloud over all commercial life, we find a woman pleading with Carver to force Thompson to return her investment of $1,000, made five years previously. Carrie Kirtley to Carver, Atlanta, Dec. 15, 1930. Carver's associates did succeed in getting him patents for one cosmetic and two pigments made from clay and iron, dated Jan. 6, June 9, and June 14, 1925.

201 **other peanut derivatives . . . future:** Carver to Pammel, Sept. 20, 1926; Carver to C. A. Goodwin, Feb. 12, 1927.

201 **comforting to the stomach:** Carver to D. Jacobs, June 10, 1928.

202 **had never found . . . that was effective:** Pauline Brown (Office of Dr. D. H. Brown) to Carver, Jacksonville, FL, July 29, 1925.

202 **as much Penol as Carver could send:** E. Jones to Carver, Mobile, Sept. 6, 1926; S. J. Rosenbaum to Carver, New York, Jan. 8, 1926.

202 **keep them straight . . . manufacture:** Carver to Courtenay DeKalb, Apr. 1, 1926; Emmett Jones to Carver, Mobile, Sept. 6, 1926; S. J. Rosenbaum to Carver, New York, Jan. 8, 1926.

202 **never made a profit:** J. H. Moorman, Publisher, to Carver, Mobile, June 2, 1928; see also J. T. Hamlin, President of Penol, to Powell & Powell concerning the failure of the enterprise due to distribution problems, Sept. 29, 1937.

202 **we know it foundered:** Carver to R. H. Edmonds, July 11, 1928; F. O. P. Theander to Carver, Thibodaux, LA, Aug. 31, 1928.

202 **He was naive and trusting:** John Sutton to Dr. John W. Kitchens, San Antonio, June 3, 1975, George Washington Carver Monument Archives, Diamond, MO.

202 **bears out Sutton's judgment:** J. T. Hamlin to Carver, Danville, VA, Oct. 7, 1940; A. J. Murray to Herb-Juice Penol Co., Inc., Washington, D.C., July 16, 1940; Carver to J. T. Hamlin, Oct. 12, 1940; Carver to Victor Schoffelmayer, Nov. 25, 1940.

202 **"I know practically nothing about":** Carver to Henry Overton, Feb. 16. 1927; see also Carver to C. H. Howard, Oct. 17, 1927.

203 **"Don't tell anybody, absolutely":** Peter Duncan Burchard, interview with James J. Lawson, Boyds, MD, Oct. 16, 2004; interview with Sheridan Howard Settler, Tuskegee, Oct. 26, 2004, Carver Oral History Project, GWC Monument Archives; Carver to W. B. Purcell, Dec. 15, 1924, GWC Papers, Tuskegee Archives.

203 **zinc for yellows and whites:** Carver to C. H. Howard, Tulsa, Oct. 17, 1927; C. T. Bennett to Carver, Sept. 4, 1929; Carver to Hon. Raymond Courtenay, May 4, 1929.

203 **letters . . . from Africa:** Carver to Moton, Feb. 27, 1929; Carver to McNeill and Libby Co.,

Mar. 4, 1929; see also Springfield Fire and Marine Insurance Co. to Carver, Springfield, MA, Sept. 13, 1928; Kemmers-Graham Co. to Carver, Cincinnati, May 20, 1929; Mabel Evelyn Gay to Carver, St. Petersburg, FL, July 5, 1933; Metoriola Adeleye to Carver, Oke-Efon, Abeokuta, Nigeria, June 6–10, 1932.

204 **I am getting along . . . like I used to:** "Carver," IX, pp. 28–29, Lucy Cherry Crisp Papers.

204 **harmful effects of smoking:** Carver to Mr. Andrews, Feb. 20, 1925; C. P. Crumb to Carver, Philadelphia, June 19, 1924.

204 **blizzard of loving letters:** Some of these students had gone on to found their own schools on the Tuskegee model and looked to Carver for advice, so that he had some influence on the pedagogy of his time. Martin A. Menafee of Voorhees Institute in South Carolina, William H. Holtzclaw of Utica Institute in Mississippi, and one who was not a former student, Rev. Lyman Ward, who founded the Southern Industrial Institute for the Training of White Youth at Camp Hill, Alabama, were all friends who remained close to Carver over many years.

205 **son had been arrested:** James Fowler to Carver, Scotlandville, LA, May 15, 1929; Dr. R. B. Daniel to Carver, Columbus, GA, July 23, 31, 1930; Carver to Dr. R. B. Daniel, Aug. 9, 1930; Pansie Buck to Carver, Hattiesburg, May 23, 24, 1929.

205 **"without a doctor's permission":** Carver to V. H. Power, Dec. 17, 1925; Oriental students of Cornell to Carver, Ithaca, Dec. 17, 1925; Carver to R. E. Brown, July 7, 1925; Unhoo Publishing Co, to Carver, Brooklyn, Aug. 20, 1925.

205 **He continued . . . the experiment station:** Carver gave up working the six-acre experiment station plot in 1925, although he was ready several years earlier. His lab work continued as before. Carver to Business Committee, Dec. 14, 1925.

205 **passing the collection plate:** Moton to Carver, Mar. 20, 1933.

205 **stinginess toward him:** Burchard, interview with Gwendolyn Henderson, Oct. 22, 2004, Tuskegee; interview with Bernice Fields, Oct. 31, 2004, Tulsa; with Helen Bratcher, Oct. 28, 2004, Nashville, GWC Monument Archives.

205 *Life of George Washington Carver:* Boston, 1929.

206 **begging loans . . . acquaintances she met there:** First National Bank of Neosho to Cal Jefferson, July 3, 1923, GWC Monument Archives.

206 **"much love to you and your wife":** First National Bank of Neosho to Cal Jefferson, Nov. 25, 1919; June 26, 1922; May 3, 1923; July 3, 1923. Expense account: 1920, 1921, 1922, 1923. Earlier letters from Mariah to Cal read as follows: "Dear Sir, I feel so much better since I had such a good time at your house yesterday. I never enjoyed anything so much. Riding in the car helped me so much. I want you and your wife to come over here Saturday afternoon. Sis Porth is going away and all her neighbors and friends are going to . . . tell her goodbye. They are going to have ice cream and I want you and your wife here . . . Much love, goodbye, and don't fail to come." Mariah Watkins to Cal Jefferson, Neosho, Oct. 22, 1922, GWC Monument Archives. See also bills to Mariah from Midway Grocery, 1898, Wells Fargo, 1912, City of Neosho water company, 1912, and the county tax assessor, 1924; Harry O. Abbott Papers, GWC Monument Archives.

206 **knew nothing of her troubles:** There is one letter and one telegram from Carver to Mariah, both with illegible dates, in Miscellaneous Documents, ibid.

206   **self-sufficiency in food:** Jack E. Boyd to Carver, CO, June 2, 1928, GWC Papers, Tuskegee Archives.

206   **Soviet Union . . . to work on cotton production:** The Soviets wanted the specialists in cotton to remain in the country for two years. Carver sent the recommendations but did not go himself, nor did he accept repeated invitations to tour the country; C. J. Golden to Carver, New York, Dec. 18, 1930, Apr. 18, 1931; Carver to John Sutton, Jan. 26, 1931; Carver to C. J. Golden, May 7, 1931; Carver to the *Afro-American*, Jan. 16, 1934; Sept. 24, 1934, GWC Papers, Tuskegee Archives; see also, Burchard, interview with Dr. John Hope Franklin, GWC Monument Archives.

206   **courage . . . to send . . . to the Soviet Union:** John Sutton to Dr. John W. Kitchens, San Antonio, June 3, 1975, GWC Monument Archives.

207   **finally in 1946 remarried:** John Sutton to Carver, Kapacuogap, Ceb-Kab, Soviet Union, July 1, 1932. The year after his arrival in the USSR, 1931, Sutton (1897–1978) married Ilyena Vasilievna. His second wife was Bessie Brandon. Sutton died in his hometown of San Antonio; John Wesley Sutton Collection, Manuscripts Division, Howard University, Washington DC.

207   **"and his anger was gone":** Sutton to Dr. John W. Kitchens, GWC Monument Archives. Mark Hersey takes on the question of whether Carver was a real scientist and concludes that his value was as an ecologist with visionary conservation ideas. Mark Hersey, *My Work Is That of Conservation* (Athens, GA, 2011).

207   **"hang himself . . . help Tuskegee":** Dr. "Ludy" Johnson, quoted by Sutton, Sutton to Kitchens, GWC Monument Archives.

207   **turning aside . . . invitations to lecture:** Carver to Amos Hall, Sept. 7, 1928, GWC Papers, Tuskegee Archives.

207   **"spelling and grammar . . . respectable":** Carver to Dr. M. L. Ross, Apr. 7, 1930.

208   **"take pleasure in recasting it":** Carver to Mrs. M. B. Owens, Apr. 10, 1930.

208   **thanks for his apology:** Atchison, Topeka, and Santa Fe Railways to Carver, June 20, 1930; Carver to Jack Thorington, Feb. 18, 1930. The incident did not stop the railroad from denying berths to other black patrons.

208   **little to say . . . beyond small talk:** Carver to Dr. M. L. Ross, Feb. 17, May 17, June 3, 14, July 4, 27, 1930.

208   **he exhorted them:** Burchard, interview with Elaine Freeman Thomas, Tuskegee, Oct. 24, 2004, GWC Monument Archives.

209   **protest . . . reported in the papers:** Wilson Newman to Carver, Birmingham, Dec. 7, 1929.

209   **"I'm afraid you're doomed now":** Barry to Carver, Columbus, GA, June 8, 1931.

CHAPTER THIRTEEN. "Passion Pure and Simple"

Unless otherwise noted, letters to and from Carver are located in the George Washington Carver Papers, Tuskegee Institute Archives.

210 **"The Christ in you, of course"**: Carver to Hardwick, Oct. 19, 1923, Apr. 5, 1924, George Washington Carver Monument Archives, Diamond, MO. Hardwick graduated from Virginia Tech in 1920. For this and other details about Hardwick, I am indebted to Dr. William C. Davis and the librarians of Virginia Tech.

210 **cheered his name**: Peter Duncan Burchard, interview with Thomas B. Hargrave, Oct. 18, 2004, Silver Spring, MD, Carver Oral History Project, GWC Monument Archives.

210 **"love of Jesus Christ"**: Lucy Cherry Crisp, "Carver," unpublished manuscript, Section IX, p. 27, Lucy Cherry Crisp Papers, Special Collections, Joyner Library, East Carolina University, Greenville, NC.

211 **"handsome, marvelous, spiritual Boy"**: Carver to Hardwick, July 11, 1931, George Washington Carver Papers, Tuskegee Archives.

211 **"things He has created"**: Carver to Jack Boyd, Mar. 1, 1927.

211 **strung together Bible references**: "Poor Luther Burbank—how our hearts go out in pity for his soul, for whom Jesus died." (Burbank had made an agnostic remark in a lecture.) There follows a list of thirty-three citations from the Gospels. M. F. Riuker to Carver, Los Angeles, July 1, 1926.

211 **"feel the flame of eternity in my soul"**: W. P. Nickell to Carver, Nashville, Dec. 18, 1930.

212 **"right thinking is in the kingdom of heaven"**: Ethel A. Mackert to Carver, Pittsburgh, Dec. 12, 1933.

212 **"I think of you in connection with it"**: Carver to Hardwick, Apr. 5, 1924, GWC Monument Archives.

213 **"and is still meaning to me"**: Carver to Pammel, June 8, 1922, Feb. 22, 1924, Louis Pammel Papers. Special Collections, Iowa State University Library.

213 **Wallace . . . unabashed affection**: Carver named one of his amaryllis hybrids "The Wallace." In 1921 he reported to Wallace that he was experimenting with 400 bulbs. Carver to Wallace, Apr. 3, 15, 1921, Record Group 6, National Archives, Washington, DC; Carver to Wallace, Jan. 6, 1924, University Archives, Iowa State University Library; see also Carver to Dr. Ross, Jan. 27, 1924, GWC Papers, Tuskegee Archives.

213 **only on special occasions**: Carver to McCord, June 11, 1929.

214 **"come to me when I needed you most"**: Carver to Hardwick, Oct. 29, 1923, GWC Monument Archives.

214 **wrote every few days**: Carver described an incident in which a white man from Birmingham came to tell Carver how much the professor had helped him succeed in life. He had brought along his lawyer. Carver had the domestic science students prepare dinner for them but did not join them because of the traditional barrier between the races dining together. He was astonished that the gentleman sent for him, insisting that he join them, which, however, Carver declined to do. Carver closed by reaffirming his love for Jim, "because there is so much Christ in you." Carver to Hardwick, Nov. 1, 1923.

214 **"keep you from coming to see me"**: Carver to Hardwick, Jan. 7, 1924.

214 **"belong to another race"**: Carver to Hardwick, Apr. 5, 1924.

215 **thought of you . . . collecting them**: Carver to Hardwick, Apr. 21, 1924: "I am working now with orange, lemon, and grapefruit peelings and getting some wonderful things out

of them. 25 or 30 precious stones have been sent to me from Michigan. Stonecutters and geologists, they say, are puzzled to know what they are . . . It will take some time to work them out, but I'm sure I can do it. They are, however, not diamonds as they think . . . Pray for me that I may determine them correctly." Carver eventually made long reports on the minerals. His assertions were verified subsequently by Michigan geologists. Though he had never been in Michigan, he traced the minerals to an ancient riverbed and assigned names to them.

215 **be with you just as much as possible:** Carver to Hardwick, May 24, 1924.

215 **have your picture before me now:** Carver to Hardwick, Nashville, May 21, 1924.

215 **"you understand me thoroughly":** Carver to Hardwick, May 25, Nov. 11, 1924, GWC Monument Archives.

216 **sprained ankles for treatment:** Carver to I. W. Bergthold, Atlanta, Aug. 5, 1924, GWC Papers, Tuskegee Archives.

216 **letter was signed "Son":** Son to Carver, June 18 [1932?].

216 **"feel nearer to the other":** Carver to Mrs. Booker T. Washington, Feb. 14, 1924.

216 **"What a responsibility":** Carver to Hardwick, Aug. 27, 1924.

217 **"seek the Christ in you":** Carver to Hardwick, July 10, 1924, GWC Monument Archives.

217 **"gold tried by fire":** Carver to Hardwick, Dec. 12, 1923, GWC Papers, Tuskegee Archives.

217 **all his other fan mail:** Carver to J. Berghold, June 26, 1926.

218 **"my love for you is just the same":** Carver to Hardwick, Sept. 8, 1924.

218 **received your fine letter:** Carver to Hardwick Jan. 20, 1927, GWC Monument Archives.

218 **ten miles after receiving Jim's letter:** Fainting spells: Carver to E. C. Roberts, May 24, 1921; long walk: Carver to Pammel, Mar. 18, 1927, Pammel Papers.

218 **Carver . . . wrote few letters:** Carver to Hardwick, Mar. 9, 1928, GWC Monument Archives.

219 **"a heart so full of love":** Though Carver had by then been awarded many honors and was known all over the country, he nevertheless expressed surprise to Hardwick that the Birmingham Chamber of Commerce had invited him to speak in a fine theater and had even sent out handsome invitations; one thousand of Alabama's elite whites attended the talk. "Think of it!" he effused. Ibid.

219 **"wondering what you are doing":** Carver to Hardwick, May 16,1928, GWC Papers, Tuskegee Archives; Carver to Hardwick, June 2, 1928, GWC Monument Archives.

219 **Of course . . . lady friend . . . time is left to me, if possible:** Carver to Hardwick, June 10, 1928, GWC Papers, Tuskegee Archives.

219 **"can hardly wait for the time to come":** Carver to Hardwick, June 26, 1928.

220 **"God's love makes your eyes . . . heavenly brightness":** Ibid.

220 **Hardwick sent . . . but did not come:** "My dear friend, you are to me the greatest figure in the whole country, impressing by simplicity of life, creative work, and selfless love, what God really is . . . I cannot thank you for what you are. I can thank God and try to give to other men something of what you have given to me." Miscellaneous Documents, GWC Papers, Tuskegee Archives.

220 **Hardwick remained in Iowa:** Carver to Hardwick, Aug. 6, 1928, ibid.

220 **"sorrowfully disappointed":** Carver to Hardwick, Oct. 6, 1928, ibid.

220   "lonesome this evening": Carver to Hardwick, Nov. 26, 1928, ibid.

220   see him again "someday": Carver was recovering from a severe case of flu. In the same letter he notified Jim that he would not be able to attend the yearly YMCA conference which was yet three months away. Several of the Blue Ridge boys were planning to visit him, however. "I would love to read nature with you and your boys. I do hope that someday I will be able to do so." Carver to Hardwick, Apr. 1, 1929,

220   worsened into pneumonia: The Ruths to Carver, Fondress, MS, Feb. 1, 1929; Carver to Ross, Sept. 25, 1933.

220   promising to keep more in touch: "Old friend," he wrote to Carver, "I haven't let you hear much about me but many times I have thought about you and have drawn strength from you for my work. I really want to keep in closer touch with you this year. I hope to write more. I don't want to burden you with writing to me so much because I know you are increasingly busier." Hardwick to Carver, Aug. 13, 1930, Blacksburg.

220   "I do not recall . . . happy," Carver asserted: Carver to Hardwick, Dec. 15, 1920.

220   no arrest . . . for a year: Carver to Hardwick, June 14, 1931.

221   all of his teeth removed: G. C. Blanks to Carver, Natasulga, AL, Sept. 26, 1933.

221   "What would I do without you?": Carver to Hardwick, Jan. 5, Feb. 15, 1931.

222   He picked one . . . included Jim: Carver to Hardwick, Mar. 20, Apr. 1, May 20, 1931.

222   knitted together in God's tapestry, etc.: Carver to Hardwick, Feb. 28, 1931.

222   wallpaper made from peanut skins: Carver to Tom Huston, Oct. 16, 1928, GWC Papers, Tuskegee Archives.

222   "flatter it gets": Carver to Huston, Jan. 7, 1930, May 16, 1931.

223   "precious boy . . . May 28": Carver to Hardwick, May 19, 1931.

223   "I do not feel equal to it": Barry to Carver, May 14, 1931; Carver to Hardwick, May 11, 1931.

223   "can't hurt people's feelings": Green and Ledicott to Carver, London, Oct. 20, 1930, GWC Papers, Tuskegee Archives; Viking Press to Carver, New York, June 4, 1930; Carver to Mr. George Oppenheimer, July 3, 1930; John Sutton to Dr. John W. Kitchens, San Antonio, June 3, 1975, GWC Monument Archives.

223   Swift . . . trying to make the meat more marketable: The public's rejection of peanut-fed pork was costing Alabama farmers $400,000 each year. Seth P. Storrs to Carver, Montgomery, Sept. 16, 18, 1920; Barry to Carver, Sept. 22, 1930; Swift and Co. to Carver, Moultrie, GA, Sept. 23, Dec. 6, 1930; Carver to Swift and Co. Sept. 24, 26, 29, 1930; H. H. Dowell, Moultrie, GA, Feb. 25, 1931, GWC Papers, Tuskegee Archives; Peter Duncan Burchard, interview with Louis A. Rabb, Tuskegee, Oct. 26, 2004, Carver Oral History Project, GWC Monument Archives.

224   Charlie Hyne . . . invitation . . . withdrawn: Linda O. McMurry, George Washington Carver (Oxford, MS, 1982), p. 210.

224   lost the scholarship . . . student: When Mississippi University for Women cancelled the talk, Hardwick approached various white churches for permission to use their facilities and was rebuffed. The talk was finally held at a black high school. Mrs. Paul Christtensen to Mrs. Ethel Edwards, Michigan, Oct. 6, 1948, GWC Monument Archives.

224   treatment for gum disorders: Carver to Ross, Oct. 1, Apr. 23, May 17, 1930, GWC Papers, Tuskegee Archives.

224   **peanut fungi . . . affecting other crops:** Frank E. Deems to Carver, Detroit, Jan. 30, 1934. A patent existed for a pavement containing cotton, although Carver developed his product independently. Carver to Ross, Aug. 26, 1930; Carver to USDA, Oct. 15, 1930.

224   **refill their prescriptions:** Grace L. H. Smith to Carver, Richmond, Dec. 1932; M. A. Nembhard to Carver, Belize, July 2, 1931; D. Marshall Lewis to Carver, Muskogee, OK, Aug. 21, 1931.

225   **desultory secondary education:** J. S. Hockert to Carver, Sutherland, IA, Mar. 17, 1933.

225   **most of them never to return:** Jack Moss Bridges to Carver, Headland, AL, Jan. 14, 1932.

225   **schools . . . eight months a year:** Albert White to Carver, Hattiesburg, Mar. 5, 1932.

225   **trench mouth . . . cavities:** *Montgomery Advertiser,* Sept. 14, 1930.

225   **$1.06 a day:** Ibid., Nov. 1, 1930. Less than 10 percent of teachers stayed to their third year. The policy of requiring teachers to be single was common in many counties of the state.

225   **Black Draught . . . one cent a dose:** *Tuskegee News,* Sept.–Oct. 1930.

225   **signed herself "Daught":** Alice Carter Simmons to Carver, Mississippi, Apr. 12, 1930, GWC Papers, Tuskegee Archives.

225   **salary reduced . . . $87:** "Teacher's Monthly Statement," Dec. 31, 1932, Miscellaneous Documents, Tuskegee Archives.

225   **jobless rate . . . 1.4 percent:** Sept. 2, 1930.

226   **"some poor hungry, jobless soul":** L. Bowden to Carver, Columbus, GA, Dec. 5, 1931, see Carver to Ross, Dec. 7, 1931.

226   **Al Capone . . . for the unemployed:** *Associated Press,* July 13, 1930; *Montgomery Advertiser,* Nov. 15, 1930.

226   **"whom we must rehire first":** "Al" to Carver, Milwaukee, June 6, 1933.

227   **Ittner approved . . . Fascists . . . along those lines:** Ittner did not call the movement by its name. The Technocracy idea started in New York and gained widespread adherents between 1921 and 1933. It sought to replace politicians as managers of the economy. The movement declined with the rise of Franklin Roosevelt's New Deal. Ittner to Carver, Little Valley, New York, Dec. 21, 1932.

227   **Ford sent to Carver . . . what could be done:** C. Newton Berry to Carver, Detroit, Mar. 6, 1933; Barry to Carver, Columbus, Apr. 10, 1933.

227   **"Are We Starving" . . . article:** *The Peanut Journal,* Jan. 1932.

228   **"Make up your mind . . . surplus to sell":** "Back to the Farm" (final draft of article for publication), Carver to Asa Vaughn, Jan. 21, 1931, GWC Papers, Tuskegee Archives.

228   **what the next six months will bring me:** I. B. Talton to Carver, Denver, June 16, 1931.

228   **Barry . . . "some use for living each day":** Barry to Carver, Columbus, GA, June 11, 1931, Nov. 28, 1932.

229   **gave Huston technical direction, as usual:** Barry to Carver, Columbus, Jan. 22, 1931.

229   **of Huston finding it later on:** Toby Fishbein, interview with Austin Curtis, Detroit, Mar. 3, 1979, Carver Oral History Project, GWC Monument Archives, Diamond, MO.

229   **a room full of Carver's life:** L. S. Kunze to Carver, Columbus, Dec. 29, 1931, GWC Papers, Tuskegee Archives; *Journal of Chemical Education,* June 1946.

229   **$19.50 to start college work:** E. D. Morrison to Carver, Los Angeles, Dec. 19, 1932; Leo Shoemaker to Carver, Flint, Mich., Dec., 1932; Ida Odom to Carver, Richton, MI, Mar. 3,

1933; Jack Bridges to Carver, Headland, AL, Jan. 14, 1932; A. J. White to Carver, Hatties-burg, Aug. 31, 1933.

230 **he was wiped out:** Carver to Mrs. Chisholm, Dec. 9, 1932, Jan. 15, 1933; Warren Logan to Carver, Dec. 8, 1932; Valley Savings Bank to Carver, Des Moines, May 6, 1931, Apr. 25, 1932; E. C. Meredith to Carver, Tuskegee, June 6, 1931; Macon County Bank to Carver, July 6, 1931; Carver to Ross, Feb. 7, 1933.

230 **lost an additional $500:** John Drakeford, Bank of Tuskegee to Carver, May 21, 1931; Wm. Carter to Carver, Jan. 21, 1932; Warren Logan to Carver, Feb. 20, 1932. Carver was the largest depositor in the Macon County Bank when it closed in May 1931. When liquidat-ing, the bank gave its depositors land instead of cash which it rented out and managed for them. The proceeds were small but grew over time. E. C. Meredith to Carver, Oct. 8, 1934; R. A. Crawford to Carver, Des Moines, Jan. 22, 1935.

230 **audience paid to get in:** Carver to Hardwick, Kansas City, Feb. 12, 1932, GWC Monument Archives.

231 **"caught the vision" . . . one or another:** Carver to Hardwick, Oct. 12, 1933.

231 **trips he had planned with Jim:** Carver to Hardwick, Oct. 8, 1933; Carver to Hardwick, Nov. 29, 1933; Carver to Hardwick, July 29, 1933, GWC Papers, Tuskegee Archives.

231 **"given up their lives, as we term it":** Carver to Hardwick, Apr. 9, 1932, May 8, 1933.

231 **that water-ducking business:** Carver to Hardwick, July 29, 1933.

232 **"God will be . . . near you . . . this week":** Carver to Hardwick, June 19, 1933, GWC Monument Archives; see also, July 15, 1931: "I even went to bed, "drempt" about you and rose this morning with a feeling that God will fulfill his promise to guide us in all of our ways if we only trust him wholly." Apr. 1, 1933: "This is real and not an April fool. I have only had spiritual messages from you for a long time. Just send me a few lines at least."

232 **"sensitive to change":** Carver to Hardwick, Feb. 6, 1931.

233 **"many years to come. Jim Hardwick":** Hardwick to Carver, Dec. 18, 1932.

233 **"sixteen days together" . . . to Jim's mother:** Carver to Helena Hardwick, Mar. 22, 1935, Harry O. Abbott Papers, GWC Monument Archives.

233 **" 'Jimmie's' marriage":** Carver to Mrs. Hardwick, Dec. 16, 1934, ibid.

234 **one felt very little in his presence:** Helena Hardwick to Ethel Roberts, Blacksburg, VA, Mar. 3, 1948, ibid.

234 **thanks for restoring their health:** Henry J. Sullivan to Carver, Montgomery, Mar. 17, 1931, GWC Papers, Tuskegee Archives.

234 **physician in Tupelo . . . to good effect:** Carver to Moton, June 23, 1933; T. J. Lilly to Carver, Tupelo, July 29, 1933.

234 **"a new man of you physically":** Carver to Hardwick, Feb. 6, 1931.

234 **superintendent . . . treatment for four months:** Carver to Hardwick, Mar. 4, 20, 1931.

235 **without . . . assistance:** Carver to Mrs. Hardwick, Dec. 16, 1933, GWC Monument Archives.

235 **St. Vitus's Dance . . . irregular growth:** Albert Andrews to Carver, Birmingham, Apr. 12, 1932; G.C.M.A. to Carver, Sept. 26, 1932, GWC Papers, Tuskegee Archives.

235 **roaring in the ears:** M. A. Malcomb to Carver, Andalusia, AL, Dec. 31, 1933.

235 **male organ:** Hugh G. Hother to Carver, Shiner, TX, Jan. 1, 1933.

235   **massage to Franklin D. Roosevelt:** Hazel Hancock Maddox to Carver, Savannah, GA, Nov. 26, 1933.

235   **"horrible looking":** Burchard, interview with Patricia McIntosh-Bell, Tulsa, Oct. 31, 2004.

236   **"demonstrations of its efficacy":** McGinnis United Press to Carver; Carver to United Press, Nov. 3, 1933.

CHAPTER FOURTEEN. "Suffering Humanity"

Unless otherwise noted, all correspondence to and from Carver is located in the George Washington Carver Papers, Tuskegee Institute Archives.

237   **any sort of medical treatment:** *Montgomery Advertiser,* Oct. 2, 1930; statistics from the Alabama Society for Crippled Children reporting on the number awaiting charitable financial aid. A week later (Oct. 10, 1930), the same newspaper reported that in 1930 there were 810,000 school age children in the state, 515,000 white and 295,000 black. Of these, 100,000 were illiterate: 34,000 white and 65,000 black.

237   **stay away . . . gathering places:** Ibid., Sept. 28, 1930.

237   **front pages . . . Montgomery to Milwaukee:** See from Dec. 31, 1933, to Jan. 5, 1934, *Birmingham News, Baltimore Sun, Atlanta Journal, Montgomery Advertiser, Cincinnati Enquirer, Los Angeles Herald, Dallas Morning News, Tuskegee News, Detroit News, Durham News, The Congregational Magazine* (Yorkshire, Eng.) *Mission Field* Magazine, *Columbus (GA) Ledger,* Polio Chronicle (pub. 1931–1934).

238   **"working out its. . . value":** *Birmingham News,* Jan. 1, 1934.

239   **"let me know at once":** Sarah Little to Carver, Tupelo, MS, Jan. 20; Mrs. W. C. Harrison to Carver, Merry Hill, NC, Jan. 21; Mattie Harris to Carver, Atlanta, Mar. 20; Blanche M. Wiley to Carver, Utica, NY, Apr. 3; Mrs. W. B. Lee to Carver, Opelika, AL, Jan. 11; Dr. H. L. Cress to Carver, Van Wert, OH, Jan. 1; H. R. Smith to Carver, Wilmington, NC, Jan. 1; Mrs. Mattie Parks to Carver, Birmingham, Jan. 12; [Name illegible] to Carver, Braddock, PA, Mar. 19, 1934, George Washington Carver Papers, Tuskegee Institute Archives.

239   **seemed to be intelligent:** Mrs. Emma Watts to Carver, Moultrie, GA, Jan. 18; Mrs. W. M. Lunday to Carver, Columbus, GA, Jan 28; George Knight to Carver, Kannapolis, NC, Jan. 30; J. R. Beally to Carver, Harlem, GA, July 27, 1934.

239   **please Rite Me at once:** Mrs. E. W. Bowen to Carver., Merry Hill, NC, July 16; [Illegible name] to Carver, Eatonton, GA, Jan. 21; Nellie Allen to Carver, Denison, TX, Jan. 22; Jessie Ellis to Carver, Henderson, TX, Jan. 13, 1934.

240   **which ones Carver should see:** Peter Duncan Burchard, interview with Carolyn Ford (whose mother served as Carver's mail sorter), Tuskegee, Oct. 24–25, 2004, Carver Oral History Project, George Washington Carver Monument Archives, Diamond, MO.

240   **send a doctor's statement . . . their problems:** Carver to Mrs. Mays, Mar. 19, 1935; Carver to Ivan J. Kneeland, May 30, 1935.

240   **even treated their relatives:** Mrs. Blanks's brother suffered from severe asthma and bronchitis, which doctors could not relieve. No doctor's statement was asked of him. Mrs. G. C. Blanks to Carver, Notasulga, AL, Jan. 8, 1935.

240 **would not accept payment . . . or the oil:** See, e.g., Carver to O. H. Stevenson, Jan 18, 1935.

240 **people with other disorders:** Carver to Dana and Cecil Johnson, July 24, 1934.

240 **massage women . . . "obvious reasons":** Carver to Mrs. Adahlia Johnson, Nov. 12, 1935.

240 **hay fever and skin problems:** During one of his frequent hay fever attacks, Carver anointed the inside of his nostrils thoroughly and lay down so that the oil could drain into his sinuses. It worked. Carver to Fischer, July 31, 1935.

240 **hands . . . completely healed:** Carver to Hardwick, Apr. 29, 1934.

240 **fifty-two in one day alone:** Carver to Raleigh Merritt, July 12, 1934.

240 **one young man's acne:** Edward C. Croft to Carver, Charleston, SC, Sept. 27, 1934.

240 **Within a month . . . 1,500 letters:** Carver to Dr. Shear, Mar. 24, 1934, GWC Monument Archives.

241 **He plays football . . . now as large:** Carver to Dr. Ross, Sept. 10, 1934.

241 **up and down steps without help:** Carver to Dr. Fischer, June 24, 1935. "Some months ago they brought a young man to me that was in an automobile accident and had his back broken," Carver recounted. "I refused to do anything at all, as you know I am not a doctor and am not practicing medicine, and I didn't see what I could do as he had been to a number of physicians and they gave him no encouragement at all." Carver was always careful to reassure his physician friends that he was not himself playing doctor. "The boy's mother and the boy himself begged me so hard to fix some oil for them, and they would do the massaging. This I did with great reluctance, as I felt that the young man would not last but a few weeks at the most. X-ray pictures showed that the spinal cord was almost severed. Much to my astonishment he came to see me last Saturday. He does not look like the same person in appearance. He was sitting up, riding in an automobile, and told me that he had been in swimming." One Jack Harris, paralyzed on his right side, wrote his first reports to Carver in a barely legible scrawl. But during the following year, his penmanship became normal; he wrote of improved flexibility and strength throughout his arm and hand, improvements that anyone who saw his earlier handwriting could believe.

241 **"The patient . . . just what to do":** Carver to Dr. Ross, Mar. 31; Carver to Hardwick, Apr. 18, 1924, GWC Papers, Tuskegee Archives; Carver to W. S. Sherrill, Apr. 25, 1934, W. S. Sherrill Correspondence, Franklin Delano Roosevelt Presidential Library and Museum, Hyde Park, NY.

241 **"simply a scientist . . . efficacy of peanut oil":** Carver to Dr. Ross, Nov. 11, 1934.

241 **"9 days, then use the oil again":** Carver to Dr. Dibble, Oct. 2, 1934.

241 **"dissecting it out":** Rackham Holt, *George Washington Carver* (New York, 1948), p. 299.

242 **"still unable . . . from the floor":** Lillian Wilcox to Carver, Montgomery, June 4, July 16, 1935. A boy who had come to him with a withered hip and leg was almost well, according to his physician, who saw him again in a large Texas clinic. Carver to Moton, July 30, 1934.

242 **"peripheral neuritis":** Dr. S. O. Black to Carver, Spartanburg, SC, Jan. 31, 1934.

242 **fourteen physicians . . . to Carver:** Dr. O. B. Wunschow, Chattanooga, Jan 9, 1934; Dr. W. F. Boddie, Forsyth, GA, Jan 12, 1934; Dr. S. G. Stubbins, Portland, OR, Jan. 12, 1934; Dr. R. M. Brannon, Greensboro, NC, Jan. 12, 1934; Dr. J. S. Pugh, Dallas, Jan. 16, 1934; Dr. E. H. Hunter, Niles, MI, Jan 16, 1934; Dr. W. O. Harris, Cleveland, Jan. 22, 1934; Dr. W. E. Chandler (dentist), Jan. 30, 1934; Dr. Carl S. Frischkorn, Norfolk, Jan. 25, 1934; Drs. Thomas

and Martin, Cleveland, Jan. 25, 1934; Dr. Charles King (dermatologist), Birmingham, Jan. 30, 1934; Dr. Franklin C. Rasmussen, Fort Myers, FL, Jan 30, 1934; Dr. S. O. Black, Spartanburg, SC, Feb. 6, 1934; Dr. F. E. Christopher, Bolinger, AL, Feb. 6, 1934; Dr. E. Wood Ruggles, Rochester, NY, Feb. 7, 1934; Dr. Wilmont Littlejohn, Birmingham, Apr. 14, 1934.

242 **"My little baby . . . led by its mother":** Dr. Ross to Carver, Topeka, Oct. 7, 1934, Mar. 16, 1935. "The next time I hope to order five or six gallons . . . I shall keep strict records of results, etc. I will be picking up every cripple I see and see if I can help them."

242 **described many cases to Fischer:** "A father brought his little boy to me about three weeks ago. The right side was stricken with Infantile Paralysis. He limped considerably, the limb somewhat perished away, the arm also. He held his hand crumpled up. It could be straightened, but as soon as it was released it would curl up again . . . Yesterday the little fellow held out his hand with the fingers practically straight of his own accord, and holds them there without much effort." Carver to Dr. Fischer, July 22, 1935.

243 **Emmett Cox . . . driving a car:** Carver to W. S. Sherrill, Apr. 25, 1934, Sherrill Correspondence, Franklin D. Roosevelt Library, Hyde Park, NY.

243 **"I will be able to walk . . . near future":** Emmett Cox to Dr. Fischer, Atlanta, June 28, 1935.

243 **peanut oil . . . the best:** "My arm is much improved." [Name illegible] to Carver, Georgia State Industrial College, Sept. 17, 1934; Carver to R. Wens, June 13, 1936; Carver to Dr. Ross, May 14, 1934.

243 **but rather the massage:** "Other oils bought commercially would be fine. The discovery is simply the efficacy of using oils pharmaceutically," Carver to Ross, May 24, 1934.

243 **equip a special section . . . treatment:** "I gave him the names of a number of my patients," Carver informed Dr. Moton. "He investigated them at his own expense . . . He came down last Tuesday week, spent the entire morning with me, and brought one of his patients for me to go over with him." Carver to Moton, July 23, 1935.

244 **withdraw any interest . . . in your work:** Fischer to Carver, Atlanta, Mar. 16, 1936; Carver to Fischer, Mar. 21, 1936.

244 **victims of other afflictions:** Carver to Raleigh Merritt, May 2, 1934.

244 **large quantities of a fair price:** Carver to Moton, Sept. 1, Nov. 27, 1934; Philip Eye to Carver, Mar. 5, 1935.

245 **"conditioning of the muscles . . . have never functioned":** Carver to Fischer, July 19, 1935.

245 **no further progress . . . detected:** Mrs. Lomnick to Carver, Attalla, AL, Sept. 10, 1934; O. H. Stevenson, Roanoke, AL, Jan. 17, 1935.

245 **"general improvement is noticeable":** Edward B. McGowan to Carver, New York, Aug. 28, 1934; see also Mrs. Virginia Johnson to Carver, Atlanta, Dec. 12, 1934; D. N. Patillo to Carver, Loachapoka, AL, Dec. 4, 1934.

246 **Morris Fishbein's approval . . . refused:** T. H. Alexander to Carver, Mar. 17, May 19, May 31, July 18, July 19, 1936; Carver to Alexander, May 20, June 4, July 16, 1936; Fishbein to Fischer, June 13, 1936; Fischer to Carver, June 1, June 4, June 6, June 12, 1936; Carver to Fischer, June 10, June 16, 1936.

247 **Camel exhibit . . . AMA convention:** *Time* (cover Morris Fishbein), June 21, 1937, and "Medicine, AMA Indicted," Jan. 2, 1939; A. R. Hale, *These Cults: An Analysis of the Foibles of Dr. Morris Fishbein* . . . (New York, 1926).

247   "all the way up in the same leg": Carver to Moton, June 7, 1934.

247   "Prejudice . . . melting away": For remarks about his Klan patients, see Carver to Hard-wick, Jan. 29, Feb. 24, Feb. 7, 1934, Harry O. Abbott Papers, GWC Monument Archives.

248   "fakir . . . well known in the East": Churchill made the remarks in an address to the Council of the West Essex Unionists on Feb. 23, 1931. For more entertainment from Churchill on Gandhi, see Arthur Herman, *Gandhi and Churchill* (New York, 2008).

248   resemblance between Carver and Gandhi: Richard B. Gregg to Carver, South Natick, MA, May 24, 1935; Carver to Gandhi, July 27, 1935, GWC Papers, Tuskegee Archives; Toby Fishbein, interview with Austin Curtis, Mar. 3, 1979, Carver Oral History Project, GWC Monument Archives.

248   "my arm is about to give out": Carver to Mrs. Milholland, Apr. 10, 1934; Carver to Dana and Cecil Johnson, July 24, 1934, GWC Monument Archives.

248   3,000 letters . . . about massage therapy: Carver to Dana and Cecil Johnson, Dec. 27, 1935, ibid., confirmed by the number in GWC Papers.

249   dying in the Salton Lake: Frank E. Deems to Carver, Detroit, Jan. 30, 1934; Carver to Ross, Mar. 4, 1934.

249   peanut butter . . . roof of the mouth: E. E. Overhold, Washington, DC, to Carver, May 31, 1936.

249   "100 Years Free of Disease": Randle to Carver, Greensboro, NC, Mar. 19, 1934.

249   "you are entirely too young for me": Carver to Helen Chisholm, June 12, 1934.

249   "also a compound microscope": Mabel Harding, Crowell Publishers to Carver, New York, June 12, 1934.

249   Moton . . . prostate gland with it: Carver to Ross, Dec. 10, 1934; Carver to Moton, June 7, July 23, Aug. 7, 1934; Moton to Carver, Capahosic, VA, June 19, 1934.

249   so they could write biographies of him: See I. S. Calwell, to Carver, Wrens, GA, June 30, 1934.

250   Midwesterner . . . effort she put into it: Crisp to Carver, Aug. 8, 1934.

250   the two obsessions they shared: Lucy Cherry Crisp, "Carver," unpublished manuscript, Lucy Cherry Crisp Papers, Special Collections, Joyner Library, East Carolina University, Greenville, NC. A prolific poet, Crisp frequently sent Carver examples of her work; see Crisp to Carver, Falkland, NC, July 24, 1934.

251   "It is your great spirit": Carver to Hardwick, Feb. 24, 1934; see also Mar. 8, 26, Apr. 3, 18, 1934, Jan. 12, Feb. 7, 1935, GWC Monument Archives.

251   "write freely to you about this": Crisp to Carver, Greensboro, NC, July 9, 1934, GWC Papers, Tuskegee Archives.

251   "should be very happy for him": Crisp to Carver, Falkland, NC, July 22, Aug. 8, 1934.

251   "than I myself realized": Crisp to Carver, Falkland, NC, July 22, Aug. 8, 1934.

251   in the form of prayer: Lucy Cherry Crisp (1899–1977) received a BA from the Women's College of the University of North Carolina in 1919 and later studied at Columbia University, Boston University, and Radcliff College. For ten years after graduation, she taught piano and supervised music programs in schools in North and South Carolina and then worked in church programs and student religious activities. From 1938 to 1963, she was engaged in arts administration for galleries and museums in North and South Carolina.

252 **"he is on the road":** Carver to Helena Hardwick, Mar. 22, 1935, Harry O. Abbott Papers, GWC Monument Archives.

CHAPTER FIFTEEN. "Fame and Its Discontents"

Unless otherwise noted, correspondence to and from Carver in located in the George Washington Carver Papers, Tuskegee Institute Archives.

253 **"You may realize another dream":** L. H. Haywood to Carver, Waycross, GA, Dec. 14, 1928, George Washington Carver Papers, Tuskegee Institute Archives.

253 **"your caressing voice":** Howard to Carver, Waycross, GA, Apr. 11, 1933, Apr. 27, 1934.

254 **she thought were messages from God:** Ibid, Apr. 27, 1934.

254 **"George Washington Carver, Jr.":** Ibid.

255 **He particularly regretted . . . especially his botany textbook:** At his death, Carver left unfinished notes and sketches for several other articles or books. Miscellaneous Documents, George Washington Carver Monument Archives, Diamond, MO.

255 **he did not interfere with his research:** Carver complained to Abbott regarding the Tuskegee printing office, "I have been wholly unable to get anything out of it since you left." Dec. 12, 1938, Harry O. Abbott Papers, GWC Monument Archives.

255 **plants grown in Macon County:** Booker to Carver, Mar. 14, 1912.

255 **fuming . . . after years had gone by:** Abbott to Carver, Chicago, Dec. 31, 1939, GWC Monument Archives.

256 **Ford . . . its appalling poverty:** G. Lake Imes (former secretary of Tuskegee Institute), "I Knew Carver," c. 1944, ms., Abbott Papers, GWC Monument Archives. At the same time, the training course for elementary teachers was extended from two to four years. *Montgomery Advertiser*, Sept. 20, 1930.

256 **"they'll pay me more":** Toby Fishbein, interview with Austin Curtis, Detroit, Mar. 3, 1979, Carver Oral History Project, GWC Monument Archives.

256 **"appreciation . . . what you mean to her":** Abbott to Carver, Chicago, Dec. 31, 1939, Abbott Papers, GWC Monument Archives.

257 **you will see how very urgent . . . help me:** Carver to Mrs. Walcott, Jan. 21, 1937, GWC Papers, Tuskegee Archives.

257 **Mrs. Walcott . . . his apartment:** Carver to Abbott Aug. 31, 1938, Nov. 17, 1939, Abbott Papers, GWC Monument Archives.

257 **"without first engaging . . . and prayer":** John Sutton to Dr. John W. Kitchens, San Antonio, June 3, 1975, GWC Monument Archives.

258 **drawn back . . . work again with Carver:** Carver had been the first black "teaching scholar" at Iowa State; Sutton was the second. Ibid.

258 **after his return in 1938:** Carver to John Sutton, Jan. 26, 1931, ibid.

258 **Christian Scientists . . . could not prove:** Sutton examined some letters written by Carver to a Mrs. Arthur Liston, a Christian Scientist in California, and to another member of the church, dating from 1938 right up to Carver's death.

259   **the brouhaha subsided:** *Oklahoma City Black Dispatch,* Feb. 13, Aug. 14, Aug. 21, 1930;
        W. J. Black to Abbott, Mar. 6, 1930; W. B. Storey to Carver, June 27, 1930; Carver to Storey,
        June 27, 1930; Abbott to Black, July 2, Aug. 29, Sept. 14, 1930; Black to Abbott, July 31,
        Sept. 8, 1930, Abbott Papers, GWC Monument Archives.

259   **"that I had planned for us to do":** Carver to Abbott, July 8, Aug. 9, 1937, ibid.

260   **unless Abbott could accompany him:** Carver to Abbott, Sept. 17, 1937, ibid.

260   **the years at Carver's side:** "You are a prophet, a seer, a man among men, and truly a man
        of God," he wrote. "And to me . . . it has been the man side, the human side" that meant
        most. Abbott to Carver, Dec. 31, 1939, GWC Papers, Tuskegee Archives.

260   **"I wanted to see you there":** Carver to Abbott, Dec. 27, 1939, July 31, 1937; GWC Monu-
        ment Archives.

260   **"barbecued to a turn":** Carver to Abbott, July 10, Jan. 7, 1941, Feb. 22, 1940, ibid.

260   **imaginary sandwich prepared:** "Now, this sandwich that I would like to have had was a
        generous slice of fat-back between the right kind of bread with a slice of onion on top, and
        leave out all the tomatoes, mayonnaise, French dressing, and various other concoctions
        that go into sandwiches at the present time, but just good old-fashioned plain fat-back
        sandwiches such as you make and others know nothing about." Carver to Abbott, June 11,
        1941, Abbott Papers, GWC Monument Archives.

261   **contented himself . . . three regular coffees:** Mrs. James T. Hardwick to Mrs. Ethel Ed-
        wards, Blacksburg, VA, Mar. 3, 1948, GWC Monument Archives; Mrs. Hardwick to Carver,
        Mar. 22, 1935, Abbott Papers, GWC Monument Archives; Carver to Henry Ford, Apr. 29,
        1941, GWC Papers, Tuskegee Archives.

261   **lasted him for several suppers:** Carver to Abbott, Oct. 2, 1939, GWC Monument
        Archives.

261   **samp . . . a good long time:** He described how samp was made: The corn is hulled, dried,
        ground, and sifted. The fine particles that go through the first screen are called grits and
        are very fine. The particles in the second sifting are coarser and are called hominy grits,
        though Carver remarked that he had not seen them in a long time. The particles remain-
        ing after the third sifting is the samp and is very coarse. That was the kind he wanted.
        Carver to Abbott, Nov. 1, 1937; [date illegible], 1937, Abbott Papers, GWC Monument
        Archives.

261   **out of debt . . . end of 1940:** Carver to Abbott, Feb. 28, 1938, Nov. 17, 1939, Dec. 7, 1940,
        ibid.

261   **"other things that I want you to know":** Carver to Abbott, Nov. 8, Nov. 25, 1938, ibid.

262   **"how inseparable we are":** Carver to Abbott, Dec. 17, 1937, ibid.

262   **"advisable for me to leave":** Fishbein, interview with Austin Curtis, Detroit, Mar. 3, 1979,
        Carver Oral History Project, GWC Monument Archives; Abbott to Carver, Chicago, Dec.
        31, 1939, GWC Monument Archives.

262   **"That was within his power":** Carver to Patterson, July 23, 1935, GWC Papers; Fishbein,
        interview with Austin Curtis.

262   **student dorm, Rockefeller Hall:** Fishbein, interview with Austin Curtis.

262   **Curtis had begun working with him:** Carver to Abbott, Dec. 30, 1937, Abbott Papers,
        GWC Monument Archives.

263   **expected to find less prejudice:** Ibid.

263   **heard the program in Chicago:** John Hix to Carver, July 24, Dec. 20, 1935, GWC Papers, Tuskegee Archives.

263   **patent . . . peanut coffee:** Carver to Merritt, July 24, 1935.

263   **800 collections . . . confined to bed:** Paul A. Lentz and John A. Stevenson, "A Resumé of the Fungus Collections of George W. Carver," *Oklahoma City Black Dispatch*, Feb. 13, Aug. 14, Aug. 21, 1930.

264   **the brochure . . . book-length biographies:** Major publishing houses today commonly print a first run of 15,000 copies of a book to be distributed to three times the 1935 population.

264   **"mixing and dissolving to get his formula":** Fischer to Carver, July 27, 1935, GWC Papers, Tuskegee Archives.

264   **after hiring black kitchen help . . .** *Montgomery Advertiser*, Sept 5, 1930.

265   **"and what he is doing":** Quoted by William Pickens, "George Washington Carver: What Keeps a Man Alive," brochure, n.d., Miscellaneous Documents, GWC Papers, Tuskegee Archives.

265   **in conversation was "interesting":** Peter Duncan Burchard, interview with Henry Deane, Tulsa, Oct. 31, 2004, Carver Oral History Project, GWC Monument Archives.

265   *Time, Life,* **and in the newspapers:** Burchard, interview with Frank Godden, Los Angeles, CA, Nov. 6, 2004; *Time,* May 30, 1937; *Life,* Mar., June, 1937.

265   **"individual who is yet living":** Carver to Mrs. Hardwick, May 27, 1937, Abbott Papers, GWC Monument Archives.

265   **a work . . . enjoyed "so much":** Carver to Hardwick, May 9, 1933, GWC Monument Archives.

265   **Curtis remarried:** Carver to Dana Johnson, Sept. 21, 1936; Carver to Abbott, Aug. 9, 1938, Abbott Papers, GWC Monument Archives.

266   **"Bye. Yours Lovingly":** Birdie Johnson to Carver, Waycross, Feb. 12, 1936, GWC Papers, Tuskegee Archives.

266   **would not allow him to travel:** Hardwick to Carver, Montgomery, undated, 1937, GWC Papers, Tuskegee Archives; Carver to Hardwick, Aug. 26, 1937, GWC Monument Archives.

266   **a spate of honors:** Carver was awarded honorary membership in the Mark Twain Society, the National Technical Association, and the New York Academy of Sciences; he received an Alumni Merit Award from the Chicago Alumni Association of Iowa State, a Distinguished Service Key from Phi Beta Sigma fraternity, and special recognition at the 75th Anniversary of Negro Progress.

266   **opened the door to his apartment:** Fishbein, interview with Austin Curtis.

266   **"what complexion he is":** Quoted without citation, Linda O. McMurry, *George Washington Carver* (New York, 1981), p. 293.

267   **"and how I hate it":** Carver to Abbott, Aug. 26, 1937, Feb. 28, 1938, Abbott Papers, GWC Monument Archives.

267   **withdrew the . . . proposal:** A smaller Hollywood company without MGM's distribution resources attained Carver's approval and made a dramatized biography, offering a smaller fee than the one Curtis had rejected from MGM. Carver liked the movie. William J. Orr to

Carver, May 17, Sept. 20, 1937; Austin Curtis to Orr, May 25, Sept. 1, 1937; Jerry Fairbanks to Carver, Sept. 28, 1937, GWC Papers, Tuskegee Archives; Carver to Abbott, Sept. 3, 1940, Abbott Papers, GWC Monument Archives.

268 **outside many rooms . . . end of his life:** Lucy Cherry Crisp, "Carver," unpublished manuscript, Section IV, p. 313, Lucy Cherry Crisp Papers, Special Collections, Joyner Library, East Carolina University, Greenville, NC.

269 **"diligent in business," and sat down:** "Seest thou a man diligent in his business? He shall stand before kings . . . Such a man is Secretary Wallace" ("Carver," V, Lucy Cherry Crisp Papers). Carver subsequently wrote several letters thanking Wallace for the visit and for sending him some amaryllis bulbs; he wished him success with his farm relief program. Paul H. Appleby [assistant to Wallace] to Carver, Aug. 5, 1933; Carver to Wallace, Aug. 8, 28, 1933, Feb 28, Nov. 8, 1933, Henry A. Wallace Papers, National Archives, Washington DC.

269 **artificial scarcity seemed outrageous:** "Subsidized scarcity" did raise farm income, but the whole confused enterprise drew bitter criticism. Some of the slaughtered pork was distributed as relief food, but much of it was simply used for fertilizer. In 1936 the Supreme Court declared certain provisions of the act unconstitutional, destroying it, for all practical purposes.

269 **"there are thousands . . . these comforts," he wrote:** Carver to Helen Chisholm, Dec. 29, 1934, GWC Papers, Tuskegee Archives.

269 **"right out the side door":** Burchard, interview with Edward Pryce, Oct. 23, 2004, Carver Oral History Project, GWC Monument Archives.

269 **address . . . quite respectfully:** Wallace addressed Carver as "George." Fishbein, interview with Austin Curtis.

269 **Carver postage stamp:** Wallace to Franklin Delano Roosevelt, Nov. 13, 1939, Henry A. Wallace Papers, University Archives, Iowa State Library.

270 **new edition of his book:** Mary Huse (secretary to Wallace) to Raleigh Merritt, Washington, DC, Mar. 24, 1943, ibid. "The most unique thing to me about Carver is the depth of his faith and the sweetness of his spirit. He has always seen God moving in nature and therefore has always had a reverential attitude toward nature."

270 **not his great science:** James Hale Porter wrote to Wallace several times asking for his endorsement of Carver's massage therapy. Although the vice president was guarded concerning the therapy, he expended some effort to get funding for it from the National Foundation for Infantile Paralysis.

270 **race issue in his campaign:** "I have received a number of requests from political parties sponsoring the Vice-President asking me to write an article." Carver to Lucy Crisp, Oct. 31, 1940, GWC Papers, Tuskegee Archives.

270 **"a great scientist":** Telegram: Wallace to Clarence C. Sharpe (NAACP), Washington, DC, Feb. 13, 1943; Wallace to Mrs. Cornelius D. Scully, Washington, DC, Dec. 22, 1943; Wallace to Raleigh Merritt, Washington, DC, Mar. 24, 1943, GWC Papers, Tuskegee Archives.

270 **"I doubt . . . practical value came out":** Wallace to Luzanne Boozer, Dec. 7, 1948, quoted by McMurry, p. 254.

272 **Lou Gehrig's disease:** Henry A. Wallace Papers, Franklin D. Roosevelt Library; John C. Culver and John Hyde, *American Dreamer: The Life and Times of Henry A. Wallace* (New

York, 2002); Samuel Walker, *Henry A. Wallace and American Foreign Policy* (Westport, CT, 1976).

CHAPTER SIXTEEN. "Miles to Go"

Correspondence between Carver and Harry Abbott is mainly located in the Harry O. Abbott Papers, George Washington Carver National Monument Archives, Diamond, Missouri. Other letters to and from Carver, unless otherwise noted, may be found in the George Washington Carver Papers in the Tuskegee Institute Archives.

273 **"There is so much . . . what we have in mind":** When Carver was taken to the hospital, he instructed Emile Hooker to notify Harry Abbott. Carver's condition was regularly described in the newspapers, but Abbott received bulletins directly from the sickbed; he became a minor celebrity in Chicago as a reliable source of Carver information. Abbott to Carver, Dec. 13, 1939; Carver to Abbott July 8, 1938, Harry O. Abbott Papers, George Washington Carver Monument Archives, Diamond, MO.

274 **"beat them . . . frying salt meat":** Abbott to Carver, Dec. 13, 1939, George Washington Carver Papers, Tuskegee Institute Archives.

274 **contained polecat musk:** The polecat musk was "blended so skillfully that under no circumstances do you get that polecat odor," just a fragrance that is "fascinating." Carver to Abbott, Aug. 1, 1939.

274 **"You have put one over . . . you certainly did":** Two weeks later, Carver reported, "I do not care for the hulls (of the English horse bean), as with all that coloring matter, I am not sure whether it is the best thing to put that into your stomach." Carver to Abbott, Mar. 27, 1940.

274 **"real dirt farmer," . . . from his bed:** Carver to Abbott, Jan. 13, 1937, Feb. 25, 1942.

274 **"Portia . . . is doing much to help herself":** Carver to Abbott, n.d.; Carver to Abbott Mar. 1, 1940. The stamp was issued Apr. 7, 1940; Carver to Abbott, Oct. 15, 1940. The younger Washington, the grandson of Booker's adopted brother James, died the following year, July 1941, to be followed two months later by his mother, whom Carver mourned. Carver to Mrs. J. B. Washington, July 14, 1941; Carver to C. C. Hart, July 18, 1941, GWC Papers, Tuskegee Archives.

274 **"Just drop me a card . . . time for more":** Carver to Abbott, Feb. 15, 1940, GWC Monument Archives.

275 **"It is like emerging . . . ," he said:** "It is difficult to realize how desperately ill one can be and then come back again." Carver to Dana Johnson, June 30, 1938, GWC Monument Archives.

275 **spinning wheel . . . his only memento of her:** Carver to Abbott, Oct. 7, 1938; Peter Duncan Burchard, interview with Dana Johnson, Newport Beach, CA, Nov. 4, 2004, Carver Oral History Project, GWC Monument Archives.

275 **The windows . . . sounded just like his door:** Carver to Abbott, Apr. 25, 1940.

275 **Carver noticed . . . until the scar diminished:** Burchard, interview with Robert E. Garrett, Chicago, Nov. 3, 2004, GWC Monument Archives.

275 **Frank Godden:** Burchard, interview with Frank Godden, Los Angeles, CA, Nov. 6, 2004, GWC Monument Archives.

276 **He couldn't stand . . . missed one of his papers:** Safety pins: Harry D. Thompson to Mack Shepard, McAllen, TX, Sept. 20, 1943, GWC Monument Archives. Papers: Braye, who grew up to become a veterinarian, was the grandson of Carver's old colleague, C. W. Greene. Burchard, interview with Edward Braye, Tuskegee, Oct. 26, 2004, GWC Monument Archives.

276 **Carver and his unsatisfactory heart . . . for the long trip:** Carver to Abbott, Jan. 18, June 14, 1939. After the Minneapolis trip, he was obliged to decline several prestigious awards that would have required going back to New York at once.

276 **and see the Abbotts:** Carver was appointed by the governor of Alabama to represent the state on the National Negro Achievement Commission of the World's Fair.

277 **honors that washed over him:** He was obliged to decline membership in the New York Academy of Sciences, but he was present when the Tom Huston Peanut Company presented a bronze bas-relief of Carver to a black high school named for him in Columbus, GA. Carver to Eunice Thompson Miner, Mar. 31, 1938. By summer 1939, he was strong enough to give a talk in Hampton, Virginia. In 1939 the American Inventors Society made him an honorary member. He was elected to membership of the National Institute of Social Sciences in spring 1940.

277 **talking about his work with plants:** *Pittsburgh Courier, Des Moines Tribune, Chicago Defender,* Sept. 30, 1939; *Louisiana Weekly,* Nov. 4, 1939; Austin Curtis to Hotel New Yorker, Sept. 8, 1939; Lloyd Fitzgerald to Austin Curtis, Sept. 14, 1939; Leo Molony to Harvey J. Hill, Office of the President of Northfield College (in response to a letter protesting Carver's treatment), Oct. 18, 1939, GWC Papers, Tuskegee Archives.

277 **Carver, well-spoken and articulate . . . Science Forum:** Carver appeared with Edgar Guest in 1937; NBC aired a series from the Smithsonian Institute in 1938. In 1939 he was also featured on *Ripley's Believe It or Not.* In 1941 he was on *A Friend in Deed* and on *Freedom's People,* a fervently patriotic show by and about black Americans. In 1942 the film *Wings Over Jordan* was widely distributed. He was heard in many random coast-to-coast broadcasts. Patterson to Carver, Oct. 10, Nov. 7, 1941; Carver to Bernard C. Schoenfeld, Jan. 6, 1942.

277 **longer than the show's twenty-five minutes:** The show was based on the cartoons of John Hix, cartoons that were typically one large panel illustrating an unusual fact.

278 **The medal . . . Carver was ecstatic:** "A most unusual and inspiring event of my life." Carver to Eunice Adams, Mar. 1, 1940.

278 **"did not expect to get back to Tuskegee alive":** Carver to Lucius Boomer, Aug. 7, 1940.

279 **They tried to see each other . . . Ways, Georgia:** Carver to Mrs. E. B. Clossen, Dec. 31, 1937, GWC Monument Archives.

279 **Ford's . . . who liked to pose as a plebian:** Carver's first visit to Dearborn was in 1937. Carver to Dana and Cecil Johnson, Aug. 8, 1942, Abbott Papers, GWC Monument Archives.

279 **made them buy their own uniforms:** Carol Gelderman, *Henry Ford: The Wayward Capitalist* (New York, 1981), p. 288.

279   **from all sides simultaneously:** Reynold M. Wik, *Henry Ford and Grass Roots America* (Ann Arbor, 1972), p. 2.

280   **"I just turned around and came on back":** Carver to Abbott, Mar. 18, Apr. 25, 1940, GWC Papers, Tuskegee Archives.

280   **This depends . . . how the heart is working:** Carver to Clarence Hart, Feb. 21, 1940; Carver to W. W. Thompson, Mar. 27, 1940.

280   **"large quantities"—three per day:** Carver to Abbott, Feb. 15, 1940; Carver to Harvard Fatigue Laboratories, May 4, 1940, GWC Papers, Tuskegee Archives.

280   **glass of milk twice a day:** Carver to Abbott, Feb. 22, 1940, Abbott Papers, GWC Monument Archives; Carver to J. Otis, May 1, 1940; Carver to Mr. and Mrs. Logan, Aug. 14, 1941, GWC Papers, Tuskegee Archives.

280   **concoctions . . . his hapless students:** Burchard, interview with Dr. Paul Buck, Tulsa, Oct. 31, 2004, GWC Monument Archives.

280   **When his dinner . . . soybean soup:** Carver to Curtis, July 1, June 25, 1940.

280   **"It is something to be proud of":** Carver to Abbott, Dec. 7, 1940; Mar. 11, 1940; July 10, 1941; Sept. 4, 1940.

281   **"kind of sick at heart":** Carver to Abbott, Nov. 8, 1938, Mar. 4, 1939, GWC Monument Archives; Carver to Patterson, Jan. 3, 1941, GWC Papers, Tuskegee Archives.

281   **One friend . . . isolating food from rocks:** Roscoe Dunjee to Carver, July 11, 1941.

281   **Carver thought . . . attached to the main museum:** R. H. Powell to Carver, Jan. 12, Feb. 2, 1940. He was adamant that the art collection should not be lent out or broken up by housing some of it in a different museum or location. Carver to Patterson, July 16, 1942; Patterson to Carver, Aug. 6, 1942.

282   **"My greatest ambition . . . and our race":** Carver to Patterson, Feb. 27, 1940; Sept 25, 1941; Carver to Jas. Hale Porter, May 11, 1940.

282   **"its full duty toward you":** Abbott to Carver, Dec. 31, 1940. Carver had been given some land by the bank in compensation for his losses in the crash. That land appreciated and had been collecting rent under the supervision of bank officials, so that in addition to Carver's savings of $33,000, another $27,000 was part of the estate he left to the Carver Foundation. After Carver's death, the movie star Edward G. Robinson played a major role in fund-raising by personally soliciting contributions toward a 2 million dollar endowment; see Carver Correspondence, Dec. and undated, 1943, and Jan.–Mar. 1944, GWC Papers, Tuskegee Archives.

282   **"you will see, not myself":** Carver to Abbott, undated [1940], GWC Monument Archives.

282   **"did not think of me":** Carver to Abbott, Aug. 1, 1939, GWC Monument Archives.

282   **For seven months . . . could be protected:** Carver to Patterson, Mar. 3, 11, Oct. 8, 1940; May 5, July 28, 1941, GWC Papers, Tuskegee Archives.

282   **"be duplicated if they disappear":** Carver to Lloyd Isaacs, Apr. 9, 16, 1940.

282   **"without anybody to look after them":** Carver to Patterson, May 2, 17; Sept. 5, Sept. ?, 1940. He contemplated lending the collection to the State Department of Archives and History in Montgomery for safekeeping, but he finally decided against that move because he feared that once the objects left Tuskegee, the school would never be able to get them back. Carver to Lloyd Isaacs, July 19, 1940.

282   **"has kept my old heart alive":** Carver to Patterson, Aug. 10, Oct. 20, 1940, May 5, 1941; Carver to J. R. Otis, July 30, 1940; Powell to Carver, July 19, Aug. 9, 12, 1940; Carver to Powell, July 22, 1940; "George Washington Carver: What Keeps a Man Alive," undated brochure in Miscellaneous Documents, GWC Papers, Tuskegee Archives.

283   **priceless gift to Tuskegee Institute:** Carver to Patterson, Dec. 23, 1942; Patterson to Carver, Nov. 18, 1941.

283   **arrived at Tuskegee in 1896:** "The Carver Creative Research Laboratory," undated typescript, GWC Monument Archives.

283   **example of creative imagination:** The lab was not covered by fire insurance, though it had to be rebuilt after the 1947 fire. General letter by R. W. Brown, Director of the George Washington Carver Foundation, Jan. 5, 1948, GWC Papers, Tuskegee Archives.

283   **As for himself . . . his own work in massage:** Carver to Dr. John Chenault, n.d., 1939; Carver to Mary C. Hanscom, Apr. 10, 1940; Carver to James Hale Porter, Sept. 24, 1940; Carver to Margaret Gale, Nov. 24, 1942; Carver to Charles S. Kirkpatrick, President, McClean County Infantile Paralysis Foundation, Jan. 25, 1942.

284   **a warm letter of apology:** Carver to Chenault, Apr. 10 1941; Chenault to Carver, Apr. 11, 1941.

284   **Carver got "better":** Carver to Crisp, Mar. 5, 1940.

284   **"kept people away from me":** Carver to Abbott, Apr. 25, 1940, Abbott Papers, GWC Monument Archives.

284   **Physicians . . . in Mexico . . . paralysis in children:** Dr. Alejandro Luque to Carver, Teapa, Tabasco, Mexico, Nov. 14, 1940; Carver to Dr. Luque, Dec. 12–17, 1940; Dr. E. Wheadon, to Carver, Taft, CA, Feb. 23, 1940, GWC Papers, Tuskegee Archives.

284   **"the area . . . has stayed well":** N. B. Powell, M.D., to Carver, New Orleans, Sept. 16, 1941.

285   **"Please help me":** Susie Harris to Carver, Detroit, Apr. 1, 1940.

285   **they believed God listened to him:** Carver to McGhee Anderson, Jan. 10, 1941; Lena Johnson to Carver, New York, NY, Apr. 6, 1942.

285   **By 1940 . . . to some 6,000:** Carver to Rev. Walter E. Hollett, Mar. 23, 1940.

285   **"unless you run up against them face to face":** Carver to James Hale Porter, June 12, 1941, May 11, 1940; James Hale Porter to Editor, *Montgomery Advertiser*, Chicago, Dec. 3, 1941.

285   **"And did Dr. Carver . . . a concert pianist?"** Roland L. Pearman to Carver, Richmond, VA, Mar. 22, 1941, GWC Papers, Tuskegee Archives.

286   **Carver, certain that the peanut . . . never set it aside:** Carver to Editor, *San Antonio Express*, Nov. 25, 1940; Carver to Mrs. E. Hewlett, Aug. 22, 1941.

286   **He longed . . . no funds . . . for such work:** Carver to Hon. R. H. Powell, July 14, 1941; Carver to Grady Porter, Nov. 5, 1940; Carver to S. H. Wright, Jan 29, 1941; Carver to Victor H. Schoffelmayer, Editor, *Dallas Morning News*, Aug. 2, 1941; Carver to V. P. Sydenstricker, M.D., Aug. 12, 1941.

286   **root stimulant for flowering plants:** Carver was advising some bakers who were trying to produce the bread. Carver to Ogden Geilfuss, Apr. 19, 1940; Carver to John J. King, Apr. 29, 1940; E. O. Holland, Western Auto Supply Company to Carver, July 12, 1941.

286   **A U.S. senator . . . analysis of the acids:** Carver to Hon. Lister Hill, Jan. 22, 1942; Carver to Reuben Blumenfeld, Jan. 30, 1942.

286   **"for matters of greater importance":** Carver to Patterson, June 24, 1941; George P. Hoffman, U.S. Department of Agriculture to Carver, Washington, DC, Dec. 11, 1940; Carver to Victor H. Schoffelmayer, *Dallas Morning News*, Dec. 23, 1941; Carver to Dr. Brooks, Jan. 6, 1942; Carver to G. H. Schoenleber, President, Ambrosia Chocolate Company, Aug. 4, 1942, GWC Papers, Tuskegee Archives.

286   **a list of 115 plants . . . and the parts used:** Carver to Victor H. Scheffelmayer, *Dallas Morning News*, Jan. 16, 1942.

286   **peanut coffee and the rest:** Carver to Manily B. Updike, Publisher, *Deep South Magazine*, Dec. 30, 1940.

287   **curing athlete's foot:** Carver to Franklin Billman, Aug. 4, 1941; Carver to Patterson, Mar. 26, 1941; Carver to Prof. W. L. Burlison, Nov. 6, 1941; Carver to Whom It May Concern, Apr. 19, 1941; Carver to W. M. Danner, July 16, 1941, GWC Papers, Tuskegee Archives.

287   **Carver's extraordinary fungus collection:** Paul Miller to Carver, Aug. ?, 1940.

287   **"could not even see the lines of the paper":** Carver to Thomas Campbell, Oct. 18, 1940.

287   **"What a real joy . . . as skillful as yourself":** Carver to Dr. R. Beecher Costa, Apr. 16, 1940.

287   **"3:00 p.m., when I go back again":** Carver to T. A. Feeley, Tate Iron and Steel Co., July 8, 1941. Sometimes his doctor prescribed a series of intro-muscular injections "which I naturally hate." Carver to Patterson, Oct. 20, 1940.

288   **"before I can catch myself":** Carver to Patterson, Nov, 20, 1939; Carver to Crisp, Aug. 21, 1940.

288   **medicaments . . . to the dismay . . . physician friends:** Carver to James T. Gordon, Oct. 7, 1940; to Joseph W. Booker, Nov. 18, 1940; to McGhee Anderson, Nov. 22, 1940; to Mrs. Harry Cohen, July 8, 1942.

288   **Five motherless kittens . . . breakfast and dinner:** Carver to Mary R. Schmiedemdorf, Sept. 23, 1941.

288   **Carver's favorite . . . was the japonica:** Carver to L. H. Williams, Feb. 2, 1937, GWC Papers, Tuskegee Archives; Burchard, interview with Dr. Sheridan Howard Settler, Oct. 26, 2004, Carver Oral History Project, GWC Monument Archives; Carver to C. R. Stephens, Aug. 24, 1942; Carver to Mrs. H. G. Richey, Oct. 28, 1942, GWC Papers, Tuskegee Archives.

288   **reports for the USDA:** Carver to George J. Hope, Nov. 27, 1940; Dec. 30, 1940; Carver to M. W. Hendricks, Sept. ? 1941, GWC Papers, Tuskegee Archives; Carver to Harry Abbott, Oct. 9, Nov., 1940, Abbott Papers, GWC Monument Archives; Carver to George Hope, Nov. 27, 1940; Carver to Dr. J. A. Stevenson, Senior Mycologist, Dec. 22, 1941, GWC Papers, Tuskegee Archives.

288   **"dish rag gourd":** Carver to Reuben E. Blumenfeld, Jan 12, 1942; Patterson to Carver, Aug. 14, 1941; Julian C. Miller, LSU Horticultural Research to Carver, Baton Rouge, LA, July 27, 1942; Carver to *Montgomery Advertiser*, Aug. 31, 1942.

288   **Mrs. Jessie . . . a relative of Harry:** Carver to Charles H. Albert, Nov. 11, 1941, GWC Papers, Tuskegee Archives; Carver to Abbott, Feb. 15, 1940; July 11, 1942, Abbott Papers, GWC Monument Archives.

289   **"Dr. Carver would either be cutting . . . early morning hours":** Burchard, interview with Dana Johnson, Newport Beach, CA, Nov. 14, 2004; interview with Eliot Battle, Columbia, MO, Nov. 9, 2004, Carver Oral History Project, GWC Monument Archives.

289   **Others announced their cures for cancer:** D. T. Sykes to Carver, Dallas, TX, Jan. 21, 1940; Philip Berlin to Carver, Atlanta, Mar. 19, 1941; Carver to Mrs. J. H. Rodgers, Aug. 27, 1942; Carver to William Paul Allen, Jan. 24, 1942; Carver to Arthur Kemp, Apr. 22, 1940, GWC Papers, Tuskegee Archives.

289   **inspired . . . give another one a haircut:** George A. Dingus, Taft, OK, to Carver, Feb. 8, 1941.

289   **"Your Truly. God Bless us All":** Merittie Houston, Philadelphia, Jan. 5, 1940. It bears repeating that ungrammatical letters from black people were in the minority, despite the miserable education afforded to segregated people of color. Usually, it is impossible to discern the race of Carver's correspondents, who were nearly all pretty good writers.

290   **"absolute reserve and discretion," he wrote:** "A" to Carver, Mexico City, Apr. 3, 1940.

290   **Abraham Lincoln's home:** Carver to Abbott, June 1, 1940. In April 1941, a new Agricultural Extension Service building in Washington, DC, was dedicated to him, but Austin Curtis had to read Carver's speech. T. M. Campbell, Washington, DC, to Carver, Apr. 9, 1940. J. A. Landon gave Carver the gavel and an ashtray made from part of Lincoln's tin roof. Carver to Ida R. Elliott, July 24, 1941, GWC Papers, Tuskegee Institute Archives.

290   **a slew of university presidents:** Robert Hobday, Pres., Thomas A. Edison Foundation to Carver, Washington, DC, Jan. 27, 1942.

290   **sent Curtis . . . with an acceptance speech:** The Catholic Council of the South solved Carver's travel problem in giving him its award. The ceremony was broadcast on radio from Birmingham, but Carver's acceptance was broadcast all over the South from Tuskegee "Why I should be so signally honored is more than I can figure out. I have just endeavored to do my little bit in the world as fast and as thoroughly as the Great Creator of all things gave me the light and strength." Apr. 1941, GWC Papers, Tuskegee Archives.

290   **Carver saw them . . . in Tuskegee:** Abbott to Carver, Dec. 13, 1939; Carver to Abbott, Sept. 3, 1940.

290   **several large blocks of stamps:** Mrs. Wallace Simpson to Carver, Atlanta, Feb. 17, 1940.

290   **at liberty to authorize its use:** Sherman Dubose to Carver, Palmetto, FL, Oct. 5, 1940; Carver to Dubose, Oct. 7, 1940.

290   **the people . . . could have filled Wyoming:** See Heffelginer Radio Features to Carver, Feb. 1, 1941; George Dewey Lipscomb to Carver, New York, Aug. 11, 1942; the Macmillan Company to Carver, New York, Aug. 12, 1942; Ralph J. Bunche (on behalf of the Carnegie-Hyrdal Study) to Carver, New York, Jan. 27, 1940.

290   **escaped learning about him:** J. A. Hill to Carver, Sept. 16, 1942.

291   **"so much from thin air":** Enoch B. Garey to Carver, Washington DC, Aug. 11, 1942.

291   **Arkansas School for the Deaf . . . club after him:** Willie Earl Davis to Carver, Little Rock, Nov. 10, 1941.

291   **"you will have been all of these":** Engraved on a milestone marker at the GWC Monument, Diamond, Missouri.

291   **manufacture his own buttons:** "Odds and Ends," undated typescript in the GWC Monument Archives.

291 **sent biblical quotations:** John 8:32: "And ye shall know the truth and the truth shall make you free." He appended his own paraphrase: "And you shall know science and science shall set you free, because science is truth." Carver to Rev. T. G. Parish, Sept. 30, 1935, ibid.

291 **"how much I can do while living":** Carver to Abbott, Apr. 15, 1942, Abbott Papers, GWC Monument Archives.

291 **to the spirit of life and to the butterfly:** "How to Search for Truth," undated typescript, GWC Monument Archives.

291 **"Great God who made all of us":** 1941 quotation engraved on a marker at the GWC Monument, Diamond, Missouri.

292 **"that was it":** Carver to Abbott, Mar. 27, 1941, Abbott Papers, GWC Monument Archives; Carver to Harvey Hill, Mar. 27, 1941, GWC Papers, Tuskegee Archives.

292 **Ford . . . plans for nutrition research:** Carver to R. H. Powell, Mar. 11, 1941, GWC Papers, Tuskegee Archives. Carver lamented that he never had a chance to introduce Abbott to his "most inspiring" friend. Carver to Abbott, Mar. 27, 1941, Abbott Papers, GWC Monument Archives.

292 **$1,000 to the Carver Foundation:** Carver to Ida R. Elliott, July 2, 1941, GWC Papers, Tuskegee Archives.

292 **"the most colossal . . . ever witnessed":** Carver to Glenn Clark, May 12, 27, 1941.

292 **"alone in his bewilderment":** Clark Howell to Carver, May 27, 1941.

292 **"You can imagine how thrilling it was":** Carver to Eugene Connelly, n.d., 1941.

293 **The president . . . to confer the degree:** President Alan Valentine to Carver, Rochester, NY, Mar. 6, 1941; see also Carver to Valentine, Jan. 27, 1941; Valentine to Carver, Jan. 31, 1941.

293 **"stranger than fiction":** The announcement, usually made in December for the following year, was given out six months early because of Carver's precarious health.

293 **for the price of three dollars:** W. C. Handy to Carver, New York, July 1, 1941, GWC Papers, Tuskegee Archives.

293 **for chewing insects . . . would be poisoned:** Carver to Z. Boys, Sept. 16, 1942; Carver to E. E. Mead, Sept. 22, 1942; Carver to J. A. Franklin, Dec. 8, 1941.

293 **Students . . . with onions and eggs:** Burchard, interview with Helen W. Bratcher, Nashville, Oct. 8, 2004, GWC Monument Archives.

293 **laughed . . . along with everyone else:** Carver to Dana Johnson, Jan. 14, 1942, GWC Monument Archives.

294 **"I regret . . . we both think of him":** Carver to Crisp, July 2, 1941, GWC Papers, Tuskegee Archives.

294 **from time to time Crisp . . . and her paintings:** Crisp to Carver, Mar. 3, 1940. *Lullaby:* "Rest you now, my Dear One, / Night and stars are near, / Darkness now enfolds you / Close and warm and dear . . ."

294 **at twenty-seven miles per hour:** Crisp to Carver, undated [1939?]; Christmas, 1939; Jan. 11, 1940; Carver to Crisp, Aug. 21. 1940.

294 **to write about the end of his life:** Carver to Crisp, Mar. 5, 13, 1940; Crisp to Carver, Mar. 5, 1940; Carver to Mrs. Clossen, Mar. 6, 1937.

294 **two-dollar royalty to the Carver Foundation:** Crisp to Patterson, Dec. 24, 1942.

295   **his definitive biography:** In the years preceding Carver's death, there appeared countless
       articles in magazines and biographical dictionaries, and several booklets, notably Glenn
       Clark's *The Man Who Talks With Flowers.* A number of biographies for children were in
       preparation, but only one full-length biography for adults had appeared, Raleigh Mer-
       ritt's *From Captivity to Fame.* Carver articles appeared in *Time, Life, Saturday Evening Post,
       Readers Digest, Colliers, American Magazine, Liberty, Chemist, Pathfinder, Southern Workman,
       Literary Digest, Christian Century,* and *Service.*

295   **Curtis serving as the intermediary:** Toby Fishbein, interview with Austin Curtis, Detroit,
       Mar. 3, 1979, Carver Oral History Project, GWC Monument Archives.

295   **she got under his skin:** Memo of telephone conversation, Rackham Holt and Dr. Ather-
       ton Lee, Feb. 6, 1944. Holt requested an interview with Wallace for a magazine article.
       Wallace's secretary replied, "We are not to give Mrs. Holt an appointment; she has been
       pushing for one for a long time—wanted the VP to 'practically write' her book on Dr.
       Carver." Henry A. Wallace Papers, Franklin D Roosevelt Library, Washington, DC.

295   **Holt stated . . . every day for several hours:** U.S. Senate and House of Representatives,
       Joint Committee Meeting on Public Lands and Surveys, Feb. 5, 1943, Washington, DC,
       GWC Monument Archives.

296   **Carver and Curtis . . . records about his early life:** Carver called her attention to an
       article in the *Kansas City Times,* for example, which he thought had accurate information.
       Carver to Holt, Sept. 14, 1942; *Kansas City Times,* Sept. 9, 1942.

296   **"his valuable work is preserved":** Curtis to Mrs. Grace L. Benjamin, Apr. 14, 1937, GWC
       Papers, Tuskegee Archives.

296   **"then he had his own family to look after":** Carver to Abbott, Apr. 25, 1940, Abbott Pa-
       pers, GWC Monument Archives.

297   **"He is certainly a very dear boy":** Carver to Mrs. Curtis, May 31, 1940, GWC Papers,
       Tuskegee Archives.

297   **dining hall food:** Carver to Mr. and Mrs. Austin Curtis Sr., Oct. 25, 1941. Curtis's second
       wife, Oreta, was the art teacher at Tuskegee. Burchard, interview with Helen W. Bratcher,
       Nashville, Oct. 28, 2004, GWC Monument Archives.

297   **dishes were derived from peanuts:** Toby Fishbein, interview with Austin Curtis, Detroit,
       Feb. 1, 1979, GWC Monument Archives.

297   **Chinaberry . . . never tried to patent:** Burchard, interview with Robert L. Judkins, Tuske-
       gee, Oct. 27, 2004, GWC Monument Archives.

297   **development of this memorial:** Curtis to Clarence H. Schultz, Superintendent, GWC
       National Monument, Detroit, May 10, 1960, Austin W. Curtis Papers, 1896–1971, Bentley
       Historical Library, University of Michigan, Ann Arbor. I am indebted to Samuel Ferraro
       for researching the Curtis Papers for this biography.

298   **"no improvement over Buster whatever":** Carver to Curtis, June 15, July 1, 1940, GWC
       Papers, Tuskegee Archives.

298   **"you can be of great service":** Carver to Dr. Frank E. Steele, Mar. 11, Oct. 9, 1940; Carver
       to Dr. Waddell, Apr. 11, 1941; Carver to Austin Curtis, May 24, 1941; Carver to Mrs. Wat-
       kins, Apr. 25, 1940.

298   **"get absolutely exhausted":** Carver to Rev. Richardson, Sept. 21, 1940.

299   "sorry to have to leave him": Patterson to Carver, Oct. 19, 1940, Aug. 14, 1941; Carver to Patterson, Sept. 1, 1941; Carver to Mrs. Patterson, June 5, Sept. 8, 1941.

299   "Your speech . . . as it always is": Patterson to Carver, Mar. 17, 1941.

300   "requires the highest type of intelligence": Carver to H. A. Spicely, Nov. 13, 1941.

300   massive student strike . . . 1941: Burchard, interview with Jeanne Goodwin, Tulsa, Oct. 30, 2004; interview with Robert E. Garrett, Chicago, Nov. 3, 2004, GWC Monument Archives. "On account of my condition they kept the strike activities away from me as much as possible. I could hear them from my room, however, and some of the demonstrations from my office, but naturally, I didn't attempt to go out. Everything seems quiet now." Carver to Abbott, Feb. 28, 1941, GWC Papers, Tuskegee Archives.

300   "live out of the garbage receptacles": Carver to Walter G. Benz, Oct. 5, 1940.

300   "eating out of the trash can": Burchard, interview with Robert E. Garrett.

301   "wrap them up . . . throw them down to him": Carver to Mrs. L. V. Sutton, undated [1941?].

301   nor send the Jews back to Germany: Gladwyn Murray Childs to Carver, Lobito, Angola, Jan. 1, 1940.

302   "eating weeds": "I have never in all my experience had a bulletin to receive the real ovation like the bulletin on 'Weeds.'" Carver to Rackham Holt, Aug. 4, 1942, GWC Monument Archives.

302   "Nothing definite . . . establishing a birthday": Carver to Abbott, July 15, 1940, June 14, 24, 1942, Abbott Papers, GWC Monument Archives.

302   what might happen at any moment: Carver to Abbott, June 24, 1942, GWC Monument Archives.

302   boarding a train for Michigan: Carver to Abbott, July 11, 1942, GWC Papers, Tuskegee Archives.

303   excessive chemicals in the air and food: Burchard, interview with Dana Johnson, Newport Beach, CA, Nov. 4, 2004.

303   "my nutritional laboratory," in Dearborn: As Ford became more involved in the manufacturing uses of plant products, the word "nutritional" seems to have been dropped from the name.

303   "Just to think . . . possession of such a thing?": Carver to Dr. Walter Crump, Sept 25, 1942.

303   "an indefinite stay": Austin Curtis to Charles Easton, County Agent, undated, 1942.

303   time and tenacity: Carver to Dana Johnson, Feb. 14, 1942, GWC Monument Archives.

303   "I am still holding on": Carver to Glenn Clark, Aug. 28, 1942, GWC Papers, Tuskegee Archives.

CHAPTER SEVENTEEN. "A Million Thanks"

Unless otherwise indicated, Carver's correspondence is found in the George Washington Carver Papers, Tuskegee Institute Archives.

304   **always disappointed them:** Peter Duncan Burchard, interview with Helen W. Bratcher, Nashville, Oct. 28, 2004, Carver Oral History Project, George Washington Carver Monument Archives, Diamond, MO.

304   **both the ink and the paper could be reused:** Reynold M. Wik, *Henry Ford and Grass-roots America* (Ann Arbor, 1972), p. 143.

304   **"thinks the same way I do":** Rackham Holt, *George Washington Carver* (New York, 1943), p. 314.

305   **Ford left school . . . erudition:** Information about Henry Ford is taken from one objective biography, Carol Gelderman, *Henry Ford: The Wayward Capitalist* (New York, 1981); one rather more critical biography, Reynold M. Wik, *Henry Ford and Grass-roots America* (Ann Arbor, 1972); one highly critical biography, Keith Sward, *The Legend of Henry Ford* (New York, 1968); and one favorable biography, Alan Nevins and Frank Ernest Hill, *Ford: The Times, the Man, the Company* (New York, 1954).

305   **Frank Campsall:** Campsall had composed fifty form letters to choose from in responding to general mail. Ford himself saw only those few letters that his secretaries selected as being of particular interest.

305   **Grand Cross . . . from Hitler:** Ford blamed either the Jews or the Communists for foisting on civilization everything he hated: the Great War, Darwinism, bobbed hair, short skirts, lipstick, Wall Street, ragtime, jazz, and the liquor business. According to Sward, p. 451, he thought "the Jews" had been behind the assassination of Abraham Lincoln.

305   **Carver . . . respected learning and learners:** Ford's newspaper, *The Dearborn Independent,* ran a series of ninety-one virulently anti-Semitic articles. Meanwhile, Carver wrote to Mrs. Milholland, "I believe the Jews are going to come into their own. I am glad you are interested in them." *The Dearborn Independent,* Harry O. Abbott Collection, George Washington Carver Monument Archives.

306   **cruel ridicule . . . city dwellers:** Gelderman, p. 200.

306   **daily income of $264,000:** Wik, p. 103, citing *The Detroit News,* Jan. 13, 1924.

306   **"if they use it for the benefit of others":** Wik, p. 44.

306   **standing in bread lines every day:** Wik, p. 188, citing Mayor Murphy's report to the federal government.

307   **He said . . . Community Chest . . . condemned:** Sward, p. 224, ff.

307   **real lions . . . in his den:** The manager and head of the service department was Ford's constant companion, Harry Bennett, an ex-boxer with ties to the underworld. Bennett controlled a gang that the *New York Times,* with some exaggeration, called "the largest private quasi-military organization in existence" (Jan. 26, 1937). Bennett's house contained secret passages, tunnels, and the den with wild animals.

308   **enforcing a rough discipline:** See the scathing satire of Ford's assembly line in John Dos Passos, *U.S.A.: The Big Money* (New York, 1969). Men could be dismissed for violating a hundred arbitrary rules—talking on the job, sitting down or leaning on a post during equipment failures, forming close friendships with other workers, driving any car other than a Ford. Lunchboxes were searched for union leaflets.

308   **"history that excluded harrows . . . think so yet":** Gelderman, p. 277.

309 **each kind of article . . . 1607:** Ibid., p. 276.

310 **"Woodsy" . . . students into the school:** Burchard, interview with Gwendolyn Woods Butler, Tuskegee, Oct. 27, 2004, GWC Monument Archives.

310 **first buckwheat cakes . . . since childhood:** Carver to Crisp, Apr. 13, 1940, George Washington Carver Papers, Tuskegee Institute Archives.

311 **Ford's alternative . . . jitterbug:** Gelderman, pp. 279, 283.

311 **could only walk over . . . on "good" days:** Carver to Ford, Apr. 30, 1940; Mar. 12, July 28, Aug. 25, Dec. 8, 1941; Aug. 10, 27, 1942.

312 **meats, vegetables, and starches . . . the same meal:** Reported by Wik, p. 152, without citations.

312 **"bad mixtures in the stomach":** Sward, p. 108.

312 **It is certain . . . innovations . . . also numerous:** Even while Ford was immersed in trying to recreate the past, he continued to carry out enlightened projects, such as a mission house to treat alcoholics and drug addicts. He lent tractors to schools and vocational colleges in several states. All of these much-publicized efforts were on a very small scale, however, considering that the Ford Company was a worldwide enterprise.

313 **"come and go, come and go":** Burchard, interview with Dr. Walter Hill, Tuskegee, Oct. 27, 2004, GWC Monument Archives.

314 **"My heart goes out to you . . . realize":** Carver to Mr. C. H. Blake, Sept. 3, 1942; Carver to Mr. Gover, July 8, 1942, GWC Papers, Tuskegee Archives.

314 **none of the heat of evangelism:** Carver to Chenault, May 30, 1941; Chenault to Carver, Birmingham, June 2, 1941.

314 **"especially when I am doing creative things":** Clark to Carver, St. Paul, Dec. 16, 1939; Carver to Clark, Dec. 28, 1939, Feb. 4, 1941.

314 **"go over these marvelous things":** From Glenn Clark: "Oh little ant that fell on me / Out of this lovely tall elm tree, / Would you could hear the things I say / Of the wonders of God on this beautiful day." From *Koronis (MN) Sparks* 1, no. 7 (Aug. 13, 1941); Carver to Clark, Sept. 9, 1941.

315 **Clark was sending . . . to receive them:** Clark to Carver, Jan. 9, 1942.

315 **win out in the "crusade":** Carver to Clark, Jan. 23, 1942.

315 **From 1939 . . . Franklin D. Roosevelt:** Theodore Roosevelt to Carver, Oyster Bay, New York, Dec. 19, 1939; Fort Devens, MA, June 18, 1941; Carver to Theodore Roosevelt, June 27, 1941; Theodore Roosevelt Papers, Manuscripts Division, Library of Congress, Washington, DC; Wallace to Carver, Washington, DC, Jan. 3, 20, 1940, Henry A. Wallace Papers, University of Iowa Archives; Carver to Mrs. Franklin D. Roosevelt, Mar. 14, 1941, Franklin D. Roosevelt Library and Museum, Hyde Park, NY. "I had a fine letter from the President which came last Saturday. He says that he is using the peanut oil from time to time and that he is sure that it helps." Carver to Dana Johnson, Mar. 30, 1941, GWC Monument Archives.

315 **shared his predicatory impulses:** See Harvey Hill to Carver, Minneapolis, Sept 26, 1941; Jan. 23, 1942.

316 **"birds" . . . U.S. postal service:** Ross to Carver, Topeka, Jan 30, 1940; Carver to Ross, July 18, 1942.

316 **handwritten letters . . . valuable:** Envelope, 1905, Miscellaneous Documents; Carver to Mrs. Clossen, Feb. 14, 1942, both in GWC Monument Archives

316 **Much as he liked . . . Second World War:** Carver to Clark, May 20, 1940.

316 **"mean it just in that light":** Carver to W. A. Duff, undated, 1940.

316 **a Carver postage stamp:** Burchard, interview with Abdul-Salaam Muhammad, Los Angeles, Nov. 6, 2004, GWC Monument Archives.

317 **event . . . cancelled at the last minute:** "During the time of your ceremony I was not expected to live an hour." Carver to Dana Johnson, Jan. 5, 1940, GWC Monument Archives.

317 **"lives of you dear boys . . . mean yet":** Hart to Carver, Atlanta, Dec. 31, 1941; Carver to Dr. Charles Albert, July 17, 1941; Carver to Dana H. Johnson, Jan. 5, 1940, GWC Papers, Tuskegee Archives.

317 **"including . . . Wilson":** Carver to Mrs. L.V. Sutton, n.d., 1940; Wilson Newman to Carver, Dec. 20, 1940.

317 **little community of Tuskegee Institute:** Carver to Abbott, Dec. 17, 1937; Jessie Abbott to Harry Abbott, Jan. 1, 1942, Harry O. Abbott Papers, GWC Monument Archives.

317 **two saints . . . Booker T. Washington and George Carver:** Scott to Carver, Washington, DC, June 17, 1941; Peter Duncan Burchard, interview with Frank Godden, Los Angeles, CA, Nov. 6, 2004, GWC Monument Archives.

317 **according to . . . pushed him out of his company:** Walter Richards to Carver, Columbus, GA, July 18, 1940.

317 **"Jim Hardwick . . . where he is":** Carver to Al Zisler, May 23, 1941.

318 **"I do not know his address":** Carver to Mrs. Hardwick, Oct. 1941, GWC Monument Archives. Carver remarked, "She assured me that he had not forgotten that I existed and that he was going to write to me, but as yet he has not done it. I do not know where he is." Carver to Rev. Wallace Fridy, Dec. 15, 1941, GWC Papers, Tuskegee Archives.

318 **"not heard from him . . . two years":** Carver to Mrs. Helena Hardwick, Jan. 7, 1942, GWC Monument Archives.

318 **"you are tall and splendid to look at":** Birdie Howard to Carver, Mar. 14, 1940, GWC Papers, Tuskegee Archives.

319 **grandfather . . . far away:** Birdie to Carver, Dec. 31, 1939; Oct. 14, 1940.

319 **Hooker, and, of course, Birdie:** Carver spoke to his lawyer of making out just such a list of bequests, but at his death the lawyer remarked that no such list was ever found.

319 **"would like to leave you something":** Birdie to Carver, Mar. 14, 1940.

320 **" a credit . . . to all people":** Carver to Birdie, Mar. 25, 1940.

320 **"tan remover" to make it fade:** Birdie to Carver, Mar. 14, 1940; July 19, 1942.

320 **"dream was interpreted correctly":** Carver to Birdie, June 21, 1940.

320 **"your letters . . . anybody can ever be":** Birdie to Carver, June 18, 1940; Carver to Birdie, June 26, 1940; Birdie to Carver, June 18, 1940.

321 **"A million thanks for everything":** Birdie to Carver, Jan. 20, 1941.

321 **walk . . . around his room:** Carver to Birdie, Jan 8, 1941.

322 **give you the strength to make the trip:** Ibid.

322 **that she was seething:** Birdie to Carver, June 23, 1941; Carver to Birdie, June 18, 1941.

322 **"I hope you are still fine":** Birdie to Carver, Oct. 12, 1941.

323   **"I'll hear it in your heart":** Ibid.

323   **"Home Sweet Home":** Carver to Birdie, July 11, 1942; Birdie to Carver, July 19, 1942.

323   **pleaded with him . . . let alone help him:** Jessie Abbott to Harry Abbott Jan. 3, 1943, GWC Papers, Tuskegee Archives.

324   **used motor oil and clay:** Carver to I. E. Castellanos, Jan. 5, 1943.

324   **"Dr. Carver just passed":** Burchard, interview with Dr. Frederick Kennedy, San Pedro, CA, Nov. 5, 2004; interview with Arnold Williams, Tulsa, Oct. 30, 2004, GWC Monument Archives.

324   **claimed to be . . . cousin:** Burchard, interview with Jeanne Goodwin, Tulsa, Oct. 3, 2004, GWC Monument Archives.

324   **insisted . . . on the colored side:** R. T. Bagby to President Patterson, Birmingham, Jan. 20, 1943, GWC Papers, Tuskegee Archives.

325   **"gave his discoveries to the world":** *Tuskegee News*, Jan 14, 1943. Telegram: Franklin Delano Roosevelt to President Patterson, Franklin D. Roosevelt Library, Hyde Park, NY.

325   **"and still no holidays":** Burchard, interview with Helen W. Bratcher, Nashville, Oct. 28, 2004, GWC Monument Archives.

Epilogue

327   **"the world has ever known":** "Writings About Carver, 1945–1975," undated, microfilm in Tuskegee Archives; Peter Duncan Burchard, interview with Helen W. Bratcher, Nashville, Oct. 28, 2004, Carver Oral History Project, GWC Monument Archives.

327   **"life more significant":** Quoted in Rackham Holt, *George Washington Carver* (New York, 1948), p. 267.

327   **"kind-hearted soul":** Abbott to Carver, Dec. 31, 1937, George Washington Carver Papers, Tuskegee Institute Archives.

BIBLIOGRAPHY

MANUSCRIPTS

Harry O. Abbott Papers. George Washington Carver Monument Archives, Diamond, MO.

Joseph Lancaster Budd Papers. Special Collections. Iowa State University Library, Ames.

Carver Oral History Project, 2004. George Washington Carver Monument Archives, Diamond, MO.

George Washington Carver Collection. George Washington Carver Monument Archives, Diamond, MO.

George Washington Carver Papers. Tuskegee Institute Archives. A copy of these papers is available at Iowa State University Library.

Lucy Cherry Crisp Papers. Special Collections. Joyner Library, East Carolina University, Greenville, NC.

Austin W. Curtis Papers, 1896–1971. Bentley Historical Library, University of Michigan, Ann Arbor.

Fuller, Robert P., and Merrill J. Mattes. "The Early Life of George Washington Carver, Part I," report for the National Park Service, 1957. George Washington Carver National Monument Archives, Diamond, MO.

Iowa State University Office of Institutional Research, Miscellaneous Documents.

Seth Low Papers. Butler Library, Columbia University, New York, NY.

Louis Hermann Pammel Papers. Special Collections, Iowa State University Library.

W. S. Sherrill Correspondence. Franklin Delano Roosevelt Presidential Library, Hyde Park, NY.

Theodore Roosevelt Papers. Library of Congress, Washington, DC.

William Howard Taft Collection. Library of Congress, Washington, DC.

John Wesley Sutton Collection. Manuscripts Division, Howard University, Washington, DC.

United States Department of Agriculture. G.S.A. National Archives and Records Services, Washington, DC.

United States Department of the Interior: Toogood, Anna Coxe, "Historic Research Study and Administrative History, George Washington Carver National Monument, Diamond, Missouri," July 1973, National Park Service, Denver, CO.

United States Senate Committee on Public Lands and Surveys and the House of Representatives Committee on Public Lands, Washington, DC. Feb. 5, 1943; *Congressional Record*, January, 1921, Library of Congress.

Papers of Henry A. Wallace. National Archives, Washington, DC.

Henry A. Wallace Papers. Franklin D. Roosevelt Library, Washington, DC.

Henry A. Wallace Papers. Franklin Delano Roosevelt Presidential Library, Hyde Park, NY.

Henry A. Wallace Papers. University of Iowa Archives.

Booker T. Washington Collection. Division of Manuscripts, Library of Congress. Washington, DC.

Booker T. Washington Papers. Tuskegee Institute Archives, Tuskegee, AL.

James A. "Tama" Wilson Papers, 1835–1920. Special Collections, Parks Library, Iowa State University.

James A. Wilson Collection. National Archives, Washington, DC.

NEWSPAPERS

Atlanta Constitution, 1895, 1923, 1931, 1933–1943

Atlanta Journal, 1933

Baltimore Sun, 1924, 1925, 1930–1943

Birmingham News, 1933

Birmingham Reporter, 1924

Black Dispatch (Oklahoma City), 1930

Chicago Defender, 1939

Chicago Tribune, 1916, 1919, 1928, 1937, 1941

Cincinnati Enquirer, 1933, 1923–1925, 1943

Columbus (GA) Ledger, 1896

The Dallas Morning News, 1924, 1933, 1940–1943

The Dearborn Independent, 1919–1927

Des Moines Tribune, 1928, 1939

The Detroit News, 1919, 1924, 1927, 1937

Durham Morning News, 1943

Fort Scott (KS) Daily Monitor, 1879

Kansas City Times, 1942

Louisiana Weekly (New Orleans), 1939

Los Angeles Herald Examiner, 1924, 1933, 1943

Montgomery Advertiser, 1896, 1898, 1904, 1905, 1930, 1933, 1941

New York Times, 1915–1920, 1923–1937, 1943–1944

Pittsburgh Courier, 1939

The Register (Des Moines, Iowa), 1899

Times-Democrat (New Orleans), 1901

The Tribune (Des Moines), 1928, 1939

The Tuscaloosa News, 1930, 1933, 1943

The Tuskegee News, 1896, 1905, 1920, 1924–1930, 1933–1944

The Tuskegee Student, 1900

The Vindicator (Youngstown, Ohio), 1943

Washington Herald, 1939

West Liberty (IA) Index, 1896

MAGAZINES

The American Magazine (New York), 1932

Christian Century (Chicago), 1939–1943

Colliers (New York), 1940

The Congregational Magazine (Yorkshire, England) 1895–1925

Cornell Countryman (Cornell University) 1902–1903

Deep South Magazine (Lafayette, LA), 1940

Liberty (New York), 1930–1942

Life (New York), 1940–1944

Literary Digest (New York), 1941

Pathfinder, 1939

The Progressive Farmer (Birmingham, AL) 1942

Reader's Digest (New York), 1937, 1939, 1942

Review of Reviews (New York), 1902–1903

Saturday Evening Post (Indianapolis), 1939–1943

Service (New York), 1940–1943

Southern Workman (Hampton Institute), 1895–1896

Time (New York), 1924–26, 1930, 1933, 1937, 1941–1943

JOURNALS AND BULLETINS

Annual Report of the Agricultural Experiment Station of the A&M College, Auburn, Alabama, 1898

Bulletins of the Iowa Agricultural Experiment Station (Ames), 1894–1895, 1895–1896, 1896–1897

Publications of the Iowa Horticultural Society (Ames), 1893, 1896

Journal of Chemical Education (Washington, DC), 1946

Journal of Mycology, 1902, 1903

Journal of the National Medical Association (Silver Spring, MD), 1999

National Education Association Journal (Washington, DC), 1946

The Peanut Journal (Columbus, GA), 1924, 1932

Polio Chronicle, 1931–1934

Report of the New York State Agricultural Experiment Station (Geneva), 1895

In the years just before Carver's death there appeared numerous articles and book chapters about Carver's life, articles in biographical dictionaries, and several booklets, notably Glenn Clark's *The Man Who Talks With Flowers* (62 pages). A number of Carver biographies for children were published, including Shirley Graham and G. D. Lipscomb, *Dr. George Washington Carver, Scientist* (New York, 1944); Evangeline Harris, *Little Tot's Story of George W. Carver* (Terre Haute, IN, 1940); and Augusta Stevenson, *George Carver, Boy Scientist* (Indianapolis, IN, 1944). The booklets included Harvey Jay Hill, *He Heard God's Whisper* (Minneapolis, MN, 1943), 80 pages; J. P. Hunter, *Saint, Seer and Scientist* (Grand Rapids, MI, 1939), 32 pages; G. Lake Imes, *I Knew Carver* (Harrisburg, PA, 1943), 24 pages; Basil Miller, *George Washington Carver: God's Ebony Scientist* (Grand Rapids, MI, 1943); A. M. Pullen, *Despite the Color Bar: The Story of George Washington Carver, Scientist* (London, 1946), 121 pages.

BOOKS

African American National Biography. Vol. 5. Oxford, 2008.

Alexander, Adele Logan. *Ambiguous Lives.* Fayetteville, AR, 1991. Contains guarded but unique observations about the author's grandmother, who was Carver's close friend.

Bond, Horace Mann. *Negro Education in Alabama: A Study in Cotton and Steel.* New York, 1969. Very interesting statistics.

Boorstin, Daniel. *The Americans.* New York, 1965. A lively picture of the Midwest during Carver's homesteading years by one of this country's foremost social historians.

Burchard, Peter Duncan. *Carver: A Great Soul.* Fairfax, CA, 1998. An impressionistic little book that lacks critical information but imparts the warmth of Carver's personality, by the man who conducted most of the interviews for the Oral History Project of the National Park Service.

Citro, Joseph F. *Booker T. Washington's Tuskegee Institute.* Rochester, NY, 1972. Both this book and the master's thesis on Tuskegee Institute which preceded it are painstaking, fair-minded, and exhaustively researched. Gives a balance sheet of Washington's accomplishments and failures in running the school, with an abundance of fascinating details.

Culver, John C., and John Hyde. *American Dreamer: The Life and Times of Henry A. Wallace.* New York, 2002.

Dos Passos, John. *U.S.A.: The Big Money.* New York, 1969. Contains his famous, bitter poem about Henry Ford.

Encyclopedia of Arkansas History and Culture. Little Rock, 1954. Offers much information about the eradication of hookworm in the South.

Fellman, Michael. *Inside War: The Guerilla Conflict in Missouri During the American Civil War.* New York, 1989. A splendid study in every way.

Garraty, John A. *The New Commonwealth.* New York, 1968.

Gelderman, Carol. *Henry Ford: The Wayward Capitalist.* New York, 1981. Fair-minded and well researched. Fills in gaps in Raymond Wik's biography.

Hale, A. R. *These Cults: An Analysis of the Foibles of Dr. Morris Fishbein . . .* New York, 1926. An expose of the bogeyman of the American Medical Association.

Harlan, Louis R. *Booker T. Washington.* 2 vols. New York, 1972–1983. The definitive biography: fair, balanced, thorough, and altogether brilliant.

Harlan, Louis R., and Raymond W. Smock, eds. *The Booker T. Washington Papers.* 14 vols. Urbana, IL, 1972.

Hays, Samuel P. *The Response to Industrialism, 1885–1914.* Chicago, 1957.

Herman, Arthur. *Gandhi and Churchill.* New York, 2008. Refreshing and entertaining look at two very controversial and imperfect public men, irrespective of their current status as public saints.

Hersey, Mark. *My Work Is That of Conservation.* Athens, GA, 2011.

Holt, Rackham. *George Washington Carver.* New York, 1948. The absence of citations is a serious limitation of this readable biography, and the author was entirely too fond of Carver for us to trust her uncritical characterization of him. Nevertheless, her close acquaintance with him allowed her to give a more detailed portrait than can be found in any other work.

Johnson, Charles. *Shadow of the Plantation.* Urbana, IL, 1934. An early, now neglected work with a wealth of specific information about sharecropping and tenant farming in Macon County, Alabama.

Kellogg, J. H. *Plain Facts for Old and Young.* Burlington, IA, 1888. Most entertaining is his "Treatment for Self-Abuse . . ." essay. Booker T. Washington swore by him.

Kennedy, David M., Lizabeth Cohen, and Thomas A. Bailey. *The American Pageant.* 13th ed. New York, 2006. Especially useful for an overview of the country during the settlement of the West, the Reconstruction Era, and the Great Depression.

Kremer, Gary R. *George Washington Carver.* Santa Barbara, CA, 2011. Very short and superficial.

———, ed. *George Washington Carver in His Own Words* (Columbia, MO, 1987). Attempts to prove the thesis that Carver was extremely egotistical by a sly arrangement of quotations from Carver interspersed with the author's own interpretation of them.

McMurry, Linda O. *Carver.* New York, 1982. A hatchet job that attacks Carver's reputation as a scientist and an original thinker. McMurry claims he had an out-of-control ego to boot. One of the greatest flaws of the work is the author's unquestioning acceptance of Booker T. Washington's criticisms of Carver.

Merritt, Raleigh H. *From Captivity to Fame.* Boston, 1929. Valuable for those most interested in Carver's recipes and nutritional research.

Nevins, Alan, and Frank Ernest Hill. *Ford: The Times, the Man, the Company.* New York, 1954. Unexceptional, despite Nevins's deserved reputation as an eminent historian.

Nichols, Bruce. *Guerilla Warfare in Civil War Missouri, 1862.* Jefferson, NC, 2004. A good compendium of hard-to-find information and analysis.

O'Kieffe, Charley. *Western Story: The Recollections of Charley O'Kieffe, 1884–1898.* Lincoln, NE, 1960. Conversational and very readable description of the inconveniences of life on the Missouri-Kansas-Nebraska frontier.

Scopes, John T. *The World's Most Famous Court Trial . . .* New York, 1971. The trial as seen by the major participant before it was reworked in the stage and screen versions.

Scott, Emmett J., and Lyman Beecher Stowe. *Booker T. Washington, Builder of a Civilization* New York, 1917. Hagiography.

Smock, Raymond W. *Booker T. Washington.* Chicago, 2009. Louis Harlan's collaborator revisits Washington's life in the light of current skeptical opinions.

———, ed. *Booker T. Washington in Perspective: Essays of Louis R. Harlan.* Jackson, MS, 1988. The cogent observations of the man who spent a lifetime unraveling the complicated skein that was Washington.

Stokes, Anson Phelps. *Tuskegee Institute: The First Fifty Years.* Tuskegee, AL, 1931.

Sward, Keith. *The Legend of Henry Ford.* New York, 1948. A particularly fierce hatchet job that should be read with a degree of skepticism.

Walker, Samuel. *Henry A. Wallace and American Foreign Policy.* Westport, CT, 1976.

Washington, Booker T. *Up From Slavery.* New York, 1901.

———. *The Story of My Life.* Chicago, 1900.

———. *My Larger Education.* New York, 1911.

Wik, Raymond M. *Henry Ford and Grass Roots America.* Ann Arbor, 1972. Balanced and fair biography; the missing parts of Ford's life are provided by Gelderman's biography.

INDEX

CHRISTINA VELLA holds a Ph.D. in modern European and U.S. history from Tulane University in New Orleans, where she is currently Visiting Professor. A consultant to the U.S. State Department, she also lectures widely on a range of historical and biographical topics and occasionally serves as an adviser to NPR, PBS, The History Channel, and A&E. She is the author of *Intimate Enemies*, a biography of the Baroness Pontalba, *The Hitler Kiss*, a memoir of the resistance, *Indecent Secrets: The Infamous Murri Murder Affair of 1905*, and numerous book chapters. For information, please see www.christinavella.com.